D0026171

ENCYCLOPEDIA OF
AMERICAN BUSINESS HISTORY

VOLUME I

CHARLES R. GEISST

An imprint of Infobase Publishing

Encyclopedia of American Business History

Copyright © 2006 by Charles R. Geisst

Facts On File, Inc.
An imprint of Infobase Publishing
132 West 31st Street
New York, NY 10001

Library of Congress Cataloging-in-Publication Data

Geisst, Charles R.
Encyclopedia of American business history / Charles R. Geisst.
p. cm.
Includes bibliographical references and index.
ISBN 0-8160-4350-7 (hardcover : alk. paper) 1. United States—Commerce—History—Encyclopedias. 2. Business enterprises—United States—History—Encyclopedias. 3. Industries—United States—History—Encyclopedias. I. Title.

HF3021.G44 2005
338.0973'03—dc22   2005003309

Text design by Cathy Rincon

Cover design by Cathy Rincon

Illustrations by Sholto Ainslie

Printed in the United States of America

VB Hermitage 10 9 8 7 6 5 4 3 2 1

This book is printed on acid-free paper.

CONTENTS

CONTRIBUTORS*

JAMES BARTH, Auburn University
JONATHAN BEAN, Southern Illinois University
MANSEL G. BLACKFORD, Ohio State University
HOWARD BODENHORN, Lafayette College
E. N. BRANDT, Michigan
MARCELO BUCHELI, Stanford University
MARTIN CAMPBELL-KELLY, Warwick University,
  England
ANN CARLOS, University of Colorado
ROBERT J. CHANDLER, Wells Fargo Historical
  Services
ALBERT CHURELLA, Ohio State University, Lima
DANIEL C. CLARK, Oakland University
JAMES W. CORTADA, IBM Corporation
MACEO DAILY, University of Texas at El Paso
RENE DE LA PEDRAJA, Canisius College
JEAN DERMINE, INSEAD Fountainbleau, France
ALEXANDER J. FIELD, Santa Clara University
WILLIAM FRASER, University of Florida
JOHN FREDRIKSEN, independent scholar
ANDREA GABOR, Baruch College
MARGARET A. GEISST, Budd, Larner, P.C., Short
  Hills, N.J.
DONALD G. GODFREY, Arizona State University
LEE GRADY, Wisconsin Historical Society
H. ROGER GRANT, Clemson University
JEFFREY E. GRELL, Leonard, Street & Deinard
PETER Z. GROSSMAN, Butler University
WAYNE GROVE, Syracuse University
THOMAS HARKINS, Duke University
PAUL HARRISON, Brandeis University
DIANA HENRIQUES, *New York Times*
JENNIFER HOLMES, University of Texas, Dallas

ROGER HOROWITZ, Hagley Museum and Library
HERBERT HOVENKAMP, University of Iowa College
  of Law
LAWRENCE HUGGINS, Manhattan College
ROBERT JACKSON, State University of New York,
  Oneonta
SUSAN JOHNSON, Ohio State University
IRVING KATZ, Indiana University
AUSTIN K. KERR, Ohio State University
LEE KORINS, University of Northern Colorado
PAUL LAGASSE, Baltimore, Maryland
PAUL J. LEBLANC, La Roche College
TIMOTHY J. LECAIN, Montana State University,
  Bozeman
FRANK LEWIS, Queens University, Canada
JAMIE LEWIS, Forest History Society
FIONA MACLACHLAN, Manhattan College
NIKKI MANDELL, University of Wisconsin,
  Whitewater
VICTOR MATHESON, College of the Holy Cross
AJAY K. MEHROTRA, University of Chicago
MARY MICHEL, Manhattan College
SHARON ANN MURPHY, University of Virginia
MICHAEL NAMORATO, University of Mississippi
ROGER OLIEN, University of Texas at the Permian
  Basin
STEVE PEREZ, California State University,
  Sacramento
RONNIE J. PHILLIPS, Colorado State University
PAUL H. RAKES, West Virginia University
  Institute of Technology
JONATHAN REES, Colorado State University, Pueblo
PRISCILLA ROBERTS, University of Hong Kong

* Articles not specifically credited to a contributor were written by Charles Geisst.

PETER L. ROUSSEAU, Vanderbilt University

JAMES M. RUBINSTEIN, Miami University of Ohio

THOMAS SADLER, Manhattan College

MARTHA SAUNDERS, University of West Florida

JULIANN SIVULKA, University of South Carolina

AMANDA SMITH, Washington, D.C.

JEFF SMITH, Washington University in St. Louis

PETER SPITZ, independent scholar

THOMAS STANTON, Johns Hopkins University

CHRISTOPHER STERLING, George Washington University

CLAIRE STROM, North Dakota State University

PETER TEMIN, Massachusetts Institute of Technology

STEVEN TOPIK, University of California, Irvine

GLENN UTTER, Lamar University

JENNY WAHL, Carleton College

DENNIS B. WORTHEN, Lloyd Library and Museum

JEFFREY YOST, Charles Babbage Institute, University of Minnesota

LIST OF ENTRIES

INTRODUCTION

Over the last 15 years, business history has exploded as a discipline, while much business history also was made during the boom economy of the 1990s. As a result, the need for a business history encyclopedia has become more important as a means of chronicling these events and showing their antecedents, stretching back to American independence.

The *Encyclopedia of American Business History* is the first serious attempt in several decades to describe the major business events, institutions, and individuals in American history. Readers will find entries crossing all of the traditional categories—descriptions of individuals, events, companies, legislation, and movements that have had a significant impact on American history and business life. Each entry is accompanied by a short bibliography that will enable the reader to pursue the topic further. They reference the best known or most general books or articles and have been chosen as the next logical place for a reader to look up information. But in some cases, little information has been written about the entries to date, although they have been included because of their importance. A more general bibliography is included at the end of the volume.

Because much of business history is still in the making, we have tried to make the entries in this volume as up-to-date as possible. In some cases, this required arbitrary decisions about what material was included and excluded. The guiding principle used here was to include material that was developed enough to allow the reader to pursue the subject in greater detail.

Some of the more recent material may stand the test of time, while other recent entries may disappear in the future. Not all material once thought relevant has weathered the decades and centuries well.

This encyclopedia's entries begin with the period after American independence. Beginning a historical timeline is always difficult, but the founding of the Bank of New York and the New York Stock Exchange is a convenient general time at which to start. A few entries precede this period, but the overwhelming majority of entries date from the late 18th century. Encyclopedia entries traditionally are narrow in their scope except for the entries on trends or time periods. In order to allow readers to get a broader sense of their importance, each entry is cross-referenced to other entries of related importance so that by reading them together, readers can get a better sense of their importance and effects on business life. A timeline has also been included so that the major events in business history are presented visually.

The vast majority of these entries center around individuals, companies, laws, and trends in business. In a few cases, readers will find entries that are not necessarily American but are universally known and well-established tools used in business practice. Their effect on American business and finance is indisputable, and they have been included in the list of entries.

*   *   *

Traditionally, much of business history has been dominated by finance, and this current volume reflects that influence to an extent. In the 19th century, record keeping was not exact, and many of the records and accounts that were bequeathed to posterity were passed down by institutions like the New York Stock Exchange, the country's oldest surviving business institution (along with the Bank of New York). As a result, many financial and banking events were duly recorded, while other areas of business, like accounting and advertising, were mainly ignored until more recently.

Other than finance, the area of business that received the most attention in the 19th and early 20th centuries was manufacturing, traditionally considered an American strength and an area of innovation as well as national pride. Many innovations were uniquely American, while others were borrowed from Europe but refined to the point where many people tended to consider them as American. One of the hallmarks of American business and industry was an ability to produce vast quantities of manufactured goods, giving the country a distinct advantage over the European competition. In many cases, the easy availability of many of these goods, such as steel and automobiles, led many casually to believe that they had their origins in the United States.

Only when manufacturing and production were well established did the management theorists enter the business scene, beginning early in the 20th century. Efficiency became the goal of business when it became apparent that production was no longer a serious issue. Management theory also rose at a time when organized labor was flourishing, giving more credence to efficiency theories and new ideas about production and distribution of goods, since labor costs were rising as the unions pushed for better wages and benefits for their members. In order to cover the increasing costs, business had to adopt new methods that would produce better economies of scale and reduce fixed and variable costs.

Advertising and marketing also began to develop in the 20th century. In the 19th century, billboard and print advertising were the major methods of informing customers about new products. After World War I, consumerism exploded on a scale not witnessed before; getting a message to consumers about products became increasingly difficult and competitive. This led many marketers to begin studying consumer behavior and buying patterns. In addition to marketing, the field of public relations also grew substantially, demonstrating that image was becoming as important as quality. Many industrialists and financiers hired public relations experts, as did many companies keen to show themselves in the best possible public light.

The 1920s became a crucial decade for the development of American business, both positively and negatively. Automobiles, radios, and new home building led the charge during the decade, and production reached historic highs, fueled by a booming stock market and low interest rates. A property boom in Florida also attracted many investors and speculators and led to the rapid development of infrastructure in the state. Consumer credit also was introduced, allowing many customers traditionally relying on cash to pay for consumer durables on time. But the party ended abruptly in October 1929, when the stock market crashed. Asset values declined precipitously from their inflated levels, and the country quickly sank into the Great Depression and would not fully recover until the years following World War II, when production levels again increased to, and often exceeded, those of previous years.

The 1920s also are crucial in understanding business history. Modern consumer society was born during the decade. Consumption reached two-thirds of gross domestic product, and the role of the consumer and consumer financing became entrenched. Equally important for students of business history (but less well known) is the fact that better record keeping began in the 1920s, as the government began collecting more systematic and uniform business statistics than was previously the case. Economic statistics especially began to replace the anecdotal evidence used heavily in the past by commentators and writers, especially those who wrote about finance and the markets. Although somewhat rudimentary by later standards, this record keeping and statistics gathering also marked the beginning of the modern era in business, when soft numbers and ideological preferences gave way to a more empirical method of studying business phenomena.

Although the Great Depression and World War II interrupted this cycle, it would resume again in the 1950s and continue unabated until the present. As business developments continued at a dizzying pace for the rest of the century, the standard areas of business inquiry were established. Manufacturing and production, finance, advertising and marketing, management science, and accounting were all well entrenched and would be joined by the new art of computer science later in the century. Internet-based business would follow in the 1990s.

While the 1920s remain a crucial decade for business history, another more general event is also crucial to understanding the evolution of business and the modern corporation. In the second half of the 19th century, a process began that built momentum as the years passed. This was the phenomenon known as the rise of managerial capitalism. As companies grew larger, the need for capital for expansion grew, as did the need for bringing in managers from outside the close ranks of the company or the family members who founded it. These professional managers marked the rise of managerial capitalism and ushered in a new period of American business history. Labor was now more divided than ever before in many firms, and these managers were employees rather than owners of the company. Often, they brought an expertise badly needed if their companies were to survive and prosper. The concomitant rise of management theory early in the 20th century certainly helped the movement toward professionalism within the managerial ranks. And business schools began to be founded, catering first to graduate students and then undergraduates, seeking to produce new generations of potential managers imbued with theory at early stages in their careers.

Some events became watersheds in American history and have received emphasis in the entries that follow. In the 20th century, the stock market crash of 1929 and the Great Depression set off a chain of events that profoundly altered business for the rest of the century. The precipitous market collapse and the string of bank failures that had been occurring throughout the 1920s set off a torrent of new legislation in the Hoover administration and the first administration of Franklin D. Roosevelt. New securities and banking laws were established, and the new accounting standards required by the Securities Exchange Commission, itself a product of the new legislation, established generally accepted accounting principles that survive to the present day.

Even when the crises were not created by the stock market or domestic events, the ramifications could be felt throughout the business community. The currency exchange crisis occurring in the summer of 1971 resulted in a realignment of the world's major currencies, a subsequent change in American bank regulation, and the eventual introduction of the euro as the world's second major reserve currency behind the dollar. These events often are overlooked by business historians, who tend to concentrate on domestic issues, but are included here because of their far-reaching effects on American business and history.

While finance and manufacturing remain the two oldest fields in business history, recent developments in accounting history and advertising history have given a more complete picture of American business over the last two centuries. Also, scandal has often interrupted to make these once arcane fields more important. The collapse of the Enron Corporation and WorldCom early in the 21st century made vital a reexamination of the long-standing securities laws and accounting principles established since 1933, especially since they occurred while what were widely believed to be the most stringent securities and accounting principles in the world were in effect.

Business history also attests to the legacy that immigrants left on American affairs. Although many of those names today are assumed to be American, readers will notice that Alexander Graham Bell, Alexander Brown, Andrew Carnegie, John Jacob Astor, Samuel Insull, Jacob Schiff, Cyrus Vance, and Alexander Hamilton, to name but a few, all came to the United States at various stages in their lives and left an indelible imprint. Whether they came as children or as adults, all were able to capitalize on the opportunities afforded them and build empires based on steel, telephones, fur trading, and finance. Many of the original institutions they built, especially in fur trading and finance, were designed after European models preceding them but would emerge as uniquely American institutions.

Many of the opportunities immigrants as well as established Americans were able to exploit occurred in a growing economy free of many of the regulations known today. Railroad regulation did not occur for several decades after the lines were first widely used, and many regulations over other industries did not occur until the first third of the 20th century. Congress did not enact the first permanent income tax until 1913, so that many early entrepreneurs had already built substantial fortunes, and their families were well established by the first world war. When combined with the lack of meaningful statistics about many American industries and government, this only added to the highly anecdotal nature of American business. After early attempts at regulation, the introduction of the income tax, and closer study of the nature and character of business, attitudes began to change in the era of managerial capitalism, which had already entered its third generation.

Until the period following World War I, the United States was an importer of capital, dependent upon Europeans for money for long-term infrastructure investments, such as railroads and communications. As a result, many banking houses arose to channel European investments into the country. Although many of them are long since departed, either gone out of business or absorbed by other larger institutions, their historical record prior to World War I is important for understanding the nature of the United States before it emerged as a world power.

In the 1980s, this trend was reversed, and the United States again became dependent on foreign capital as its trade and budget deficits began to increase and foreign investment in both tangible assets and domestic securities became vital. Although the issue raised much attention and debate that continues to the present, in business history it is not a new topic, only the current chapter in American trade and foreign investment.

Beginning in the same decade, deregulation became the avowed policy of both Republican and Democratic administrations, and many New Deal and Progressive-era regulations fell by the wayside. Regulation of certain industries, which began a slow and often tortuous history in the 19th century, fell by the wayside in favor of deregulation in the name of freer markets. Globalization of the marketplace also occurred rapidly, helping to integrate many of the world's markets in both tangible and intangible products and services. Both trends demonstrated that business history to date has been a mix of the old and the new. The rapid pace of change has made the need for an encyclopedia encompassing these events, personalities, and companies more important than ever.

advertising industry American advertising is a huge and powerful industry with expenditures approaching $250 billion in 2001 in the United States alone, with more than $450 billion spent worldwide. The biggest advertisers are the nation's manufacturers of automobiles, food, soft drinks, beer, and tobacco. Advertising expenditures pass through thousands of advertising agencies that primarily create the ads and buy the space or time in the media. Some agencies have formed global corporations with worldwide connections, while other, smaller agencies have chosen to specialize in retailing, direct mail, and minority markets, among other services.

European colonists brought the idea of advertising with them to America, but the concept was slow to take hold. Colonists had little need to advertise their goods and services for sale over a wide area. In 1704, the first known newspaper advertisement appeared in the *Boston Newsletter,* offering real estate for sale. During the 18th century, the *Pennsylvania Gazette* was the first newspaper to print advertisements with illustrations. And the first magazine advertisement appeared in the May 1741 issue of *General Magazine.*

The majority of advertising centered on land, runaways (slaves and indentured servants), and transportation. Notices selling slaves also constituted a good percentage of these advertisements. The remaining ads were lists of goods offered for sale by local merchants and descriptions of books newly published. These simple announcements basically answered the readers' two questions—where and when? Advertising then changed dramatically.

The Industrial Revolution brought bigger and faster steam presses, lithography, new methods of paper-making, and color reproduction techniques that made volume printing cost-effective by the mid-1800s. At the same time, the country's burgeoning urban population, booming economy, and western expansion created a demand for news about business, travel, entertainment, and the availability of goods and services. This led many newspaper publishers to consider advertising as a vital source of revenue; some even included the word "advertiser" in the paper's name. The typical newspaper page looked much the same as our present-day want ads or legal announcements, with little white space and few illustrations to separate the ads.

A key development in the newspaper world was the introduction of the "penny paper," which cost only 1 cent compared to the more common 5 or 6 cents. At this low price, the papers planned to sell a lot of advertising to subsidize revenue. The result was that newspapers sold enormous amounts of space in one-inch chunks. Unlike newspapers, magazines made most of their money from subscriptions and did not accept paid notices until the 1870s.

With improved methods of transportation, manufacturers distributed their goods over wider areas and thus required sales promotions that reached beyond their local region. Advertisers found that the media arrangements needed to print their announcements included a myriad of details and time-consuming tasks. These included identifying effective newspapers, negotiating rates, directing the printer, confirming the insertion, and sending in payment. To fill this need, newspapers began paying agents to sell space to advertisers and thereby gave birth to an entirely new business, the advertising agency.

The first advertising agent in America was Volney B. Palmer, who started in Boston in 1841 and soon opened offices in New York and Philadelphia. Still, there were barely a half-dozen

Advertisement for farming equipment, ca. 1870 (Library of Congress)

such agencies as late as 1865. By the last part of the century, however, the newly opened agencies began to offer their services to advertisers, promising help with writing the ads, seeing that they were placed in the best possible locations, and trying to get the best possible deal with the paper. Like today, the agency is typically paid a commission by the newspaper, magazine, or television company. The advertising agency collects the money for the bill from the advertiser, takes out a 15 percent commission, and passes what is left to the newspaper or magazine or media station.

Many did not consider advertising an honorable practice. Without any formal regulation, advertisements for dubious health remedies, get-rich-quick schemes, and other outrageous fakery filled the pages of national newspapers and magazines. The ad copy, commonly called "puffing," had no limit to the claims it made. This image was not helped much by advertising for patent medicines, which were the first products to heavily advertise on a national scale. However, the patent medicine companies, desperate for places to advertise, recognized that pages in magazines could efficiently promote their products.

Ads also provided a new source of income to magazine publishers. At this point, the role of the magazine publisher changed from being a seller of a product to being a gatherer of consumers. For example, *Collier's, Ladies' Home Journal, Saturday Evening Post, American Magazine, Woman's Home Companion,* and *The Delineator* were promoted in the business world as being created primarily as vehicles for advertising. These new magazines created new opportunities for national advertisers as well as new demands on agencies.

With the rise of national advertisers and the advent of new media, advertising agencies changed to meet the demand of American business. Agencies expanded beyond their initial role as sellers of newspaper space. Some agents formed billposting companies, which erected their own boards and leased space. Others organized streetcar and magazine advertising, selling the media on a national basis. Agencies also learned how to create advertising campaigns and plan marketing strategies.

This activity led to the creation of national, and sometimes global, advertising organizations. New York City, the nation's leading city in domestic and foreign trade, emerged as the center of advertising as major agencies opened up shop: N. W. Ayer & Son (1869); J. WALTER THOMPSON (1871); George Batten Co., later BBDO (1891); and Bates Agency (1893). Mathilde C. Weil, Mary Compton, and Meta Volckman operated their own agencies in New York, while other women found places in business as copywriters, advertising artists, publishers, agents, and representatives.

After the Civil War, industrialization, rapid urbanization, and massive immigration changed patterns of social life and the character of the American middle class. Manufacturers began to exploit people's desire for fashionable things, as material goods became visible symbols of personal worth and identity. Marketers soon recognized that with a memorable brand name and attractive packaging, they could charge a higher price for their products; in turn, they urged consumers to accept no substitutes. Nationwide advertising put the trademark before the readers, and the copy told why the product was better. As a result, customers knew the brand they wanted before entering the store. Thus, early manufacturers boxed and advertised hundreds of cereals, packaged soaps, flour, cigarettes, matches, canned vegetables, fruits, milk, and soup.

By the turn of the century, manufacturers routinely introduced new brand-name products with a wave of advertising. Advertisers also gradually began to turn their advertising entirely over to agencies. With full responsibility for campaigns, the advertising agencies evolved into their present-day form within the first decade of the century. Advertisements now were but one component of planned campaigns that had to be integrated into appropriate and sound marketing strategies. Skilled copywriting, layout, and illustration became important in achieving continuity and strengthening selling appeal. The role of account executive also expanded from simply bringing in new business to providing a needed liaison between the business-oriented client and creative staff, while space brokers continued to shop around for the lowest bids for each media schedule. Market research, however, proved slower in getting started than copywriting, layout, and account management.

When four-color front and back covers and one- or two-color interior ads became standard by 1900, magazines exploded with color. While humor, jingles, and trademark characters kept the names of products in the public's mind, they did not always sell them. A new advertising approach, called "reason-why" copy, shifted the focus of ads to sales arguments designed to overcome any resistance.

This hard-sell style was in sharp contrast to the simple brand-name identification campaign that sold the product name to the public. The print copy then had to convince customers they should buy the product, and at the same time, the sales pitch had to convince the merchant that he could make money by stocking it. In short, the copy style was straightforward and direct. It stated firmly what the product did and how it would benefit the buyer. In the process, reason-why practitioners John E. Kennedy, Claude Hopkins, and Albert Lasker established the copywriter as crucial to ad agency operations.

Until 1906, the advertising of this period was completely unregulated. In that year, Congress passed the Pure Food and Drug Act, which required manufacturers to list the active ingredients of their products on their labels. Still, advertisers could continue to say just about anything—and did.

The emergence of advertising as a legitimate enterprise was perhaps evidenced with the outbreak of World War I, when "patriotic" businesses, citizen groups, and even the government kept company names in the public eye and created national advertising programs to gain public support. After the 1918 armistice ended the war, manufacturers increased their advertising budgets and spurred the return to a consumer economy.

Following a brief depression in 1921, the economy took off on a period of rising prosperity. People's newly acquired affluence also provided manufactures with a ready-made mass market. Ads sold cosmetics and goods to improve appearance—and an endless stream of new inventions to save time, eliminate the need for servants, permit the wife to leave the home, and improve the life of everyone. It was also a time of the general distribution of the telephone, electric light bulbs, electric phonographs, and cameras. The radio, another invention in this era, would have a profound effect on advertising and society.

Agencies seeking to gain a professional standing for their work supported the trend toward scientific advertising. National advertisers with multimillion-dollar budgets sponsored market and psychological research to ensure that their advertising proved an effective marketing tool. Professional journals advised the advertising industry that 80 percent and more of the readers of advertisements were women. Also, women were emotional; therefore, ads should portray idealized versions rather than prosaic realities. Keep the copy personalized and intimate. To fit these requirements, ads were filled with short stories where the woman was concerned about the impression she was making, her success in holding her husband, and the health or intelligence of her children.

Newspapers and magazines dominated mass communications until the first commercial radio broadcast in 1920. Over the course of the decade, radio emerged as a major industry through both the marketing of radio sets and the selling of airtime to advertisers. Most early station managers and many public officials, however, did not welcome commercial advertising messages, fearing that the dignity of radio would be compromised by the advertising chatter. But broadcast operating costs and pressure from the potential advertisers forced the issue, and commercial messages on radio eventually became acceptable. Ever since, radio has accepted advertising's financial support.

At the same time, J. Walter Thompson led the ad industry in both innovative copy styles and the variety of services offered to clients. The agency's billings more than tripled, from $10.7 million in 1922 to $37.5 million by the end of the decade, making it the industry leader in total billings, a position it maintained for the next 50 years.

The end of the Roaring Twenties was signaled by the stock market collapse of October 1929. In the worst depression in American history, a staggering number of people were unemployed, there was little money to spend, and few goods were sold. For the rest of the decade, until World War II broke out, the economy remained largely stagnant, and advertising suffered like any other sector of the economy. The total volume of advertising revenue plunged nearly 70 percent—from a 1929 high of $3.4 billion to a low of $1.3 billion in 1933.

Admakers faced the difficult task of promoting products that Americans either could not afford or were hesitant to purchase. In response, admakers increasingly resorted to hard-sell and even sensationalist campaigns. Ads of the 1930s were jammed with text, threatening slice-of-life stories, contests, premiums, prizes, and two-for-one promotions. This resulted in a surprising backlash. New government regulations created heavy supervision and control over the way advertising was practiced, while a consumer revolt produced a series of commercially popular books that dramatized the most questionable advertising practices.

Another notable event during these years was the emergence of radio as a significant advertising medium. Different from present television formats, in which each commercial sells only one product, in 1930s radio the whole show advertised one product. Soap operas, begun in 1932, and so named for the soap companies that created and sponsored them, dominated daytime. Comedies and variety shows played in the evenings.

Advertising contributed to the World War II effort as well. After the attack on Pearl Harbor, the U.S. government revived the poster and ad programs that had been successful in World War I. The Office of War Information formed the War Advertising Council in 1942, producing the most extensive advertising campaign in history, promoting war bond sales, internal security, rationing, housing solutions, and precautions against venereal disease. As defense production increased, many wartime advertisers also found that the themes of patriotism and conservation fostered consumer loyalty and sold goods. With the defeat of Germany and Japan, the productive wartime economy slowly transformed into an even stronger consumer economy.

Following World War II, advertising realized its greatest prosperity since the 1920s. Between 1945 and 1960, gross annual advertising expenditures quadrupled, and automobiles replaced packaged goods and cigarettes as the most heavily advertised products. During this period, many advertising agencies merged, opened offices overseas, and expanded their services. This trend toward mergers arose as clients demanded more services such as research, sales analysis, package design, and publicity. Advertisers also competed in an increasingly cluttered marketplace as business boomed. For every new product four or five major competitors already existed. In order to sell more, businesses advertised more and demanded that marketing and advertising departments claim a scientific basis for their work.

And then there was television. Its rise from pre–World War II science experiments to a television set in nearly every home occurred in the 1950s. The developers of the new medium tapped the experience of the early radio broadcasters. Recognizing that shoestring operations characteristic of many radio stations were no longer feasible, TV established networks of affiliated stations. Initially, the national commercial networks were limited to the big three—CBS, NBC, and ABC.

As had been the case with radio, the television networks at first served merely as production and transmission facilities, while advertisers controlled the programs. Philip Morris cigarettes, for example, owned *I Love Lucy,* General Mills sponsored *Betty Crocker's Star Matinee,* and Dutch Masters cigars funded the *Ernie Kovacs Show.* By 1950 TV advertising revenue reached $100 million; soon thereafter TV revenues overtook those of radio. Four years later, in 1954, television became the leading medium for advertising. By 1960 nearly every home had a television set.

The first television ads were simply televised radio commercials, and sometimes the announcer could even be seen holding the script. These commercials, as well as most programming until 1957 (except filmed entertainment), aired live because videotape recording had not yet been invented. Animated commercials also reached a zenith in the late 1950s, in part because they were less costly than glamorous models and actors. Advertisers also targeted children as a specific market to sell toys, cereals, and candies.

Full sponsorship of commercial entertainment faded from television during the 1960s when most advertisers decided that programs were too expensive to sponsor and strategically ran their messages on several other programs. When the networks took over the responsibility for programming from advertisers, they at first referred to advertisers whose commercials appeared during their programs as "participating sponsor." Today most broadcast advertising is simply sold as spot announcements or "spots"— that is, the breaks between the programs.

Scenes of modern life, sentiment, and a reliance on science and technology characterized advertisements of this era. Two of the most significant advertising personalities of this period were Rosser Reeves of the Ted Bates Agency and consultant Ernest Dichter, best known for his motivational research (MR). Reeves emphasized science and research, and his ads typically featured simple repetition of a single theme, or the "unique selling proposition" (USP). Also, Reeves pioneered the use of the new medium of television as a force in American political campaigns.

In 1952, he sold presidential candidate Dwight Eisenhower in the same way that he promoted toothpaste, with a USP: "Eisenhower, man of peace."

Consumer researcher Ernest Dichter pioneered the MR approach, replacing the statistical techniques of polling and counting with concepts derived from psychology and psychoanalysis. MR examined what triggered people to make choices on the subconscious and unconscious levels. Noted for his work on Chrysler, for example, Dichter deduced that more men bought a sedan even though they were attracted to a convertible, because they associated the hardtop with their wife and the sportier vehicle with a mistress. But MR was not without its critics. The publication of Vance Packard's best seller *The Hidden Persuaders* (1957) warned the public that large-scale efforts were manipulating people "against their free will."

Advertisers, too, reinforced traditional family values. A profusion of ads pictured idealized versions of the mythic conventional family with well-behaved children and narrow gender roles. However, in the following decade people turned from science to inspiration, youth rebelled, and women and African Americans demanded inclusion and fairness.

Advertising during the 1960s was slow to respond to the massive social changes of the era. While the nation was struggling with civil rights, the Vietnam War, and the sexual revolution, advertising often portrayed women and minorities in subservient roles. It appeared that only white people bought and used products, and that women had few aspirations beyond the home and family.

What was revolutionary about advertising in the 1960s was "creatives" (art directors and copywriters) having a bigger say in agency management. Since the unique style of the ad design was so closely identified with a single artist and a single copywriter, the new project teams worked better in small agencies rather than in huge advertising companies. The result was that accounts moved their work from old-line, traditional agencies and took their campaigns to innovative, boutique advertising companies that were fast and flexible. And a wide variety of products, notably Pepsi, traded on youth and the idea of youth. The creative revolution, and the look it produced, is most often associated with four famous advertising agencies: Leo Burnett, Ogilvy & Mather, Doyle Dane Bernbach, and Wells Rich and Green.

In 1935, copywriter Leo Burnett opened his shop, Leo Burnett Co., in Chicago. Like Reeves, Burnett focused on the product but also sparked interest with good artwork, information, recipes, and humor. Burnett's campaigns used a host of continuing characters called "critters," as well as jingles, in both print and television ads. Likeable, animated characters created by Burnett include the Jolly Green Giant, Tony the Tiger for Kellogg's Frosted Flakes, and Snap! Crackle! And Pop! for Kellogg's Rice Krispies. The familiar cowboy, the Marlboro Man, became one of the great campaigns in advertising history.

When David Ogilvy opened his agency on Madison Avenue in 1949 (later Ogilvy & Mather), he believed that an ad should be a dignified explanation of what was being sold. The ad followed the Ogilvy formula: a handsome picture, a long headline, and straightforward, low-key copy. Ogilvy also devised unique hooks to capture the reader's attention, and then repeated them to link his ads together. For example, the Hathaway man's eyepatch, the Schweppes salesman's Van Dyke beard, and the quietly ticking clock in the dignified Rolls-Royce all became identified with their brands.

The innovative approach of Bill Bernbach and his New York–based agency Doyle Dane Bernbach (DDB) represented another leading force in advertising. His ads were humorous, limited to a single selling point, and sometimes used only one sentence or two to a page. There were the campaigns for Volkswagen, Levy's Rye Bread, and Alka-Seltzer. He believed that the purpose of an ad was to persuade people to buy, and anything that detracted from that idea and those words was bad design. Admakers need to simplify and to dramatize the selling idea to make memorable the message of the advertisement.

Mary Wells's agency Wells Rich and Green started as one of the first major agencies ever headed by women. Wells produced memorable commercials for Alka-Seltzer's "Try it, you'll like it." And for the Braniff International Airlines "Flying Colors" campaign, she painted the planes pastel shades and dressed the stewardesses in Pucci outfits.

It was also the beginning of the merger movement that swept the industry throughout the 1970s and into the next. Advertising agencies grew rich in the 1960s and early 1970s as corporations poured their money into creative campaigns. The ad agencies then poured their profit into in-house research, and they got larger. But that trend changed in the mid-1970s, when a severe recession and double-digit inflation stifled the economy. What had started as small, flexible idea-houses in the 1960s had become large and sluggish. The need for costly research activities and the huge sums of money resulting from advertising contracts set the agencies up for a wave of mergers and takeovers in the 1980s, combining them into a far smaller number of huge corporations.

At the same time, the civil rights movement led to more cultural diversity throughout the advertising industry. The most noticeable reform involved presenting African Americans in a range of normal occupations and tasks rather than as demeaning stereotypes. However, few African Americans worked on Madison Avenue in any capacity, professional or clerical. To address this imbalance, agencies created new training programs and white-collar positions for minorities. Several national African-American agencies also opened. In 1956, Vince Cullers had started the nation's first African American–owned full-service agency, followed by Burrell, Inc., in 1971 and UniWorld headed by Bryon Lewis.

Women also took a cue from the successes of the civil rights movement, and the second wave of the feminist movement hit Madison Avenue. The women of the 1960s were a new phenomenon, better educated and more socially and politically aware. They also represented almost half of the total workforce in the country. In terms of marketing and advertising, women were not going to be influenced by the same advertising and promotional messages. But advertisers continued to address women in terms of "idealized roles" rather than "reality situations." Feminist criticism did not abate until the advertising industry began to pay attention to feminist concerns with gender issues. By the mid-1970s, ads not only depicted the professional woman at work but also increasingly pitched her cars, homes, and insurance.

By the late 1970s, many women had opened their own agencies. Among these were Shirley Polykoff, Jane Trahey, Paula Green, Jo Foxworth, Lois Geraci Ernst, and two African-American adwomen, Joyce Hamer and Caroline R. Jones.

Advertisers faced still other challenges in the health hazards associated with tobacco and a revived consumerism. In 1964 the surgeon general announced that cigarette smoking was a health hazard that required remedial action. For advertisers this meant that warning notices had to be printed on every pack, and cigarettes could no longer be advertised on television and radio.

The 1970s also resulted in added REGULATION. First, a group of Boston women founded the Action for Children's Television, which lobbied the government to limit the amount and content of advertising directed at children. Also, the FEDERAL TRADE COMMISSION and the industry's National Advertising Review Board demanded higher standards of honesty and disclosure from the advertising industry. Most notable among the campaigns judged to be misleading were Warner-Lambert for Listerine, Campbell Soup, and Anacin.

A final point that needs to be made is that both consumers and formal regulatory agencies restricted advertising, yet technological advances posed unprecedented opportunities. The development of the VCR, cable television, and the laser disc all occurred during this period. Also, advertisers learned how to reach more specific audiences through the diversity of new cable TV programming such as ESPN, CNN, TBS, and Nickelodeon. In the 1980s, television advertising was influenced by the rapid-cut editing style of MTV, while infomercials presented a long advertisement that looked like a talk show or a half-hour product

demonstration. Then came personal computers, laptops, and hand-held computer systems.

The success of Silicon Valley and the emergence of Pacific Rim countries also led to a flood of creativity from the West Coast. For the first time, New York City no longer dominated the creative scene. Creative marketers could now be found at the offices of California agencies such as Chiat/Day,

Large billboard advertisements in New York City (SPENCER/GETTY IMAGES)

Hal Riney, and Foote Cone & Belding. Other innovative agencies also appeared in such cities as Minneapolis, Dallas, Atlanta, and Portland.

In the 1980s, glamour, wealth, and power were back in style. Well-heeled, well-traveled consumers expected quality goods, fashions, furniture, and architecture. Despite rising production costs and an increasingly cluttered marketplace, manufacturers spent a great deal of money on image building for cosmetics, perfume, and fashion. Advertisers no longer described how their products worked or why they were better or different; rather, powerful images alone were expected to evoke confidence in the brand.

In 1987, however, the downturn on Wall Street signaled the "good life" was out and the "simple life" was back. The recession of the late 1980s continued into the 1990s and led to far reaching changes in the industry. Global competition also put American corporations under pressure to restructure, consolidate, and simplify.

The economic realities of the 1990s, combined with changing demographics and lifestyles, have created a new breed of savvy consumers. Advertisers also had to adapt to the concept that consumers have greater control of the information they receive about products and brands—and consumers give information back to the firms, for example, through e-mail and tracking of Internet surfing. The proliferation of cable television, direct marketing technology, and the growth of interactive, wireless, and broadband technologies has further fragmented the media. A growing investment in advertising has resulted in so much clutter that promotion options, such as online communication, brand placement in film and television, point-of-purchase displays, and sponsorships, are more attractive to advertisers.

As new technology presents new communication options, advertising as a process has not changed. So far, advertising is still a paid, mass communication effort to persuade and inform. As a business process, advertising continues to be one of the primary marketing tools that contribute to profits by stimulating demand and nurturing brand loyalty.

Further reading

Fox, Stephen. *The Mirror Makers: A History of American Advertising and Its Creators*. New York: Vintage Books, 1983.
Goodrum, Charles, and Helen Dalyrymple. *Advertising America: The First Two Hundred Years*. New York: Harry N. Abrams, 1990.
Lears, Jackson. *Fables of Abundance: A Cultural History of American Advertising*. New York: Basic Books, 1995.
Marchand, Roland. *Advertising the American Dream*. Berkeley: University of California Press, 1985.
Pope, Daniel. *The Making of Modern Advertising*. New York: Basic Books, 1983.
Presbrey, Frank. *The History and Development of Advertising*. Garden City, N.Y.: Doubleday, Doran, 1929.
Sivulka, Juliann. *Soap, Sex, and Cigarettes: A Cultural History of American Advertising*. Belmont, Calif.: Wadsworth, 1998.

Juliann Sivulka

airline industry The U.S. airline industry is responsible for transporting more than 600 million passengers and 18 million pounds of freight per year, and employs approximately 600,000 people nationwide. In 1997, passenger and freight revenues exceeded $89 billion. The industry is comparatively young, just over 80 years old; its robust performance is the result of constant interplay between technological innovations, government regulations, and evolving customer requirements.

The first scheduled air service in the United States was a small Florida air taxi service that began in 1913. However, the modern airline industry dates from 1918, when the U.S. Army inaugurated, and the U.S. Post Office acquired, the Air Mail service. Benefiting from advanced airplanes and engines developed during World War I, the Post Office established a scheduled coast-to-coast network. The Post Office gradually expanded its airmail routes for the next five years.

In the mid-1920s, federal legislation designed to stimulate commercial aviation considerably influenced the development of airlines. The Air Mail Act of 1925 authorized the Post Office to contract with private companies for mail delivery along regional Contract Air Mail (CAM) routes. Ford Air Transport flew the first CAM flight in 1926. Other airlines awarded CAM routes included Western Air Express, Pacific Air Transport, and Varney Speed Lines. Beginning in 1927, PAN AMERICAN AIRWAYS flew international airmail.

Shortly after scheduled services began, the Air Commerce Act of 1926 transferred authority for operating the airmail system to the Department of Commerce. The transfer was complete by 1928. Advances in aviation technology during the 1920s improved the proficiency and reliability of airlines. Blind flying and radio navigation capabilities permitted nighttime and cross-country flights. Many airlines received grants from the Daniel Guggenheim Fund for the Promotion of Aeronautics to finance the development and purchase of airplanes.

Supportive legislation and operating subsidies encouraged financiers to view airlines as sound investments. As a result, larger, more viable regional airlines appeared. When Jack Maddux acquired Transcontinental Air Transport and Western Air Express in November 1929, the resulting company—TWA—became a major national airline.

Charles Lindbergh's 1927 solo Atlantic flight generated popular interest in air travel. The Air Mail Act of 1930 capitalized on this interest by establishing a premium for airlines that flew passengers as well as mail. Airlines encouraged the AIRPLANE INDUSTRY to develop suitable multi-engine aircraft, the ancestors of today's airliners. Among them were the Douglas DC, the Lockheed "Electra" series, and the BOEING 247. During the mid-1930s, airlines shifted their focus from airmail to passengers as their primary source of revenue.

Further rearrangement came in 1934, when Congress canceled all domestic airmail contracts due to collusion between the postmaster general and several airlines. New bids were eventually sought, but due in part to this scandal antitrust regulations required all airline operators to divest their aircraft and engine manufacturing holdings. For example, United Aircraft & Transport split into United Aircraft Corporation and United Air Lines. This structure has remained the industry's standard.

Comprehensive federal REGULATION of air commerce began in earnest with the Civil Aeronautics Act of 1938. This act established the Civil Aeronautics Authority (CAA) under the Department of Commerce. One of the purposes of the CAA was to ensure fair competitive practices in the comparatively small industry. Two years later an independent Civil Aeronautics Board was established to control routes, fares, safety, and entry by new airlines.

Developments during World War II significantly influenced the postwar industry. After 1945, airlines had access to larger aircraft with more powerful engines, produced by companies with substantially greater output capabilities. New international agreements and a reorganized CAA favored expansion. Airlines benefited from improved navigation and landing aids. Charter, freight, and regional services appeared, using inexpensive surplus transports.

Jet propulsion, an important wartime technological innovation, significantly altered the industry in the mid-1950s. Fuel efficiency and power initially limited commercial applications, but the development of the Pratt & Whitney JT-3 engine allowed Boeing and Douglas to develop commercial airliners around it: the 707, which entered service in 1958, and the DC-8 in 1959. Though conversion to jetliners proved expensive, by the early 1960s jet aircraft began to dominate air travel and enabled the major airlines to overtake railways and ocean liners as the primary method of long-distance passenger transportation. Concurrent with the development of jetlin-

Aerial view of a Boeing B-47 Stratojet (LIBRARY OF CONGRESS)

ers, an independent Federal Aviation Agency (later Administration; FAA) superseded the CAA in January 1959. The FAA later became part of the Department of Transportation.

In response to the need to carry more passengers more cost-effectively, wide-body airliners were introduced in the early 1970s. However, the oil crisis and an economic recession slowed airline growth; when airlines sought fare increases to offset losses, industry critics cried that regulation had turned airlines into inefficient, monopo-

listic sluggards. In 1978, Congress passed the Airline Deregulation Act, which ended more than 50 years of direct federal oversight of the industry. The resulting competition inspired innovations such as hub-and-spoke systems, frequent flier miles, and computer reservation systems.

By 2000, airlines were generally prospering. Despite shakeups and mergers, competition thrived, and airlines turned small but consistent profits. New airlines competed and collaborated with major carriers to provide domestic and international service. Nevertheless, concerns about the quality of safety and service led to increasing tensions between airlines and travelers and even the airlines' own employees. Concerns about industry competitiveness in the global marketplace inspired a new round of consolidations. Observers are uncertain whether problems will increase now that airlines answer to stockholders rather than to the government or to customers.

The terrorist attacks of September 11, 2001, in which the world watched transcontinental airliners become weapons of mass destruction, will likely alter for at least a generation the relationship of air travel to American life. Increased security and heightened passenger unease appear to be the new norm. In addition, the price of jet fuel has steadily increased, on top of which several airlines have been embroiled in labor disputes with airline employee unions over salaries and pension plans. All of these factors came into play when United Airlines—the third-largest airline in the United States—declared bankruptcy in 2002, from which it is still trying to recover. The larger airlines are also suffering from the competition being presented by low-cost carriers such as Southwest Airlines and Jet Blue. These smaller airlines have found ways to cut costs, lower fares, and remain profitable—forcing the larger airlines to match their lower fares and thereby reducing profits. As the industry recovers from the losses of both revenue and reputation, however, it will likely resume its pattern of change in response to new competitors, markets, and opportunities.

See also EASTERN AIRLINES.

Further reading
Gittell, Jody Hoffer. *The Southwest Airlines Way: Using the Power of Relationships to Achieve High Performance.* New York: McGraw-Hill, 2003.
Millbrooke, Anne. *Aviation History.* Englewood, Colo.: Jeppeson Sanderson, 1999.
Morrison, Steven, and Clifford Winston. *The Evolution of the Airline Industry.* Washington, D.C.: Brookings Institution, 1995.

Whitnah, Donald R. *Safer Skies: Federal Control of Aviation, 1926–1966.* Ames: Iowa State University Press, 1967.

Paul Lagasse

airplane industry   The manufacture of aircraft, missiles, and related systems is a high-profile and a high-risk industry. Aerospace sales account for nearly 2 percent of the nation's GDP, generating more than $155 billion in sales and $10.8 billion in profits in 2000. Success factors include science and technology, the state of the economy, competition, and customer priorities.

The army issued the country's first airplane production contract to the Wright brothers in 1908. Airplane companies were not profit-making manufacturing ventures, but rather small-scale establishments. Many short-lived companies appeared prior to 1917, along with more durable firms such as Martin and BOEING. World War I accelerated industry growth and cemented a permanent relationship with the military. Airplane orders rose dramatically; most were for license production of superior European designs. Because of wartime production control by the automobile industry, airplane production levels never reached anticipated levels. After the armistice, the government canceled more than $100 million in contracts, and many companies folded.

Growing legislative support, a strong economy, and technological innovations helped the postwar airplane industry grow. New firms capitalized on novel approaches to design or manufacturing. Many of these companies, including Douglas, Lockheed, and Northrop, gained publicity through races and record-breaking flights. Legislation in the 1920s stimulated the industry to design transport aircraft and ensured the continuity of government orders. Popular interest in aviation grew, and financiers began investing in manufacturers. Research led to faster, safer, and more fuel-efficient airplanes. Large trusts such as United Aircraft and Transport Corporation, North American Aviation, and Curtiss-Wright appeared, consolidating airplane manufacturers and airlines under one corporate umbrella. These lasted until 1934, when antitrust legislation permanently separated manufacturers from airline operators.

Through the 1930s, domestic and foreign demand for airliners and warplanes grew dramatically. As the government's call for defense-related manufacturing intensified, companies frequently sought government aid to build and staff new factories.

After Pearl Harbor, production came under government control. Companies relied on subcontracting and licensing to fulfill mass-production orders. More than 300,000 complete airplanes, 800,000 piston engines, and 700,000 propellers were manufactured between 1940 and 1945. However, as with World War I, sudden contract cancellations at war's end threatened the survival of many manufacturers.

Renewed demand for commercial aircraft softened the blow for several companies. Douglas, the largest prewar manufacturer of airliners, returned immediately to airliner manufacture, as did Lockheed. Attempts by other firms to enter the airliner market proved unsuccessful. Other firms survived by moving into niche markets such as helicopters, light aircraft, and subassemblies.

The president's Air Policy Commission in 1947 issued a report calling for the maintenance of a strong airplane industry to supply the armed forces. Firms began experimenting with jet propulsion and high-speed aerodynamics. The Korean War allowed airplane manufacturers to gain experience mass-producing jet aircraft. The decline in military orders after the war was offset by a rise in demand for commercial aircraft. The stage was thus set for the introduction of jet airliners, which revolutionized not only commercial air transport but also the economics of the industry.

In the mid-1950s, Boeing parlayed its experience with mass-producing jet bombers into the design of the 707 airliner, which entered service at the end of the decade. Douglas introduced its DC-8 jet airliner a year later. Other transitional designs appeared as firms sought to discover a new equation of efficiency, economy, and reliability to accommodate jet engines.

Beginning in the late 1950s, the airplane industry became the aerospace industry as a result of increased military demand for missiles and related technologies. Manned and unmanned spaceflight represented a high-profile opportunity for many firms to succeed in a new field.

Despite efforts to diversify, by the 1960s increasing project costs and decreasing unit quantities per order threatened to bankrupt many companies. There were several high-profile mergers, including McDonnell Douglas and Martin Marietta. Firms came under intense criticism for controversial military projects that were called too costly, over-managed, and unnecessary. By the 1970s, military and commercial sales had stabilized at $20 billion. Although the number of aircraft produced dropped considerably; critics claimed the industry operated at overcapacity. Manufacturers sought to improve economies of scale by introducing intercontinental widebody airliners. Boeing's 747 was the first, followed by McDonnell Douglas's DC-10 and Lockheed's L-1011. However, with rising fuel costs airlines could barely afford them. Efforts to develop supersonic transports were halted by predictions of low passenger yield, poor fuel economy, and potential environmental hazards.

The doldrums of the 1970s were overcome by the effects of airline deregulation and increased military spending, beginning in the early 1980s. The trend toward fewer numbers of increasingly expensive aircraft continued into the 1990s, exemplified by the Rockwell B-1 and Northrop B-2 bombers and the McDonnell Douglas F-18 and Lockheed F-117 fighters. The "make-or-break" nature of such contracts, and the relaxation of antitrust scrutiny in the face of international competition, resulted in more joint projects and mergers in the 1990s. For example, the team of Lockheed/Boeing/General Dynamics developed the YF-22 fighter for the air force; the rival YF-23 was developed by Northrop and McDonnell Douglas. Shortly thereafter, Northrop and Grumman announced their merger, followed by Lockheed and Martin Marietta that same year. In 1997, McDonnell Douglas merged with long-time commercial rival Boeing to create the world's largest aerospace firm.

Private and business aviation was never as lucrative as commercial and military aviation. By the late 1970s, major manufacturers had left the field to smaller, specialist companies such as Piper, Cessna, and Lear. After years of strangulation caused by product liability litigation, domestic purchases have risen steadily due to recent legislation designed to reduce the impact of liability suits.

The future of the aerospace industry will likely be oriented toward increasing international competition. Newly opened markets in Asia and eastern Europe represent both opportunities and challenges. U.S. firms will doubtless face tough competition from overseas private and state-owned manufacturers for the civil and military markets of the new millennium.

Further reading

Biddle, Wayne. *Barons of the Sky: From Early Flight to Strategic Warfare, the Story of the American Aerospace Industry.* New York: Simon & Schuster, 1991.

Pattillo, Donald M. *Pushing the Envelope: The American Aircraft Industry.* Ann Arbor: University of Michigan Press, 1998.

Rae, John B. *Climb to Greatness: The American Aircraft Industry, 1920–1960.* Cambridge, Mass.: MIT Press, 1968.

Paul Lagasse

American Express Company   The American Express Company is one of the most visible companies in the world. Known primarily for its widely used green charge card and blue box logo, American Express provides travel and financial services to millions of people and businesses each year.

The American Express Company has a long history. It was founded in 1850 to carry packages and financial instruments mainly on the RAILROADS; the express offered direct delivery and insurance for its consignments. The new firm was actually a merger of smaller companies run by three legends of American business history: Henry Wells, William Fargo, and John Butterfield. The first two went on to found WELLS FARGO & Company, while Butterfield organized the Overland Mail, the first effort at a land postal link between the West Coast and the East. The three men fought each other often but the benefits of the merger were so apparent that the company survived its internal strife and grew rapidly. By the late 1860s, American Express had formed a CARTEL along with four other express firms (Adams Express, United States Express, Southern Express, and Wells Fargo) to divide territory and control competition within the express business. These efforts at cartelization were remarkably successful, and the five dominated the business for more than 50 years.

The express cartel was able to control its business because federal law barred the United States Post Office from carrying packages over a certain weight. But the Post Office spurred American Express toward an important innovation. In an effort to win a greater share of financial transport, and to prevent the theft of letters containing cash, the Post Office introduced the postal money order in 1864. This eroded a lucrative part of the express business, and in 1881, the new president of American Express, James Congdell Fargo (William's younger brother), authorized the creation of an express money order that quickly won a large market share of the money order business.

Several years later, Fargo was traveling abroad and found it difficult and expensive to change small sums of money from one currency to the next. He returned home determined "to do something" about it. He turned to Marcellus Fleming Berry, the man who had devised the express money order system. Berry created the

American Express Traveler's Cheque, a money order with a specific face value and (originally at least) a guaranteed conversion rate into all of the major European currencies. The traveler's cheque—the TC in company parlance—is the most significant original product idea in the company's history.

The traveler's cheque (the company chose the British spelling of "check") was launched in 1891 at a time when Americans were just beginning to travel abroad in large numbers. The cheque was a huge success. In order to service cheque holders, as well as to conduct an international express business, American Express began to establish offices in Europe, which led in a short time to a more general business for travel and tourism throughout the world.

The success of the TC, money order, and travel businesses could not have been more opportune for American Express. In 1905, the express industry was brought under the regulatory supervision of the INTERSTATE COMMERCE COMMISSION; eight years later it faced competition from the Post Office's parcel post; and finally, in 1918, under the stresses of war, the U.S. government forced a merger of all express operations into a separate entity, the American Railway Express Company. But American Express was able to survive the change and expanded its financial and travel operations. By the 1920s, it had a worldwide network of offices.

In the 1920s and for more than 30 years thereafter, the traveler's cheque was the company's main source of profit. The TC's profitability came not from small service charges the company gained on each sale, but rather from the fact that people bought cheques one day but redeemed them later, often weeks later. This meant there was always a balance of money for uncashed cheques, a "float" that could be reliably tracked and invested in safe interest-bearing instruments. By the early 1950s, the TC float had reached more than $250 million and was invested mainly in municipal bonds, guaranteeing the company several million dollars in annual income.

In the 1950s, the company wondered whether a new device for travel and entertainment, a universal charge card pioneered by Diners' Club, posed a threat to the TC, and there was a running debate within the company over how to respond to the threat. Many younger executives wanted to acquire Diners' Club, while some senior officials wanted to create an American Express card. But the only opinion that mattered was that of the chief executive, the autocratic Ralph Reed, and he seemed to oppose any involvement in the "credit card" business. Late in 1957, however, he authorized the creation of an American Express credit card (as they called it then), which was launched the following year.

The effort was so poorly thought out that the card led to millions of dollars in losses over the first five years, and Reed's successor, Howard Clark, tried to sell the card operation. When that effort failed, Clark instead found a skilled manager who turned the unit profitable, and the company embarked on an aggressive market program. The tag line, "Don't leave home without it," became one of the most famous ad slogans of the 20th century, and the card soon surpassed the TC as the company's principal moneymaker.

The success of the card gave the company a high stock price and an urge to use it for acquisitions. Clark acquired the Fireman's Fund Insurance Company, while his successor, James Robinson, added brokerage companies, private and investment banks, and financial advising operations. By the 1980s, American Express was hailed as a "financial supermarket," one of the strongest diversified financial companies in the world.

But the various parts of the company did not always mesh, and before long American Express divested itself of insurance, brokerage, and investment banking subsidiaries. As income fell, commentators wondered whether American Express could survive as an independent entity, especially since the card's profitability seemed in doubt.

But American Express has had a knack for surviving. Over the years, it was threatened by government regulation, a takeover attempt by the Chase National Bank, and a scandal in a small warehousing subsidiary that almost led to the company's bankruptcy. But American Express survived those crises as well as recent downturns in its fortunes. At the end of 2002, it was still independent, still very profitable, and, with a market capitalization of more than $50 billion, still a force to be reckoned with in the financial world.

Further reading

Burrough, Bryan. *Vendetta: American Express and the Smearing of Edmund Safra*. New York: HarperCollins, 1992.

Carrington, Tim. *The Year They Sold Wall Street*. Boston: Houghton Mifflin, 1985.

Friedman, Jon, and John Meehan. *House of Cards: Inside the Troubled Empire of American Express*. New York: Putnam, 1992.

Grossman, Peter Z. *American Express: The Unofficial History of the People Who Built the Great Financial Empire*. New York: Crown, 1987.

Peter Z. Grossman

American Federation of Labor   The American Federation of Labor (AFL) was the predominant labor organization in the United States from the late 1880s until 1936, when a split occurred that generated the Congress of Industrial Organizations. It was rooted in a culture of labor radicalism that flowed from the post–Civil War period to the Second World War, but in time it became an increasingly moderate, even conservative, force representing particularly (though not exclusively) skilled workers in craft unions.

The founding of the organization can be traced to 1881, when a national gathering in Pittsburgh, Pennsylvania, came together under the banner of the Federation of Organized Trades and Labor Unions of the United States and Canada (FOTLU). It replaced the National Labor Union that had existed from 1866 to 1872 but had been pulled apart by the lure of divergent electoral strategies. FOTLU veered away from

electoralism, also seeking to be more efficiently organized and more narrowly focused than the more expansive labor reform group, the Knights of Labor. While some dedicated socialists were prominent among its founding members, other key founders were not, and the federation as a whole helped to consolidate the trend toward an increasingly nonradical "pure and simple" unionism in the U.S. labor movement.

"We have numberless trades unions, trades' assemblies or councils, Knights of Labor and various other local, national, and international unions," declared the call for the national conference that formed FOTLU. "But great as has been the work done by these bodies, there is vastly more that can be done by a combination of all these organizations in a federation of trades." Among the key architects of the new organization were Samuel GOMPERS and Adolph Strasser of the Cigarmakers Union and Peter J. McGuire (often credited as initiating both May Day and Labor Day) of the Carpenters Union. All had come out of the socialist movement, and the influence of Karl Marx is clearly perceptible in the preamble of the FOTLU constitution: "A struggle is going on in the nations of the civilized world between the oppressors and the oppressed of all countries, a struggle between capital and labor . . . This history of the wage-workers of all countries is but the history of constant struggle and misery engendered by ignorance and disunion; whereas the history of the non-producers of all ages proves that a minority, thoroughly organized, may work wonders for good or evil. . . . Conforming to the old adage, 'In union there is strength,' the formation of a Federation embracing every trade and labor organization in North America, a union founded upon a basis as broad as the land we live in, is our only hope."

This preamble was carried over into a new constitution in 1886 that reorganized the organization under a new name—the American Federation of Labor. The AFL's president, from its founding until his death in 1924 (with a one-year hiatus) was the tough-minded Samuel

Gompers, who moved in an increasingly prag-matic direction.

Initially, many associated FOTLU and the AFL with the socialism that had significant influ-ence in some working-class circles of the time. Socialism—favoring replacement of capitalism by social ownership and democratic control over the economy—was not viewed positively in this era of triumphal industrial capitalism. Gompers explained that the allegation of his being part of a socialist conspiracy was a slander based partly on a misunderstanding. "In those early days not more than half a dozen people had grasped the concept that economic organization and control over economic power were the fulcrum which made possible influence and power in all other fields," he later wrote in his autobiography. "Control over the basic things of life gives power that may be used for good in every relationship of life. This fundamental concept on which the AFL was later founded was at that time not for-mulated in men's minds, and the lines between Socialists and trade unionists were very blurred."

Indeed, during the 1880s, Gompers became known not as an advocate of socialism but as an advocate of what became known as "pure and simple trade unionism." This meant organizing workers into unions that would focus on strug-gles at workplaces around issues of higher wages, fewer hours of work, and improved working con-ditions—to the exclusion of radical social causes, whether socialism or anything else. When asked what the labor movement wanted, Gompers once replied simply: "More." Yet Pennsylvania Federa-tion of Labor president James Maurer has left this record of one of Gompers's many "pure and sim-ple" union speeches: "If a workingman gets a dollar and a half for ten hours' work, he lives up to that standard of a dollar and a half, and he knows that a dollar seventy-five would improve his standard of living and he naturally strives to get that dollar and seventy-five. After that he wants two dollars and more time for leisure, and he struggles to get it. Not satisfied with two dol-lars he wants more; not only two and a quarter,

but a nine-hour workday. And so he will keep on getting more and more until he gets it all or the full value of all he produces."

Despite the underlying militancy of this per-spective, however, Gompers steered the federa-tion into what labor radicals would denounce as a "class-collaborationist" course. He sought posi-tive relations with business leaders in organiza-tions such as the National Civic Federation, and—with the slogan of "support our friends and punish our enemies"—backed "capitalist politi-cians" willing to take pro-labor positions. By the early 1900s, he was openly and vehemently denouncing socialists and socialism (though always expressing admiration, even in his end-of-life autobiography, for Karl Marx). Nor was he above siding with employers and government authorities in efforts to destroy the radical Indus-trial Workers of the World (IWW) during World War I. More than this, and despite an expansive rhetoric about the U.S. labor movement embrac-ing all workers, Gompers and those around him adopted bigoted attitudes toward blacks, Asians, and new immigrants from southern and eastern Europe, as well as toward women. By contrast, he was quite vocal and proactive—from the 1917 Russian Revolution onward—in opposing com-munism within the labor movement as well as globally. Many saw the AFL as white, male, and "100% American"—and while Gompers never argued for such a position, his policies con-tributed to making this a reality.

The policies pioneered by Gompers were con-tinued by William Green, who assumed the AFL presidency with the death of Gompers in 1924. As an official in the UNITED MINE WORKERS OF AMERICA, Green had favored industrial unionism and union involvement in broad social reform efforts, but as AFL president he would become the foremost standard bearer of the dominant AFL orientation: narrow craft unionism and a "pure and simple" focus on seeking to improve wages and conditions at the unionized work-place. This contributed to the erosion of AFL membership, as skilled trades in many sectors of the economy were being sidelined by the rise of mass production industries.

For many, "pure and simple" unionism had evolved into an exclusive concern for the narrow economic interests of unions' own members, with a disregard for larger social questions. An approach sometimes called "business unionism" often predominated: Not only were union leaders very pro-business (seeking far-reaching accommodations with employers), but also they saw the union itself as a business providing services to its paying members, with union representatives being called "business agents" and notions of democratic control by the membership being replaced by a notion of hierarchical "businesslike" efficiency. With the phenomenal growth of gangsterism in the "roaring twenties," corruption and racketeering made significant inroads among some unions in the federation. And in the conservative political atmosphere of the decade, the AFL inclined toward an acceptance of the dominant laissez-faire philosophy—rejecting the idea of government programs to help disadvantaged workers.

Within AFL ranks, voices of dissent and opposition to craft union conservatism grew. A. Philip Randolph, leader of the all-black Brotherhood of Sleeping Car Porters, successfully fought to get his union into the AFL, and then consistently protested against racist practices in the ranks of organized labor. With the devastating impact of the decadelong Great Depression that began in 1930, increasing numbers joined socialists and other radicals in challenging laissez-faire and pro-business perspectives. Most significantly, a number of unions organized on an industrial basis (including all skill levels and occupations within a given industry) began arguing against the narrow craft orientation of the AFL. This included John L. LEWIS of the United Mine Workers, David Dubinsky of the International Ladies Garment Workers, and Sidney Hillman of the Amalgamated Clothing Workers, who spearheaded the formation of a Committee for Industrial Organization in 1935.

The reaction of Green and other AFL officials to the industrial union challenge was to denounce and finally expel them, only to see the industrial unions transform their committee into the Congress of Industrial Organizations (CIO). The CIO embraced a spirit of union militancy and radicalism (allowing the active participation of various socialists and communists as CIO organizers) that engendered—throughout the late 1930s—a series of dramatic strikes that organized millions of unskilled and semiskilled workers into a variety of new unions: the United Auto Workers (UAW), the United Electrical Workers (UE), the United Steelworkers (USWA), the National Maritime Union (NMU), the Transport Workers Union (TWU), the International Longshoremen's and Warehousemen's Union (ILWU), and many others.

CIO staff member Shirley Quill's description of AFL union officials conveys profound cultural differences between the two federations: "The AFL leaders were exactly what they appeared to be. Representing plumbers, carpenters, electricians and dozens of the old-line organizations, they were crafty, comfortable, conspicuously well-fed, successful powerbrokers in their own fiefdoms. They competently negotiated contracts covering wages, hours, working conditions and pensions, and stared blankly when such arcane subjects as discrimination, minority rights, seniority for women and voter registration appeared on the agenda."

And Victor Reuther (brother of UAW leader Walter REUTHER) later reminisced: "AFL officials periodically journeyed to Florida to spend several weeks, spending a few hours each morning in formal session, then going to the races or golf course or whatever for the rest of the day. The CIO Executive Board, under Philip Murray and then under Walter, usually met in a hotel conference room in some northern industrial city—Pittsburgh, Chicago, New York, or Washington—never too far removed from industrial workers who wanted to come before it to discuss urgent problems."

"Labor's civil war" generated much debilitating conflict and destructive "raiding" practices—

often with AFL unions signing backdoor contracts with employers who were interested in keeping out the more militant CIO. Yet the CIO challenge also played an important role in galvanizing sectors of the AFL (most dramatically the International Brotherhood of Teamsters) to organize on an industrial basis, and in modernizing itself in a variety of ways. More than this, elements of the CIO ferment and experience were brought into the AFL when some of the industrial rebels rejoined the federation. Most dramatic (though quite short-lived) was the return of John L. Lewis and the United Mine Workers. Earlier and more sustained was the "coming home" of David Dubinsky, the liberal-minded ex-socialist, who brought with him not only the ILGWU but also the former communist leader Jay Lovestone. Lovestone would become the architect and director of the AFL's fiercely anticommunist foreign policy, which soon became interwoven with efforts of the U.S. State Department.

An additional point of convergence was the full support that both labor federations gave to the U.S. war effort during World War II—establishing "no strike" pledges and participating in the War Labor Board, for example. Both had also become aligned with the Democratic Party, thanks to pro-labor policies advanced by President Franklin D. Roosevelt. With the end of the war and the beginning of the cold war, a development in the CIO would establish another point of convergence: the massive and thoroughgoing purge of communists and communist-led unions, and the marginalization of other left-wing influences. Not long after, the AFL would take measures to check the influence of racketeering. These developments—and the deaths in 1952 of AFL president William Green and CIO president Philip Murray—set the stage for a merger.

The AFL was now led by ex-plumber George MEANY, of whom more than one CIO leader had a low opinion. Phil Murray had described Meany as "some kind of loud-mouth bum from New York," commenting, "I can't stand him . . . [I] don't want to have anything to do with him." The younger and more dynamic Walter Reuther—one-time socialist, bristling with innovations and idealistic rhetoric—was now president of the CIO. When the merger came, however, and the AFL-CIO came into existence in 1955, it was George Meany, a master of organizational maneuver and expertise, who quickly asserted himself as the dominant force. With the merger, about 36 percent of the U.S. labor force was unionized, an all-time high.

Meany's comments shortly after assuming the AFL-CIO presidency reflect the triumph of an extreme variant of the AFL's "pure and simple" ideology. "I stand for the profit system; I believe in the profit system. I believe it is a wonderful incentive," Meany declared to a group of U.S. businessmen. "I believe in the free enterprise system completely. I believe in the return on capital investment. I believe in management's right to manage." Rhetorically asking "what there is to disagree about," Meany concluded: "It is merely for us to disagree, if you please, as to what share the workers get, what share management gets from the wealth produced by the particular enterprise." Despite the dissatisfaction of labor dissidents, this orientation would be predominant in the AFL-CIO for years to come.

Further reading

Buhle, Paul. *Taking Care of Business: Samuel Gompers, George Meany, Lane Kirkland, and the Tragedy of American Labor.* New York: Monthly Review Press, 1999.

Dubofsky, Melvin, and Warren Van Tine, eds. *Labor Leaders in America.* Urbana: University of Illinois Press, 1987.

Kaufman, Stuart Bruce. *Samuel Gompers and the Origins of the American Federation of Labor.* Westport, Conn.: Greenwood Press, 1973.

Le Blanc, Paul. *A Short History of the U.S. Working Class, From Colonial Times to the Twenty-First Century.* Amherst, N.Y.: Humanity Books, 1999.

Reuther, Victor G. *The Brothers Reuther and the Story of the CIO, A Memoir.* Boston: Houghton Mifflin, 1979.

Robinson, Archie. *George Meany and His Times, A Biography.* New York: Simon & Schuster, 1981.

Paul J. Le Blanc

American Stock Exchange The Curb Exchange, as the American Stock Exchange (AMEX) was known in its early days, was one of the most colorful attractions in New York. The exchange was actually operated on the street, hence the term *curb,* and orders for execution were yelled down, or hand signaled, to brokers from clerks in windows of the offices overlooking the street. Brightly colored jackets or hats were also worn by the brokers on the street, so that clerks could more easily identify their own broker—a custom still in use on most stock exchange floors around the world today. Hand signals thus became an integral part of this exchange and continue to be used to this day, despite the advent of electronics on the floor. Like other organized stock exchanges, the exchange uses the auction method of buying and selling stocks, whereby all orders pass through a specialist on the floor. After many years of rain, sleet, and snow, the exchange moved indoors in 1921 and was officially renamed the American Stock Exchange in 1953.

For many years, the AMEX served as an incubator for issues that would eventually get listed on this exchange after a period of trading in the "over-the-counter" market. It was from the American Stock Exchange that maturing issues then moved to the NEW YORK STOCK EXCHANGE (NYSE). In the 1960s, that progression began to change when some small companies became listed on the AMEX and grew into investor favorites but never changed their listings. With the growth of the NATIONAL ASSOCIATION OF SECURITIES DEALERS Automated Quotations market (NASDAQ) and the aggressive listing efforts of the NYSE, this long-standing procedure has become dormant in recent years. Stocks stay on NASDAQ or move directly to the NYSE, with few stopping at the American Stock Exchange in between. This has slowed the growth of the AMEX in recent years and forced it to search for other markets and other products.

In 1975, it became the second exchange in the United States to trade listed options, and this has been the exchange's bright spot for the last three decades. Today the AMEX is the second largest volume trader of listed options, behind the Chicago Board Options Exchange, and has been the creator of many innovative derivative products. In addition to options, the exchange has successfully experimented with other hybrid types of instruments that combine features of stocks and MUTUAL FUNDS, especially those that represent a basket of market indicators. These are known as index funds and market baskets.

As a result of pressures created by the 1990s bull market, the exchange needed to establish links with other exchanges in order to survive. The need for capital to expand was intense because of the need for new communications and computer systems. Finally, in 1996 the AMEX was merged with the NASDAQ. The marriage between the two different types of market was initially unsuccessful, and the NASDAQ began searching for a buyer for the exchange. The growth of the AMEX in the future will be intimately tied to its ability to find a suitable merger partner and to continue to develop new investment vehicles that can engender trading in new derivative instruments if not stocks.

See also STOCK MARKETS.

Further reading
Sobel, Robert. *Amex: A History of the American Stock Exchange.* New York: Weybright & Talley, 1972.
———. *The Curbstone Brokers: The Origins of the American Stock Exchange.* New York: Macmillan, 1970.

Lee Korins

American Telephone & Telegraph Co. (AT&T) The American Telephone and Telegraph Co. at its peak in the 1970s was the largest

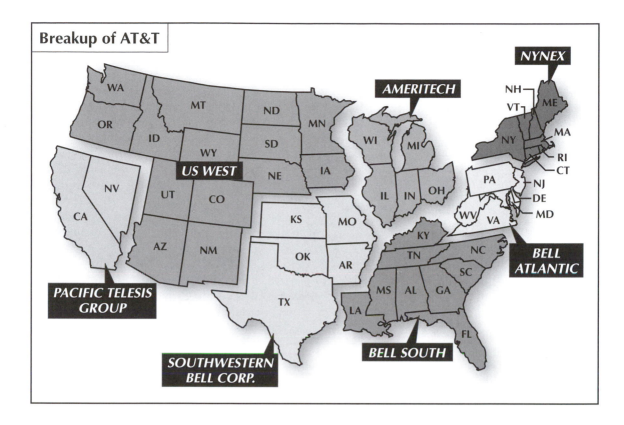

Breakup of AT&T

company on Earth. It had more than 1 million employees and was active in every state of the union. It provided telephone service to almost all Americans, manufactured and leased telephone equipment, and conducted research that led, among other things, to the development of modern computers through the invention of transistors at Bell Labs. It took AT&T a century to reach this position and only a decade to fall from it.

AT&T was formed in the 1870s to exploit Alexander Graham Bell's telephone patents. It was very successful, but met vigorous competition when the original patents expired. AT&T became the dominant telephone company early in the new century by focusing its attention on the intercity telephone network and, no doubt, some hard competing. Most telephone traffic was local, given the nature of economic life at the time and the primitive nature of long-distance

telephony, but AT&T's unique network gave it a distinct competitive advantage.

Bell's original company was organized as the Bell Telephone Co. in 1878. Its first general manager was Theodore Vail, hired away from the U.S. Post Office by Thomas A. Watson, one of Bell's early colleagues. From that point, the company developed quickly, based upon Vail's management expertise and far-sightedness. When he took the reins, less than 26,000 telephones were in service. Over the course of the next 10 years, Vail imposed his own design on the company, transforming it into a system rather than just a telephone company. Of its several original components, the American Telephone & Telegraph Company proved to be the most functional. Other parts of the company, namely the New England Telephone Company, sold licenses to smaller companies.

As the Bell System, composed of AT&T subsidiaries, grew to dominate the national telephone scene, it was subject to its first antitrust prosecution. In a consent decree in 1913, AT&T agreed to stop buying telephone companies and instead connect them to its network. During and after the Great War, the government decided to work with AT&T as a regulated monopoly rather than to promote competition. The dream of Theodore N. VAIL, president of AT&T in 1885–87 and again in 1907–19, of "one system, one management, universal service," was on its way to fulfillment.

AT&T was subject to its second antitrust prosecution after the Second World War, focusing on the market power of Western Electric, AT&T's manufacturing arm. The suit was settled by a consent decree in 1956 in which AT&T restricted itself to the telephone business. This appeared to be a minor constraint since AT&T had sold off its interests in radio, movies, and television, all promoted by research done in AT&T's Bell Labs, before the war. As computer and telecommunications technology grew less distinguishable, however, the constraint became more troublesome.

AT&T also agreed to transfer revenues from long-distance calls to Bell operating companies to keep local rates low, allowing some of the benefits of rapid technological advance in long distance telephony to be realized by local services. The resulting relatively high price of interstate calls attracted other smaller companies who saw a profit opportunity under the price umbrella formed by the high long-distance rates. An early challenge to AT&T was mounted by MCI, one of the small companies that initially wanted to use the phone company's lines. Discussions with AT&T proved fruitless, and the challenge was taken to court. The FCC encouraged MCI and other aspiring companies as a way to reintroduce competition into telephony. The third antitrust prosecution of AT&T started initially from concerns about Western Electric's equipment monopoly, but it quickly added MCI's accusations of unfair treatment. The suit dragged on for almost a decade and resulted in a consent decree that ended the Bell System.

Finally, AT&T agreed to settle the suit with the Justice Department after prolonged legal battles. The Modification of Final Judgment of 1982, so called because it was cast as a modification of the 1956 consent decree, allowed AT&T to retain Western Electric and Bell Labs in return for divesting itself of the Bell operating companies. The Bell operating companies were grouped together into seven Regional Bell Operating Companies, or RBOCs. Until 1996, the RBOCs were enjoined from competing directly with AT&T in long-distance service, and AT&T was unable to compete effectively with the RBOCs for local service. AT&T has attempted to enter local telephone markets, in competition with its former subsidiaries, which offered long-distance service of their own in competition with their former parent. In 2004, AT&T announced it would no longer be selling telephone services to residential customers and would concentrate on core businesses such as voice and data services to large corporations. AT&T, once the biggest company on Earth, is now only one telecommunications company among many.

See also BELL, ALEXANDER GRAHAM; WATSON, THOMAS A.

Further reading

Boettinger, H. M. *The Telephone Book: Bell, Watson, Vail & American Life.* New York: Stearn Publishers, 1977.

Coll, Steve. *The Deal of the Century: The Breakup of AT&T.* New York: Atheneum, 1986.

Temin, Peter. *The Fall of the Bell System.* New York: Cambridge University Press, 1987.

Peter Temin

American Tobacco Co.   Founded by Washington Duke after the Civil War, American Tobacco grew to be the largest company of its type in the world by the end of the century. The original company was located in Orange County, North Carolina. Duke served in the Confederate Army during the Civil War. After his return from a Union prison, he and his family rebuilt the family farm, which had deteriorated during the war, and began growing leaf tobacco suitable for smoking. His original product was called "Pro Bono Publico." Within a year of the war's end, his farm was producing more than 15,000 pounds annually. By the early 1870s, he was producing more than 100,000 pounds annually.

In 1874, Duke moved his operation to Durham, the capital of the North Carolina tobacco business. His sons Brodie and James B. Duke were active in the family business, and Duke rapidly became one of the richest men in the county. His major competitor manufactured the famous Bull Durham brand of smoking tobacco, and in order to compete with that company Duke admitted an outside investor and expanded his company. It became known as W. Duke, Sons & Co. In 1881, it began manufacturing cigarettes in addition to pipe tobacco.

The company became automated in 1884, when Duke purchased a machine capable of rolling cigarettes. After the machine succeeded in reducing labor costs, James B. Duke opened a branch operation in New York City. This helped the company gain access to a national market, and the branch became crucial to the company's further success. Encouraged by the business expansion of the period and the growth of large trusts in the late 1880s, Duke and his four major competitors decided to merge, forming the American Tobacco Co. in 1890. The consolidation was typical of the period of trust growth, although it would draw the attention of trustbusters in Congress and government. Before the merger, the companies produced more than 90 percent of the nation's tobacco. After the merger was complete, the company became known as the "tobacco trust" because of its dominance of the market.

American Tobacco was also the largest producer in the world by 1890. Washington Duke left the company to his sons in order to pursue other interests, including philanthropy. But the company's success was challenged by ANTITRUST forces in the administration of Theodore Roosevelt, and a suit was filed seeking the breakup of the company in 1908. Lower courts ruled in favor of the Justice Department, and the case was appealed to the Supreme Court. In 1911, two weeks after the Standard Oil Company decision, the Court upheld the lower courts and ordered the breakup of the company—the second monumental decision ordering the breakup of a major monopoly that year.

As a result, four major companies were created in the wake of the order—the new American Tobacco Co., Liggett & Myers, P. LORILLARD & COMPANY, and R. J. Reynolds. The creation of new companies, spun-off from the old parent, was similar to the breakup of Standard Oil. Recognizing the antitrust sentiment in the country, James B. Duke had by that time branched out into other interests, including electric power production in the South. Since 1904, he had been involved with the establishment of the Southern Company, a major utility. But his tobacco company became a significant economic force in the South, especially in North Carolina, and became the standard for the industry.

Further reading

Durden, Robert F. *The Dukes of Durham, 1865–1929.* Durham, N.C.: Duke University Press, 1987.
Porter, Patrick G. "Origins of the American Tobacco Company." *Business History Review* 43 (1969).

antitrust   Characterizing the process of reviewing MERGERS to decide whether they violate antimonopoly laws. The name derives from the period of trust creation in the United States, from 1875 to 1911, when many large "trusts" were formed in order to consolidate various industries by merging companies in similar lines of business. The trusts eventually gave way to the modern HOLDING COMPANY, but the term *antitrust* survives, dating from the passage of the Sherman Antitrust Act in 1890.

The SHERMAN ACT was the first major antitrust legislation passed in the United States. Previously, the only way to attack monopoly in the courts had been through the COMMERCE CLAUSE in the Constitution, which brought mixed results because of its limited potential applications. After the act was passed, trust creation continued, and a record number of mergers were consummated during the McKinley administration in the late 1890s. But after Theodore Roosevelt became president, more antitrust cases were mounted, initiated by the Justice Department. Actions were initiated against the Northern Securities Company, American Tobacco Company, Standard Oil Company, and the United States Steel Corp. among others. The first decade of the 20th century became known as the golden era of antitrust.

Two of the most notable antitrust cases—against Standard Oil and American Tobacco—were upheld by the Supreme Court in 1911, and both companies were ordered to be broken up. In 1914, more antitrust legislation was added when Congress passed the CLAYTON ACT in an attempt to prevent price discrimination, interlocking directorships, and vertical mergers, topics not specifically covered by the Sherman Act. The Clayton Act prohibited companies from acquiring the stock of others in order to prevent competition. Like the Sherman Act, the law was vague in places and did not always prevent horizontal combinations from taking place. Congress also created the FEDERAL TRADE COMMISSION (FTC) in 1914 to help prevent price discrimination and protect consumers by issuing cease and desist orders against companies that had complaints filed against them for unfair trade practices. The agency was intended to enhance the Sherman Act and give the government a method of preventing unfair practices short of filing suit under the 1890 legislation. Today antitrust actions on the federal level can be initiated by the Antitrust Division of the Justice Department or the FTC.

Antitrust laws were complemented by antitrust policy, as seen in the political attitude of the administration holding office toward big business and mergers in particular. In some cases

when administrations in office were friendly to business, as in the case of McKinley, mergers were allowed to proceed at a rapid pace. In other cases, such as the administration of Theodore Roosevelt, "trust busting" was in vogue, and many cases were brought before the courts in keeping with the administration's progressive leanings. During the 1920s, another burst of mergers occurred as successive Republican administrations did not pursue antitrust in the courts, especially after U.S. Steel was ruled a "good trust" by the Supreme Court, ending a decade-long court fight in favor of the company. The friendly attitude toward mergers lasted until the NEW DEAL.

Antitrust policy was given a boost during Franklin D. Roosevelt's second administration when Thurman Arnold of the Yale Law School was named head of the Antitrust Division of the Justice Department. The staff and budget of the division were increased dramatically, and new cases were pursued. During the first FDR administration, antitrust laws had been relaxed in favor of pursuing economic recovery during the Depression, but another RECESSION occurred in 1937 that convinced many in the administration that business was to blame. Stronger antitrust actions followed. An inquiry into industrial concentrations in 1939, investigated by the Temporary National Economic Committee (TNEC), discovered that many major industries were dominated by a few large firms, despite previous attempts to level the playing field. But after the outbreak of World War II, antitrust activity again fell as economic activity concentrated on the war effort. The one law that was passed during the 1930s—the ROBINSON-PATMAN ACT (1936)—was aimed mostly at the expansion of CHAIN STORES and did not have any substantial applications until after the war.

After the war, industry began to expand, and many large CONGLOMERATES were formed. Unlike horizontal or vertical mergers, these companies were an amalgam of many different types of companies and as such did not fall under any of the

Cartoon depicting Uncle Sam trying to control the monopolies, 1887 (LIBRARY OF CONGRESS)

existing antitrust laws. As a result, Congress passed the Celler-Kefauver Act in 1950, seeking to slow the growth of conglomerates. The act did not succeed in preventing their growth, however, and it was not until the Nixon administration took office in 1969 that antitrust activity again became more vigorous. Most of the focus of the administration's policies was on protecting larger, more established companies from the predatory tactics of many of the newer conglomerates. Attempts were made or discussed, unsuccessfully, to prevent mergers among the top 200 companies so that the conglomerates could not take over the largest companies using their high prices in the stock market to acquire larger firms without using cash.

Another attempt to protect companies from predatory takeovers by conglomerates was made when Congress passed the Williams Act in the late 1960s, requiring companies acquiring more than 5 percent of another company's stock to register with the Securities & Exchange Commission. While not able to prevent takeovers, especially hostile takeovers, the law required a waiting period of 20 days while the SEC reviewed the filing, allowing some breathing space for the target companies.

During the 1960s and 1970s, many actions were brought against a wide range of companies. Among the largest and best-known were those against the IBM Corp. and AT&T as well as actions against such smaller but well-known companies as Schwinn and the Brown Shoe Company. The case against IBM was eventually dropped, but the case against the telephone company was pressed until it finally agreed to a breakup in 1982. When it did, the Antitrust Division scored its biggest victory since the landmark cases of 1911. The case also helped establish DEREGULATION as a trend in business generally, especially during the Reagan administration after 1982. The AT&T breakup encouraged Congress to begin deregulating other protected industries, a process that continued well into the 1990s.

During the 1990s in the Clinton administration, antitrust activities began strongly again with actions against a number of companies, including Intel and Microsoft Corporation. These cases proceeded while Congress passed legislation to help deregulate other industries, notably the TELECOMMUNICATIONS INDUSTRY and the UTILITIES industry. The cases were brought both by the Justice Department and the Federal Trade Commission. The case against Microsoft was upheld in the courts, making it another significant victory in antitrust, although the company was penalized rather than broken up. Throughout its history, antitrust has scored notable successes and failures against companies charged with price fixing and other anticompetitive practices. Often it has been most effective in blocking mergers before they could be consummated. Once mergers have been consummated, it is more difficult to seek antitrust remedies.

Further reading

Adams, Walter, and James Brock. *Dangerous Pursuits.* New York: Pantheon, 1989.

Geisst, Charles R. *Monopolies in America.* New York: Oxford University Press, 2000.

Kovaleff, Theodore Philip. *The Antitrust Impulse: An Economic, Historical, and Legal Analysis.* Armonk, N.Y.: M. E. Sharpe, 1994.

Whitney, Simon. *Antitrust Policies.* New York: Twentieth Century Fund, 1958.

Astor, John Jacob (1763–1848) *fur trader, real estate developer, and financier*   Astor was born in Waldorf, Baden (today Germany). He arrived in the United States at age 21, landing in Baltimore in 1784. On the voyage to New York, his ship was frozen in Chesapeake Bay for part of the winter. While on board, he met someone who told him stories of fur trading in the Pacific Northwest, and he became determined to enter the business. Although often thought to have arrived in America as a penniless youth, within two years he had established a musical instrument business, suggesting at least some moderate means.

With the Treaty of Paris in 1763 and then the American War of Independence, many of the existing business structures in North America were changing. Understanding the changing market conditions as a result of the Revolution, Astor moved into the fur business, selling furs and purchasing trade goods in New York, Albany, and Montreal, then transporting them to New York for direct sale in Europe.

By 1790, Astor also became involved in the China trade, along with Montreal merchants. He held a small but guaranteed share in China ships along with Alexander Henry, and McTavish, Frobisher and Company. With the profits from these ventures, Astor began to buy land both in Lower Canada and in the Mohawk Valley. The business pattern that emerged by 1794 of trading furs, the China trade, and land, would continue into the future and earn Astor a large fortune.

The implementation of Jay's Treaty in 1794 between the United States and Canada led to a further reorganization of trade and a break with the North West Company. In the next 20 years, Astor began profitably to expand his involvement in the China trade and to expand his fur trading activities. These activities in many ways mirrored the westward movement of the new republic. In 1808, the American Fur Company was chartered in New York and by the end of 1811 had established Astoria at the headwaters of the Columbia River. In that same year, Astor became a partner in the South West Company. Throughout this period, Astor used some of his profits to buy land in New York City. His purchases made him one of the city's largest landowners, and parts of the city were eventually named after him, especially in the borough of Queens.

The War of 1812 led to a number of changes. Although the American Fur Company would continue to operate for decades, Astoria was sold to the North West Company in 1813. In New York, Astor became involved in war financing, buying and selling government bonds profitably, along with Stephen GIRARD and the American representative of BARING BROTHERS, the British bank. He subsequently became involved in the Second BANK OF THE UNITED STATES and its branch in New York.

With the death of his grandson in 1819, Astor's direct involvement in his business affairs was reduced. Leaving them in the hands of his son, William, he sailed to Europe, where he stayed on and off for much of the remainder of his life. He became known as the wealthiest American of his day, and his fortune was one of the first significant ones to be accumulated in the 19th century. He was reputed to be the first American millionaire. When he died in 1848, John Jacob Astor had a net worth of $20 million. In his will, he bequeathed $400,000 for the establishment of a reference library in New York City.

Astor also began a family dynasty that continues to this day. Astors have become prominent in publishing, real estate, and British politics as well.

Further reading

Haeger, John Dennis. *John Jacob Astor: Business and Finance in the Early Republic.* Detroit: Wayne State University Press, 1991.

Smith, Arthur D. Howden. *John Jacob Astor, Landlord of New York.* New York: Blue Ribbon Books, 1929.

Madsen, Axel. *John Jacob Astor: America's First Millionaire.* New York: John Wiley & Sons, 2001.

Ann M. Carlos and Frank D. Lewis

automotive industry   In 1900, motor vehicles were built one at a time by hundreds of start-up companies for sale to rich people as novelties.

Most of these manufacturers disappeared by the 1920s, and except for a brief period after World War II, three companies—GENERAL MOTORS, Ford, and Chrysler—controlled around 90 percent of the U.S. market between the 1929 stock market crash and the 1973 oil crisis.

Into the 21st century, the two surviving U.S.-owned motor vehicle producers—GM and Ford—held only one-half of the U.S. market. New competitors from Asia and Europe had begun selling and making motor vehicles in the United States, using efficient production methods that resulted in high-quality products.

Controversy surrounds the identity of the builder of the first workable gasoline-powered motor vehicle in the United States. Claimants during the early 1890s included Henry Nadig in Allentown, Pennsylvania (1891), John William Lambert in Ohio City, Ohio (1891), Gottfried Schloemer and Frank Toepfer in Milwaukee, Wisconsin (1892), Charles H. Black in Indianapolis, Indiana (1893), and Elwood P. Haynes in Kokomo, Indiana (1894).

The first company organized in the United States for the purpose of producing and selling motor vehicles was the Duryea Motor Wagon Co. of Springfield, Massachusetts. Duryea sold four cars in 1895 to lead all U.S. producers. Its reputation was enhanced by winning the first important motor vehicle race in the United States, in Chicago in November 1895.

European manufacturers clearly had a head start on their American counterparts during the late 19th century. In France, De Dion–Bouton & Trépardoux pioneered production of steam-powered vehicles in 1883. Panhard & Levassor started building and selling the first "modern" motor vehicle in 1892, with the engine mounted in the front rather than under the driver.

Carl Benz and Gottlieb Daimler debated who was first in Germany during the 1880s. Daimler was the first to design a four-cycle gasoline-powered engine in 1883; he received the first German patent on a three-wheeled gasoline-powered vehicle in 1885, but did not start manufacturing vehicles until 1890, three years after Benz. Benz made the first authenticated tests of a vehicle with three wheels and a one-cylinder gasoline engine in 1885, patented it in 1886, started sales in 1887, and built a four-wheeled vehicle in 1893.

Motor-vehicle sales grew rapidly in the United States during the first decade of the 20th century, from 2,300 in 1900 to 120,000 in 1910. More than 3,000 firms were organized to manu-

facture motor vehicles, though only a few hundred achieved commercial production and sales of more than a handful.

First to sell more than 1,000 in a single year—in 1900—was the Columbia, an electric car built in Hartford, Connecticut, by the Pope Manufacturing Co., founded by Col. Albert A. Pope, the nation's leading bicycle manufacturer. A year later, the steam-powered Locomobile became the second to exceed sales of 1,000.

Charging the battery of a Detroit electric automobile (LIBRARY OF CONGRESS)

Southeastern Michigan quickly emerged as the center of U.S. auto production early in the 20th century. The amount of national production clustered in southeastern Michigan reached 80 percent in 1913. Michigan's edge came in part from expertise with gasoline engines. Of the roughly 4,000 motor vehicles sold in the United States in 1900, 40 percent were powered by steam, 38 percent by electricity, and only 22 percent by gasoline. By 1908, the three-way competition was over: Gasoline engines accounted for 83 percent of sales, and the other two power sources soon disappeared altogether.

Michigan had become a center for production of gasoline engines for agricultural and marine uses during the late 19th century. The Olds Motor Works in Lansing was a leading producer of small stationary engines to operate farm implements. Olds was the first to build motor vehicles in Detroit, in 1899, but when the factory burned two years later, the company moved back to Lansing, where it became a prominent community fixture for most of the 20th century. The Oldsmobile Curved Dash was the first large-volume low-priced car, hitting peak sales of 4,700 in 1903.

Henry M. Leland, head of Leland & Faulconer Manufacturing Co., the nation's leading producer of marine gasoline engines, also in Detroit, organized the companies responsible for the two surviving U.S.-made luxury vehicles: Cadillac in 1903 and Lincoln in 1917. Leland & Faulconer was also a major supplier of engines, transmissions, and other components to early motor vehicle manufacturers.

For five years, while he experimented with motor vehicles, Henry FORD was in charge of keeping generators in operation at one of the Edison Illuminating Company's Detroit power plants. Ford became good friends with Thomas EDISON, who despite his role in developing electricity encouraged Ford to use gasoline to power his cars.

Michigan also became the center of the motor vehicle industry because of expertise in building bodies. Flint in particular was a center for pro-duction of horse-drawn wagons and carriages. Largest was Durant-Dort Carriage Co., organized in 1886 by William C. DURANT and J. Dallas Dort. Early motor vehicles had bodies adapted from horse-drawn carriages.

Anticipating the demise of the horse-drawn carriage, Durant entered the motor vehicle industry by taking control of a struggling Flint-based Buick Motor Company in 1904. David Buick, a plumbing parts producer, had started the company bearing his name, but was unable to make it profitable. Under Durant, Buick became the best-selling brand in 1909.

Availability of investment capital also influenced the clustering of motor vehicle production in Michigan. Wall Street bankers regarded investing in motor vehicle producers as too risky because of the high failure rate. In Michigan, start-up funds came from wealthy investors who had made their fortunes in Michigan's extractive industries, such as copper, iron, and lumber.

From the thousands of companies trying to enter the motor vehicle industry during the first decade of the 20th century, two quickly emerged as the leading manufacturers: FORD MOTOR CO. and General Motors. These two companies were the sales leaders in the United States and worldwide nearly every year through the 20th century and into the 21st century.

After two failures, Henry Ford established the successful Ford Motor Co. in 1903. Ford's priority from the beginning was to build low-priced vehicles affordable for working people and practical in reducing their daily tasks. This strategy went against the conventional wisdom that luxury cars were more profitable to build. Only very wealthy people could afford cars in 1900, and they were used primarily for recreation. Henry Ford's genius was to recognize that the desire to own a motor vehicle was nearly universal.

After several years of experimentation, Ford brought out the Model T in 1909, priced at $650, at a time when the average American vehicle cost $2,000. One-half of the cars in the world were Model Ts during the 1910s, and more than 15 million Model Ts were sold before production ended in 1927 (when it was priced at only $290).

Despite its low price, the Model T was extremely profitable because of innovative mass production techniques, especially the moving assembly line, which Ford installed at his Highland Park, Michigan, factory in 1913. Each worker was given a specific task to perform, repeated every few seconds throughout the day. Workers were arrayed along the line based on the logical sequence of tasks to be performed, and the moving line brought the needed materials in turn to each of them. Ford reduced the amount of time needed to build a car from 1,260 person-hours in 1912 to 533 in 1915 and 228 in 1923.

Ford passed the benefits of the moving assembly line to the public through lower prices, thereby stimulating universal demand for vehicles in the United States, and in turn swelling Ford's gross receipts. Ford also passed on benefits to his workers by more than doubling their wages to $5 a day in 1914.

The $5 a day wage made Henry Ford a folk hero in the United States. A lifelong pacifist, Ford sailed to Europe in 1915 to try to stop World War I. He barely lost a race for the U.S. Senate from Michigan in 1918 to an opponent, Truman Newberry, who spent a fortune and was forced to resign the seat a few years later because of fundraising irregularities during the election.

Success with MASS PRODUCTION and the Model T gave Henry Ford a belief in the absolute infallibility of his judgment. He insisted on selling only the primitive Model T until 1927 despite the advice of his son Edsel and other top advisers, nearly all of whom left the company. He refused to adopt modern cost accounting, bookkeeping, or billing practices.

Ford's eccentric behavior took a more sinister turn during the 1920s. He criticized bankers, teachers, lawyers, doctors, insurance, charity, sugar, and jazz. Ford's "Sociological Department" investigated the living conditions and personal habits of his workers to certify them as worthy of the $5 a day wage. Ford published about 90 anti-

Semitic articles. Ford's Service Department, led by ex-convicts and organized crime figures and staffed by thugs, monitored worker behavior, even trips to the bathroom.

General Motors was created in 1908 by Flint carriage maker William C. Durant, who had already turned Buick into the best-selling brand. Recognizing economic benefits resulting from large size, Durant acquired numerous parts makers to supply Buick and moved them to Michigan. In 1908, Durant brought the leading motor vehicle manufacturers to a Detroit hotel room and proposed that a "trust," or monopoly, be created, much as had occurred in steel, telephone, and other industries. When Henry Ford demanded cash for his company, the deal collapsed. Durant then established General Motors in 1908 as a HOLDING COMPANY to acquire as many carmakers as possible to supplement Buick.

Durant started with Olds, which had lost its sales leadership after Ransom E. Olds left the company in a dispute with his financial backers. Durant bought the Pontiac-based Oakland Motor Car Co. a few days before its owner, Edward Murphy, died in 1909. Oakland struggled until it brought out a popular low-priced model called Pontiac in 1931. Cadillac was acquired from Henry Leland in 1909.

Unable to repay all the loans he had secured to pay for GM's rapid expansion, Durant was forced by the bankers to resign in 1910. Durant organized several new companies, including Chevrolet, which was based on a prototype developed by a famous race driver, Louis Chevrolet.

In one of the most remarkable events in American industrial history, Billy Durant, through his Chevrolet Motor Co., regained control of General Motors in 1916. By all accounts an extremely charming man, Durant convinced GM stockholders to turn over their GM shares to him in exchange for Chevrolet stock and a promise of greater profits.

Durant again overextended GM and again was forced to resign, this time for good. After another failed attempt to create a car company,

Durant died in poverty and obscurity. Control of GM passed to DuPont. Alfred P. Sloan, president and then chairman of the board of GM between 1923 and 1956, pioneered modern management practices, including decentralized day-to-day decision making and a standardized accounting system.

Sloan created a "car for every purse and purpose," assigning a distinctive price segment to each of the company's products, from the low-priced Chevrolet, which displaced Ford as the country's best-selling brand, to the dominant luxury car brand, Cadillac. GM introduced the annual model change, in which mostly cosmetic "improvements" were unveiled once a year amid fanfare, thereby convincing many motorists to trade in their otherwise serviceable older models for brand new ones. To facilitate frequent trade-ins, GM also pioneered selling cars on credit.

In 1929, a record 4.3 million vehicles were sold in the United States. The 1929 sales record would not be exceeded for 20 years. Sales declined to 1.3 million in 1932, at the depth of the Great Depression, and halted altogether between 1942 and 1945 for World War II. Ford and GM had established themselves as the two industry giants during the 1910s. They were joined during the 1920s by Chrysler Corp., which grew rapidly after its incorporation in 1925. They became known as the Big Three carmakers.

Walter Chrysler, who had run GM's Buick division and Willys-Overland Co., became president of Maxwell-Chalmers Co. in 1923. In 1924, he introduced a line of cars named Chrysler, which became so successful that he changed the name of the company to Chrysler Motors Co. in 1925, and dropped the Maxwell line of cars altogether in 1926. Chrysler passed Ford during the 1930s as the second leading carmaker behind GM.

High unemployment and poor working conditions in the plants still open during the 1930s fueled union organizing activities. Skilled craftspeople had put together early motor vehicles by hand. Along the mass-production moving assembly line, work was repetitive and automatic, with a specified number of seconds allocated to perform each task. Workers were expected to exercise little thought, judgment, or skill. Unskilled labor was supplied by immigrants to Detroit, especially African Americans from the U.S. South and eastern Europeans.

The United Automobile Workers (UAW) union successfully organized General Motors following a 44-day sit-down strike in early 1937 at a Flint Fisher Body plant. Chrysler and smaller producers quickly recognized the UAW. Ford held out until 1941. The UAW initiated a "pattern bargaining" process during the 1950s in which it picked one of the Big Three for intense negotiations. To add pressure, the union would call a strike against only the targeted company while its competitors could continue to produce and sell vehicles. The contract signed with the targeted company served as a pattern for contracts negotiated with the other two of the Big Three.

The Big Three were hit hard by the Depression. Sales declined between 1929 and 1932 from 1.5 million to 322,000 at Ford, from 1.4 million to 522,000 at GM, and from 400,000 to 200,000 at Chrysler. However, smaller companies were even more devastated and were forced to cease production altogether. By the mid-1930s, Chrysler, Ford, and GM sold 90 percent of the vehicles in the United States, and they would continue to account for nearly 90 percent of sales in most years through the 1960s.

Immediately after World War II, several smaller companies together captured one-fourth of the market, taking advantage of the enormous pent-up demand for motor vehicles. But the independents fell by the wayside once the Big Three completed conversion from military to civilian production and introduced newly designed postwar models. Among the smaller independents, Studebaker merged with Packard in 1954 and ceased production in the mid-1960s. Also in 1954, Nash and Hudson formed American Motors, which hung on until acquired by Chrysler in 1987.

GM's position in the post–World War II market was especially dominant. After Henry Ford's death in 1947, the Ford Motor Co. began a modernization program under grandson Henry Ford II. A strong group of managers known as the "Whiz Kids" were brought in to revive Ford. Chrysler's sales slipped behind Ford into third place when its redesigned postwar cars proved less appealing and less well built than its competitors.

Had it engaged in aggressive price-cutting, GM might have driven every other carmaker out of business. But the company decided that it could not exceed its 50 percent market share without incurring the wrath of congressional antitrust watchdogs. Therefore, GM used its dominant position to raise prices and swell profits. GM's annual rate of return during the quarter-century after World War II was more than twice as high as other carmakers and other U.S. manufacturers. By far the world's largest parts maker, GM further added to its profits by selling spark plugs, bearings, air conditioners, automatic transmissions, and other parts to Ford, Chrysler, and the smaller independents.

GM set up an Art and Color Section in 1927 led by Harley J. Earl, the industry's most influential designer for the next four decades. Innovative styling such as tailfins, chrome trim, and hardtop bodies (no pillar between the front and back doors) took precedence over engineering improvements. The dominance of General Motors at mid-century was best captured by its president, George Wilson, at 1953 U.S. Senate hearings to confirm his appointment as secretary of defense in the Eisenhower administration: "[F]or years I thought what was good for our country was good for General Motors—and vice versa."

GM's power reached its peak during the 1960s, when it tried to smear Ralph NADER, who had argued in his 1965 book *Unsafe at Any Speed* that the company was more concerned with profits than safety in developing its Corvair model. GM's campaign backfired, and the company ended up settling an invasion of privacy suit for $425,000, which Nader used to set up consumer advocacy programs.

A 1956 Ford Crown Victoria automobile (LIBRARY OF CONGRESS)

Prior to 1973, the Big Three regarded foreign cars as a minor nuisance. British sports cars such as MG and Triumph had style and flair, but imports—nearly all from Europe—were in general objects of ridicule and held a combined total of only 1 percent of the U.S. car market in 1955. Reliability was abysmal: Broken-down foreign cars sat for weeks until replacement parts arrived from Europe by boat.

The one exception during the 1950s and 1960s was Volkswagen, whose U.S. sales increased from 26,000 in 1955 to 156,000 in 1960 and 569,000 in 1970. The German carmaker's appeal touched two rapidly expanding groups of U.S. consumers: households seeking an economical second car and baby boomers seeking an alternative to their parents' massive "land cruisers." The Big Three blunted the growth of foreign car sales by introducing smaller models of their own in 1960, including Ford's Falcon, Chrysler's Plymouth Valiant, and GM's ill-fated Chevrolet Corvair.

The OPEC oil embargo during the winter of 1973–74 and rapid oil price rise during the rest of the 1970s induced many Americans to trade in their gas-guzzling U.S. models for fuel-efficient foreign cars. But Volkswagen was not the beneficiary of this increasing interest in foreign cars; its U.S. sales declined to 294,000 in 1980 and 159,000 in 1982. Rather, Japanese companies, led by Toyota and Honda, increased their U.S. sales from 300,000 in 1970 to 2 million in 1980. GM and Ford lost money for the first time since the Great Depression, and Chrysler was saved from BANKRUPTCY by federal government loan guarantees.

U.S. companies were mandated to raise fuel efficiency from 12 miles per gallon in 1975 to 27.5 miles per gallon in 1985. As memories of high prices and shortages of petroleum faded, the Big Three were unable to recapture market share from Japanese companies. Americans were initially attracted to Japanese cars because of higher fuel efficiency, but they continued to buy them because of higher quality.

The Big Three denied the existence of a quality gap during the 1980s. They blamed the perceived gap on consumer magazines, Ralph Nader, and biased questionnaires. Japanese companies were challenged to "level the playing field" by building cars in the United States with American workers. A dozen Japanese-owned and -managed assembly plants were built in the United States during the 1980s, and quality remained high. Most telling was a joint venture between Toyota and GM called New United Motor Manufacturing Inc. (NUMMI) in Fremont, California. Under GM management, the plant had a reputation for poor quality and a dysfunctional workforce. Under Toyota management, the same workers produced high-quality cars efficiently.

Most influential in changing the attitude of U.S. carmakers was *The Machine That Changed the World*, a 1990 report by the International Motor Vehicle Program (IMVP). Funded by U.S. and European carmakers and government agencies, the IMVP identified why Japanese carmakers were able to produce better-quality vehicles more efficiently than U.S. or European firms. The IMVP team called the Japanese system "lean production."

Under lean production, Japanese firms organized workers into teams, each trained to perform a variety of operations that rotated among team members. Teams were given more control over immediate workspace, such as arrangement of machinery, and authority to address problems, including stopping the moving assembly line if necessary. Parts made by independent suppliers arrived at the assembly plant on a just-in-time basis, shortly before needed, eliminating the need to stockpile expensive inventory. Under lean production, new models were developed more quickly in response to changing consumer preferences, and assembly lines were flexible enough to accommodate model changes without a costly and time-consuming changeover period.

The Big Three adopted many lean production principles during the 1990s, thereby closing—but not completely eliminating—the productivity and quality gaps with Japanese carmakers. The economic fortunes of the Big Three improved during the 1990s primarily because of consumer interest in trucks, which increased from 20 percent of the U.S. market in 1974 to 50 percent in 2000. The Big Three ceded sales leadership in traditional four-door "family" passenger cars to the Japanese, especially Honda and Toyota, while concentrating on highly profitable sport utility vehicles and pickups.

For their part, Japanese companies struggled during the 1990s because lean production led to lean profits. Under the principle of *kaizen* (continuous improvement), productivity and quality were improved without regard for cost effectiveness. Higher profit margins were achieved by adopting optimum lean production, which combined elements of lean and mass production. More parts were standardized, products were consolidated onto fewer distinctive platforms (chassis and underpinnings), and development and assembly times were sharply cut.

Into the 21st century, the Big Three's most significant competitive disadvantage was heavy pension and health-care costs that added $1,200 to every vehicle. UAW contracts maintained generous benefits for current and retired workers and their families while permitting the Big Three to reduce their workforce. UAW membership declined from a peak of 1.5 million in 1979 to 639,000 in 2002. In contrast, Japanese companies had fewer retirees and a workforce with fewer health care needs and little interest in joining a union.

The U.S. motor vehicle industry has become part of a global system. U.S. and Canadian motor vehicle production has been fully integrated since the 1960s, while the 1993 NORTH AMERICAN FREE TRADE AGREEMENT (NAFTA) eliminated trade barriers in and out of Mexico. More goods arrive in the United States across the Detroit-Windsor Bridge than through any other port of entry in the country, largely because of Canadian-made motor vehicles and parts. In the aftermath of the September 11, 2001, terrorist attacks, however, U.S. borders with Canada and Mexico became less easy to cross, jeopardizing further integration of the North American motor-vehicle industry.

Asian- and European-owned companies build and sell vehicles in the United States, while U.S. companies are major producers in Europe and own controlling interests in several Asian carmakers. The sale of Chrysler to the German carmaker Daimler-Benz in 1997 effectively erased meaningful differences between the Big Three "domestics" and "foreign" manufacturers.

Control of the world's motor manufacturing is expected to further consolidate into a handful of multinational companies. Sales and production are not expected to increase in North America, western Europe, and Japan in the 21st century; but rapidly rising consumer demand in developing countries, especially the two most populous, China and India, is expected to fuel further expansion of the world's motor vehicle industry. Another challenge facing the automotive industry comes from concern that the increasing number of gasoline-powered automobiles is damaging the Earth's environment with their tailpipe emissions. This has prompted the U.S. government to start imposing higher mile-per-gallon regulations on automobiles (the strictest state being California), which in turn is forcing the automakers to explore new fuels and technologies—such as hydrogen and "hybrid" vehicles—to meet these changes.

Further reading
Cray, Ed. *Chrome Colossus.* New York: McGraw-Hill, 1980.
Flink, James J. *The Automobile Age.* Cambridge, Mass.: MIT Press, 1988.
Nevins, Allan. *Ford: The Times, the Man, the Company.* New York: Charles Scribner's Sons, 1954.
Rubenstein, James M. *The Changing U.S. Auto Industry: A Geographical Analysis.* London: Routledge, 1992.
———. *Making and Selling Cars: Innovation and Change in the U.S. Automotive Industry.* Baltimore: Johns Hopkins University Press, 2001.
Womack, James P., Daniel T. Jones, and Daniel Roos. *The Machine That Changed the World.* New York: Rawson, 1990.

James M. Rubenstein

B

Babson, Roger Ward (1875–1967) *statistician and stock market analyst* Babson was born into a well-established New England family. His father was a successful dry-goods merchant who did not believe in the principles of higher education. He was undisciplined as a youth and was a member of a street gang for a brief period before obtaining his high school diploma. He then attended MIT because it provided a "technical education," which was more acceptable. After graduating in 1898, he went to work for a Boston stockbroker. He was soon fired for his overly analytical methods and independent spirit. After working for himself briefly in New York City, he returned to Massachusetts to work for another Boston broker. He then established Babson's Statistics Organization with $1,200 in 1904. The company was later known as Babson's Reports. The original company was one of the first to accumulate and analyze business statistics and sell the service to subscribers. It was so successful that he was able to diversify his interests after several years in business.

Following the Panic of 1907 on Wall Street, Babson, already wealthy because of his service's success, expanded it to include stock market reporting and advice. The service included business and stock market predictions and made Babson very well known in investment circles. He was one of the few market analysts to accurately predict the stock market crash of 1929 although many on Wall Street did not agree. In the 1920s, statistical analysis was not universally accepted. Many Wall Street bankers did not accept that business conditions were anything less than ideal before the crash and continued to believe in a rosy future even after 1929.

In addition to his analytical services, Babson was also interested in public service. He served in Woodrow Wilson's administration as an assistant secretary of labor and advocated joining the League of Nations. Later in life, he ran for president on the National Prohibition Party ticket in 1940. But he was best known for his stock market services. In addition to his service, Babson also wrote on financial matters in regularly scheduled articles. From 1910 to 1923, he wrote about business and other matters as a regular columnist for the *Saturday Evening Post*. He also contributed to the *New York Times* and to the newspapers owned by the Scripps Syndicate. He eventually formed his own syndicate, the Publishers Financial Bureau, to distribute his writings to papers across the United States. His reputation was enhanced in the late 1920s when he began predicting a strong stock market reaction to the speculative bubble. After the crash, his reputation grew, and he became one of the most sought-after market analysts.

During his lifetime, Babson authored 47 books, including his autobiography, *Actions and Reactions*. His writings covered a wide array of social and economic topics in addition to his statistical and forecasting work. He founded Babson Institute (today Babson College) in Massachusetts in 1919 and was also instrumental in establishing Webber College for Women in Florida, in part because of his wife's support for women's education. His success opened the field to a wide array of newsletters and market analyses that created an industry of information services surrounding Wall Street and business cycles.

See also STOCK MARKETS.

Further reading

Babson, Roger W. *Actions and Reactions.* New York: Harper & Brothers, 1949.
Smith, Earl. *Yankee Genius: The Biography of Roger W. Babson.* New York: Harper & Brothers, 1954.

Baker, George F. (1840–1931) *banker* Born in Troy, New York, on March 27, 1840, Baker went to live with relatives in Massachusetts when his family moved to Brooklyn and his father became a newspaperman. While living with relatives, the young boy noticed that an uncle did no apparent work, preferring to live off interest income instead. From an early age, he, too, decided that he would live off interest despite his middle-class background.

After attending the Seward Institute in Florida, a private school, Baker became a clerk in the New York State Banking Department. While working there, he became familiar with a New York banker, John Thompson, who invited him to join in a new banking venture established during the Civil War in New York City. The new institution was established in order to participate in the sale of TREASURY BONDS during the war through the national banks newly created by the National Banking Act. The bond program was run by Salmon Chase, secretary of the Treasury, who used Jay Cooke & Co. as his primary selling agent. The First National Bank of New York was established on Wall Street in 1863, and the young Baker bought shares in the company with his savings. He became its cashier and a board member in 1865 and quickly began to work his way to the top of the bank's management. During the Panic of 1873, the bank's president, Samuel Thompson, feared for the bank's survival, and Baker decided to begin buying his stock, having faith that the bank would weather the storm. As a result, he became the major figure at the bank, and in 1877 he became its president.

In the early 1880s, firmly established, Baker began buying shares in various railroad companies. He specialized in buying and selling companies after helping reorganize them and earned a

George F. Baker (LIBRARY OF CONGRESS)

good deal of his fortune in that manner. He also had extensive holdings in other banks and insurance companies. By the turn of the 20th century, he held directorships in 43 banks and corporations, making him a charter member of what became known as the "money trust" in New York banking circles. He was also the largest shareholder in the U.S. STEEL CORP. after it was organized by J. P. Morgan in 1901. He remained a close associate and confidant of Morgan. He retired from active management of the bank in 1909 but remained as its chairman. Because of his banking connections and affiliation with Morgan, he became a star witness at the Pujo hearings conducted by Congress in 1911, investigating what was known as the "money trust," the close relationships among New York bankers and their role in allocating credit and capital.

During World War I, Baker helped Benjamin STRONG of the New York Federal Reserve Bank manage operations in the money market, which included determining how much call money would be made available to the stock market. In 1916, he was indicted along with others for looting the New York, New Haven, and Hartford Railroad, but the charge was ultimately dismissed when his attorney proved that while he attended directors' meetings, he usually slept through most of them and took no part in their deliberations. Unlike many other bankers, Baker kept some distance between his bank and the securities business directly, establishing an untarnished reputation that earned him the honorary title the "Dean of Wall Street" during the 1920s. At his death, his estate was valued at $75 million, making him one of the richest bankers in the country. He also gave substantial sums to many colleges and universities, including the Harvard Graduate School of Business Administration. His son, George F. Baker Jr., succeeded him as chairman at the bank, which was a major New York City institution before later merging with the National City Bank. After other MERGERS, it is a part of Citigroup today.

See also CITIBANK; MORGAN, JOHN PIERPONT.

Further reading

Chernow, Ron. *The House of Morgan: An American Banking Dynasty and the Rise of Modern Corporate Finance.* New York: Simon & Schuster, 1990.

Logan, Sheridan A. *George F. Baker & His Bank, 1840–1955.* New York: privately published, 1981.

Bank Holding Company Act   Passed in 1956, the act was concerned with the nonbanking activities of bank holding companies (BHCs), whereas the BANKING ACT OF 1933 (Glass-Steagall Act) had dealt with the relationship between commercial and investment banks. The TransAmerica Corporation, a large California-based HOLDING COMPANY that owned the BANK OF AMERICA, was a major target of the BHCA since it had banking operations, insurance underwriting, manufacturing, and other commercial activities. The purpose of the BHCA was to regulate and control the creation and expansion of BHCs, separate banks from nonbanks within the BHC, and minimize the dangers of the concentration of economic power.

The major provisions of the BHCA were: (1) The board of governors of the Federal Reserve System (FRB) was given authority to regulate and examine BHCs, (2) the ownership of shares in corporations other than banks was generally prohibited, (3) prior approval of the FRB was required for acquisitions involving more than 5 percent of the stock of the acquired firm, (4) BHCs could acquire banks only in their home state unless the laws of another state specifically allowed them to expand into the new state though existing interstate companies were not required to divest the banks they already held, (5) transactions between BHCs and their affiliates were limited, and (6) the act reserved the rights of states to exercise jurisdiction over BHC activities. Although states did not have laws allowing interstate acquisition in 1956, they began adopting them in the 1980s and typically grandfathered companies such as Northwest Bancorporation in Iowa and First Interstate, which was operating in several western states.

The major loopholes in the legislation were the exemption of one-bank holding companies (OBHC) and the definition of a BHC as a company owning 25 percent or more of the stock of two or more banks. Without these exemptions, the law would have applied to many more financial organizations. Banks later exploited the OBHC loophole as a legal way for banks to acquire nonbanking businesses. The OBHC loophole was plugged by the BHCA Amendments of 1970.

Many of the provisions of the BHCA are no longer in effect because they have been superseded by passage of the Riegle-Neal Interstate Banking and Branching Efficiency Act of 1994, which allows bank acquisitions nationwide and interstate branching, and the Gramm-Leach-Bliley FINANCIAL SERVICES MODERNIZATION ACT of 1999, which allows organizations that can qualify as financial holding companies to enter upon any activities that are financial in nature (as opposed to closely related to banking under the original BHCA). During the period of DEREGULATION in banking during the 1980s and 1990s, and before the Financial Modernization Act was finally passed in 1999, the BHCA was the primary tool employed by the FEDERAL RESERVE to allow liberalization in the banking system. More recently, its importance has faded as the financial services industry has entered a deregulatory stage while the Federal Reserve has adopted a more liberal policy of regulating bank holding companies.

See also INTERSTATE BRANCHING ACT.

Further reading

Phillips, Ronnie J. "Federal Reserve Regulatory Authority over Bank Holding Companies: An Historical Anomaly?" *Research in Financial Services* 8 (1996).

Shull, Bernard. "The Origins of Antitrust in Banking: An Historical Perspective." *Antitrust Bulletin* 41, no. 2 (Summer 1996): 255–288.

Spong, Kenneth. *Banking Regulation: Its Purpose, Implementation, and Effects,* 5th ed. Kansas City, Mo.: Federal Reserve Bank of Kansas City, 2000.

Ronnie J. Phillips

Banking Act of 1933 (Glass-Steagall Act)

The law passed during the first months of Franklin D. Roosevelt's administration that defined the scope of American banking for the rest of the century. It was passed as a result of congressional hearings (the Pecora hearings) investigating the causes of the crash of 1929 and the banking and stock market problems of the 1920s and 1930s. An act of a similar name passed Congress the previous year relating to the gold reserves of the United States.

The act defined the bounds of American banking. It listed the activities that a commercial bank could carry out while restricting others. Specifically, it effectively prohibited commercial banks from engaging in INVESTMENT BANKING, requiring banks that practiced both sides of the business to decide within a year which side they would choose. It did so through Section 20 of the law prohibiting commercial banks from being "engaged principally" in underwriting or trading equities, meaning that they could earn only a limited amount of their total revenue from equity related activities. The section effectively made dealing or investing in stocks impossible for commercial banks and precluded them from the investment banking business.

The exclusion was aimed at the large New York money center banks, notably J. P. Morgan & Co., which traditionally had practiced a mix of commercial and investment banking and had holdings in insurance companies as well. The National City Bank and the Chase National Bank were also heavily involved in both commercial and investment banking and were the focus of the hearings and the new law. By excluding commercial banks from holding equity, the act made expansion into other related financial services difficult and in many cases impossible.

The Banking Act also created deposit insurance through the FEDERAL DEPOSIT INSURANCE CORPORATION. Almost half of all American banks failed during the Depression, and several hundred per year were failing on average before the act was passed. As a result, many depositors withdrew their funds at a crucial time, and many banks were short of funds for lending. The "money horde" was responsible for the diminution of credit when unemployment was rising and capital expenditures waning, and the introduction of deposit insurance on a national scale helped restore faith in the banking system. There was much criticism of deposit insurance at the time, with some detractors calling it socialist or simply not necessary. But when the act passed, after a weeklong banking holiday, depositors began to return to banks.

Also included in the act was Regulation Q (Reg Q) of the FEDERAL RESERVE, which allowed the central bank to set interest rate ceilings on deposits in order to prevent banks from entering a bidding war for savers' funds. In the following decades, this provision protected banks from paying the market rate for deposits and effectively protected the banks' cost of funds. Interest on checking accounts was also prohibited. These regulations lasted for more than 40 years.

The major restrictions in the Glass-Steagall Act were lifted gradually over a period of years. In 1980, the DEPOSITORY INSTITUTIONS DEREGULATION AND MONETARY CONTROL ACT increased the amount covered by deposit insurance and permitted interest-bearing checking accounts. Reg Q was also phased out by the act and disappeared after the DEPOSITORY INSTITUTIONS ACT was passed in 1982. It was not until 1999, when the FINANCIAL SERVICES MODERNIZATION ACT was passed, that commercial banks were again free to own investment banking and insurance subsidiaries, although the Federal Reserve had been allowing the practice on a de facto basis since the early 1990s. In response to pressures from the marketplace, Congress passed that act, effectively rolling back the major restrictions of the Glass-Steagall Act and creating a more liberal banking and investment banking environment.

The Banking Act of 1933 was the most restrictive banking law ever passed. When combined with the McFadden Act of 1927, it created a peculiarly American style of banking found nowhere else. For decades, it was considered part of the "safety net" that protected savers and the banking system itself.

See also COMMERCIAL BANKING.

Further reading

Benston, George J. *The Separation of Commercial and Investment Banking*. New York: Oxford University Press, 1990.
Kennedy, Susan Estabrook. *The Banking Crisis of 1933*. Lexington: University Press of Kentucky, 1973.
Geisst, Charles R. *Undue Influence: How the Wall Street Elite Put the Financial System at Risk*. Hoboken, N.J.: John Wiley & Sons, 2005.
Wicker, Elmus. *Banking Panics of the Great Depression*. New York: Cambridge University Press, 2000.

banknotes   The issuance of banknotes was an integral part of commercial bank operations until the mid-20th century, when the FEDERAL RESERVE monopolized their issuance and circulation. The global history of banknotes can be divided into three periods.

Paper money, made from the bark of mulberry trees, was introduced in China sometime between A.D. 650 and 800. By about A.D. 1000 redeemable banknotes were issued by at least 16 different banks. Overissue led to inflation, which may have ultimately led to the downfall of the Sung Dynasty. Governments in later dynasties also issued paper money, though not necessarily banknotes, but the Chinese experiment with paper money lapsed between 1644 and 1864.

In Europe, the earliest paper money was issued by goldsmiths who took in deposits for safekeeping and issued certificates of deposit that developed into currency. Modern banks first appeared in mid-14th-century Italy, but the Stockholm Bank of Sweden is often credited with having been the issuer of the first banknotes in Europe in 1661, redeemable in local copper coins or silver thalers. Banknotes were introduced to the British Isles by the Bank of England shortly after it opened in 1694 and by the Bank of Scotland in 1695. Whereas the Bank of England's first issues were certificates of deposit for gold issued in the specific amount of the deposit in pounds, shillings, and pence, the Bank of Scotland almost immediately issued notes in round denominations between £5 and £100, a practice employed by the Bank of England only in 1745. A £1-note was first issued by the Bank of Scotland in 1704. Given the poor state of the coinage in the late 17th and early 18th century, banknotes issued by reputable bankers became an attractive and convenient means of payment and constituted an important part of the money supply. When coin shortages grew acute, Scottish banknotes were reputedly torn into quarters and halves and accepted as the equivalent of 5 or 10 shillings, respectively.

Banks put their notes into circulation by giving them to borrowers who took out loans. So long as the bank maintained a reputation for redeeming its notes, the public was willing to hold them because they were easier to transport and transact with than gold and silver coins of various quality and uncertain value. In holding a bank's notes, the bank effectively received an interest-free loan from the note-holding public even while it earned interest from borrowers who circulated the notes on the bank's behalf. Thus, both banks and the public benefited from the issuance of banknotes. Banks earned a return from issued and as-yet unredeemed notes, and the public experienced the reduced cost of transacting through barter or with coins of uneven quality. In addition, the replacement of banknotes for coins freed precious metals for use in alternative productive activities.

The earliest paper money used in the New World was issued by the Massachusetts colony in December 1690 to pay troops recruited for an expedition against Canada. Although gold and silver, mostly of Spanish origin, circulated in the colonies, it was typically of low quality and in short supply. The money supply was regularly augmented by issues of paper money by colonial governments.

During the American Revolution, the Continental Congress issued paper money that rapidly depreciated in value during the wartime overissue and massive inflation. It was this wartime experience that led the framers of the Constitution to ban the issuance of bills of credit (paper money) by the individual states. The federal government did not issue paper money again until the exigencies of the Civil War forced its hand in 1861. In the interim, banks supplied a large fraction of the U.S. circulating medium through the issuance of banknotes. As early as 1820, banknotes represented about 40 percent of the U.S. money supply (coins + banknotes + deposits). Individual states provided corporate charters to joint-stock banks, which were given the authority to print and circulate their own notes. Most states limited banknote issues to a multiple of a bank's paid-in capital, but a few imposed explicit reserve requirements in terms of legal tender coins.

One of the most interesting and remarked-upon periods for U.S. banknotes was the Free Banking Era (1837–63). During this era, 18 states allowed banks to issue notes limited only by the value of government bonds the banks were willing to deposit with a regulatory body as collateral and the banks' willingness and ability to meet redemption calls in coin. The number of banks expanded rapidly to about 1,600 in 1860, each of which issued a half-dozen or more different denomination banknotes.

The diversity of banknotes during the Free Banking Era led to two problems: redemption of notes issued by faraway banks and counterfeiting. Redemption of notes that had traveled far from the issuing bank was often handled through interbank clearing relationships, whereby one bank would take in another bank's notes on deposit and later return them to the issuing bank. The Suffolk Bank of Boston established a region-wide clearing system across New England. Less comprehensive systems were put in place in New York, Philadelphia, and other major cities. Eventually, these clearing agreements developed into formal arrangements out of which clearinghouse associations evolved. In addition to formal inter-bank clearing arrangements, private brokers, known as banknote brokers, emerged who bought notes issued by faraway banks for coin or notes of local banks. It is believed that brokers set prices to reflect transportation and transaction costs, redemption risks, and a normal rate of return. In doing so they provided liquidity and monitoring functions.

The counterfeiting problem is often thought to have been rampant. Several banknote brokers published weekly or monthly newspapers that reported all known counterfeits, with a typical issue providing descriptions of several dozen to as many as several hundred known and suspected counterfeits.

In 1863, Congress passed the National Banking Act, which effectively instituted free banking on a national scale. Between 1863 and 1936 any bank meeting federal guidelines could issue its own notes, subject to a number of regulatory conditions. To reduce transaction costs and counterfeiting, all notes were produced by the Bureau of Engraving and Printing, using a common design for all banks. The only features that differentiated the notes of one bank from another were the issuing bank's name, its federal charter number, signatures of its officers, and the seal of the bank's home state. Otherwise, the pattern was identical.

The Federal Reserve Act of 1913 introduced a new currency—the Federal Reserve note—which remains the principal circulating currency in the United States up to the present. Since the first Federal Reserve notes appeared in 1914, the bank's notes have changed in size and appearance and added colors other than green, beginning with the $20-note in 2003. In most developed countries, such as the United States, central banks such as the Federal Reserve have gained a government-mandated monopoly of the money supply. Scotland remains a notable exception. Even up to the present, individual banks in Scotland issue their own currency.

What lies in the future for banknotes? Some scholars contend that the INTERNET is likely to generate media that resemble banknotes, otherwise known as virtual banknotes. PayPal, for instance, already acts like a deposit bank, and its transaction services are increasingly like those offered by the goldsmiths of a much earlier era. From here, it is only a short step to providers of on-line transaction services offering on-line currencies that will circulate freely among buyers and sellers on the Internet.

Further reading

Bodenhorn, Howard. *A History of Banking in Antebellum America: Financial Markets and Economic Development in an Age of Nation Building.* New York and Cambridge: Cambridge University Press, 2000.

———. *State Banking in Early America: A New Economic History.* New York and Oxford: Oxford University Press, 2003.

Dillistin, William H. *Bank Note Reporters and Counterfeit Detectors, 1826–1866.* New York: American Numismatic Society, 1949.

Mackay, James A. *Paper Money.* New York: St. Martin's Press, 1975.

Quinn, Stephen F., and William Roberds, "Are On-Line Currencies Virtual Banknotes?" *Federal Reserve Bank of Atlanta Economic Review* (Second Quarter 2003): 1–15.

Howard Bodenhorn

Bank of America   California bank founded by A. P. Giannini (1870–1949) in San Francisco in 1904 as the Bank of Italy. The son of Italian immigrants, he established the bank with $150,000 in borrowed money in order to serve the retail immigrant community in the city. His reputation was enhanced quickly when he managed to stay open during the great earthquake and fire that struck the city in 1906, by rescuing the bank's money, loading it in a horse-drawn vegetable cart, and taking it home with him. When other bankers refused to open their institutions after the quake, Giannini insisted on opening and extended credit to customers based on a handshake and a signature.

Not to be confused with a New York bank having the same name in the earlier part of the century, the bank remained primarily a California institution. In 1919, Giannini changed the name of the institution to BancItaly Corp. and again in 1928 put it under the umbrella of a HOLDING COMPANY called the Transamerica Corp. so that it could expand nationally. He then bought the older Bank of America in New York and adopted its name. Because of subsequent laws forbidding interstate branching passed by many states and the McFADDEN ACT, the bank conducted almost all of its business within California, although it was aided after 1927 by the size of the state, enabling it to have one of the largest branch networks of any bank in the country. But other subsidiaries did operate on a national basis, although most of Transamerica's activities were concentrated in western states. Giannini's fame spread in California after making loans to the wine industry and the new MOTION PICTURE INDUSTRY in the 1920s.

Prior to World War II, the bank made great inroads into consumer lending especially, being one of the first banks to offer customers consumer loans at relatively low rates when compared to other lenders. He was among the first bankers to offer auto loans and consumer loans to small customers.

After World War II, the bank began to expand into other financial services and international banking. In the late 1940s, it was the largest bank in the country. But Transamerica was the target of many antitrust inquiries, and when the BANK HOLDING COMPANY ACT was passed in 1956 the empire was restricted to operations in California. In the mid-1960s, the Bank of America developed the Visa card, a credit card that extended revolving credit to customers, unlike the established CREDIT CARDS that demanded full payment upon billing. The bank's forays into international banking were less successful, and it was significantly exposed by many loans to less-developed countries in the late 1970s and 1980s, becoming one of the largest single lenders to Mexico before its debt crises began. It suffered a financial and organizational crisis as a result and had to have new management installed.

In 1998, the bank agreed to merge with NationsBank of North Carolina to create the first coast-to-coast banking operation in the country. The name Bank of America remained although the merger was actually a takeover by Nations-Bank. In 2004, Bank of America acquired Fleet-Boston, creating the third-largest financial institution in the United States.

See also COMMERCIAL BANKING.

Further reading

James, Marquis, and Bessie Rowland. *Biography of a Bank: The Story of Bank of America, 1891–1955.* New York: Harper & Bros., 1954.

Johnston, Moira. *Roller Coaster: The Bank of America and the Future of American Banking.* New York: Ticknor & Fields, 1990.

Nash, Gerald D. *A. P. Giannini and the Bank of America.* Norman: University of Oklahoma Press, 1992.

Bank of New York Founded in 1784, the bank is the oldest existing banking institution in the country. The bank's charter was written by Alexander HAMILTON, who practiced law in New York City at the time. When he became the first Treasury secretary under George Washington, he began a series of borrowings for the government, and the bank was used as an intermediary. The bank did the borrowing, and the government issued warrants on the bank. The technique helped establish the credit of the United States at a time when few foreign investors were interested in doing business with the new government.

From its inception, the bank was capitalized "in specie only," meaning that its capital was money coined in silver or gold rather than land. Its first shareholders were New York businessmen who intended that the bank be founded on a reputation for prudent management so the notes it issued would be backed by specific proportions of specie. The bank issued stock, one of the first companies in the United States to do so, and it was traded on the New York stock market, which was conducted out-of-doors along Wall Street. In 1792, it began loaning money to the Society for Establishing Useful Manufactures, which planned a group of factories to be built in Paterson, New Jersey. It was also a lender to the two major canal projects, the Morris Canal in New Jersey and the ERIE CANAL in New York. Many of the steamship companies operating around New York also received loans from the bank. Most of the loans it originally made were short-terms, maturing in months rather than years. Its stock remains listed on the NEW YORK STOCK EXCHANGE today.

Before the Civil War, the bank was a major clearing institution for gold trading and settlements. After the war, the bank provided loans to a host of infrastructure investments, including the RAILROADS and utility companies. Of crucial importance to New York City, the bank also provided funds for its subway system, which opened in 1904. Before the BANKING ACT OF 1933 was passed, the bank merged with the New York Life Insurance & Trust Co. in 1922. It later merged with Fifth Avenue Bank in 1948 and with the Empire Trust Co., also in 1948, enabling it to strengthen its trust services even further. As COMMERCIAL BANKING began to expand in the post–World War II years, especially in the late 1950s and 1960s, the bank established a HOLDING COMPANY in 1969 and began to open branches around the New York metropolitan area. It also added an international office in London at the same time.

The bank's major acquisition was the Irving Bank Corporation in 1988, one of New York's best-known banking institutions. In the 1980s, the bank became one of the largest clearers of federal funds in the country and a major factor in the funds clearance system. Its business remains primarily wholesale although it does maintain a retail banking operation and branches.

Further reading

Domett, Henry W. *A History of the Bank of New York 1784–1884.* New York: Bank of New York, 1884.

Nevins, Allan, ed. *History of the Bank of New York & Trust Co.* New York: privately published, 1934.

Bank of the United States, The   The Bank of the United States (BUS) was actually two separate banks—the First BUS (1791–1812) and the Second BUS (1817–41). The First Bank, envisioned by Alexander Hamilton, the nation's first Treasury secretary, received its 20-year charter from Congress in February 1791. The mixed (20 percent public- and 80 percent privately owned) corporation was capitalized at $10 million, which exceeded the combined capital of all state-chartered banks, insurance companies, and canal and turnpike companies of the time. Investors were permitted to tender newly issued federal bonds as payment for $400 shares in the bank, and this innovation helped to bring U.S. debt securities, which had only three years earlier sold at deep discounts, back to par. In doing so, the fledgling bank contributed to one of Hamilton's most important achievements—restoration of the credit standing of the United States.

In the first decade of its existence, the BUS served as a safety net for the federal government, standing ready to make loans when necessitated by low tax collections. It opened branches in New York, Boston, Baltimore, and Charleston in 1792, and later in Norfolk, Savannah, Washington, and New Orleans. By 1805, half of the bank's capital was managed by the branches. Starting with the sale of 55 percent of its shares on the open market in 1796, the federal government reduced its dependence on the bank, and the bank shifted its focus toward business lending. In the first decade of the 1800s, the bank and its branches operated essentially as a large commercial bank. It nevertheless would on occasion make specie loans to other banks when liquidity needs arose, and provided some unofficial control over note issues by regularly collecting notes of state banks and presenting them for redemption.

The establishment of a "national" bank had been a contentious political issue in 1790. At that time, those suspicious of the centralized power

First Bank of the United States (New York Public Library)

that such an institution might imply, led by Thomas Jefferson and James Madison, questioned its very constitutionality. By the time that the bank was up for recharter in 1811, these abstract issues were supplemented by a distrust of foreign ownership in the bank, which had exceeded 70 percent by 1809, and questions about its economic necessity in light of large budget surpluses. The latter arguments were pivotal in Congress's defeat of the act to recharter by the vice president's tie-breaking vote. President Madison, bound by his ideology at the time of the bank's founding, privately supported recharter but remained publicly neutral. The defeat forced the bank to wind up operations in 1812. As the bank had consistent net earnings of 9 percent over its 20-year existence and had declared dividends of 8 percent regularly, its closing proceeded in an orderly and timely manner. State banks quickly arose in its aftermath to assume its commercial banking functions. The strains of financing the War of 1812, however, led Congress soon to reconsider the efficacy of a quasi-central bank.

The Second BUS received a federal charter in 1816 with a capitalization of $35 million, and operated under this charter from February 1817 until March 1836. The Second Bank, like the First, was established to restore order to the currency, but also to facilitate the holding and disbursement of the government's funds by acting as its banker. Aside from overexpanding note issues shortly after opening and a near-suspension of specie payments in 1819, the bank assumed its role effectively until 1829, when rhetoric over recharter escalated between Nicholas BIDDLE, who led the bank from 1823 until 1839, and President Andrew Jackson. Jackson was "afraid of all banks" and the possibility of default on their note issues, and was suspicious of an institution in which individuals could profit by lending the public treasure. The smoldering conflict led Biddle to seek early recharter of the bank in the latter part of Jackson's first term. When the recharter became a campaign issue in 1832, Jackson responded by vetoing the act on July 10, 1832.

Upon reelection, Jackson ordered the removal of all government deposits from the Second Bank in 1833 and placed them with selected state-chartered (i.e., "pet") banks. With its federal charter near expiration, the bank lost much of its regulatory zeal, allowing the pet banks to use the new deposits to expand note issues. With no impending threat of note redemption by the BUS, these issues combined with inflows of specie from abroad to produce a rapid inflation between 1834 and 1836 that ended in the financial Panic of 1837. In the meantime, the Second BUS obtained a state charter from Pennsylvania in 1836 and continued operations until 1841. As bank president and still the nation's most influential banker, Biddle actively criticized Jackson's 1836 policy of requiring specie payments for the purchase of public lands, mostly in the West, to curb speculation, and even made unsolicited and apparently unwelcome attempts to steer President Van Buren away from the impending crisis immediately after Jackson left office in the spring of 1837. In the aftermath of the panic, "Biddle's Bank" used its resources and international reputation to engage in active speculation in the cotton market, and heavy losses from these activities contributed to a second financial panic in 1839. The bank's capital stock appears to have been a total loss when the doors closed on February 4, 1841.

When the Whigs regained the White House in 1841, Henry Clay quickly moved an act to charter a third bank through Congress, but it was vetoed unexpectedly by President John Tyler, who ascended to office after President Harrison's death shortly after inauguration. The nation's central banking "experiment" would not be again attempted until the founding of the Federal Reserve in 1913.

Further reading

Catterall, Ralph C. H. *The Second Bank of the United States.* 1903. Reprint, Chicago: University of Chicago Press, 1960.

Hammond, Bray. *Banks and Politics in America.* Princeton, N.J.: Princeton University Press, 1957.

Smith, Walter Buckingham. *Economic Aspects of the Second Bank of the United States.* New York: Greenwood Press, 1953.

Taylor, George Rogers. *Jackson versus Biddle: The Struggle over the Second Bank of the United States.* Boston: D. C. Heath, 1949.

Peter L. Rousseau

Bank of United States A New York bank, located in Manhattan, which failed in 1930 at the beginning of the Great Depression. At the time, it was the largest bank failure in American history and became one of the primary causes behind the banking reforms passed by Congress in 1933 in the first weeks of Franklin D. Roosevelt's administration.

The bank was purposely named after the long defunct BANK OF THE UNITED STATES, although it omitted "the" from its name. Many of its offices and branches were decorated with flags, giving the impression that it somehow was an official institution. The bank was located primarily in Manhattan, with branches located mostly in working-class and immigrant neighborhoods. It had about 60 branches and several subsidiaries

that served 400,000 depositors. The management of the bank used the deposits to help purchase the bank's own stock in the market. When the stock market crashed in October 1929, the bank's stock price fell substantially. Since the purchases were funded with customer deposits, it also wiped out many of the deposits as well.

Although the bank was a member of the Federal Reserve Bank of New York, the collapse came too unexpectedly for an effective bailout. Many of the major New York City banks refused to help stabilize it, adding to the resentment of the large banks that was building in the early 1930s. Initially, more than $300 million in deposits was lost, representing the savings of many working-class and first-generation Americans.

New York banking authorities attempted to rescue the bank but were too late in preventing runs on its branches. Newspapers around the country published pictures of lines that formed outside the branches as anxious depositors lined up to withdraw their funds. The publicity led many depositors in other parts of the country to withdraw their funds from banks, adding to a national liquidity problem that developed, depriving banks of the funds necessary to make new loans. The superintendent of banks in New York was indicted for not acting quickly enough to prevent the problem. Eventually, he was exonerated and some of the deposits were partially reimbursed, but the crisis became the impetus for nationwide deposit insurance that was included in the BANKING ACT OF 1933.

The bank became the best-known failure of its day and paved the way for future legislation, although it was fraudulently managed and probably would have failed even without the market crash. Although the abuses of the bank were somewhat isolated, its problems did underline the risks to which customer deposits could be subjected by unscrupulous bank management. For that reason, the Glass-Steagall Act separated investment from COMMERCIAL BANKING when it was written, a separation that lasted until 1999. The bank became the symbol of the fragility of the financial system during the late 1920s and early 1930s, a period of thousands of bank failures.

See also NEW DEAL.

Further reading
Werner, M. R. *Little Napoleons and Dummy Directors: Being the Narrative of the Bank of United States.* New York: Harper & Bros., 1933.
Wicker, Elmus. *The Banking Panics of the Great Depression.* New York: Cambridge University Press, 1996.

bankruptcy A legal condition whereby an individual or corporation legally claims that it is no longer able to pay its creditors. Bankruptcy laws usually allow the filer to claim protection while it reorganizes in order to continue doing business, a different stage of bankruptcy than declaring that the business or economic enterprise is no longer able to continue. Creditors may force a company into bankruptcy in order to protect the priority of their claims against it. In either case, bankruptcy is legally declared.

Bankruptcy is defined by the U.S. Bankruptcy Code, written and periodically updated by Congress. Originally, bankruptcy laws dealt harshly with those declaring insolvency. Congress passed bankruptcy laws in 1800, 1841, and 1867. The first was passed after a stock market panic in the outdoor market conducted in New York, caused by William DUER, resulting in him being sent to debtors' prison where he eventually died. The law was repealed three years later. The next two were passed in the wake of stock market panics and were repealed several years later. The 1841 law was repealed three years after being enacted. The 1867 law was the first to include protection for corporations. It, too, was repealed.

A more substantial law was passed in 1898, which gave companies the opportunity of seeking protection from their creditors. However, it required a period of great economic instability and distress to pass new laws designed to give further protection. During the Great Depression, Congress passed two more laws, one in 1933 and the other in 1934. Then the Chandler Act was passed in 1938, allowing for the possible reorganization of businesses rather than their dissolution.

For the next 40 years, bankruptcy laws did not undergo major changes because the number of major bankruptcies was very small. The major exception was the filing by the Penn Central Railroad in 1970. A major reform was added to the code in 1978 when Congress passed the Bankruptcy Reform Act, which streamlined the procedures used for filing and increased the number of bankruptcy courts. Once a bankruptcy proceeding has been initiated, the questions arise of exactly what to do with the failing entity. Generally, two types of proceedings follow.

Under a Chapter 11 proceeding, the company is protected from its creditors while it reorganizes under the auspices of the court. When a bankruptcy plan has been approved by the courts and the SEC, the firm's creditors then must also approve the plan. If reorganization proves unfeasible, then the company enters Chapter 7 of the law and must liquidate itself in order to satisfy creditors. Other amendments to the act followed. The Bankruptcy Amendment Act of 1984 limited the right of companies to terminate labor contracts. In 1986, another chapter was added to account for farms.

Sometimes filing for Chapter 11 bankruptcy has been used as a defense against large claims against a company. By freezing its assets and protecting current creditors and shareholders, a company can immunize itself against a large product liability claim or other anticipated lawsuit. This tactic was employed during the 1980s to protect some drug and medical device manufacturers against claims from customers. In the 1980s and 1990s, many well-known companies filed for bankruptcy, some being household names. Included among them were EASTERN AIRLINES, Continental Airlines, Allied Stores and Federated Department Stores, Greyhound, R. H. Macy, and PAN AMERICAN AIRWAYS. Another filing by Texaco was instigated as part of a corporate defense against an unwanted takeover. To date, the longest-standing bankruptcy proceeding was by the LTV Corporation, which declared Chapter 11 in 1986 and was reorganized only in 1993. The company was forced to file again in 2001.

Another reform was passed with the Bankruptcy Reform Act of 1994. This act includes increased streamlining procedures and also addresses individual bankruptcies more than its predecessors. It created a National Bankruptcy Commission to report on continuing bankruptcy reform. The 1994 act contains many new provisions for both businesses and individuals, including provisions to expedite bankruptcy proceedings and provisions to encourage individual debtors to use Chapter 11 to reschedule their debts rather than use Chapter 7 to liquidate.

Further reading

Balleisan, Edward. *Navigating Failure: Bankruptcy and Commercial Society in Antebellum America.* Chapel Hill: University of North Carolina Press, 2001.

Coleman, Peter. *Debtors and Creditors in America: Insolvency, Imprisonment for Debt and Bankruptcy 1607–1900.* Washington, D.C.: Beard Books, 1999.

Mann, Bruce H. *Republic of Debtors: Bankruptcy in the Age of American Independence.* Cambridge, Mass.: Harvard University Press, 2002.

Skeel, David A. *Debt's Dominion: A History of Bankruptcy Law in America.* Princeton, N.J.: Princeton University Press, 2001.

Warren, Charles. *Bankruptcy in United States History.* Cambridge, Mass.: Harvard University Press, 1935.

Baring Brothers   A British banking house founded in 1763, originally as a merchant business specializing in textiles and commodities. The firm shifted to the merchant banking business under the guidance of Francis Baring in 1776. The partnership served as the major banker to the gentry, British businesses, and the Crown of England. By the time of the Napoleonic Wars, the bank was called the "sixth great power" in Europe along with the major European governments.

Baring was a major factor in British-American trade in the late 18th and 19th centuries. The bank served as banker and often principal in many major financial transactions, including the Louisiana Purchase. It was the major conduit for British funds to be invested in the United States, often through local agents. Local bankers with ties to the bank acted as investment agents, and substantial funds were invested. It often acted as intermediary for the British Crown, which had funds invested in the United States. In the late 18th and early 19th centuries, many Americans feared the influence of Baring because it was assumed that the bank represented the interests of George III, whose mental state deteriorated after the loss of the American colonies. The British remained major suppliers of capital to the United States until the 1890s.

Among Baring's agents in the United States were David Parish of Boston, Kidder Peabody & Co. of Boston, and Lee Higginson & Co., also of Boston. After the Civil War, Kidder was its main agent and helped funnel British funds into railroad investments as well as property and farms. Its major competitor as supplier of funds to the United States was another well-established European bank, the House of Rothschild, whose agent in the United States at the time was August BELMONT.

Baring's influence began to wane after the bank failed during a financial crisis in 1890. It had become heavily invested in South American bonds and was saved only by a bailout by the Bank of England. After that incident, the bank's influence in the United States began to wane as it retrenched its operations. The bank continued to operate in Britain until 1995, when a major trading scandal in its Singapore office forced it to close its doors. It was absorbed by the Dutch financial services group ING and operates as a subsidiary of that company presently.

The main contribution of Baring to the development of the American economy was as a conduit for British overseas investment throughout the 19th century. The strength of the European bankers in this respect illustrated how dependent the United States was on the inflow of long-term investment capital for much of that century, until its own financial markets became developed. The American merchant banks that served as its principal agents in the United States also became major banking institutions until the House of Morgan began to supercede them in the 1890s and early 1900s.

See also FOREIGN INVESTMENT; ROTHSCHILD, HOUSE OF.

Further reading
Hidy, Ralph W. *The House of Baring in American Trade & Finance.* Cambridge, Mass.: Harvard University Press, 1949.
Ziegler, Philip. *The Sixth Great Power.* New York: Knopf, 1988.

Barron, Clarence W. (1855–1928) *newspaperman* Born in Boston, Barron's father was a teamster. He graduated from Prescott Grammar School and the Graduate English High School in 1873 and went to work for the *Boston Daily News* and then the *Evening Transcript.* From 1878 to 1887, he was a reporter covering many beats but then began gravitating toward financial reporting. He became financial editor of the *Boston Transcript.* Recognizing the need for sound financial news, he founded the Boston News Bureau in 1887 and in 1897, the Philadelphia News Bureau. In 1893, he wrote his first book, *The Boston Stock Exchange.*

Financial news at the time was spotty and dominated by journalists often paid by Wall Street interests, who planted stories with journalists in order to affect the prices of stocks. Barron, however, saw the role of financial journalist as defending "the public interest, the financial truth for investors and the funds that should support the widow and the orphan." As a result, he became one of the first journalists to see his role as a conduit of nonbiased financial information as well as a commentator on financial markets.

In 1902, he purchased control of Dow Jones & Co., publisher of the *Wall Street Journal,* for $130,000 following Charles Dow's death. The paper's circulation was about 7,000; by 1920 it reached 18,750. In 1912, he became president of Dow Jones and the *Wall Street Journal.* Barron introduced new printing equipment, and the newsgathering side of the company expanded. By the end of the 1920s, more than 50,000 copies of the paper were in daily circulation. In 1921, he founded the weekly financial newspaper that bears his name—*Barron's.* He served as the paper's editor in addition to being president of Dow Jones and publisher of the *Wall Street Journal.* The newspaper was an immediate success, reaching a circulation of 30,000 in its sixth year.

Barron testified before the Massachusetts Public Service Commission in 1913, when it was investigating the New Haven Railroad, and in 1920 he helped expose the investment racket conducted by Charles PONZI. He was the subject of a $5 million libel suit for his 1920 muckraking exposes of Ponzi. The suit was dropped after Ponzi's arrest and conviction.

Barron is widely considered the father of American financial journalism. Many of his anecdotes and stories about the financiers of his period can be found in *They Told Barron* (1930) and *More They Told Barron* (1931). He also wrote several other books, including *War Finance, As Viewed From the Roof of the World in Switzerland, The Mexican Problem, The Audacious War,* and *Twenty-Eight Essays on the Federal Reserve Act.* He died in a sanitarium while visiting as part of a weight-loss program.

See also NEWSPAPER INDUSTRY.

Further reading
Pound, A., and S. T. Moore, eds. *They Told Barron.* New York: Harper & Bros., 1930.
Wendt, Lloyd. *The Wall Street Journal: The Story of Dow Jones and the Nation's Business Newspaper.* Chicago: Rand McNally, 1982.

Baruch, Bernard Mannes (1870–1965) *financier and government official* Born in South Carolina, Baruch's father was a physician who moved to New York in 1881. Bernard was raised in New York City and graduated from the City College of New York in 1889. He went to work after graduation and made his first million dollars by the time he was 30. He became a governor of the NEW YORK STOCK EXCHANGE and was one of Wall Street's best-known investors in the 1920s.

Baruch's first job on Wall Street was with A. A. Houseman & Co. in 1891. He began speculating in railroad stocks and soon bought and sold American Sugar Refining. His first serious market operation earned him $60,000 and sealed his fate as a speculator. As the Spanish-American War ended, he cut short a vacation and returned to New York, sensing that the market would rise on the news. He traveled to the city on a weekend, climbed through a window at the Houseman office, and traded stocks in London while the U.S. market was still closed. Shortly afterward, he bought a seat on the New York Stock Exchange for $39,000 and opened his own office. He was so successful at making money in the market that he began to look for something more challenging to do with his time.

Following Woodrow Wilson's career since he became president of Princeton University, Baruch actively supported his presidency and was rewarded for his support. Baruch served in Woodrow Wilson's administration as chairman of the War Industries Board in 1918 and a year later served on the U.S. delegation to the Versailles peace conference. In the early 1920s, his name was linked by Henry Ford's *Dearborn Independent* to a Jewish plot to control the world, a common paranoia in the 1920s. Commenting later on the claim, he wrote that, "similar attacks were picked up and mounted by the Ku Klux Klan . . . to say nothing of Joseph Goebbels and Adolph Hitler." He continued his interest in the stock market and made a substantial reputation by being one of the major Wall Street investors to withdraw most of his money from the market before the 1929 crash. Sensing that the stock market was becoming perilously high prior to 1929, he also proposed a bankers' pool of funds to help prop it

up in the event it fell, but was turned down by Wall Street bankers.

In the 1930s, Baruch was an active supporter of the NEW DEAL but never became secretary of state, a job he coveted. He supported government institutions designed to stimulate the economy but was not a supporter of government price supports, As a result, he began to drift away from FDR and the New Deal.

During World War II, he served on a committee writing an influential report on the state of the RUBBER INDUSTRY. He also served President Harry Truman after the war on the U.S. Atomic Energy Commission studying the U.S. position on atomic energy. Despite his government service, his reputation as an investor earned him the most accolades and opprobrium, although he was always quick to point out that he paid most of his own expenses while in government service. He also donated substantial sums to educational institutions in New York City. A 1953 gift to the City University of New York resulted in the university renaming its business school after him. Despite a strong penchant for the press and self-promotion, Baruch was one of Wall Street's best-known figures who glided between New York and Washington with great ease during the two world wars.

Further reading
Baruch, Bernard M. *My Own Story*. New York: Holt, Rinehart & Winston, 1957.

Coit, Margaret L. *Mr. Baruch*. Boston: Houghton Mifflin, 1957.

Field, Carter. *Bernard Baruch: Park Bench Statesman*. New York: Whittlesy House, 1944.

Grant, James. *Bernard M. Baruch: The Adventures of a Wall Street Legend*. New York: John Wiley & Sons, 1997.

Schwarz, Jordan A. *The Speculator: Bernard M. Baruch in Washington 1917–1965*. Chapel Hill: University of North Carolina Press, 1981.

Bell, Alexander Graham (1847–1922) *inventor* The inventor of the telephone was born in Scotland. As a boy and young man, Bell was interested in speech therapy and technologies that could help those with speech and hearing problems to communicate with others. He was exposed to these problems at an early age since both his father and grandfather were interested in communications. His grandfather, Alexander Bell, wrote a book on speech and elocution, and his father was a speech teacher in Dublin. Mabel Hubbard, his mother—and a painter—was deaf.

At age 23, Bell moved to Canada with his parents. A year later he began teaching at the Boston School for Deaf Mutes. After Morse developed the TELEGRAPH, Bell began to study electrical transmission and developed the idea of a "harmonic telegraph." This sort of device, which led to the development of the telephone, envisaged sending more than one message along an electrical line directly to the recipient rather than a telegraph office, which would then have to forward a telegraph message by hand to the ultimate recipient. He teamed with Thomas WATSON, another inventor and proven technician. In 1875, they developed the first device capable of carrying sound along an electrical line. Within a year, Bell filed for a patent on his new device, which was

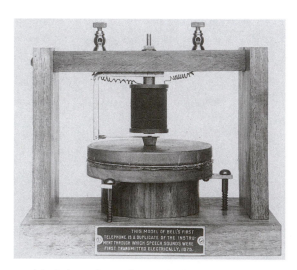

Model of Alexander Graham Bell's first telephone (LIBRARY OF CONGRESS)

granted on March 7, 1876. In the same year, the first telephone was introduced at the Philadelphia World's Fair.

Bell formed the Bell Co., which became his vehicle for carrying out telephone development. After several legal skirmishes with WESTERN UNION TELEGRAPH CO., the Bell Co. emerged victorious from the courts and became the acknowledged leader in telephone systems. The Bell Co. and its smaller affiliates were consolidated as the AMERICAN TELEPHONE & TELEGRAPH CO. (AT&T) in 1878. Its first general manager was Theodore VAIL, who would resign but later return when the company was reorganized early in the 20th century. The Bell companies held most of the patents covering telephonic technology until the 1890s, when many of them began to expire, opening communications to competition.

In 1881, Bell won France's Volta Prize and used the $10,000 award to set up the Volta Laboratory in Washington, D.C. He worked with two associates, his cousin Chichester Bell and Charles Sumner Tainter, at the laboratory, and their experiments soon produced major improvements in Thomas Edison's phonograph, allowing it to become commercially viable.

After freeing himself from the day-to-day operations of his company, Bell continued research and inventing. One of his first innovations after the telephone was the photophone, a device allowing sound to be transmitted on a beam of light. Bell and Tainter developed the device, and in 1881, they successfully sent a photophone message over 200 yards from one building to another. Bell regarded the device as his greatest invention, even greater than the telephone. The photophone was the principle upon which laser and fiber-optic communication systems were later founded.

In 1907, four years after the Wright brothers first flew at Kitty Hawk, Bell formed the Aerial Experiment Association with four young engineers whose goal was to create airborne vehicles. By 1909, the group had produced four powered aircraft, one of which, the Silver Dart, made the first successful powered flight in Canada in 1909. Bell spent his later years improving hydrofoil designs, and in 1919, he and Casey Baldwin built a successful hydrofoil.

He also lent considerable support to *National Geographic* and *Science* magazines. When he died, the country's telephone system went silent for a minute to honor him. He remains the most famous American inventor.

Further reading

Bruce, Robert V. *Bell: Alexander Graham Bell and the Conquest of Solitude*. Ithaca, N.Y.: Cornell University Press, 1990.

Grosvenor, Edwin S., Morgan Wesson, and Robert V. Bruce. *Alexander Graham Bell: The Life and Times of the Man Who Invented the Telephone*. New York: Harry Abrams, 1997.

Mackay, James A. *Alexander Graham Bell: A Life*. New York: John Wiley & Sons, 1998.

Belmont, August (1813–1890) *financier, politician, arts patron, and sportsman* Belmont was born to Jewish parents in Germany and immigrated to the United States at the age of 23. Rising from the position of office boy to confidential clerk for the Rothschilds' banking firm in Frankfurt, Belmont was in New York when the Panic of 1837 ruined the Rothschilds' agent there. He established August Belmont and Company, a private banking firm, and soon became a dominant figure on Wall Street, where his long-term connection to the Rothschilds worked to his advantage. His firm's early fortunes relied on its foreign exchange transactions, on commercial and private loans, and on investments in industrial, railroad, and government securities.

Despite being a naturalized American, Belmont harbored political and diplomatic ambitions, and he was helped in realizing some of them through his wife's uncle, John Slidell, a leading Washington Democrat. President Franklin Pierce rewarded Belmont's 1852 campaign largesse by naming him minister to the Netherlands. While at The Hague, Belmont negotiated a commercial treaty opening the Dutch East Indies to American merchants. He also played a less public role in drafting the Ostend Manifesto (1854), which some fellow American diplomats hoped would convince Spain to sell its Caribbean possession, Cuba, to the United States. Belmont continued his strong affiliation with the Democratic Party with major contributions to President James Buchanan's 1856 election campaign; he also served as chairman of the Democratic National Committee during the subsequent presidential campaigns of Stephen A. Douglas (1860), George B. McClellan (1864), and Horatio Seymour (1868).

During the Civil War, Belmont was a prominent "War Democrat" and successfully persuaded the Rothschilds and other leading European financiers to avoid any involvement with Confederate bond issues. In the postwar period, Belmont sided with the "hard money" bloc. He called for the prompt resumption of specie payments by the United States Treasury and opposed the compromises of the Bland-Allison Act (1878). When the American economy revived after a mid-1870s depression, August Belmont and Company became a leading investment banking house, often associated with J. P. Morgan and Company in underwriting syndicates that floated large issues of railroad and industrial stocks and bonds.

Belmont had a keen appreciation of the arts, especially painting and opera. He purchased many paintings to adorn his Fifth Avenue mansion. In 1878, he helped found the New York Academy of Music for operatic productions and symphonic concerts and served as head of its board until 1884.

Belmont also established for himself a major reputation in the world of sports. He was instrumental in bringing thoroughbred horse racing to the United States and supported two large horse breeding farms. It was he who began the Belmont Stakes in 1867, which subsequently became the famous "last leg" of a Triple Crown for three-year-old race horses, following the Kentucky

Derby and the Pimlico Preakness. He served for almost a quarter of a century as president of the American Jockey Club.

Belmont died on November 24, 1890, two weeks shy of his 77th birthday. He was succeeded at the family bank by his son August BELMONT II, who became equally famous in banking, social, and sporting circles.

See also ROTHSCHILD, HOUSE OF.

Further reading

Black, David. *The King of Fifth Avenue: The Fortunes of August Belmont.* New York: Dial Press, 1981.

Katz, Irving. *August Belmont.* New York: Columbia University Press, 1968.

Irving Katz

Belmont, August, II (1853–1924) *banker and sportsman* Son of New York banker and socialite August Belmont and Catherine Slidell Perry, the daughter of Commodore Matthew Perry, August II was born in New York City. He attended Harvard, graduating in 1874, and entered the family banking business, run by his father until his death in 1890. He then assumed the reins of the firm. While at college, August was an avid track runner and helped import the first spiked running shoe into the United States, which helped revolutionize competitive running.

Known mostly as a socialite, August II nevertheless continued the family banking tradition. Much of the family business was built upon the relationship of his father with the Rothschilds, and August continued the tradition. The Anglo-German banking family was a major source of FOREIGN INVESTMENT for the United States until the outbreak of World War I. In 1900, he was instrumental in helping finance the New York subway system, which opened in 1904. In addition, Belmont contributed much time and energy to the continued development of the American Jockey Club, founded by his father, and also to racing his own horses, again following in his father's tradition. He also helped finance the Cape Cod Canal, which opened in 1914. The U.S. government used the canal extensively during World War I to reduce shipping time between New England, New York, and points south. The family maintained a stake in the canal that was not sold until the 1920s.

During World War I, Belmont served as an officer in the U.S. Army, serving in Spain as a major, helping purchase livestock for the military. During his later years, he was preoccupied with horse breeding and racing. As a result, the family firm, August Belmont and Company, began to fade as a major Wall Street investment bank. The bank still made headlines in the early 1930s when it became the object of a retroactive lawsuit by the Soviet government, claiming that Belmont held a deposit from Russia that had never been returned.

Belmont died in 1924, and the family firm was closed. Its assets were liquidated to pay off debts, while his heirs chose to remain in the investment banking business at other firms rather than continue the family firm. His stables and horses were also liquidated, sold off to other prominent businessmen and socialites. His death marked the official end of Rothschild influence in American finance, although in reality it had ended some years before. Both he and his father made an indelible mark upon American finance, combining finance with extensive socializing and influencing Wall Street for years to come. They are best remembered for their contributions to American horse racing, especially the Belmont Stakes run in New York.

See also BELMONT, AUGUST; ROTHSCHILD, HOUSE OF.

Further reading

Black, David. *The King of Fifth Avenue: The Fortunes of August Belmont.* New York: Dial Press, 1981.

Bowmar, Dan, III. *Giants of the Turf: The Alexanders, the Belmonts, James R. Keene, the Whitneys.* Lexington, Ky.: The Blood Horse, 1960.

Geisst, Charles R. *The Last Partnerships: Inside the Great Wall Street Money Dynasties.* New York: McGraw-Hill, 2001.

Better Business Bureaus The Better Business Bureaus sprang from the early 20th-century "truth in advertising" movement. Advertising was then emerging as a distinct profession and hoped to elevate its low public standing. Unfortunately, the largest advertisers were patent medicine manufacturers who pioneered national marketing techniques while peddling false promises of health "cures." Muckraking exposés by *Ladies Home Journal* (1904–05) and *Collier's* (1905) revealed that the ingredients contained in these nostrums included everything from innocuous herbs to alcohol and opium. A horrified public pressured Congress to pass the Pure Food and Drug Act (1906), which required the labeling of drugs. National advertising agencies responded by dropping patent medicine accounts. Eight years later, Congress established the FEDERAL TRADE COMMISSION (FTC) to deal with unfair trade practices. The Wheeler-Lea Act of 1938 further empowered the FTC to deal with "deceptive" advertising and other misleading "acts or practices."

Local advertising clubs, meanwhile, set up volunteer "vigilance committees" (later renamed "Better Business Bureaus") to monitor advertising and retail trade. In 1914, the Minneapolis advertising club established the first full-time, professional Better Business Bureau. The concept spread to dozens of other U.S. and Canadian cities. For example, the NEW YORK STOCK EXCHANGE, seeking to eradicate stock swindlers, helped found the Better Business Bureau of New York City. The bureaus kept files on businesses, investigated scams, and reported criminal cases to the authorities. They worked closely with newspaper publishers, urging them to reject deceptive ads, and also cooperated with the American Medical Association in exposing health quackery. The Association of Better Business Bureaus (ABBB) represented the local BBBs, while a National Better Business Bureau (NBBB) focused on national advertising. In 1971, these two associations merged to form the Council of Better Business Bureaus (CBBB). The BBBs were successful at curbing fraudulent advertising and sales claims. However, cases involving borderline deception were more difficult to challenge given the subjective nature of the violations. Moreover, some large advertisers flouted the BBB code of ethics. Nevertheless, the drastic reduction in outright fraud and dishonesty, so prevalent in the early 20th century, was a major accomplishment. Member firms valued the BBB for its efforts to eliminate unfair competition and channel consumer dollars into honest businesses.

The BBBs' history is intertwined with the CONSUMER MOVEMENT. During the 1930s, consumer activists launched an unprecedented attack on advertising with best-selling books such as Arthur Kallet and F. J. Schlink's *100,000,000 Guinea Pigs*. Consumers' Research and Consumers Union tested products against their advertised claims and found many wanting. The low popular opinion of advertising was reflected in the colossal success of *Ballyhoo,* a magazine that spoofed leading advertisements. The BBBs responded to this widespread public cynicism by becoming involved in consumer education. They published buying guides and held conferences to bridge the gap between businesspeople and consumer advocates.

Consumer advocacy intensified in the 1960s and 1970s as Ralph NADER and other advocates demanded stricter government control of business. A separate critique of advertising's corrupting influence on the public, particularly children, led to calls for the censorship of commercial speech. Fearful of government control, the leading advertising associations joined the Council of Better Business Bureaus in establishing the National Advertising Review Board (NARB). The NARB is responsible for regulating national advertising content. It reviews the decisions of the CBBB's National Advertising Division. Although the NARB lacks legal authority, advertisers have abided by its judgments.

The Better Business Bureaus also arbitrate consumer disputes. Large corporations, regulatory agencies, and courts have turned over an increasing number of complaints to the BBBs.

Recently, the Council of Better Business Bureaus has worked to bring self-regulation to Internet commerce. Companies may apply for a BBB seal of approval for their Web sites. This issue will certainly grow in importance as consumers spend more money online.

The Better Business Bureaus have a controversial past. Muckraking journalists and aggrieved business owners denounced the BBBs for acting as busybody detectives. This was especially true in the 1930s, when books appeared with such sensational titles as *The Indictment of the Better Business Bureau Conspiracy* (1931) and *Rackets: An Exposé of the Methods and Practices of the Better Business Bureaus* (1933). More recently, consumer advocates have questioned whether the BBBs represent business or the consumer. Thus, by mediating between business and consumer groups, the BBBs are vulnerable to charges that they did too little, or too much, for either side.

Further reading

Kenner, H. J. *The Fight for Truth in Advertising.* New York: Round Table Press, 1936.

Smith, Ralph. *Self-Regulation in Action: The Story of the Better Business Bureaus, 1912–1962.* New York: Association of Better Business Bureaus, 1962.

Jonathan J. Bean

Biddle, Nicholas (1786–1844) *banker, legislator, and diplomat* Born in Philadelphia, Biddle was the son of a Philadelphia banker. Recognized as a child prodigy, he entered the University of Pennsylvania at age 10 and was scheduled for graduation at 13. Because of his age, he was not granted a diploma and so enrolled at the College of New Jersey in Princeton, graduating as valedictorian at age 15. He then returned to Philadelphia to study law with his brother William and jurist William Lewis. In 1804, he became secretary to John Armstrong, the ambassador to France. Adding to his resume, he also helped work on the details of the Louisiana Purchase and attended Napoleon's coronation.

Biddle also served as secretary to James Monroe, the new ambassador, in 1807. He later edited the papers of Lewis and Clark but abandoned the effort when he was elected to the Pennsylvania legislature in 1810. He also founded the literary journal *Port-Folio.* During the War of 1812, he served on the Philadelphia Committee on Defense and twice ran unsuccessfully for Congress. He also served in the Pennsylvania legislature, where he became familiar with the BANK OF THE UNITED STATES. He was appointed to the bank's board of directors by Monroe in 1819, and when Langdon Cheves resigned, he was appointed president of the bank in 1822. He remained its president for the next 14 years.

The bank was heavily influenced by his leadership, and it became known as "Biddle's Bank," a nickname that later did not sit well with President Andrew Jackson. During the 1820s, the bank was very successful, and the economy grew under Biddle's guidance. Biddle helped transform the bank, which previously had been a Philadelphia bank with branches throughout the East and South, into a central bank. He used the bank to effectively counter trends within the economy, providing liquidity when there appeared to be business slowdowns and contracting it when the economy expanded. But after the election of 1828, when Andrew Jackson took office, the new president believed the bank was unconstitutional despite an earlier Supreme Court ruling in MCCULLOCH V. MARYLAND in 1819.

Congress reauthorized the bank in 1832, but Jackson vetoed the bill. After Jackson refused to renew the bank's charter, Biddle remained with it for several years until it eventually closed its doors. It later changed its name to the Bank of the United States of Pennsylvania. He finally resigned from the greatly diminished institution in 1839. He was later charged with fraud but eventually acquitted of all charges.

The failure of the Second Bank of the United States was due in part to Biddle's inability to deal with the politics of Jackson, who once told him

In this cartoon, President Andrew Jackson refuses to renew the charter for the Bank of the United States. Nicholas Biddle, with the head and hoofs of a demon, runs to Jackson's left. (LIBRARY OF CONGRESS)

that "I do not dislike your bank any more than all banks." There was some animosity on the president's part toward wealthy men of letters, of whom Biddle was the best example of his generation. The animosity had a distinct downside since the United States was left without a central banking institution until the FEDERAL RESERVE was created in 1913. The vacuum left by the failure of "Biddle's Bank" was filled by private bankers in later years, notably by John Pierpont Morgan, whose power and influence finally led to the establishment of a true central bank almost a hundred years later.

Further reading

Catterall, Ralph C. H. *The Second Bank of the United States.* Chicago: University of Chicago Press, 1903.

Govan, Thomas P. *Nicholas Biddle: Nationalist and Public Banker, 1786–1844.* Chicago: University of Chicago Press, 1959.

Taylor, George R. *Jackson v. Biddle: The Struggle over the Second Bank of the United States.* Boston: D. C. Heath, 1949.

Wilburn, Jean A. *Biddle's Bank: The Crucial Years.* New York: Columbia University Press, 1967.

Black-Scholes model   A formula for pricing stock options. Stock options are a type of derivative instrument that provides the holder the right, but not the requirement, to buy or sell stock at a future date. Options to buy are called "call" options, and those to sell are "put" options. The Black-Scholes model was developed in 1970–71 by Fischer Black and Myron Scholes, with collaboration from Robert C. Merton. The three were young economists at the time. The model at first received a hostile reception from mainstream economists and was immediately rejected from three academic journals before finally being published in a leading economics journal in 1973. All three researchers soon became leaders in the academic field of financial economics and before long became influential Wall Street advisers.

Their research eventually earned Scholes and Merton the 1997 Nobel Prize in economic sciences. (Black died in 1995 and could not be named a recipient, although he was cited in the announcement.) The Black-Scholes model itself is mathematically complicated, but in many cases the option price depends only on the volatility (or variability) of the underlying stock. In this sense, options are said to provide the price of volatility. Greater volatility translates into greater option prices because of the very nature of options—they do not have to be exercised in the "bad" outcomes, so the option holder receives potential benefits without any downside.

The Black-Scholes model works due to an underlying arbitrage argument. Since a stock and a bond can be combined to mimic exactly the payouts of an option, the price of the option must be the same as the price of that "replicating portfolio," or there would have to be an arbitrage opportunity that investors could exploit. The results of the Black-Scholes model can also be derived from a decision-tree framework pioneered by John Cox, Stephen Ross, and Mark Rubinstein in the mid-1970s. This technique relies on computer power and Monte Carlo simulation to reproduce all the possible scenarios for the movement of a stock and made Black-Scholes more operational by allowing option pricing in more complex situations.

The Black-Scholes model quickly revolutionized the pricing of derivative securities and helped an active market develop in options. Few, if any, academic studies in economics have had a bigger impact on the "real world." In 1973, the CHICAGO BOARD OF TRADE opened a stock options exchange—the Chicago Board Options Exchange. Other exchanges quickly followed suit, and the model became associated with their development from their earliest days. The OPTIONS MARKETS quickly spread to include interest rates, and now a variety of options trade beyond those on stocks—including such new instruments as swaps, caps, floors, and swaptions. Both the over-the-counter and exchange-traded derivatives markets are among the largest in the world and currently trade trillions of dollars each year. In addition, hidden options can be found and priced in a variety of business and finance applications.

The model has also been used to price stock options granted to executives as part of their compensation packages. The controversy arising in the late 1990s over executive compensation and the use of stock options gave the model additional life as one of the few ways in which such executive compensation tools could be adequately priced for accounting purposes.

See also FUTURES MARKETS.

Further reading
Bernstein, Peter L. *Capital Ideas: The Improbable Origins of Modern Wall Street.* New York: Free Press, 1993.
Reynolds, Bob. *Understanding Derivatives: What You Really Need to Know about the Wild Card of International Finance.* New York: Financial Times, 1995.

Paul Harrison

Boeing Co.   The largest and one of the most successful American manufacturers of civilian and military aircraft. The company was founded by William E. Boeing (1881–1956) in 1916, originally to make seaplanes. Boeing had left Yale in 1903 and made his fortune in the timber industry in the Pacific Northwest. He became interested in airplanes in 1908 and spent the next several years learning about them while taking flying lessons. In 1915, he teamed with George Westervelt to build a biplane capable of landing on water and nicknamed it the B & W. They began producing the plane, and the Boeing manufacturing company was born.

During World War I, the company achieved its first notable success. In 1917, Boeing knew that the U.S. Navy needed training airplanes, and he sold the navy a seaplane called the Model C. The seaplane performed well, and the navy ordered 50 more—the company's first production order. By 1918, 337 people were on the Boeing payroll, and the company's future was more secure.

In 1919, Boeing delivered the first international air mail from Canada to the United States. The post office later rewarded Boeing with the first airmail route, from Chicago to San Francisco. He also founded Boeing Air Transport, the predecessor to United Airlines. In all cases, Boeing used his own planes in his commercial enterprises, using the revenues to aid in further aircraft development. He sold his interest in the company in 1934 to pursue other ventures, but the company retained his name.

Boeing planes became the standard in aviation. A Boeing plane was used to drop the atomic bombs on Japan, and the company's lunar orbiter and Moon Rover were used in the first Moon landing. In 1952, the company tested the B-52 prototype that was to become a standard for the military and a year later the B-47E, a jet bomber. The original presidential plane, Air Force One, was a Boeing 707, and newer models are still used by the White House. The 707 became the world's most popular long-distance jet in the mid-1950s after Pan American World Airways ordered 20 for its fleet. It revolutionized air travel, allowing many more people to fly than ever before. Although William Boeing died in 1956, the company was faithful to many of his original business strategies. It has diversified into other lines, including the building of irrigation projects and desalinization plants, and providing computer services. In addition, the company continued to produce planes and other hardware for the space program and also purchased rival McDonnell Douglas as well as Rockwell International and Hughes Electronics, a communications company.

During the post–World War II years, Boeing began developing missile systems for the military. Building upon research done in the 1940s to develop a guided missile system, whereby the missile is guided by an analog computer, the company developed intercontinental ballistic missiles and also developed the ground systems needed to house and deploy them. It won the contract for the first Minuteman missile program from the Defense Department in the early 1960s.

During the 20th century, Boeing was the world's leading aircraft manufacturer. Its most serious competition in the 1990s came from the European consortium Airbus Industries. The consolidation of the domestic aircraft manufacturing industry was due mainly to Boeing's influence and success because the company maintained a tight hold on the market with reliable aircraft and design innovations.

See also AIRPLANE INDUSTRY.

Further reading

Bowers, Peter M. *Boeing Aircraft Since 1916*. London: Putnam, 1989.

Serling, Robert J. *Legend and Legacy: The Story of Boeing and Its People*. New York: St. Martin's Press, 1992.

Taylor, M. J. H. *Boeing*. London: Jane's Publications, 1982.

Brandeis, Louis D. (1856–1941) *Supreme Court justice and social reformer* Born in Louisville, Kentucky, Brandeis's family moved to Germany in 1872, when his father sold the family business in Kentucky, anticipating the RECESSION, or panic, that would follow in 1873. Louis attended school in Germany and entered Harvard Law School when his family returned to the United States. After graduating, he initially practiced law in St. Louis but quickly returned to Boston, where he established a practice with a law school classmate, Samuel Warren. The new firm became known as Warren & Brandeis. He continued to practice law in Boston until 1916.

Adopting social and economic reform causes early in his career, he became known as "the people's lawyer." Often working pro bono, he developed strong sympathies for the trade union movement and the women's rights movement. Between 1900 and 1907, he defended the public interest against the Boston utilities and also argued successfully before the U.S. Supreme Court that labor laws applied to women as well as men. During the argument, he made use of statistics and economic information, and this sort of presentation became known as the "Brandeis brief."

Brandeis was also an ardent opponent of monopoly concentrations and the abuses of the concentration of capital by New York bankers, often referred to as the "money trust." Many of his principles can be found in his 1914 book, *Other People's Money*, in which he described how bankers used deposits for their own political ends. It was written after congressional hearings into the money trust. He also wrote *Business, A Profession* (1914), about the success of Filene's Department Store in Boston.

Before World War I, Brandeis's political leanings were seized upon by his opponents in order to portray him as an enemy of big business. He opposed bankers' control of the New England railroads. He began a long legal battle against J. P. Morgan's control of the New Haven Railroad that lasted from 1905 to 1913. In the end, Morgan was forced to divest control of most of the bank's holdings. He also became arbitrator in a strike by New York garment workers. After seeing the plight of the workers, many of whom were Jewish, he became active in Zionist causes and remained so for the rest of his life. He was the author of Woodrow Wilson's economic platform in the 1912 presidential elections and often tutored Wilson on economic matters. As a result, Wilson named him to the Supreme Court in 1916. He was confirmed as the first Jewish justice despite some anti-Semitism surrounding his confirmation.

During Franklin D. Roosevelt's presidency, Brandeis often consulted with members of the administration at a distance. He upheld many of the legal challenges to the NEW DEAL brought before the Court but did argue that the NATIONAL RECOVERY ADMINISTRATION was unconstitutional. He retired from the Court in 1939 and died two years later. While best remembered as a justice, Brandeis was the embodiment of a crusading lawyer imbued with progressive ideas who often, and successfully, challenged big business during the era dominated by the trusts.

See also ANTITRUST; MORGAN, JOHN PIERPONT.

Further reading
Gal, Allon. *Brandeis of Boston.* Cambridge, Mass.: Harvard University Press, 1980.
Mason, A. T. *Brandeis: A Free Man's Life.* New York: Viking, 1946.
Strumm, Philippa. *Louis D. Brandeis: Justice for the People.* New York: Schocken Books, 1984.
Urofsky, Melvin I. *A Mind of One Piece: Brandeis & American Reform.* New York: Scribner's, 1971.

Bretton Woods system   The international monetary structure devised at a conference held at Bretton Woods, New Hampshire, beginning in 1944. Even before World War II ended, the Allies realized that the postwar period would require a new exchange rate system in order to prevent a recurrence of the distortions that characterized the foreign exchange markets in the 1920s and early 1930s and led to World War II. The power given to the International Monetary Fund (IMF) at the conference to monitor exchange rates lasted until 1971 and was known as the fixed parity system.

The Bretton Woods conference was called in order to create a viable monetary system that would take effect when World War II ended. One of its main objectives was to create a system in which unilateral devaluations of currency would not be possible without a country consulting its major trading partners. During the 1930s, unilateral devaluations were common as many major trading countries attempted to make their exports cheaper by devaluing their currencies, adding to the international economic slowdown. Bretton Woods created two major international economic organizations—the International Bank for Reconstruction and Development (World Bank) and the International Monetary Fund (IMF). The IMF was charged with maintaining the new dollar parity system adopted by the countries attending. The World Bank originally was charged with helping rebuild Western Europe but later began making development loans to less developed countries by borrowing funds in the international bond markets.

Under the Bretton Woods system, the U.S. dollar was given a gold value of $35 per ounce, and the rate was fixed. Other currencies were then given a value in dollars that was allowed to fluctuate only ± 1.00 percent from their parity value. If a currency fluctuated from this band, the country's central bank was obliged to intervene on its behalf. The dollar thus became the new international exchange standard, although gold remained the underlying standard because of the fixed rate given to the metal in dollar terms. The major trading currencies (hard currencies) traded in the FOREIGN EXCHANGE MARKET were quoted in dollar terms.

When trade conditions warranted, some currencies could become overvalued or undervalued with the fixed parity system. If a currency was overvalued, its exports would fall while imports rose, causing an imbalance in trade suggesting that the currency needed to be devalued. Under the system, the country involved would seek permission from the IMF to officially devalue its currency in dollar terms. A devaluation by a major trading country normally meant that one of its major trading partners would have to revalue its currency, stating its dollar terms higher than in the past.

In the summer of 1971, the U.S. dollar came under severe pressure in the markets because the United States was experiencing a balance of payments deficit. Political and economic pressure mounted for the United States to devalue, but the Nixon administration maintained that it would not do so. Then in August, President Nixon announced devaluation as part of an economic package designed to fight inflation. The convertibility of the dollar was severed, and the currency began to decline in the markets. After months of uncertainty, an international monetary conference, held at the Smithsonian Institution in Washington, officially ended the Bretton Woods system of fixed parities. The old band of 1 percent was replaced by a new one of 2.25 percent and gold officially revalued at $38 per ounce. But the attempt at stability was short-lived, and within months the Smithsonian agreement collapsed. The new system that emerged was referred to as one of floating exchange rates.

Under the floating rate regime, the power of the IMF was substantially reduced over the major trading countries. Also, exchange rates for the major trading currencies were determined by market forces and used no fixed parities. Since 1972, the floating exchange rate system has become more volatile since no bands exist to constrain trading, and spot rates between currencies can fluctuate without any restraint unless a central bank decides to intervene on behalf of its own currency. The new volatility caused problems for American business since it required changes in the ways in which corporations hedged their foreign exchange exposures. Many companies began to experience wide swings on their balance sheets since their overseas assets and liabilities began to fluctuate more widely than in the past.

See also EURO; GOLD STANDARD.

Further reading

Destler, I. M., and C. Randall Henning. *Dollar Politics: Exchange Rate Policymaking in the United States.* Washington, D.C.: Institute for International Economics, 1990.

Eichengreen, Barry J. *Globalizing Capital: A History of the International Monetary System.* Princeton, N.J.: Princeton University Press, 1996.

Funabashi, Yoichi. *Managing the Dollar: From the Plaza to the Louvre.* 2nd ed. Washington, D.C.: Institute for International Economics, 1989.

Solomon, Robert. *The International Monetary System 1945–76.* New York: Harper & Row, 1977.

Brown Brothers Harriman A private banking firm founded in Baltimore in 1800 by Alexander Brown, an Irish immigrant, as a trading company specializing in textiles. His sons opened more branches of the house in other eastern cities and gradually moved into banking. The first branch was John A. Brown & Co., opened in Philadelphia in 1818. A New York office, Brown Brothers, was opened several years later and became the flagship for the other houses, which eventually closed down, leaving Brown Brothers as the premier private bank in New York before the Civil War.

A keen student of economics, Alexander Brown died in 1834. As a sign of respect for his efforts in keeping Baltimore and Maryland solvent in the wake of Andrew Jackson's refusal to extend the charter of the Second BANK OF THE UNITED STATES, all ships in Baltimore harbor lowered their flags to half-mast upon learning of his death. The firm remained under the control of family members well into the 20th century. Alex. Brown & Sons remained in Baltimore as a brokerage and is today a subsidiary of Deutsche Bank, which bought it in 1997.

The Liverpool branch of the bank was in financial difficulties in 1837 as a result of a panic in the United States, which severely affected British-American trade, and had to be bailed out by the Bank of England, with guarantees from Peabody & Co. in London, the predecessor of J. S. Morgan & Co. During another panic 20 years later, Brown Shipley, as the British firm became known, returned the favor and made a loan to allow Peabody to remain afloat after falling upon hard times.

Brown Brothers became the major private bank in the country in the 19th century until the emergence of Drexel Morgan & Co. in the 1880s. It engaged in banking, securities, and trade finance. Before the Civil War, it helped finance North Atlantic shipping, becoming principal owner in the Collins Line, a major North American shipping company sailing the North Atlantic. Several family members perished with the *Artic*,

a transatlantic steamship that sank off Newfoundland in 1854, the greatest passenger shipping disaster prior to the sinking of the *Titanic*. After the war, Brown Brothers became the target of the muckraking efforts of Elizabeth Cady Stanton and Parker Pillsbury, who charged the Browns with mismanagement of the line. The firm also became involved in railroad financing after the war.

Need for additional capital required it to merge with Harriman banking interests in 1930, and it became known as Brown Brothers Harriman. The Glass-Steagall Act of 1933 forced the bank to give up its securities operations, which were spun off to Brown Harriman & Co., later to become Harriman Ripley & Co. One of its partners at the time was Prescott Bush, father of future president George H. W. Bush and grandfather of George W. Bush. But it remained a private bank and as such was able to retain its seat on the NEW YORK STOCK EXCHANGE. It remains one of the few private banks existing today, specializing in investment management and international finance in addition to private banking.

See also INVESTMENT BANKING.

Further reading

Geisst, Charles R. *The Last Partnerships: Inside the Great Wall Street Money Dynasties*. New York: McGraw-Hill, 2001.

Kouwenhoven, John A. *Partners in Banking*. New York: Doubleday, 1968.

bucket shop A term originally used in the late 19th century to describe a place where small investors would place bets on stocks and commodity futures contracts. Bucket shops took orders from customers beginning with small odd lots, sometimes on margin as low as 10 percent of a stock or commodity's value, and would pretend to invest the money in the market. In fact, they usually did not invest it at all but simply paid the investor based on the stock's movement or sometimes disappeared, stealing investors' funds.

Often, the stock or commodity futures exchanges would find bucket shop operators on the floor of their exchanges, attempting to determine the direction of prices so that they would know what tips to give investors or how to invest their own money without assuming risk. The exchanges finally passed rules to eliminate them. Before World War I, the Chicago commodities exchanges, and particularly the CHICAGO BOARD OF TRADE, declared open warfare on the bucket shops in the courts in an attempt to drive them out of business. Often, the bucket shops would take customers' money and open a contrary position in the market, ensuring that the customers would lose their money while the bucket shop profited. The public's use of bucket shops in the pre-1920 period was relatively widespread since the shops appeared to be offering "leverage" to the man in the street.

The futures exchanges won a major victory against the bucket shops in a landmark Supreme Court case, *Board of Trade of City of Chicago v. Christie Grain & Stock Co.* in 1905. The bucket shops claimed that the exchanges and WESTERN UNION, the company that provided the wire services, were restraining trade by refusing them access to their transmitted prices. The Court ruled that the bucket shops could not use prices transmitted by the Chicago Board of Trade in their own business, pretending to be legitimate in the process. Although suffering a setback, bucket shops continued to thrive through the 1920s.

In the 1920s, their presence began to fade as the exchanges became more organized and less tolerant of their activities. Finally, the securities laws passed during the 1930s put an end to their activities. Today, the term is used to imply that a company deals for itself first rather than the clients it is supposed to represent as broker. During more recent bull markets and periods of intense speculation, many "boiler rooms" have appeared, selling worthless stocks and derivatives to unsuspecting investors, keeping the bucket shop tradition alive and well.

See also FUTURES MARKETS; STOCK MARKETS.

Further reading

Hill, John, Jr. *Gold Bricks of Speculation.* Chicago: Lincoln Book Concern, 1904.

Lefevre, Edwin. *Reminiscences of a Stock Operator.* Chicago: George Doran & Co., 1923.

Buffett, Warren (1930–) *financier* Warren Buffett was born in Omaha, Nebraska, on August 30, 1930, the son of a wealthy stockbroker. As a child he was allowed to work in his father's firm, where he absorbed useful investment principles and also dreamed of acquiring great wealth. More important, Buffett acquired an acute grasp of statistics and financial analysis that served him well throughout his long career. He passed through the University of Nebraska in 1950 and was greatly influenced by reading the book *Security Analysis* (1934) by Benjamin Graham and David Dodd. That same year he enrolled at Columbia University's business school to study under Graham and further inculcated his mentor's strategy for success on the stock market. This entailed buying stocks at no more than two-thirds of net capital and usually traded at low prices because other investors were ignoring them. Buffett was so impressed by Graham's approach that he offered to work at his investment firm without pay but was declined. He was eventually hired by Graham as an analyst in 1952, worked in New York City for four years, and then returned to Omaha in 1956. There, with $5,000 of his own money and $100,000 raised from other sources, he founded his own investment firm, the Buffett Partnership. At that time Buffett began formulating his own personal approach to investment, based on realistic appraisal of the companies in question and a determination to retain stock for as long as a firm was well managed. In time he also broke with Graham's approach of looking for statistical bargains and sought out companies that were underrated for various reasons.

From the onset, Buffett proved himself to be one of the 20th century's most brilliant investors.

His success enabled him to purchase controlling stock in the failing American Express company in 1963 and, as interim CEO, he turned it around with tremendous profit. Two years later Buffett bought out Berkshire-Hathaway, a textile firm based in New Bedford, Massachusetts. This investment repeatedly failed to realize profits, but Buffett used it as a means for raising additional capital for investments elsewhere. As usual he was spectacularly successful, and in 1969 he dissolved the Buffett Partnership to concentrate more on building his own wealth. Over the next two decades Buffett carefully acquired profitable companies such as See's Candies, various insurance companies, and numerous media outlets, all of which proved lucrative. By 1984 he was positioned to obtain controlling stock of the American Broadcasting Company (ABC) while also expanding his holdings in Time, Incorporated. The following year he orchestrated the takeover of ABC by Capital Cities and secured an 18-percent interest in the new company. In 1986 Buffett invested heavily in the Wall Street investment firm SALOMON BROTHERS, basically ignored the stock market crash of 1987, and reaped considerable profit by holding on to stock rather than selling it under adverse conditions. In 1995 Buffett fulfilled his most ambitious endeavor, that of arranging the acquisition of ABC by the Walt Disney Corporation. This resulted in formation of the world's largest media conglomeration, again with windfall profits for Buffett.

Presently, Buffett is the country's second-richest man after Microsoft chairman Bill GATES.

But for all his wealth and influence he consistently projects a simple, homespun persona and continues living modestly in a home he acquired in 1958 for $31,000. Buffett is also prone to dispensing folksy, down-to-earth advice to investors. His basic message is play the game for the long haul and ignore any notion of quick or easy profits. Investors are also advised to champion companies that are presently undervalued, yet are well managed, as these are most likely to return a steady profit on investments. He also looks unkindly upon venture capital firms as too unpredictable and feels that TV stations, advertising agencies, and newspapers are the best investment risks. Curiously, he declines to get involved with computers due to his unfamiliarity with high technology. The rumpled, down-to-earth Buffett remains the chairman of Berkshire-Hathaway and is popularly viewed in investment circles as the "Sage of Omaha."

Further reading

Buffett, Warren E. *Warren Buffett Speaks: Wit and Wisdom from the World's Greatest Investor.* New York: Wiley, 1997.

———. *Thoughts of Chairman Buffett: Thirty Years of Unconventional Wisdom from the Sage of Omaha.* New York: Harper Business, 1998.

Kilpatrick, Andrew. *Of Permanent Value: The Story of Warren Buffett.* New York: McGraw-Hill, 1998.

Lowenstein, Roger. *Buffett: The Making of an American Capitalist.* New York: Random House, 1997.

John C. Fredriksen

C

Carnegie, Andrew (1835–1919) *industrialist*
Born in Dunfermline, Scotland, in 1835, Carnegie immigrated to the United States with his family in 1848. The family settled in Pittsburgh, Pennsylvania, where Andrew went to work to help support the family rather than attend school. He took his first job in a factory when he was 13 for a salary of $1.20 per week.

After working at a telegraph company and teaching himself Morse code, Carnegie went to work for the Pennsylvania Railroad, where he was the personal assistant to Thomas Scott, later to be the railroad's president. He worked at the railroad for 12 years before striking out on his own. Recognizing that the cargo the railroad carried, especially crude oil, was more lucrative than railroading itself, Carnegie made some investments that increased his annual income to almost $50,000 per year during the Civil War. In 1862, he organized a company to build iron bridges, initially for the Pennsylvania Railroad. The company was later reorganized as the Keystone Bridge Company and became one of the first companies to build bridges made of iron rather than wood, which had been the standard. The company supplied iron for the Eads Bridge over the Mississippi River in St. Louis and the Brooklyn Bridge over the East River in New York. In 1867, he organized the Keystone Telegraph Co. to lay telegraph wires alongside railroad lines, recognizing that the railroad phenomenon had created a communication as well as transportation revolution.

In the early 1870s, Carnegie decided to expand into steel production. Steel had been improved significantly by the Bessemer process, developed in Britain by Henry Bessemer, and Carnegie decided to begin manufacturing it in the United States. Within a short period of time, he was producing steel for the RAILROADS and was quickly becoming one of the largest producers in the country. His first steel company was called Carnegie, McCandless & Co. His management style included a rigorous use of cost-cutting measures designed to make production as efficient as possible while keeping costs down. In 1889, he published the "Gospel of Wealth," in which he held that the wealthy have an obligation to guard society because of their wealth and merit. He later changed his views on social matters to more egalitarian positions. Although highly successful, a future acquisition caused Carnegie

Andrew Carnegie (LIBRARY OF CONGRESS)

eventually to reconsider his involvement in the industry.

In 1883, he acquired the Homestead steelworks in Pennsylvania but also inherited a labor dispute between the management of the company and its union, the Amalgamated Association of Iron and Steel Workers. Henry Clay FRICK was manager of the Homestead plant after Carnegie acquired it and adopted a hard-line position concerning striking workers. Frick attempted to break the union's hold on the plant and hired private Pinkerton detectives to guard against the workers. In the summer of 1892, a pitched battle broke out between the workers and guards. A total of 18 died in the battle before order was restored. The plant only reopened a year later in 1893. The public commotion caused by the affair brought labor practices in general,

and Carnegie's management of the plant specifically, under close scrutiny. The conflict tore at his interest in promoting labor's objectives on the one hand and cost efficiency on the other.

Finally, Carnegie decided to sell what had become Carnegie Steel to J. P. Morgan in 1901. He was approached by Charles SCHWAB, a close ally of Morgan, about selling the steelworks and wrote the selling price on a piece of paper that Schwab immediately gave to Morgan. Morgan agreed to the $480 million purchase price, to be paid in bonds and stock, and the deal became the largest takeover in history. The resulting company became known as U.S. STEEL and was the largest in the world. It was the first company whose balance sheet was valued at more than $1 billion. As a result, Carnegie became the richest man in the world. He also became one of the most disconsolate, at least temporarily, when Morgan later confided to him that he could have received $100 million more if he had held out for a higher price.

After selling Carnegie Steel, Carnegie engaged in philanthropy on a scale not yet seen in American business. He founded the Carnegie Institute of Technology in 1900 and endowed thousands of public libraries, colleges, and universities through the Carnegie Endowment, established in 1911. He also established the Carnegie Endowment for International Peace in 1910. He died in Massachusetts in 1919.

See also MORGAN, JOHN PIERPONT; STEEL INDUSTRY.

Further reading

Carnegie, Andrew. *Autobiography of Andrew Carnegie.* Boston: Houghton Mifflin, 1920.

Krass, Peter. *Carnegie.* New York: John Wiley & Sons, 2002.

Livesay, Harold C., and Oscar Handlin. *Andrew Carnegie and the Rise of Big Business.* 2nd ed. New York: Longman, 2000.

Shippen, Katherine. *Andrew Carnegie and the Age of Steel.* New York: Random House, 1964.

Tedlow, Richard S. *Giants of Enterprise: Seven Business Innovators and the Empires They Built.* New York: HarperBusiness, 2001.

Wall, Joseph Frazier. *Andrew Carnegie.* 2nd ed. Pittsburgh: University of Pittsburgh Press, 1989.

Carrier, Willis H. (1876–1950) *engineer and inventor* Born in Angola, New York, Carrier was from an old New England family; one of his ancestors was burned at the Salem witch trials. After finishing high school and teaching for several years he entered Cornell and graduated with a master's degree in 1901. In the same year, he went to work for the Buffalo Forge Co. as an experimental engineer. While working at the company, he met Irving Lyle, who would later be his business partner. A year later, he made his first air-conditioning installation in a Brooklyn, N.Y., printing plant. For the first few years, air conditioners were used to cool machines, not buildings as is common today.

Carrier was involved with air-conditioning throughout his life. He received his first patent for an "apparatus for conditioning air" in 1906. He presented his "Rational Psychrometric Formulae," the basis for calculations in air conditioning, to the American Society of Mechanical Engineers in 1911. Using their pooled savings of $35,000, Carrier and a group of like-minded engineers founded the Carrier Engineering Corp. in 1915.

From the beginning of his career, Carrier was concerned not only with lowering temperature but controlling humidity as well. The first commercial enterprises to install his devices were movie theaters in Texas, using the machines to cool the environment rather than industrial machines. The era of modern air-conditioning engineering began in 1922, when he developed the first safe, low centrifugal, refrigeration air conditioner using a nontoxic refrigerant. In another coup for his invention, Congress installed air conditioners in 1928. By 1930, Carrier had installed more than 300 air-conditioning units in movie theaters around the country.

Carrier's operations were moved from Newark, New Jersey, to Syracuse, New York, which lured him with local tax incentives and other inducements. In 1939, he developed a system capable of cooling SKYSCRAPERS. He held more than 80 patents during his career, including those for refrigerants as well as for mechanical innovations.

Carrier's inventions are credited with helping the United States develop its infrastructure and businesses uniformly throughout the country, regardless of climate. As air conditioners improved and became more affordable, they ceased to be a luxury item and became standard for new buildings as well as existing structures. New areas of the country were opened for development, especially in the South and Southwest, and a new phase of post–World War II migration began. Known as "The Chief," he died in New York City at age 73. His company was bought by United Technologies Corporation and remains a UTC subsidiary. His invention is one of the most significant, but overlooked, American developments of the 20th century.

Further reading

Cooper, Gail. *Air-conditioning America: Engineers and the Controlled Enviroment, 1900–1960.* Baltimore: Johns Hopkins University Press, 2002.

Ingels, Margaret. *Willis Haviland Carrier: Father of Air Conditioning.* New York: Country Life Press, 1952.

cartel A group of companies banding together to control the price of goods or services by regulating the supply. By regulating the supply, they are able to control prices and quantity. Usually, the members of a cartel are the largest producers in the industry, which may otherwise have few other members of significance. More recently, the term *shared monopoly* has been used in place of cartel.

Cartels originated during the mercantilist age when several companies sharing the same interests banded together in order to control prices. During the early years of industrialization, cartels were common because there were not enough companies existing to provide competition in some industries. The first cartel of significance in the United States was the South Improvement Co., formed in 1871 by John D. Rockefeller's Standard Oil Co. and other oil producers. The company successfully negotiated rebates with the RAILROADS that would lower their haulage costs while at the same time paying them a kickback from the fees paid by nonmembers of the company. When the new rates were accidentally posted before an announcement was made, many small oil producers discovered that their haulage rates had increased sharply and blamed the company for their plight. When the SHERMAN ACT was passed in 1890, cartels became illegal in the United States as they were considered to be organizations formed to restrain trade and fair competition. Other ANTITRUST laws, notably the CLAYTON ACT, also attempted to control cartel formation and behavior.

While antitrust laws forbid cartels in the United States, they do operate internationally, often controlling the supply and affecting prices of commodities. The best-known international cartel is OPEC (Organization of Petroleum Exporting Countries), a group of oil producers, mainly from the Middle East and Asia, that controls the output of oil from their countries. It is an example of a government-controlled cartel, organized to protect the prices and supply of the countries' major export.

Further reading

Geisst, Charles R. *Monopolies in America*. New York: Oxford University Press, 2000.
Wells, Wyatt. *Antitrust and the Formation of the Postwar World*. New York: Columbia University Press, 2002.

chain stores The name given to retail stores that establish branch operations in multiple locations, often across state lines. Originally, the term was applied to department and grocery stores that began expanding and later was applied to large all-purpose stores that sold more than one line of merchandise. Usually the stores were an expanded form of a well-known, established retailer.

Chain stores were established in the late 19th and early 20th centuries, but the 1920s proved to be crucial to their development. After World War I, many stores began expanding into branches in order to capitalize on the prosperity of the 1920s. Among the first were retailers that had started as catalog merchants. SEARS, ROEBUCK opened its first branches in 1925; Montgomery Ward began in 1926. The grocery, or food, chains were already operating extensive branch operations. The GREAT ATLANTIC & PACIFIC TEA CO. had 14,000 branches nationally by the late 1920s, while Safeway and Piggly Wiggly Stores expanded regionally. Clothing retailers such as J. C. PENNEY also expanded rapidly during the decade.

The expansion of the stores was aided greatly by the popularity of the automobile, which allowed people to drive to the stores in order to shop. The combination of the two helped revolutionize American life and contributed to the development of the suburbs. Most of the original stores were located in major cities, and they viewed the development of the suburbs as a natural expansion of their urban business. But the movement was not without its critics, many of whom maintained that the stores were destroying the small-town character of rural and semi-rural American life. The stores began a political and public information campaign to fight these attacks in the 1920s.

Many of the chain stores were financed by smaller Wall Street investment banks in the 1920s such as Merrill Lynch, GOLDMAN SACHS, and LEHMAN BROTHERS. Critics held that Wall Street was helping to destroy small-town America and that the chain stores were behaving like monopolies. The same criticism was also leveled at banks and movie theaters, both of which were also expanding. The chains became a major public policy issue in the 1930s, with critics claiming that they were destroying the American way of life by ruining small businesses while sending profits out of the community to big cities such as New York and Chicago. There was also an element of anti-Semitism in this attitude since similar arguments were leveled against Jews in Germany, who either owned or operated many large retail establishments.

Banks and cinemas ultimately faced either antitrust charges or antiexpansion legislation designed to prevent them from crossing state lines or insisting on exclusivity by showing only studio-produced films. The MCFADDEN ACT was seen as an antibank expansion law by many when it was passed in 1927. In 1936, the chain stores faced their greatest challenge when the ROBINSON-PATMAN ACT passed Congress. The act was aimed directly at the chains and became known as the "chain store act."

The stores kept expanding after World War II despite the protests and legal challenges. The stores moved into the suburbs with the general expansion of the suburbs in the 1950s and 1960s and became anchors at many newly built shopping malls. The major chains developing in the post-1970 period, such as Wal-Mart, heard similar complaints as they expanded around the country in the 1970s and 1980s. Their critics maintained that they were driving small merchants out of business by undercutting prices and establishing themselves through economies of scale that smaller merchants could not match.

See also K-MART; MERRILL, CHARLES; WALTON, SAM; WARD, AARON MONTGOMERY.

Further reading

Hendrickson, Robert. *The Grand Emporiums.* New York: Stein & Day, 1979.
Mahoney, Tom, and Leonard Sloane. *The Great Merchants.* New York: Harper & Row, 1966.

Chase Manhattan Bank   In 1799, a water company named the Manhattan Company was founded in New York. Part of its original charter also provided for a banking company, which was begun as the Bank of Manhattan Company.

Among its founding members were Alexander HAMILTON and Aaron Burr. The bank quickly became established in New York City and originally made loans to New York State to finance expansion of the ERIE CANAL.

After the Civil War, John Thompson founded the Chase National Bank, named after Salmon P. Chase, secretary of the Treasury during the war. The bank obtained its charter as a national association through the NATIONAL BANK ACT of 1864, designed to rationalize the banking system. In 1927, it became the largest bank in the country, with assets of $1 billion. Along with some other large banks, the bank delisted its stock from the NEW YORK STOCK EXCHANGE in 1928, ostensibly to prevent speculation. In 1930, Chase bought the Equitable Trust Company from the Rockefeller family, which received a substantial block of stock in return. From that time, Chase became known as the "Rockefeller bank." David Rockefeller later became chief executive of Chase in 1961.

The bank's reputation suffered in the early 1930s as it became one of the focal points of discontent after the Crash of 1929 and the early years of the Great Depression. During Senate hearings in 1933, Albert Wiggin, president of the bank during the 1920s, testified about his own activities during the stock market bubble. It was revealed that he had often traded the bank's stock for his own account even when it appeared to run counter to the bank's interests. It was he who had the stock delisted from the stock exchange, and the speculation occurred during the same period. As a result of his revelations and those of others, the BANKING ACT OF 1933 was passed. His successor, Winthrop Aldrich, helped heal the image of the bank, and he became one of the few bankers supporting financial reform during the NEW DEAL. After the new law was passed, Chase divested itself of its securities affiliates and chose the path of commercial rather than INVESTMENT BANKING like J. P. Morgan, which also chose COMMERCIAL BANKING.

Throughout the 20th century, much of the bank's growth came through MERGERS. The Bank of Manhattan Company bought the Bank of the Metropolis in 1918; Chase purchased it in 1955 and changed its name to the Chase Manhattan Bank. By 1955, the bank had purchased more than 20 smaller banks. Like many other large banks in the 1950s and 1960s, Chase wanted to expand to the suburbs, outside its Manhattan base, but was initially constrained by local New York banking laws. The bank created a HOLDING COMPANY, the Chase Manhattan Corporation, in 1969 in order to diversify its holdings and expand; that same year a change in New York State banking laws allowed banks to cross county lines, something they had been prohibited from doing in the past. As a result, the bank opened branches in Long Island and other boroughs of the city. The bank also listed its stock on the stock exchange again after an absence of 40 years.

As part of its expansion in large retail banking, the bank developed the New York Cash Exchange (NYCE), the first successful major attempt at automated teller machines (ATMs), in 1985. The bank maintained a mix of retail and wholesale banking functions. In 1996, it merged again, this time with the Chemical Banking Corp. to again form the largest bank in the country. It lost the top spot shortly thereafter when CITIBANK merged with Travelers Group.

In 2000, it completed its best-known merger when it purchased J. P. Morgan & Co. in order to gain entrance into investment and wholesale banking. The $36-billion stock-only deal closed in December 2000, ending J. P. Morgan's long history of independence. The new entity was named J. P. Morgan Chase, with the Morgan side conducting investment banking and wholesale banking business while the Chase side emphasized retail banking in its many forms. The new bank ranked as one of the top-five banking institutions in the country.

See also BANK OF AMERICA; BANK OF NEW YORK; MORGAN, JOHN PIERPONT.

Further reading

Rockefeller, David. *Memoirs*. New York: Random House, 2002.

Wilson, John Donald. *The Chase: The Chase Manhattan Bank N.A., 1945–1985.* Boston: Harvard Business School Press, 1986.

chemical industry   The U.S. chemical industry owed a great debt to Europe, where an inorganic chemical- and coal-based industry, with emphasis on synthetic dyestuffs, started to develop well before it did in this country. The domestic industry came into its own when hydrocarbons from American refineries and natural gas started to be used as feedstock for an organic chemical industry, while Europe's organic chemicals were still based on coal. World War II gave a further impetus to this so-called petrochemical industry, as North American companies built plants to produce aromatics for high-octane aviation gasoline, synthetic rubber for tires, and a variety of plastics all based on hydrocarbon feedstock. Petrochemical production processes became the growth engine for chemical production throughout the world, with the United States leading in the development and commercialization of many new technologies in this area. As chemical engineering, the science that led to the construction of very large and economical plants, was also pioneered in the United States, the country became the worldwide leader in growing a robust chemical industry. It made synthetic products—polymers and plastics, synthetic rubber, fibers, solvents, adhesives, and many other products—available at relatively low cost to consumers, thus spurring rapid growth of the industry as natural materials—wood, cellulose, glass, paper, metals—were increasingly replaced by synthetics.

Europe and Japan built a similar petrochemical industry, often based on U.S. technologies. Later, other regions and countries started to build plants of this kind, a trend that accelerated as a number of countries in the Middle East and elsewhere started to industrialize, in some cases based on inexpensive local hydrocarbons from crude oil and natural gas. The U.S. chemical industry, which had undergone an unprecedented wave of innovation, development, and growth between 1940 and 1970, entered a more mature phase by the 1980s, when technology development slowed and international competition started to become a factor.

Many petrochemical processes had started to reach the limit of further improvement, and so researchers turned their attention increasingly to pharmatechnology and biotechnology, to electronic chemicals for computers and other high-tech equipment, and to other such specialties, which had greater potential for profit. At the millennium, the U.S. chemical industry was in intense competition with many other countries and had largely lost the advantages it had originally enjoyed due to low-cost feedstocks available on the U.S. Gulf Coast. The industry is now considered largely mature, in a manner similar to that of the cement, steel, and paper industries, but it has remained one of the biggest and most important domestic industries.

The domestic chemical industry can be said to have started in the Philadelphia area when DuPont de Nemours built its first black powder plant in 1802, followed a couple of decades later by a sulfuric acid plant built in Bridesburg. In Baltimore shortly thereafter, a superphosphate plant was built, which treated bones with acid. In 1839, Eugene Grasselli, an Italian immigrant, built a lead chamber sulfuric acid plant. Tar distilleries, based on coal tar from coke ovens, started being constructed later in the 19th century, separating from tar wastes and off-gases a number of organic chemicals, such as benzene, phenol, creosotes, naphthalene, and higher aromatic chemicals, as well as ammonia. Coal-based town gas for household uses also started being produced, yielding similar materials as chemical byproducts. The Solvay process for the production of soda ash, developed in Europe, was placed into production near Syracuse, New York, in 1884, and two other plants of this kind were built at the turn of the century to supply the new plate glass industry. A Canadian, T. L. Willson,

built an electric furnace to make calcium carbide, leading to the production of acetylene and calcium cyanamide in North America in 1905, a notable producer being American Cyanamid.

Europe's chemical industry led that of the United States in a number of ways, based on a traditionally greater emphasis on chemical research in Germany, France, England, and other countries. In the late 1700s and 1800s, researchers such as Lavoisier, Berthelot, Gay-Lussac, Kekule, Sabatier, Woehler, Liebig, Perkin, Nobel, and others made many breakthrough developments that led to the establishment of plants to produce synthetic dyestuffs, human-made fibers, explosives, soda ash, solvents, and medicines, such as acetylsalicylic acid (aspirin). Synthetic dyestuffs such as alizarin and indigo, to supplant and eventually replace imported natural dyes, began production in England, Germany, and France in the 1860s and 1870s using raw materials from coal distilleries. The German chemical industry in particular became paramount not only in its own market but also in exporting to other countries including the United States. Eventually the I. G. Farben CARTEL became so powerful that it dominated world production in many chemicals, as it also established plants, joint ventures, or other cooperative arrangements (such as selling cartels) with U.S. producers DuPont, Allied Chemical, and others. The development of dynamite production by Alfred Nobel, based on nitroglycerine, led to another worldwide cartel, which included two plants in the United States by 1873.

Nitric acid was first produced by the Merrimac Chemical Company in 1905 and aniline by the Benzol Products Company in 1912. Synthetic phenol via the chlorobenzol process was made by Dow Chemical shortly after World War I, taking over from a less efficient phenol process.

The first plastics developed in England were based on nitrocellulose and camphor and known as Xylonite. In the United States, John Wesley Hyatt, looking for a substitute for the ivory used in billiard balls, established a plant in Newark, New Jersey, to make this type of polymer in

1872, giving it the name Celluloid. It was soon used to make knife handles, films, collars and cuffs, and other products. It became the most important plastic produced until 1909, when Leo Baekeland, a native Belgian who had immigrated to the United States, discovered another plastic material based on phenol-formaldehyde, which was termed Bakelite.

Monsanto had been established in 1902, first as a producer of saccharin, then of other organic and inorganic chemicals. Cellulose was also initially used to produce so-called manmade fibers and films. Cellulose acetate, first produced in France, did not become commercially important until acetone could be used as a solvent, leading to so-called acetate silk, manufactured in the United States and elsewhere around the turn of the century. The first highly successful manmade fiber, viscose rayon, based on wood or cotton pulp, was developed by Courtaulds in England in 1895 and was first produced in the United States by Avtex Fibers in 1910.

By 1914, the U.S. chemical industry had become relatively self-sufficient, with the exception of having to import potash and nitrates, as well as having essentially no dyestuffs industry. Chlor-alkalies were being produced in quantity at Niagara Falls and elsewhere, with Hooker Chemical, Niagara Alkali, and Dow as important producers. The Frasch sulfur mining process developed on the Gulf Coast, where large deposits had been discovered, started to yield large quantities of sulfur for sulfuric acid production and other sulfur compounds. Borates were produced by U.S. Borax in the West. Stauffer Chemical was making acids and phosphates, and a British firm, Albright and Wilson, was producing phosphorus and sodium chlorate. Industrial gases were produced by Air Reduction Company, affiliated with Air Liquide in France, and by Linde Air Products Company.

Union Carbide and Chemicals acquired the Presto-Lite company, which had for some time produced acetylene from calcium carbide for use in automobile headlights and street lights. Union Carbide also bought an interest in Linde and started experimenting at Linde's plant in Tonawanda, New York, to crack hydrocarbons in order to make both acetylene and ethylene from ethane, plentiful in natural gas. A commercial plant was built near Charleston, West Virginia, in 1921, and by 1927, the firm was making ethylene glycol for a product needed in antifreeze protection for automobiles. In 1923, Ethyl Corporation introduced tetraethyl lead to raise gasoline octane, making possible the development of high-compression car engines.

High-pressure synthesis work in Germany just before the war was responsible for one of the biggest chemical industry breakthroughs, the development of a process to make synthetic ammonia from hydrogen and nitrogen. While the process was patented and therefore not readily available to U.S. companies, within a decade Shell Chemical in Martinez, California, and DuPont at Belle, West Virginia, were able to build synthetic ammonia plants with successful operations achieved in 1930, using a somewhat lower pressure to skirt the BASF patents.

Dow Chemical, incorporated in 1892, had become a large producer of bromine from wells in the Midland, Michigan, area. A joint venture with Ethyl Corporation at Kure Beach, North Carolina, used a process to extract and purify bromine from seawater. In the late 1930s, Dow built the first large-scale outdoor chemical complex on the Texas Gulf Coast to extract bromine and magnesium from seawater, also making chlorine-caustic, ethylene, ethylene glycol, and ethylene dibromide, used as a solvent for tetraethyl lead (TEL).

Thermal cracking plants installed by refineries were yielding increasing quantities of ethylene, propylene, and aromatics, all ideally suited as petrochemical feedstocks. The first so-called petrochemical plant was built by Esso (now Exxon) at the Bayway, New Jersey, refinery, making isopropyl alcohol via the hydrolysis of refinery propylene, using sulfuric acid to effect the reaction. Esso at that time had strong relations with Germany's I. G. Farben combine, whereby the know-how for a number of technologies developed by the two entities was shared. For example, the German firm provided to Esso its know-how in hydrogenation reactions, while Esso shared its knowledge of making TEL. In the late 1930s, Esso started high-temperature steam cracking of crude oil fractions to ethylene and higher olefins, related to the work that Union Carbide had been doing in Charleston. Hydrogenation was used to remove sulfur from refinery streams going into gasoline and fuel oils.

Shell Chemical at its Emeryville, California, research laboratories was developing techniques to make high-octane blending components (e.g., isooctane) from propylene and butylenes using a dimerization catalyst. Other developments commercialized by Shell in the 1930s included synthetic glycerin and methyl ethyl ketone, which became an important paint solvent.

The 1930s also saw considerable progress in the field of plastics. Union Carbide and B.F. GOODRICH developed techniques to soften polyvinyl chloride (PVC) resin, the product formed by copolymerization with vinyl acetate, the latter by the development of so-called plasticizers. PVC became the first important thermoplastic resin, finding a myriad of uses in piping, seat covers, shower curtains, toys, and other applications. Meanwhile, Dow was working on technology to produce styrene, leading a few years later to production of polystyrene resins, which have much greater clarity than PVC. Dow polystyrene was put on the market in 1937.

The much-heralded work by Wallace Carothers at DuPont led in the late 1930s to the development and commercialization of a number of synthetic polymers and fibers, notably nylon. Somewhat earlier, DuPont had built a plant to make neoprene, a specialty rubber. Teflon, an inert plastic with many uses, was also developed by DuPont around the same time.

An important shift in plant design saw the construction of chemical plants in open-air sites, starting on the U.S. Gulf Coast at such places as Freeport, Texas (Dow), Texas City (Union Carbide, Monsanto), Baton Rouge (Esso, Ethyl Corporation), Orange (DuPont), and Lake Charles (PPG, Conoco). Previously, following European tradition, plants had generally been built inside buildings.

The 1930s also saw the end of U.S. chemical companies' participation in several cartels that had their origin in Europe. The Justice Department and the FEDERAL TRADE COMMISSION attacked these cartels as being monopolistic and in restraint of trade. Only export cartels, as allowed under the Webb-Pomerine Act, were allowed from that point forward.

The Second World War was a crucible for the North American chemical industry, as it became one of the most essential industries supporting the war effort. With imports of natural rubber from Japanese-controlled Malaysia no longer possible, several domestic companies developed synthetic rubbers for tire and hose production based on styrene, butadiene, and acrylonitrile. Some of this technology had also come from Esso's exchange of technical information with I. G. Farben.

Work on dimerization, dehydrogenation, and aromatization of hydrocarbon fractions produced massive amounts of high-octane blending components for aviation and automobile gasoline. Fighter planes in particular required high-octane for rapid takeoffs. A number of synthetic polymers and fibers were produced in increasing quantities, including nylon for parachutes, polyethylene for radar equipment, specialty solvents, and many other "petrochemicals." Antibiotics, more powerful than the sulfa drugs then in use, were developed during this period, with production of penicillin by Merck, Pfizer, Squibb, and Commercial Solvents Corporation, among others.

The Manhattan Project, which in 1945 resulted in the capitulation of Japan due to the bombs dropped on Hiroshima and Nagasaki, was one of the most significant achievements, as chemical engineers learned how to separate and concentrate uranium isotopes to produce fissionable materials.

The end of the war, with its shortages of consumer products and an even longer pent-up demand as a result of the Great Depression, brought about an unprecedented buying wave in durable goods such as housing, automobiles, and appliances. With synthetic materials becoming broadly available to factories that shifted their output from war materials to consumer goods, petrochemicals started a period of "double digit" growth that lasted until the late 1960s. Now, a number of companies wanted to make petro-

chemicals, which were rapidly replacing, in many applications, such conventional materials as glass, wood, natural rubber, iron, copper, aluminum, and paper. A number of old-line companies making these traditional materials (e.g., U.S. STEEL, Goodyear, B.F. Goodrich, Georgia Pacific, Pittsburgh Plate Glass) and others now entered the manufacture of petrochemicals, using technologies licensed from engineering firms and competing with the traditional chemical companies that were loath to let in these newcomers. Most of the oil companies now also established a petrochemical division. By the end of the 1960s,

Dow production plant for Saran Wrap (LIBRARY OF CONGRESS)

sales of several petrochemicals were measured in billions of pounds per year.

The 1960s and 1970s saw a rapid increase in the internationalization of the chemical industry. German, French, British, and Dutch firms made a number of acquisitions and joint ventures in the United States, such as Wyandotte Chemical by BASF; Mobay, a joint venture between Monsanto and Bayer; ICI's acquisition of Atlas Chemical; and DSM's majority investment in the fiber company American Enka. Belgium's Solvay established a U.S. subsidiary. Conversely, such firms as Dow Chemical, Union Carbide, DuPont, Gulf Oil Chemicals, Esso Chemical, National Distillers and Chemicals, and Monsanto invested in Europe, generally building plants for which exports had previously established good markets.

This was also a period when chemical producers recognized the economic advantage of scale and started to build much larger ("single train") plants than had been built to date. In ethylene, ammonia, styrene, and several other products, these large plants, which were made possible by a number of chemical engineering process and equipment breakthroughs, established new economics for the MASS PRODUCTION of these chemicals.

A pattern of consumption of chemicals was being established, and it continues to the present time. Highest production inorganics were sulfuric acid, ammonia, chlorine, caustic, phosphoric acid, hydrogen, oxygen, and nitrogen gas. Highest production organics were ethylene, propylene, ethylene dichloride, benzene, urea, and styrene. Plastics and resins included polyethylene (several densities), polypropylene, PVC, and polystyrene. Synthetic fibers were led by polyester, nylon, and olefin.

This period also saw the establishment and/or rapid growth of a number of specialty chemicals manufacturers, such as W. R. Grace, Hercules, Nalco, Petrolite, Witco, National Starch and Chemicals, and many others. These firms, generally using less complicated technologies, made various types of chemicals (e.g., adhesives, sealants, water treating chemicals, photographic chemicals, mining chemicals, personal care chemicals) that facilitated production processes or imparted special characteristics to consumer products. Fine chemicals were also produced in large quantities, in many cases as feedstocks for a rapidly growing PHARMACEUTICAL INDUSTRY, including such firms as Pfizer, Merck, Smith Kline, Wyeth Laboratories, Eli Lilly, and American Home Products.

The first oil shock in 1973 and the second in 1978–79 became landmark events for the domestic chemical industry. It soon became clear that the industry could no longer depend on very cheap, copiously available hydrocarbon feedstocks to produce petrochemicals. From a pre-1973 price of $3 per barrel, crude oil prices rose as high as $30 per barrel in 1979, eventually settling between $15 and $25 per barrel in the 1980s and 1990s. Natural gas, which had cost as little as 15 cents per million BTU, rose to a level between $2 and $2.50, following the higher crude oil prices as well as higher production costs and diminishing sources of low-cost gas.

Important changes were taking place as the U.S. chemical industry faced increasing maturity, with demand growth for its products dropping from a double-digit rate to less than twice the GDP growth and with technology innovation at a much lower level. Meanwhile, a number of countries in the developing regions of the world (Korea, Thailand, Malaysia, Taiwan, Brazil, and Saudi Arabia) were rapidly building up an internal chemical industry, either to supply local markets or for exports or both. Inexpensive hydrocarbon deposits in western Canada, the Middle East, and several other areas provided the basis for large export-oriented plants, which started to compete strongly with the once heavily advantaged U.S. petrochemical plants on the Gulf Coast. By the end of the century, the balance of trade in chemicals, once highly positive and amounting to more than $20 billion of exports over imports, had actually become negative.

A tremendous amount of industry restructuring and, to a lesser extent, consolidation took place in the 1980s and 1990s, as companies had to decide whether to stay in or to quit the production of highly competitive petrochemicals and whether to shift much of their portfolios to the production of higher-value specialties. Many old-line chemical companies (Stauffer, Allied Chemical, National Distillers, etc.) disappeared due to MERGERS and acquisitions, and a number of oil companies decided to sell or exit their petrochemical operations.

The chemical industry had also become a target of environmentalists, who pointed to the hazardous nature of its operations and the exposure of workers and the public to toxic chemicals. The industry became highly regulated at the federal, state, and local levels and was spending a large part of its cash flow on meeting environmental standards and on chemical testing.

Once the darling of the investing public due to its rapid growth and the miracles of technology that have been responsible for a plethora of new synthetic materials, the chemical industry has become increasingly embattled as it tries to operate in a manner to satisfy its various stakeholders. With exports declining due to foreign competition, and some products voluntarily phased out due to their toxic characteristics, it has remained one of the largest domestic industries, essential to our standard of living, yet increasingly on the defensive and unsure of its future.

See also PETROLEUM INDUSTRY.

Further reading

Aftalion, Fred. *A History of the International Chemical Industry*. Philadelphia: Chemical Heritage Press, 2001.

Barnes, Harry C. *From Molasses to the Moon. The Story of U.S. Industrial Chemicals Company*. New York: U.S. Industrial Chemicals Company, 1975.

Borkin, Joseph. *The Crime and Punishment of I.G. Farben*. New York: Macmillan/Free Press, 1978.

Brandt, E. N. *Growth Company. Dow Chemical's First Century*. East Lansing: Michigan State University Press, 1997.

Chapman, Keith. *The International Petrochemical Industry*. Oxford: Basil Blackwell, 1991.

Spitz, Peter H. *Petrochemicals. The Rise of an Industry*. New York: John Wiley & Sons, 1988.

———. *The Chemical Industry at the Millennium*. Philadelphia: Chemical Heritage Press, 2003.

Peter Spitz

Chicago Board of Trade (CBOT)

A commodities and futures exchange established in Chicago in 1848. Originally designed as a commodities marketing exchange, the board quickly became devoted to trading in futures contracts. During the Civil War, the exchange became prominent by buying and selling futures contracts on staple commodities such as wheat and corn. By the 1880s, the exchange was the best-known business enterprise in Chicago. Other similar exchanges were also developed in St. Louis, Kansas City, and Minneapolis.

Originally, the CBOT and other commodities exchanges traded contracts that guaranteed buyers and sellers prices and deliveries on a specific future date—but the actual contracts were not negotiable after being originated. Traders quickly developed a market, and soon speculation became the primary activity on many of the exchanges. The CBOT especially became known for corners and bear raids, massive speculative operations by traders and speculators conducted on the floor, or pits, of the exchange. In corners, traders would try to corner the entire supply of a commodity using both physical commodities and futures contracts in order to exact higher prices. In bear raids, commodity contracts were sold short, forcing down prices. These operations became so notorious that they attracted other operators who would try to entice small investors to gamble on commodities in BUCKET SHOPS. The CBOT achieved a notable victory over the incursions made by the bucket shops in a U.S. Supreme Court decision in 1905, *Board of Trade of City of Chicago v. Christie Grain & Stock Co.* The Court denied the bucket shops information generated on exchange prices and transmitted by the Western Union Company.

By the 1890s, the CBOT became the largest futures market in the world and began a drive to force the bucket shops out of business. The market prospered during World War I and began adding new contracts to those already traded in the pits. These contracts were for agricultural commodities. The exchanges were all restrained somewhat by a series of commodities trading regulations passed in the 1920s and 1930s and were limited by measures passed during World War II to restrain prices and speculation.

During World War II, exchange activity declined significantly as price controls on many commodities curtailed speculation and restricted trading in many commodities. New contracts began to develop after the war, and contracts began appearing on nonagricultural commodities that severely strained REGULATION on trading because they were not included in the Commodity Exchange Act passed in 1936.

In the 1950s and 1960s, the CBOT began adding new contracts again in order to maintain its spot as the largest futures exchange. It added contracts on livestock to the agricultural commodities it already traded. But the biggest change to its way of doing business came in the early 1970s, when it began experimenting with financial futures and options. Since options on futures contracts were prohibited at the time, the exchange helped develop the Chicago Board Options Exchange (CBOE) in 1972. The new subsidiary traded options on common stocks independently of the CBOT. The CBOE soon became the largest options exchange in the world.

Also beginning in the early 1970s, the CBOT began introducing contracts on financial instruments. It was soon trading futures contracts on Treasury securities and financial indexes. A crosstown rival, the International Monetary Market, developed by the Chicago Mercantile Exchange, established in 1919, began offering contracts on financial instruments at the same time, and the two became the largest financial futures exchanges in the country. Options trading remained on separate exchanges even after

options on futures contracts were reintroduced after the COMMODITY FUTURES TRADING COMMISSION was established in 1974. The commission became the first significant regulator of the futures exchanges, covering all futures products, not only those on agricultural commodities.

In the 1990s, many of the exchanges began experimenting with electronic trading and links with foreign futures exchanges. The CBOT retained its open outcry system in the pits, with floor traders known as market makers remaining the ultimate source of prices

See also FUTURES MARKETS; OPTIONS MARKETS.

Further reading

Geisst, Charles R. *Wheels of Fortune: The History of Speculation from Scandal to Respectability.* New York: John Wiley & Sons, 2002.

Lurie, Jonathan. *The Chicago Board of Trade, 1859–1905: The Dynamics of Self-Regulation.* Urbana: University of Illinois Press, 1979.

Taylor, C. H. *History of the Board of Trade of the City of Chicago.* Chicago: Robert O. Law Co., 1917.

Chrysler, Walter Percy (1875–1940) *industrialist*

Born in Wamego, Kansas, Chrysler began his career as a machinist's apprentice after finishing high school. His first job was as an apprentice machinist at the UNION PACIFIC RAILROAD yards, where he developed an interest in machinery that would last his entire life. He later joined the Chicago and Great Western Railroad as a superintendent. He moved again to the American Locomotive Company. He began disassembling automobiles and learning how to reconstruct them in his spare time, and that interest led him to the automobile industry.

Chrysler purchased his first car in 1908, a Locomobile, and immediately took it apart and then rebuilt it to learn as much as possible about automobile engineering. He joined the Buick Motor Company in 1912 as a manager at half of his old salary and became its president in 1916. He then joined GENERAL MOTORS as a vice president of operations. He made numerous improvements to car production since the company was still being run by carriage makers rather than by automotive engineers. He did not get along with the president of GM, William C. DURANT, and retired when the company was reorganized in 1920.

Chrysler was able to retire a millionaire, although he returned to the auto industry soon thereafter when he began to reorganize the Willys Overland Co. at a salary of $1 million per year. In 1925, he took control of the ailing Maxwell Motor Co. and transformed it into the CHRYSLER CORP. The new company produced his first car, equipped with four-wheel hydraulic brakes and a high-compression motor. Within four years it became the second-largest producer in the country. Its most notable product was the Chrysler Six, a six-cylinder engine car that became one of the most popular in the country.

Chrylser's most notable acquisition was the purchase of the Dodge Brothers' Motor Co. from Clarence Dillon of DILLON READ & CO., a New York investment bank, in 1928. Growing through acquisition would become a trademark of his company in the future. Adding Dodge to his line substantially increased the company's name and reputation and enabled it to become the second-largest carmaker. Previously, it was fifth in a very crowded market. Chrysler also added two new lines, the Plymouth and the DeSoto, after acquiring Dodge.

In the 1920s, he also financed the construction of the Chrysler Building in New York City, at the time the world's tallest building, eclipsing the Woolworth Building in southern Manhattan. He was unaware that the Empire State Building was being secretly planned to be the world's tallest building by John RASKOB, the former president of General Motors. Personal rivalries between industrialists were characteristic of the era before the 1929 stock market crash. Chrysler was president of his company from 1925 to 1935 and after relinquishing the job remained as chairman of the board of directors until his death.

Further reading

Chrysler, Walter P., and Sparkes Boyden. *Life of an American Workman.* New York: Dodd, Mead, 1950.
Curcio, Vincent. *Chrysler: The Life and Times of an Automotive Genius.* New York: Oxford University Press, 2000.

Chrysler Corp. Traditionally the third-largest American manufacturer of automobiles, behind GENERAL MOTORS and Ford. The company traces its origins to the Maxwell-Briscoe Co., formed by Jonathan Maxwell and Benjamin Briscoe in 1903 in Tarrytown, New York. The first car produced by the company was the Maxwell. In 1910, the United States Motor Car Co. was formed, consolidating several smaller manufacturers, including Maxwell, although the company failed three years later. The company was then bought by Walter Flanders, who renamed it the Maxwell Motor Co. in order to capitalize on its most popular car and brand name.

But the new reorganization did not ensure the company success. By 1920, it had fallen into financial difficulties again, and Walter CHRYSLER, the retired president of Buick and a vice president of General Motors, was tapped to form a reorganization committee. As a result, the Chrysler Corp. was formed in 1921. The company continued to produce the Maxwell and also introduced the six-cylinder Chrysler Six in 1924, which became very popular in its own right. In 1926, the company announced a luxury model, the Imperial. Two years later, it began production of the Plymouth and the DeSoto. In 1928, it also made one of its largest acquisitions to date.

Chrysler was approached by Clarence Dillon of the Wall Street firm DILLON READ & CO. The manufacturer had been owned by Dillon for several years after he bought it from the Dodge family following the untimely deaths of the Dodge brothers who had guided the company. He offered to sell it to Chrysler. The purchase price was $170 million, and Dodge became a division

The 1952 Chrysler Windsor club coupé (Library of Congress)

of Chrysler, adding to its product line. In the 1930s, the company announced new designs for its cars, including the Airflow concept, which changed cars from boxy carriages to more modern, flowing styles. Most vehicle production was devoted to the war effort in the early 1940s, but the company began introducing rapid style changes to its lines in the 1950s and 1960s.

The company began to run into financial difficulties in the late 1970s. In 1979, Lee Iacocca, a former Ford executive, was named chairman, and in the following year, the company had to be bailed out by a federal loan, one of the few ever made to the private sector. The federal government loaned Chrysler $1.5 billion under the Loan Guarantee Act. Chrysler also sold its defense division to General Dynamics. The restructuring was successful, and the company was able to repay the loan in 1983. The early 1980s were considered the turning point for the company, which was able to survive its financial difficulties.

In 1984, the first minivan was introduced, and the vehicle became one of the most impor-

tant product lines in the company's history. A year later, the company entered an agreement with Mitsubishi Motors of Japan to jointly build subcompact cars in the United States. Later in the 1980s, it established a seven-year/70,000-mile power train warranty for its cars and in 1987 completed a takeover of American Motors, absorbing the country's fourth-largest car manufacturer. The deal allowed it to acquire the Jeep line of vehicles. In 1988, the company introduced the first passenger vehicle equipped with a standard driver-side airbag.

By the 1990s, the company again was highly profitable. A prolonged takeover fight with investor Kirk Kerkorian in the 1990s shook the company and eventually caused it to seek a merger partner. Finally, in 1998 it merged with Daimler Benz of Germany in what was described as a "merger of equals." Ultimate management control of Chrysler moved to Germany as a result. The company remained the number three domestic automaker behind General Motors and Ford, although it was classified as a foreign-owned corporation.

Further reading
Hyde, Charles K. *Riding the Roller Coaster: A History of the Chrysler Corporation.* Detroit: Wayne State University Press, 2003.
Langworth, Richard, and Jan Norbye. *The Complete History of Chrysler Corp. 1925–1985.* New York: Beekman Publishers, 1985.
Moritz, Michael. *Going for Broke: The Chrysler Story.* Garden City, N.Y.: Doubleday, 1981.
Reich, Robert B., and John Donahue. *New Deals: The Chrysler Revival and the American System.* New York: Times Books, 1985.

Cisco Corporation   A manufacturer of INTERNET routing equipment founded in 1977 by two Stanford computer specialists who invented the Internet router because they could not communicate with each other over the Internet using the current technology. In less than 20 years, Cisco would become the most widely held stock in the country and at one time had the highest market capitalization of any stock in the United States.

The company began to grow exponentially, paralleling the use of the Internet, first in academia and then in general commercial use. The company grew rapidly in the 1990s, under the aegis of John Chambers. He joined Cisco in 1991, when it was already becoming known as a Wall Street favorite. Chambers became CEO in 1995 and continued the aggressive strategy that made the company a phenomenally rising star.

Rather than build from the ground up, the company adopted a growth-by-acquisition strategy in the 1990s. Using a rising stock market to good advantage, Cisco acquired many companies in related fields by paying for them with its own stock, which kept rising in the market because its earnings continued to grow. For example, the company paid $4.1 billion for StrataCom in 1996, a manufacturer of computer networking technology. At the time, the acquired company had sales of $335 million, meaning that Cisco paid a multiple of 12 times sales for the company. Paying multiples of sales or potential sales was a sign of the

"new economy," in which all tried and tested techniques of valuation were overlooked. Three years later, Chambers announced that Cisco was paying $7 billion for privately owned Cerent Corporation, a small network equipment company that had been in existence for only a year.

The strategy made Cisco the largest manufacturer of Internet routing equipment, identified closely with the Internet itself. But the acquisitions growth began to slow considerably in 2000, when the stock market indexes began to fall, and Cisco could no longer use its increasing stock value to pay for acquisitions. During the 1990s, its acquisitions were paid for with what was known as "Cisco money," highly priced stock that paid for additional acquisitions at prices unheard of in the technology industry.

Cisco began to experience competition from overseas manufacturers in the late 1990s and early 2000s but maintained its market in the face of competition. After its stock fell to a low of $9 per share, the company became identified with the excesses of the Internet age, although it remained the premier company in its industry and one of the most widely held stocks in the country.

Further reading
Bunnell, David. *Making the Cisco Connection.* New York: John Wiley & Sons, 2000.
Paulson, Ed. *Inside Cisco: The Real Story of Sustained M & A Growth.* New York: John Wiley, 2001.
Slater, Robert. *The Eye of the Storm: How John Chambers Steered Cisco through the Internet Collapse.* New York: HarperBusiness, 2003.
Waters, John K. *John Chambers and the Cisco Way: Navigating Through Volatility.* New York: John Wiley; 2002.

Citibank   Since the early 20th century, one of the three largest U.S. banks. It was established in 1812 as the City Bank of New York, a state-chartered bank. In its first quarter-century, it functioned primarily as a credit union for its merchant customers, with bad debts sometimes restricting its ability to provide services and increasing the bank's reliance upon often volatile banknotes and interbank balances. After the Panic of 1837, a dynamic new director, Moses Taylor, a wealthy merchant closely linked to millionaire fur trader John Jacob ASTOR, gradually acquired a controlling interest in the bank, holding its presidency from 1856 until he died in 1882, to be succeeded by his son-in-law, Percy Pyne. Eschewing banknotes and interbank balances, Taylor and Pyne pursued policies of strong liquidity and high cash reserves, enabling the institution—rechartered in 1865 as the National City Bank of New York—to finance their family's extensive railroad, utility, and commercial ventures.

In 1891, Pyne appointed James W. Stillman, an able New York businessman and securities underwriter with close family ties to the Rockefeller petroleum interests, president of the National City, then 12th in size among New York City banks. Stillman aggressively expanded the bank's operations; in the decade after 1895 its assets grew 22 percent annually, making it the nation's largest bank, a status he guarded jealously, and the first to acquire $1 billion in assets. Its capitalization rose from $3.4 million in 1891 to $49.3 million (with profits of $5.2 million) in 1907, with Stillman, William, and Percy Rockefeller as controlling stockholders. Stillman rapidly expanded the bank's operations into INVESTMENT BANKING, underwriting numerous securities issues for such clients as the UNION PACIFIC RAILROAD interests of E. H. HARRIMAN, which in turn provided lucrative investment opportunities for National City's growing number of corporate industrial clients, prominent among whom were large RAILROADS and the Rockefeller Standard Oil interests. On securities issues National City often worked closely with major New York investment houses, notably J. P. Morgan & Company and KUHN LOEB & COMPANY. The National City also benefited from extensive correspondent relationships with rural American banks, for whom it undertook profitable New York exchange transactions. Under Stillman, it embarked on an aggressive merger and acquisitions program, controlling or acquiring stock in the Third National Bank, the Fidelity Bank, the Hanover National Bank, the Riggs National Bank, and several others. The National City aggressively sought federal government business and by 1897 was the largest national government depository; early in the 20th century, Treasury secretaries employed such government deposits to relieve fluctuations in the money market. In the Panics of 1893 and 1907, the National City's continuing strong liquidity policies won it numerous deposits from depositors and borrowers seeking security.

In 1899, Stillman hired as vice president Frank A. Vanderlip, an innovative former financial journalist and assistant secretary of the Treasury, who became president in 1909, leaving Stillman supreme as chairman until his death. Vanderlip dramatically expanded the National City's securities business, and call loans rose from one-third of total loans in the 1890s to two-thirds in the 1900s. Vanderlip also became prominent in the movement to expand American foreign commerce and investment, building on the foreign trade department Stillman had established in 1897 and instituting a new training program designed to equip young bank personnel for overseas service. By 1907, the National City financed one-third of American cotton exports and had established an impressive foreign correspondent network. Vanderlip was among the most outspoken campaigners for a U.S. central bank system, in part because this would facilitate American banks' capacity to finance foreign commercial transactions, invest abroad, and establish overseas branches. After the Federal Reserve Act was passed in 1913 and the First World War began in 1914, Vanderlip rapidly acquired the International Banking Corporation, opened 132 branches in Asia, Latin America, and Russia, participated in extensive wartime loans to foreign governments and the financing of substantial overseas trade, and established the American International Corporation to purchase non-American businesses. These ventures' ambitious scope, along with substantial National City losses after the November 1917 Bolshevik seizure of power in Russia, alarmed both Stillman, who died in 1918, and other prominent National City directors, who in 1919 dismissed Vanderlip, who had nonetheless laid the foundations of National City's subsequent international preeminence among American banks.

Charles E. Mitchell, appointed president in 1921, built on his predecessors' accomplishments, expanding COMMERCIAL BANKING services to large corporations and wealthy individuals, but also opening branches throughout New York to attract numerous small individual depositors and offering them opportunities to purchase domestic and overseas securities. By 1929, its associated National City Company handled almost one-quarter of all such bond issues floated in the United States, though Mitchell's enthusiastic underwriting of shaky German and Latin American securities, while highly profitable throughout the later 1920s, ultimately brought National City large losses and his own dismissal and public disgrace. The 1933 Banking Act forced National City to renounce investment banking. Gradually recouping its position in the 1930s, during World War II National City handled extensive U.S. government accounts.

After 1945, the National City—renamed First National City Bank in 1956, after acquiring the First National Bank of New York, a one-branch blue-chip institution with substantial assets and several major corporate accounts—came under the dynamic leadership of the internationally minded Walter B. Wriston, who became president in 1968, remaining chief executive officer until 1984. Later renamed Citibank (in 1976), it recouped its international position, opening or reopening branches in every major overseas country. From then onward no other American financial institution could match its international interests. Wriston also aggressively sought both

large and small domestic depositors, attracting smaller customers with loan, mortgage, and credit card facilities, and pioneering the introduction of automatic teller machines in all branches. The financial deregulation of the 1980s enabled Citibank further to extend its activities, and under the Citicorp holding company umbrella it once more marketed securities and offered domestic and overseas clients a wide range of investment facilities. In the later 1990s, it launched an impressive campaign to expand its overseas operations in Asia, where many local clients believed American-based financial institutions offered greater security than their local counterparts.

In 1998, Citibank was merged with the Travelers, an insurance company run by Sanford WEILL. The merger was the largest in history at the time and marked a significant change in the ownership and operation of banking institutions. As part of the deal, the two institutions needed to comply with the relevant provisions of the BANK HOLDING COMPANY ACT and the Glass-Steagall Act. Within a year, however, the Glass-Steagall Act was replaced by the FINANCIAL SERVICES MODERNIZATION ACT, and the merger became permanent.

Further reading

Huertas, Thomas F., and Harold van B. Cleveland. *Citibank, 1812–1970.* Cambridge, Mass.: Harvard University Press, 1985.

Logan, Sheridan. *George F. Baker and His Bank, 1840–1955.* New York: privately published, 1981.

Winkler, John K. *The First Billion: The Stillmans and the National City Bank.* Babson Park, Mass.: Mass Spear & Staff, 1951.

Zweig, Phillip L. *Wriston: Walter Wriston, Citibank, and the Rise and Fall of American Financial Supremacy.* New York: Crown Publishers, 1996.

Priscilla Roberts

Clark Dodge & Co.   A merchant and INVESTMENT BANKING firm founded by Enoch Clark (1802–56) after the Panic of 1837. Clark had been a partner in the firm of S. & M. Allen &

Co., a merchant bank that failed during the panic. The Allen firm originally was a dealer in lottery tickets and became one of the first members of the NEW YORK STOCK EXCHANGE when it established permanent indoor headquarters after 1817.

Clark and his brother-in-law Edward Dodge established their bank in Philadelphia with capital of $15,000. The original firm was known as E. W. Clark Dodge & Co. While working for the Allens in their Providence, Rhode Island, office, Clark gained experience speculating on the Boston Stock Exchange that he would put to use in his own firm. The main business of the new firm was trading in gold bullion and BANKNOTES. The firm succeeded quickly and opened offices in St. Louis, New Orleans, and New York as well as other offices in the Midwest. New York soon became the main office.

Like many other small but well-connected merchant banks, Clark Dodge became prominent when it assisted the Treasury in issuing bonds to pay for a war effort. When the Mexican War began in 1846, the firm shared underwriting of TREASURY BONDS with the better-known bank Corcoran & Riggs of Washington, D.C. Employing his branch system to good use, Clark made more money floating the interest on the bonds between his different offices and the U.S. Treasury than he did by selling them.

The firm became larger as a result of its success and admitted several new members to partnership, including Jay COOKE, who was admitted in 1849. Before the Civil War, the firm also helped underwrite scores of railroad bonds, allowing the senior members of the firm to go into semiretirement. But the Panic of 1857 put the firm under severe strain, and its offices closed temporarily, then opened again when the panic subsided. When it did reopen, it was without the services of Jay Cooke, who had left and opened his own firm shortly after. Enoch Clark died in 1856, a year before the panic. Clark Dodge and Jay Cooke & Co. both played a vital part in selling Treasury bonds to finance the war, with Cooke playing the major role.

Clark Dodge became one of Wall Street's best-known names, although it never grew to a substantial size, remaining a second-tier underwriter for most of the 20th century. It opened several branch offices in the Northeast. Like many other firms, it entered the investment management business in the 1920s after the major banking and securities laws were passed and developed a substantial presence in managing investor funds. Finally, in the 1970s it was acquired by KIDDER PEABODY & CO. and merged into Kidder's investment management business.

Further reading

Clark Dodge & Co. *Clark Dodge & Co., 1845–1945.* New York: privately published, 1945.

Geisst, Charles R. *The Last Partnerships: Inside the Great Wall Street Money Dynasties.* New York: McGraw-Hill, 2001.

Clayton Act One of the three major ANTITRUST laws in the United States, the law was passed following congressional hearings in 1912 that revealed much about the nature of American business and finance. Many business combinations had been formed despite the existence of the SHERMAN ACT since 1890, and Congress decided to attempt to plug some of the loopholes.

Largely as a result of the Standard Oil decision in 1911, both conservatives and liberals were unhappy with judicial interpretations of the Sherman Act. While the Supreme Court approved the antitrust conviction and breakup of Standard Oil, it also announced a rule of reason that seemed wishy-washy to Progressives. All three political parties (Republican, Progressive, and Democrat) advocated significant congressional supplementation of the antitrust laws. Wilson's victory guaranteed that the revision would be substantial. The Clayton Act, which was passed in 1914, defined prohibited practices much more specifically than the Sherman Act had.

Section two of the Clayton Act condemned a type of PREDATORY PRICING attributed to Standard Oil, whereby the large firm charged a very low price in the victim's market, "recouping" its costs by charging higher prices in other markets where it already had a monopoly. Section three prohibited tying, or the monopolist's insistence that the buyer could purchase a desired product only if it took a second, perhaps undesired, product as well; and exclusive dealing, or a seller's requirement that the buyer take the contracted good only from that seller. Section four included an expanded right of private plaintiffs to seek treble damages plus attorney fees for antitrust suits. Section five provided that, if the government should win an antitrust case, private plaintiffs suing the same defendant need not prove the case again, but must show only their injury. Section six was designed to immunize labor unions—a form of cartel—from antitrust claims of price fixing or boycott. Section seven prohibited anticompetitive MERGERS between competing firms. Finally, section eight prohibited interlocking directorates—that is, prohibited the same person from serving on the board of directors of two competing companies.

Almost immediately the Clayton Act had a significant effect on antitrust jurisprudence, with the Supreme Court condemning several practices under the new statute, such as both tying and exclusive dealing, that had been approved under the older Sherman Act standards. The development of a more aggressive merger policy came later. The labor exemption proved ineffectual and had to be supplemented by further legislation during the NEW DEAL.

See also ROBINSON-PATMAN ACT.

Further reading

Freyer, Tony. *Regulating Big Business: Antitrust in Great Britain and America, 1880–1990.* New York: Cambridge University Press, 1992.
Keller, Morton. *Regulating a New Economy: Public Policy and Economic Change in America, 1900–1933.* Cambridge, Mass.: Harvard University Press, 1990.
Sklar, Martin J. *The Corporate Reconstruction of American Capitalism, 1890–1916.* New York: Cambridge University Press, 1988.

Herbert Hovenkamp

Coca-Cola Co. A beverage company founded by John S. Pemberton in 1886, Coca-Cola became the most recognizable brand in the world. When the company was founded, soda beverages were considered medicinal, to be taken for minor stomach ailments. Root beer had been introduced 10 years before, and Coke's major rival, Pepsi Cola, was founded 10 years later. However, when drinking alcoholic beverages became less fashionable and Prohibition became law, soft drinks became more popular, and Coke soon became the most popular brand.

Pemberton concocted the drink in a vat in his backyard and sold the first batch to Jacobs Pharmacy in Atlanta in 1886. The store sold the first drinks to customers for 5 cents each. Sales for the first year totaled around $50, but within 10 years the beverage became the most popular soda fountain drink. The script that became the company's logo was designed by Pemberton's accountant, who wrote the name longhand. An Atlanta businessman, Asa Candler, acquired ownership of the company in 1891 and then began marketing it nationwide. Three years later, the first factory to manufacture the syrup outside Atlanta was opened in Dallas.

In 1906, Coke was manufactured outside the United States for the first time, in Cuba and Panama. The Roots Glass Company designed what became the famous contoured bottle in 1915, and it, too, became a symbol of the beverage. By 1917, more than 3 million bottles were sold per day. A group of Atlanta businessmen bought the company in 1919 for $25 million. Coke had already implemented its own unique distribution system of allowing independent botwell established that by the 1960s the term *Coca-Cola imperialism* began to be used to identify the export of American pop culture.

In the early 1980s, Roberto Goizueta was named chairman, and the company began introducing other products to its line in response to the continuing challenge by Pepsi. Not all of the new products and innovations, such as the "New Coke" product and its accompanying ad campaign, proved successful, but the company retained its hold on both its market and its brand name after Goizueta's death in 1997.

Further reading

Allen, Frederick. *Secret Formula: How Brilliant Marketing and Relentless Salesmanship Made Coca-Cola the Best-Known Product in the World.* New York: HarperBusiness, 1994.

Hoy, Anne. *Coca-Cola: The First 100 Years.* Atlanta: Coca-Cola, 1986.

Pendergrast, Mark. *For God, Country and Coca-Cola.* New York: Scribner's, 1993.

Advertisement for Coca-Cola, ca. 1890 (Library of Congress)

tlers to brew and distribute the product. The franchise system of bottling and distribution became an industry standard that still exists today.

By 1920, more than 1,000 bottlers existed selling the product in the United States and abroad. Under Robert Woodruff, the company began emphasizing bottle sales, and the company began a series of promotions for which it would become famous in the advertising world. Woodruff remained at the helm of the company for six decades and was responsible for its exponential growth and popularity. In 1928, the company established a link with the U.S. Olympic Committee by donating a thousand cases to athletes. By 1940, the beverage was bottled in more than 40 countries. The brand name became so

coffee industry   Coffee has been not only one of the most valuable imports into the United States for a century and a half, but it has also become one of the most valuable industries in the United States. From a very simple commodity chain involving delivering green beans to the end users, coffee became surprisingly complicated and industrialized. Wholesale and retail grocers were the innovators in reshaping the trade. From being simple middlemen as merchants, they increasingly became industrialists, though the revolution was as much one of distribution as of production.

Coffee has had diverse appeals. Sometimes it has been a drug, other times a hospitality drink or a prestige item. It has attracted consumers on three major gradients: taste, price, and convenience. It faced various competitors (tea, alcohol, cereal substitutes, soft drinks), some of which caused coffee manufacturers to produce better coffee and others that caused market segmentation based more on price and convenience than on quality. What is meant by "coffee" has varied considerably over time. Coffee enjoyed some unusual characteristics, starting as a luxury drink and becoming a national necessity, as the federal government recognized during the two world wars. Though coffee was a mass drink, it required a good deal of effort to turn it into a mass produced and marketed product. The U.S. market was unusual, and because of its wealth and great size, it began to shape the world coffee business. Coffee in the United States was consumed mostly in homes, not in cafés as was common in much of Europe. Drunk in the home, it was the housewife who decided what coffee to purchase and serve. Hence, wholesalers and retailers have been oriented much more toward women consumers than men. With the grocery store, not the café, as the site for choosing the product, large roasters and brand names first appeared in the United States.

The United States underwent a revolution when, by the middle of the 19th century, Americans were each drinking more than five pounds of coffee a year, one of the highest amounts in the world. By 1880, the per capita total reached 8.4 pounds, and by the end of the 19th century the United States was consuming 13 pounds per capita and importing more than 40 percent of the world's coffee. (This would grow to more than 60 percent after World War II.) The U.S. population's 15-fold explosion in the first century of American independence meant that total coffee imports grew 2,400 percent. Half of the growth in world consumption in the 19th century was due to increased U.S. purchases.

With the Civil War, coffee moved slowly away from being simply a domestic drink and purely a breakfast beverage. War, combined with the growth of major cities such as New York and the spread of industry, led ever more people to drink coffee outside the home, in the field and at hotels and train stations. The Civil War also modernized production and distribution of provisions. For coffee, the timing was good. The Austrian Max

Bode had invented the spherical roaster in 1851, which improved control over even oven temperatures. More important for American troops was the pull-out roaster produced by the New Yorker Jabez Burns in 1864, allowing more regular roasting and on a much larger scale. Grocers began to roast coffee for their customers and sometimes grind it. This business seems to have grown rapidly after 1874. It is estimated that there was a 20-fold increase in roasted coffee sold in the 20 years after the outbreak of the Civil War.

The fact that the United States had by far the most developed railroad system in the world helped spread coffee drinking to the country's interior without making the beverage prohibitively expensive for the working class. The railroad also helped bring down the price of essential staples for consumers, providing greater discretionary income with which to buy former luxuries such as coffee.

The creation of the New York Coffee Exchange in 1882 institutionalized access to information. Prices and grades thereby became more generalized. Middlemen such as importers and jobbers were reduced, while the trade became more industrialized. In 1883, 90 percent of the coffee business was in green coffee sales and only 10 percent was for roasters. By 1913, the numbers were the reverse: 95 percent of the buyers at the exchange represented roasters and only 5 percent green beans.

The first packaged roasted coffee was Osborn's Celebrated Prepared Java Coffee, which started in 1860. A technological problem, as well as a lack of consumer trust and differences in consumer taste, kept large roasters from quickly dominating the national industry in the way that giant refiners dominated sugar. Although green coffee keeps for years, roasted coffee loses its aroma and taste quickly. Ground roasted coffee dissipates even faster. Consequently, roasters had to have regional distribution sites.

The packaged brand coffee spread after a major technical breakthrough came in 1898, when Edwin Norton invented vacuum packing, which allowed roasted, ground coffee to retain its flavor. This was part of a general revolution in the food industry. In 1903, Hills Brothers was the first coffee company to commercially adopt vacuum packing, though it was not yet perfected. The notion of an impersonal, distant brand was still not accepted by most housewives at the beginning of the 20th century. Distribution channels were still locally based, and most shoppers had personal relationships with their grocers, who offered them credit and premiums but not much choice.

The ability to preserve roasted coffee in vacuum packages and the creation of grocery CHAIN STORES allowed emerging national brands to occupy an ever larger place in the trade in the United States. The GREAT ATLANTIC & PACIFIC grocery chain, which began by selling tea and coffee, went the furthest in vertical integration. A & P was providing fully 15 percent of all coffee purchased in the United States by World War I and was the fifth-largest industrial corporation in the United States.

Controversies over purity in coffee as well as in other foods threatened to retard the expansion of the packing and distribution industries. The same crusade that would bring Prohibition in 1919 brought in 1907 the United States Pure Food and Drug Act. It decreed that imported coffee be marked according to its port of exit and be free of additives. Decaffeinated coffee was invented in Germany at the turn of the century as an outgrowth of the pure food campaign. The decaffeinated coffee companies such as Koffee Hag and the cereal-based substitutes such as Postum challenged traditional coffee. There was a continued advance of consumption from 8.4 pounds per capita in 1880 to 18.4 pounds in 1949, the high mark in U.S. history. A new coffee product, instant soluble coffee, also stimulated consumption.

The expansion was largely due to a Swiss company, Nestlé, which started marketing Nescafé in 1938 and quickly dominated the market. By the 1960s, as much as one-third of home-prepared coffee was soluble. Unfortunately, the convenience of instant coffee undermined the quality of the brew. Instant coffee mostly employed robusta coffee, a faster growing but more bitter species than the arabica. The growth of the coffee market continued in the 20th century because of the rise of supermarkets in the 1930s, which led to a great increase in advertising. Selling a vastly larger number of goods, the supermarket depended upon small margins but large volume. Ever more coffee companies competed on price rather than the quality of their blend and relied ever more on advertising.

As supermarkets began covering the country, General Foods (evolving from Postum) and Standard Brands (which had been Royal and Fleischmann Companies as well as Chase and Sanborn) created enormous food CONGLOMERATES. Success in the postwar mass food processing industries depended upon market power, that is, capital and access to supermarket shelves. Giant food conglomerates such as General Foods, COCA-COLA, and Ralston Purina bought up smaller successful coffee companies. They sold nationally with little attention to regional preferences. A result of the growth of conglomerates and supermarkets was that a small number of roasters dominated that trade. By the 1950s, the five largest roasters in the United States roasted more than one-third of all coffee and held 78 percent of all stocks. By the 1990s, three companies were responsible for 80 percent of the U.S. coffee market—General Foods, Proctor and Gamble, and Nestlé—and dominated much of the international market as well. Nestlé alone bought 10 percent of the world's coffee crop annually. They used market power and advertising to dominate the coffee market. By 1996, two enormous companies, Phillip Morris ($135 million) and Procter and Gamble ($95 million), spent two-thirds of the America's $354 million coffee advertising budget.

As the leading brands merged into some of the largest companies in the world, they became overshadowed by more global corporate strategies. The parent companies are not coffee concerns. Phillip Morris owns Kraft Foods, which bought

General Foods. It owns Maxwell House, Sanka, Brim, Yuban, and General Foods' International Coffee brands. Phillip Morris owns not only several competing coffee brands, but also coffee substitute brands such as Sanka and competing convenience drinks such as Kool-Aid, Capri Sun, and Crystal Light.

These companies have also expanded internationally. In 1978, the four firms' concentration ratio for the eight largest markets was 59 percent for roasted coffee and 75 percent in soluble coffee (almost all of which was produced by Nestlé and General Foods). Since then concentration has grown. However, consumption in the United States has fallen sharply from its high in 1949 (in pounds per capita) or in the early 1960s when the measure was changed to cups of coffee a day. Per capita coffee consumption in the United States was down from its peak of 3.2 cups per day in the 1960s to less than 2 cups in 1996.

There is a countertrend as well in the growing gourmet market. Joined with the fair trade movement, coffee houses emphasize high-quality, high-priced brews with some concern about the environmental impact of production techniques and the treatment of laborers. Specialty coffeepots and espresso makers are a booming market, but they entail less than a quarter of the total market. In fact, despite popular perceptions that coffee consumption is rapidly expanding and the quality is improving, the United States is one of the few areas in the world where per capita consumption is not growing. The result of this change is that while the United States is still in gross terms the world's largest coffee consumer, its share of imports has fallen dramatically. After World War I the United States imported almost two-thirds of the world's coffee and in 1961 still half. By 1993, the total had fallen to less than 20 percent. Americans still consume the most caffeine, but now it is in the form of soft drinks.

Further reading

Dicum, Gregory, and Nina Luttinger. *The Coffee Book: Anatomy of an Industry from Crop to the Last Drop.* New York: New Press, 1999.

Pendergrast, Mark. *Uncommon Grounds.* New York: Basic Books, 1999.

Steven Topik

Colgate, William (1783–1857) *manufacturer*

William Colgate was born in Kent, England, on January 25, 1783, the son of a farmer. In 1795, his father, a vocal proponent of the French Revolution, fled England with his family to avoid prosecution. They settled in Baltimore, Maryland, where Colgate was indifferently educated. His family subsequently relocated to Virginia and then New York, while he eventually resettled in Baltimore in 1798 to work as a tallow chandler in the candle-making business. Colgate proved himself both industrious and adept in business matters, and he eventually acquired his own soap works. He sold his company and moved to New York City in 1803 to work for the firm of John Slidell & Company. Colgate eventually rose to business manager there, and in 1806, he founded a new firm, William Colgate & Company. As a businessman, Colgate was cognizant that urban areas required large quantities of soap and candles, and he determined to make his products and service distinct from competitors. For example, he pioneered free home delivery of soap to ensure a steady supply of loyal customers. In 1807, he assumed a partnership with Francis Smith, and the two men profited from the Embargo and Non-Intercourse Acts directed against competing products manufactured in Great Britain. By 1813, Colgate was sufficiently profitable that he bought out his partner's share, and within four years he was the leading soap manufacturer of the New York region. Four years later he was among the first American soap manufacturers to successfully compete for a share of the European market.

Colgate also distinguished himself from competitors by an incessant willingness to upgrade and improve his line of products for consumers. Soap was then used primarily as a detergent for laundry or cleaning hands. Being made largely from ash and animal fat, it was coarse, abrasive, and smelled bad. In 1820, Colgate began experimenting with starch as a low-cost filler in his hand soap to bring down costs, and he soon became the largest starch manufacturer in the country. Eventually he became one of the first American companies to adopt the European practice of saponification, which introduced new forms of tallow and oils to the soap manufacturing process. In 1829, he copied the European practice of adding perfume to his soap products, thereby increasing their appeal to women, who were his primary consumers. Colgate's products were considerably successful, and in 1845, he was induced to build a soap-boiling pan with an internal capacity of 43,000 pounds. This was the largest such device in the world at that time and allowed Colgate to further expand both his production rates and markets. In 1847, he brought his son in as a full partner and relocated his business to New Jersey, where he had been producing starch for years. In 1850, he introduced perfumed, high-quality soap products for upscale consumers, which gave his products a greater appeal to the rising middle class. Not surprisingly, Colgate, who did all the bookkeeping, buying, and promotional activity by himself, never suffered a serious business loss.

In addition to business concerns, Colgate further distinguished himself from contemporaries by his personal commitment to philanthropy. A fervent Baptist since 1808, he regularly tithed to church interests and in 1816 helped establish the American Bible Society. In 1832, Colgate partially founded the American Baptist Home Mission Society to preach the Gospel throughout North America. In 1837, he withdrew from the American Bible Society and subsequently founded a new organization, the American and Foreign Bible Society, for religious proselytizing abroad. To that end, in 1850, Colgate funded the first major English-language translation of the Bible since the King James version. He also donated funds to the Hamilton Literary and Theological Seminary, which in 1890 was expanded into present-day Colgate University. Colgate died in New York City on March 25, 1857, the leading soap magnate of his day. As such he made indelible contributions to the rise of personal hygiene for the lower and middle classes and to the expansion of religious instruction in America. In 1928, his firm merged with Palmolive Peet Company, forming one of the largest soap and household product firms in the world.

Further reading

Brackney, William. *The Baptists*. New York: Greenwood Press, 1988.

Everts, William W. *William Colgate: The Christian Layman*. Philadelphia: American Baptist Publications Society, 1881.

Hardin, Shields T. *The Colgate Story*. New York: Vantage Press, 1959.

Williams, Howard D. *A History of Colgate University, 1819–1969*. New York: Van Nostrand Reinhold, 1969.

John C. Fredriksen

Colt Firearms   An arms manufacturer founded by Samuel Colt (1814–62) in Paterson, New Jersey. The company was founded to produce Colt's idea for a revolving-cylinder handgun, which he patented in 1836. The new invention was a radical change from handguns that used flintlock technology and were capable of firing only one round. His invention allowed five or six rounds to be fired consecutively before reloading.

Colt also manufactured carbine rifles. Despite developing several models of gun, the Paterson factory closed in 1842. The factory and equipment were sold, and Colt dabbled in other ventures, including the development of underwater ammunition, including mines, and collaboration with telegraph inventor Samuel F. B. MORSE. After the Mexican War began in 1846, Colt's firearms again became popular when the army used limited quantities of them in Texas. The U.S. Ordnance Department bought a thousand of the newly designed handguns, and Colt began producing them in Connecticut with the help of Eli Whitney Jr., son of the inventor who had originated the concept of interchangeable parts years before.

In 1851, Colt became one of the first American manufacturers to set up facilities in England in order to manufacture his products abroad. The parent company was incorporated in 1855 with the issuance of 10,000 shares, of which Colt kept all but four shares for himself. It sold its products to retailers through a sales force of agents and jobbers. When the Civil War began, Colt ceased selling his guns in the South and supplied only Union forces. In 1861, the firm had 1,000 employees and earned about $250,000 per year. Colt died shortly after the war began, and the company remained under family control until 1901, when it was sold to outside investors. In 1867, it began producing Gatling guns, a prototype of the later machine gun. A special revolver made for the Texas Rangers also proved popular and reliable. It was made in a Colt factory in Paterson, New Jersey.

During World War I, Colt collaborated with John Browning and produced Browning automatic rifles and machine guns. The company also produced the most famous of its products, the Colt .45 semiautomatic pistol. During both world wars, Colt produced more than 2.5 million of them for the government, and the weapon became famous as one of the most effective and reliable of all time. After the war, the company was purchased by the Penn-Texas Corp. and began to diversify into other areas such as machinery and even commercial washing machines.

In the 1960s, the company introduced several lines of automatic rifles, including the famous M-16. In 1964, the parent company reorganized as Colt Industries, and the firearms part became known as Colt Firearms. More automatic weapons were introduced in the 1980s, but the company suffered a setback when the Colt .45 was replaced as official government issue in 1984. After a series of unsuccessful corporate maneuvers, the company filed for Chapter 11 BANKRUPTCY in 1992. But product development

continued in the 1990s with the introduction of new automatic rifles. In the 1990s, the company also began developing smart-gun technology.

Colt produced the most recognizable handguns in the world. The original revolver is forever associated with the opening of the American West, and the automatic became the most famous handgun used in World War I and in the years following.

Further reading

Boorman, Dean K. *The History of Colt Firearms*. New York: Lyons Press, 2001.
Hosley, William. *Colt: The Making of an American Legend*. Amherst: University of Massachusetts Press, 1996.

Columbia Broadcasting System (CBS)   One of the three major broadcasting networks, founded in 1927 and developed and expanded by William S. Paley (1901–90) from 1929. Born in Chicago, Paley studied at the University of Chicago and graduated from the University of Pennsylvania in 1922. At age 27, using funds from his father's investments, Paley purchased working control of the struggling CBS radio network. A year later, more family funds helped him purchase total control of the company.

After purchasing a group of independent radio stations, Paley moved his headquarters to New York to be near the heart of the ADVERTISING INDUSTRY. He began giving his radio programs to his affiliates for free in return for advertising slots, a novel concept at the time. The strategy was very successful, and he claimed more than 70 affiliates within two years of beginning operations.

CBS took the high road to broadcasting. In 1930, the network began broadcasting concerts by the New York Philharmonic and also created Columbia Records. The label pioneered the long-playing (LP) record, introduced in 1948. The large disk revolutionized the recording industry and made Columbia the leading record company in America. Other divisions were added, including news and entertainment. When television appeared and became widespread, the company was again in the forefront and produced many quality programs in addition to a host of soap operas and quiz shows. From the 1950s, the network became known as the "Tiffany network," a compliment reflecting its high-end programming and networking standards.

The network remained at the top of the ratings race until the 1980s, when it lost its top spot to NBC, its traditional rival. Under Lawrence Tisch's leadership, the company divested its publishing and recording divisions in an attempt to become leaner and focus on its core business. Then in 1995 Tisch sold his stake in CBS to Westinghouse Electric, and the company began to regain some of its momentum. The new CEO, Mel Karmazin, merged the company with another media giant, Viacom. Paley's company now was part of an entertainment empire that included Paramount Pictures, MTV, VH1, and Nickelodeon cable companies, among others.

See also SARNOFF, DAVID.

Further reading

Paley, William S. *As It Happened: A Memoir.* Garden City, N.Y.: Doubleday, 1979.

Paper, Lewis J. *Empire: William S. Paley and the Making of CBS.* New York: St. Martin's Press, 1987.

Slater, Robert. *This . . . Is CBS: A Chronicle of 60 Years.* Englewood Cliffs, N.J.: Prentice Hall, 1988.

commerce clause   The section of the Constitution (Article 1, Section 8, Clause 3) that gives Congress the authority "to regulate Commerce with foreign nations, among the several States, and with the Indian tribes." The section became one of the most contentious parts of the Constitution in the 19th century and became a central issue in disputes between the states and the federal government.

The clause had its first serious application by the Supreme Court in a case that revolved around a ferry service between New York and New Jersey.

New York had granted an exclusive steamship monopoly to a company run by Robert FULTON and Robert LIVINGSTON and piloted by Aaron Ogden. A rival New Jersey company, run by Thomas Gibbons and piloted by Cornelius VANDERBILT, challenged the monopoly in court. Losing in the lower court, the case found its way to the Supreme Court, where Chief Justice John Marshall ruled in favor of the New Jersey company in the landmark case *Gibbons v. Ogden* (1824). Marshall held that commerce between states was more than simply traffic, it was also social intercourse and included navigation. By ruling in favor of Gibbons, the Court effectively used the clause to strike down a state-granted monopoly. In the absence of ANTITRUST legislation at the federal level before 1890, the commerce clause became one tool used to battle alleged monopolies when it could be shown that transportation companies sought to eliminate competition or fix prices by controlling interstate commerce.

The Court recognized that the power did not extend to commerce that was purely intrastate. But when interstate commerce was involved, it fell within the purview of the Congress. The issue arose again after the Civil War when the RAILROADS began to expand in the American West. The states attempted to regulate the activities of the railroads, and one case found its way to the Supreme Court in 1877. The Court ruled in *Munn v. Illinois* that certain sorts of industries, including railroads and grain storage facilities, operated in the public interest and as such were subject to its authority. Munn ran a grain warehouse and was charged with operating without a license. The Court upheld an Illinois Supreme Court ruling upholding his conviction, stating that such businesses were "clothed in the public interest." Nine years later, however, advocates of railroad regulation were disappointed when the Court ruled in *Wabash Railway Co. v. Illinois* (1886) that the states could not regulate railways simply passing through the states.

Applications of the commerce clause to railroad regulation were not used by the federal government to regulate the rails unless a case arose in which a defendant claimed that state regulations actually involved unconstitutional burdens upon interstate commerce, as in the case of *Munn*. In 1887, Congress created the INTERSTATE COMMERCE COMMISSION to oversee the railways. But the commerce clause was still a major issue even after the SHERMAN ACT was passed in 1890.

In *United States v. E.C. Knight Co.* (1896), the Court ruled that the company had not acted illegally to restrain trade or commerce despite the fact that the United States had argued that it was part of a larger trust, the American Sugar Refining Co., which actively acquired smaller companies in the 1890s. The decision led to an unprecedented merger boom. Cases that followed, notably *Addyston Pipe & Steel Co. v. United States* (1899) and *Swift & Co. v. United States* (1905), were found in favor of the government when it claimed that the companies operating locally could still affect interstate commerce by their decisions.

Further reading

Corwin, Edward S. *The Commerce Power v. States Rights: Back to the Constitution.* 1936. Reprint, Gloucester, Mass.: Peter Smith, 1962.

Frankfurter, Felix. *The Commerce Clause under Marshall, Taney and Waite.* Chapel Hill: University of North Carolina Press, 1937.

commercial banking   The term given to banking institutions that provide a full array of customer services to both retail and business customers. In the 19th and early 20th centuries, commercial banks served mostly business customers, and "commercial banking" was appropriate when describing them. Banks accept deposits from customers, and make loans at a higher rate of interest. Originally, most of the deposits accepted were from business customers, and the loans made were also to businesses for short to medium terms.

Commercial banks were organized in the late 18th century around the time of American Independence. The Bank of North America was chartered in Philadelphia by Robert MORRIS and was followed by the BANK OF NEW YORK, chartered by Alexander HAMILTON in 1784. Throughout the 19th century, banks remained partnerships and conducted business mainly with businesses and wealthy individuals. They were confined to their home states and often their home cities or counties. Interstate banking did not exist, being prevented by state banking laws that kept out-of-state banks from encroaching on local markets. In addition to the commercial banks, commercial banking on a limited scale was done by private banks—smaller banks that also conducted securities operations. Individual savers usually kept their savings at thrift institutions that were organized to grant them mortgage credit if they kept their deposits with the same thrift.

Banking was mostly a state-level affair until the Civil War. Most banks obtained a charter from and operated within their home states. In the absence of a central bank, especially after the closing of the Second BANK OF THE UNITED STATES, many state banks issued their own banknotes, backed by specie. While acceptable within the state, having different notes issued by the states sometimes slowed interstate commerce and often led to widespread forgery. Only when the Civil War broke out did Congress attempt to remedy the situation.

The first major banking law at the national level was passed by Congress in 1864, the NATIONAL BANK ACT. The law created the Office of the Comptroller of the Currency. Banks that registered with that office were allowed to carry the designation "national bank," and the comptroller also was given regulatory powers over them. Banks were also discouraged from operating in the securities markets. But in the absence of a central bank, the comptroller had only limited powers since banks that did not register with the office were not within its limited regulatory orbit. The act effectively created a two-tier banking system in the United States, with one group of banks at the state level and another at the federal level.

In the 1890s, banks played a substantial role in the general consolidation, or trust, movement, helping to merge companies and often encouraging their directors to sit on corporate boards. After the turn of the 20th century, the powerful New York banks became known as the "money trust," a name signifying that they controlled the reins of credit. They were investigated by the Pujo Committee in 1912 in an attempt to understand their effect upon the trusts and the creation of credit.

After the FEDERAL RESERVE was created in 1913, a new regulator was added, but the Fed had authority only to dictate reserve requirements and examine those banks that were registered with it. In the 1920s, the banks also began acquiring securities subsidiaries through their parent holding companies and played a major role in underwriting and selling bonds and (later) stocks, before the Crash of 1929. The period between 1921 and 1933 witnessed a large number of bank failures, with almost 15,000 banks failing or merging with others.

Bank activities were severely curtailed by the BANKING ACT OF 1933, and those with securities operations were forced to divest. The act defined the areas of finance that commercial banks were allowed to engage in. The act prohibited commercial banks from participating in corporate securities activities. The McFADDEN ACT of 1927 had already prohibited banks from opening new branches across state lines, and it seemed that bank activities were now limited in terms of both activities and expansion. But some larger banks employed holding companies to their advantage by buying banks in other states, avoiding the restriction about opening new branches. One of the most aggressive was the BANK OF AMERICA, which organized as the Transamerica Corporation in order to expand in the western states and in New York City. After several challenges to this sort of expansion, Congress finally passed a new restrictive act limiting bank expansion across state lines.

During World War II, banks changed their habits to aid in the war effort as the Federal Reserve maintained a close control over interest rate levels. The Fed pegged the level of interest rates allowed in the marketplace and relaxed reserve requirements for banks that held Treasury securities as assets rather than loans. As a result, banks became major holders of Treasury securities and remained as such until the Korean War, when the interest rate peg was abolished, and banking returned to its peacetime business.

In 1956, the BANK HOLDING COMPANY ACT further defined the role of the Federal Reserve in regulating the activity of bank holding companies. Banks continued pressure on regulators to expand but now had to satisfy the Federal Reserve Board. Throughout the 1960s and 1970s, banks expanded into areas permitted by the Fed and also expanded substantially overseas.

High interest rates in the mid- and late 1970s had a negative effect as many savers withdrew their cash in favor of higher yields in money market mutual funds. Pressures caused by this phenomenon prompted Congress to pass the DEPOSITORY INSTITUTIONS DEREGULATION AND MONETARY CONTROL ACT, deregulating interest rates and expanding the power of the Federal Reserve. The perennial problem of who regulated the banks was closer to being solved since all banks now were subject to the Fed's reserve requirements, regardless of location or charter. Usury laws began to crumble in many states as well, as high interest rates were now tolerated by state legislators, who feared losing banks in their states if they did not loosen the decades-old restrictions. CITIBANK began opening credit card facilities in states that did not have usury ceilings, and the door swung open for New York and other major banking centers to roll back their laws.

In the 1980s, commercial banks were beset with loan problems. Many had made loans to developing countries in South America and Asia that had to be rescheduled or written off, leaving the banks with record losses. Many loans had been made at variable rates of interest that soared to record levels between 1981 and 1984. As a result, many banks were forced to increase their base capital, following an increase in capital requirements made by the Bank for International Settlements in 1988 in conjunction with the Fed and the Bank of England. Those American banks that could not meet the requirements were forced to merge or close their doors. As a result of the loan and capital problems, many banks began to seek new avenues of business in fee banking, the sort usually reserved for investment banks. Many commercial banks also purchased smaller savings and loans, hard hit by the junk bond scandal in the later 1980s, giving them a stronger foothold in the residential mortgage market.

In the 1990s, commercial banks began to expand their activities into investment banking under liberal interpretations of the holding company act made by the Federal Reserve. This included underwriting of corporate securities, forbidden since the Banking Act of 1933. However, full integration of banking, INVESTMENT BANKING, and insurance did not occur until Congress passed the FINANCIAL SERVICES MODERNIZATION ACT in late 1999. The law liberalized and expanded the list of permissible activities for a bank; as a result, the industry began to offer "universal" banking services under one roof for the first time.

When banks entered the RECESSION following the stock market drop of 2001, they were exposed to the financial markets and the loan markets for the first time since the early 1930s. Several large banks suffered notable losses on both their loan portfolios and in the securities markets, leading critics to suggest that re-regulation was needed to prevent further erosion of the financial system.

See also CHASE MANHATTAN BANK; MORGAN, JOHN PIERPONT.

Further reading

Bodenhorn, Howard. *A History of Banking in Antebellum America.* New York: Cambridge University Press, 2000.
Calomiris, Charles. *U.S. Bank Deregulation in Historical Perspective.* New York: Cambridge University Press, 2000.
Rothbard, Murray N. *A History of Money and Banking in the United States: The Colonial Era to World War II.* Washington, D.C.: Ludwig von Mises Institute, 2002.
Wright, Robert E. *The Origins of Commercial Banking in America, 1750–1800,* New York: Rowman & Littlefield, 2001.

commercial paper   A short-term debt instrument, maturing between 30 days and 270 days from original issue date. A liquid secondary market for it, along with other money market instruments, exists among banks and investment banks, which maintain prices in the secondary market. Commercial paper is issued by corporations with investment-grade credit ratings and represents the cheapest cost of funds attainable for companies in the short-term.

Commercial paper dates to the 19th century, when New York merchants began selling their short-term notes payable to intermediate dealers, who would buy them at a discount and resell them to another investor, usually a bank. When the note matured, the borrower paid back face value to the investor. The first money market dealer to buy these notes was Marcus Goldman, whose GOLDMAN SACHS & CO. became one of the largest dealers in the country after the Civil War. Until the Second World War, commercial paper was used by the FEDERAL RESERVE in its open market operations, along with Treasury bills, to sell or buy from recognized dealers in order to affect the amount of bank reserves in circulation.

During the 1950s and 1960s, the number of companies issuing commercial paper increased steadily, and it became the most popular instrument in the money market. Parallel with its development was the development of consumer credit, mainly through the use of CREDIT CARDS. Many of the finance companies offering credit card facilities to customers borrowed the money necessary to finance card operations through commercial paper and then purchased credit card receivables from merchants. The amount charged to customers was often substantially higher than the cost of borrowing.

Commercial paper can be sold directly into the market by issuing companies (directly placed), or it may be sold through an intermediary dealer (dealer placed). In the 1980s, a debate developed over whether banks that acted as dealers were in violation of the BANKING ACT OF 1933 by underwriting this short-term corporate paper in the market even though commercial paper was defined by the Securities and Exchange Commission as short-term corporate debt of less than 270 days to maturity and thus not a bond.

Today, the commercial paper market is the largest single source of short-term financing for corporations along with loans provided by commercial banks. It is the major source of short-term financing for most large corporations with credit ratings high enough to access the market on a regular basis. It is also the main source of funds for credit card lending and many other forms of short-term loans, both for consumers and companies alike.

See also INVESTMENT BANKING.

Further reading

Endlich, Lisa. *Goldman Sachs: The Culture of Success.* New York: Knopf, 1999.

Goodhart, Charles A. *The New York Money Market and the Finance of Trade, 1900–1913.* Cambridge, Mass.: Harvard University Press, 1969.

Commodity Futures Trading Commission (CFTC)

The regulatory body overseeing the FUTURES MARKETS. Created by Congress in 1974, the commission is an independent agency whose five-member body operates in a manner similar to that of the Securities and Exchange Commission (SEC) by regulating the activities on futures exchanges as well as overseeing operating procedures in the futures industry. Members of the commission are appointed by the president for five-year terms.

The futures markets have been under federal REGULATION since the 1930s. In 1922, Congress passed the Grain Futures Act, putting the commodities exchanges under the authority of the Department of Agriculture. The law loosely regulated the trading of contracts but did little to curb trading practices on the exchanges. As a result, the Commodity Exchange Act was passed in 1936 regulating the exchanges themselves for the first time. The law was intended to be similar to the Securities Exchange Act passed in 1934 regulating stock exchanges.

Until the 1960s, the markets added contracts on new commodities in moderate fashion, but the late 1960s and early 1970s witnessed an explosion in the types of contracts and commodities available. The old regulatory legislation was designed to control only grain futures, so any new contracts had no effective regulation. Precious metals trading began in the late 1960s and was often marred by trading irregularities, since the contracts were not regulated. Inflation and the rapid internationalization of the financial markets in the late 1960s and early 1970s underlined the need for hedging instruments that investors could employ to offset risk. Contracts were added in interest rate futures, other financial futures, and a wider array of commodities as well as options on futures, a long-standing problem for the futures exchanges. These new products extended beyond the scope of the original regulation, and the CFTC was formed to cope with the expanding markets.

The CFTC was given additional powers, especially with over-the-counter derivatives futures, in the Commodities Futures Modernization Act passed in 1999. Areas of dispute with the SEC over futures on equities especially were made more flexible, and jurisdictional disputes over options were remedied. The jurisdiction of the CFTC itself needed to be clarified for fear that if the markets were not well-regulated and clear to participants, then business could move overseas and domestic investors would be susceptible to fraud in unregulated overseas markets.

See also CHICAGO BOARD OF TRADE.

Further reading

Geisst, Charles R. *Wheels of Fortune: The History of Speculation from Scandal to Respectability*. New York: John Wiley & Sons, 2002.

Community Reinvestment Act (CRA)   A law passed by Congress in 1977 in response to perceived failings of banks in meeting the credit needs of the communities in which they operate, especially low- and moderate-income neighborhoods. The act is intended to encourage depository institutions to meet the credit needs of the communities within the framework of operating safe and sound financial institutions. It requires the federal supervisory agencies (the FEDERAL DEPOSIT INSURANCE CORPORATION [FDIC], the Office of the Comptroller of the Currency [OCC] and the Board of Governors of the Federal Reserve System [FRB]) to evaluate an institution's CRA performance.

The Riegle Community Development and Regulatory Improvement Act of 1994 (CDRIA) substantially amended the CRA statute to satisfy critics of the original CRA rating system and to provide some regulatory relief for small institutions. CRA performances are evaluated under one of four possible scenarios: (1) streamlined procedures for small institutions, (2) three-tiered test for large retail institutions, (3) limited-scope test for "special-purpose" institutions, and (4) strategic CRA plans. After the CRA performance of an institution is evaluated under these procedures, it is rated as "outstanding," "satisfactory," "needs to improve," or "substantial noncompliance." In recent years, more than 90 percent of institutions have received outstanding or satisfactory ratings.

The CRA provides incentives for institutions to serve the community credit needs, but the law does not grant the supervisory agencies enforcement authority. An institution's CRA rating can be taken into account whenever an institution requests to open or relocate, establish a bank HOLDING COMPANY, or engage in merger and acquisition activity. The agencies also must solicit public comment on, and publicly disclose, an institution's CRA performance.

The CRA was modified by the Gramm-Leach-Bliley FINANCIAL SERVICES MODERNIZATION ACT of 1999 (GLBA) by setting forth a graduated schedule of decreasing frequency of CRA examinations of certain small-sized banks (less than $250 million in assets) commensurate with their record of meeting CRA "community credit needs." Generally, small institutions are evaluated every four years if their current CRA rating is satisfactory and every five years if their most recent rating is outstanding.

CRA's renewed focus on mortgage, small business, and small farm loans has meant that institutions must collect and annually report their small business and farm loan activity, as well as their community development loans. As with the Home Mortgage Disclosure Act (HMDA) data, the regulatory agencies prepare a report on each institution and make it and the aggregate lending data available to the public.

In response to charges that community groups use the CRA application comment process to coerce institutions into making financial and other commitments to their organizations, GLBA attempts to prevent abuses by requiring public disclosure of written CRA agreements between an insured depository institution or affiliate and another party, such as a community group or an individual. Community groups or individuals may face stiff penalties for willful and material noncompliance or for the diversion of funds or resources for personal gain.

Further reading

Papadimitriou, Dimitri B., Ronnie J. Phillips, and L. Randall Wray. "A Path to Community Development: The Community Reinvestment Act, Lending Discrimination, and the Role of Community Development Banks," Jerome Levy Economics Institute of Bard College, Public Policy Brief No. 6, 1993.

Spong, Kenneth. *Banking Regulation: Its Purpose, Implementation, and Effects*. 5th ed. Kansas City, Mo.: Federal Reserve Bank of Kansas City, 2000.

Ronnie J. Phillips

computer industry   While the U.S. computer industry began as a direct result of large-scale Department of Defense spending on electronic digital computing research during and shortly after World War II, and the vision of a small number of engineers and entrepreneurs to commercialize this research, in large part it was facilitated and extended by technological and marketing capabilities built in the American office machine industry during the previous six decades. The U.S. office machine trade consisted of manufacturers of accounting machines, TYPE-WRITERS, cash registers, tabulators, and other devices used to record, store, process, and retrieve information. America's relative shortage of labor compared to European countries, coupled with America's embracement of labor-saving technology, resulted in the United States's strong international leadership in the production and use of OFFICE MACHINES from the late 19th century forward.

In the 1880s, Herman Hollerith, an engineer who worked at the U.S. Patent Office, invented a punched-card tabulating machine, and in doing so gave birth to electromechanical information processing. A subsequent version of Hollerith's machine demonstrated major efficiencies after it won a competition to be used on the largest information processing task of its time—the 1890 U.S. Census. Its success on this application led Hollerith to form the Tabulating Machine Company in 1896, a firm that produced punched-card tabulation machines for U.S. and other censuses, various government agencies, and a small number of large corporations. In 1911, Hollerith sold this successful company, which after several MERGERS became the Computer-Tabulating-Recording Company (C-T-R). In 1924, C-T-R's management changed the firm's name to INTER-NATIONAL BUSINESS MACHINES (IBM) to reflect its broadening line of office machine products and its growing international installations (both sales and leases). IBM, the global leader in tabulating machines, along with other firms that had led in particular office machine segments since the late

19th century, such as Burroughs Adding Machine, Remington Typewriter, and National Cash Register (NCR), would all become significant contributors to the U.S. computer industry.

During World War II, the army's Ballistic Research Laboratory (BRL) was limited to using analog computers (such as Vannevar Bush's differential analyzer) and other mechanical calculating machines to aid human calculators in solving the thousands of equations necessary to produce ballistic firing tables. These machines and methods proved wholly inadequate with regard to speed and accuracy. John Mauchly and J. Presper Eckert, both researchers at the University of Pennsylvania Moore School of Electrical Engineering, proposed developing an electronic digital computer to meet the BRL's calculating needs. Based on their strong proposal and some fortuitous connections, the army provided a $400,000 contract for a project that began in the early 1940s to build the Electronic Numerical Integrator and Computer (ENIAC)—the first fully operational digital computer. The machine, powered by 18,000 vacuum tubes, was not completed until early 1946.

Later that year, Eckert and Mauchly established the Electronic Control Company, soon renamed the Eckert-Mauchly Computer Corporation, to design and sell digital computers.

Man prepares a UNIVAC computer, 1959 (LIBRARY OF CONGRESS)

Almost simultaneously, engineers who had worked as cryptographers for the U.S. Navy during the war established Engineering Research Associates (ERA) for the same purpose. Over the next half decade both firms produced a small number of expensive mainframe computers for government departments and agencies and a few corporations. In the early 1950s Remington Rand (formerly Remington Typewriter) acquired the two pioneering computer firms and became the first of the office machine companies to enter into the U.S. computer industry. Burroughs and NCR soon followed by acquiring relatively small start-up computer firms during the mid-1950s.

IBM, as a result of its lease structure and steady revenue from punched cards, fared far better than other office machine firms during the Great Depression. At the end of World War II, IBM was by far the most profitable office machine maker in the world. The company specialized in what almost immediately became the key input-output technology (punched cards and tabulators) for computers, had an unparalleled sales and service organization, possessed a large and varied customer base, and during the late 1940s began to make substantial investments in electronics research. These factors placed it in a strong position to thrive in the computer industry during the succeeding decade. In the early 1950s, it won the primary computer contract for the Department of Defense's Semi-Automatic Air Ground Environment (SAGE) computer networked communication system, a project that was coordinated by engineers from MIT's Lincoln Laboratory. While Remington Rand was selling its million-dollar UNIVAC computer to a modest number of customers in the early 1950s, IBM was furthering its already strong capabilities in anticipation of producing computers that could sell or lease in large volume.

In the mid-1950s, IBM came out with several lower priced computers that leased for between $3,000 and $15,000 per month. In 1959, the company announced its 1401 computer, a machine that would achieve more than 10,000

installations during the 1960s and establish IBM's leadership in the computer industry. The IBM 1401, like a small number of other computers of its time, took advantage of transistor technology, which had been perfected in the decade following its invention by scientists at Bell Laboratories in 1947. Further innovations to transistor technology led to the integrated circuit (IC) during the first half of the 1960s. Behind the strength of the integrated circuit, domestic computer installations grew from 240 in 1955 to 11,700 in 1963. This growth would continue and represented a transition from the nearly exclusive scientific computing market of the early 1950s to the adoption of computers for many business purposes by the end of the decade and into the 1960s.

The IBM System/360 series, announced in 1964, was a watershed for the firm and the industry. It consisted of a series of compatible computers with varying processing powers and prices. This solidified IBM's industry leadership and led to its achieving a peak of around 70 percent of the domestic industry by 1970. A combination of leading office machine producers, a couple of late 1950s start-up firms, and two electronics giants represented IBM's primary competitors. These competitors developed some successful machines but provided only a modest challenge to IBM. IBM and its chief competitors (Burroughs, National Cash Register, Remington Rand/Sperry-Rand, Control Data, Digital Equipment Corporation, GENERAL ELECTRIC and RCA) were frequently referred to as "IBM and the Seven Dwarves" in the business press to emphasize the leader's dominance. The two electronics firms, General Electric and RCA, showed only a partial commitment to the computing business during the 1960s, lost money in this area, and divested from the field at the beginning of the 1970s.

As IBM solidified its dominance, a growing number of firms sought to imitate its computers, as RCA did with its Spectra-70 series. Two new computer firms, both formed in 1957, took a different path and initiated divergent new segments of the computer industry: minicomputing (Digital Equipment Corporation) and supercomputing (Control Data Corporation).

Some of Sperry-Rand's leading engineers and managers departed and formed Control Data Corporation (CDC) to build computers of unprecedented power to target the smaller but still substantial and growing scientific computing market. Though IBM continued to sell to scientific users, the firm chose not to enter the supercomputer business and to concentrate its resources on the business computing field.

CDC would dominate supercomputing in the 1960s but would be displaced from this area as its focus changed increasingly to computer peripherals and service businesses in the 1970s. Early in this decade, their star engineer, Seymour Cray, who had designed the advanced circuitry on the firm's supercomputers, would leave to form Cray Research. This company soon became the supercomputing leader. From the first supercomputer, the CDC 6600, to a wave of new machines by Cray Research in the 1970s and early 1980s, supercomputing expanded possibilities for modeling the Department of Defense's nuclear war scenarios, weather forecasting, and other areas requiring extensive processing power.

Kenneth Olsen and Harland Anderson, both MIT Lincoln Laboratory engineers who had worked at overseeing IBM's SAGE contract, formed the Digital Equipment Corporation (DEC). Olsen, DEC's longtime leader, recognized an opportunity to use advanced circuitry to make small computers of modest processing power for a significantly lower cost than mainframe computers. Along with Silicon Valley, which was emerging as a semiconductor center, Route 128 near Boston had also defined itself as a leading electronics development region. DEC and other minicomputer firms would add greatly to the reputation of the Boston area as a fundamental center for particular sectors of electronics and computing.

Early DEC computers sold for around $100,000, but integrated circuits of the mid-1960s and DEC's innovative designs allowed the firm to produce and sell its PDP-8 minicomputer for a mere $18,000. The PDP-8 made computers affordable to many previously excluded organizations, selling more than 40,000 units during its product life. Its success led a number of firms to enter the minicomputing field, from established companies such as Hewlett Packard and IBM to new entities such as Data General (formed by DEC PDP-8 designer Edson de Castro in the late 1960s). During the 1970s, there were more than 100 producers of minicomputers, most of which were small firms or small divisions of larger companies. Minicomputing not only extended the use of computers in hospitals, smaller laboratories, and mid-size firms, it also created a class of users who identified with operating their own machines. The minicomputer, in terms of size, cost, power, and its user community, more nearly matched the personal computer of the late 1970s and early 1980s than it did mainframes of the past.

Computers are useless without the programming that allows them to do various types of calculations and data processing tasks. In the second half of the 1950s, Sperry-Rand (the outgrowth of Remington Rand's merger with Sperry Gyroscope in 1955), IBM, and other firms and organizations began developing programming languages, such as Fortran and Cobol. These tools helped with the arduous task of programming computers. Much programming in the first decade and a half of digital computers was done by software developers at mainframe computer manufacturers or by the sophisticated organizations purchasing or leasing these machines. Early in the next decade a number of programming or software service firms emerged to produce one-of-a-kind software and systems for clients' computers. A shortage of programmers emerged as the number of computer installations expanded. This shortage, along with bugs and cost overruns, led to a real but media-exaggerated "software crisis." Software products, or standardized systems and applications for many users, emerged in the second half of the 1960s to help address high programming costs and shortages of programmers. The software products industry gained great momentum when IBM unbundled (priced and sold separately from hardware) most software beginning in 1970. Unbundling facilitated the growth of software products firms such as Informatics, Applied Data Research, Cincom, and Cullinane—many of which were later acquired by Computer Associates or other contemporary software giants. IBM and other mainframe producers also developed and sold or licensed a large number of significant software products.

The semiconductor, which gave rise to minicomputing, became a fundamental industry that grew alongside the computer. Fairchild Semiconductor became a virtual training center for producing top engineers and executives of new semiconductor companies in Silicon Valley. Three former Fairchild engineers, Robert Noyce, Andrew Grove, and Gordon Moore initiated one such firm, Intel, in 1969. Two years later, Intel invented the microchip, or "a computer on a chip." The microchip, also called a microprocessor, established a further wave of advances in computer power, miniaturization, and cost-effectiveness. Much of the microchip's history has lent credence to Gordon Moore's simple equation, Moore's Law, which states that computer processing power doubles every 18 months relative to cost. Intel's microprocessor gave rise to the personal computer kits of the mid-1970s, the emergence of new personal computer manufacturing start-ups (such as Apple Computer) in the second half of the 1970s, and IBM's entrance into the field in 1981 with the IBM PC.

In 1980, IBM sought a software industry partner to help refine its Disk Operating System (DOS) for its soon to be released PC. The first company they called on, Digital Research, balked at the opportunity (apparently it was unwilling to sign a nondisclosure agreement), and IBM went with a 32-person outfit called Microsoft that was led by cofounders William (Bill) Gates and Paul Allen. Microsoft went on to produce

MS-DOS for the PC and has been able to maintain a near-monopoly on IBM PC and PC-compatible operating systems ever since. Only recently has Microsoft faced competitive challenges from open-source systems such as Linux. IBM, while continuing to manufacture mainframes, minicomputers, and personal computers in the 1980s and 1990s, increasingly shifted its focus to software and services as revenue generators, and not just as tools to sell hardware.

Soon after IBM came out with the PC, firms such as Compaq and Hewlett Packard built compatible systems (or clones) that used Intel microprocessors and Microsoft operating systems (initially MS-DOS, and then MS Windows—a Microsoft operating system that mirrored certain graphic elements of Apple Computer's Macintosh operating system). As a result of these IBM clones, and the origin of these machines' processors and systems, the term *Wintel* (Windows and Intel) came into common usage. It signified both the powerful position of these two firms in the computer industry and the fact that IBM clone "manufacturers" were mere assemblers, marketers, and deliverers of commodity products (or "boxes").

Independent producers of software applications and recreational software (particularly computer games) tended to design products for the PC-platform first and the Apple platform second, if at all. This challenge was a major factor in Apple's personal computer market share dipping from double-digits, at the height of its early years, to lower single digits in the past 10 years. Recently, with the growth of Advanced Micro Devices and several other microprocessor competitors of Intel, Microsoft alone has been the focus of consumer and government scrutiny with regard to its domination of markets and its potential anticompetitive practices. This scrutiny came from Microsoft's dominance of operating systems, certain popular applications (MS Word for word processing and MS Excel for spreadsheets), INTERNET browsers (MS Explorer), and most importantly, its apparent efforts to link together these products to lock in customers and lock out competitors.

Like the mainframe and minicomputer, U.S. government funding would prove critical to cultivating the underlying technology for the advent of the personal computer and the networking that would help transform this machine into a ubiquitous communication technology. In response to cold war concerns over the Soviet Union's scientific and technological accomplishments of the late 1950s and early 1960s (particularly Sputnik in 1957), the U.S. Department of Defense (DoD) became all the more interested in advancing U.S. science and technology, including computing and computer networking. In 1962, the DoD initiated the Information Processing Techniques Office (IPTO) as part of its Defense Advanced Research Projects Agency (DARPA). In the following seven years the IPTO funded a Boston engineering firm, Bolt Beranek and Newman (BBN) and some key academicians to build a major computer network, the ARPANET, in order to allow scientists to communicate by computer as well as to provide a redundant computer communications network for defense purposes. The ARPANET became linked with other computer networks in the 1970s and early 1980s to form a network of networks known as the Internet.

In the early to mid-1990s, MIT scientist Tim Berners-Lee (in residence at CERN Laboratory in Switzerland) developed hypertext markup language (HTML). This provided a structure for sending graphics and text files and resulted in the World Wide Web. By early in the 21st century, the majority of Americans accessed the World Wide Web on a weekly if not daily basis. Network equipment demand expanded quickly, leading to rapid growth for CISCO Systems, the leading manufacturer of routers, devices that facilitate network traffic. Back in the 1960s and 1970s the IPTO had also funded significant graphics work. That, along with subsequent technological inventions and innovations at Xerox PARC and SRI, such as windows, icons,

pull-down menus, and the computer mouse, greatly advanced the possibilities for future computer graphics and the ease of use for personal computers and the World Wide Web. Soon after Berners-Lee's invention, several Internet browsers were developed to facilitate access to the growing information on the Internet. These included MOSAIC, Netscape's Navigator, and slightly later, Microsoft's Explorer. Microsoft made Explorer a standard feature on its Windows operating system, which led to the "net wars" with Netscape and the U.S. Department of Justice's antitrust suit against Microsoft for bundling products to eliminate competition. In 2001, Microsoft settled the federal suit and became subject to a consent decree but still faces litigation from other jurisdictions.

The World Wide Web has not only transformed the way in which many people communicate (e-mail instead of letters) and their leisure activities (interactive games and chat rooms), but has also brought about both real and perceived changes in how people engage in business. Many e-commerce firms began operations in the last few years of the 20th century, only to fall victim to the dot-com collapse that began in early 2000. The overvaluation of e-commerce firms had a precursor in the run-up of software services and products company stock during the late 1960s. Like this earlier high-technology stock market bubble and burst, a small number of industry leaders survived and thrived based on superior capabilities, first-mover advantages, established customer relationships, and a host of other factors. Today companies with dominant positions, such as E-bay in the electronic auctioning market, Google in commercial search engines, and Dell in personal computers (benefiting from its unparalleled supply management and service) have demonstrated that financial and inventory excesses of an industry do not hit world-class innovators and executors to the same degree as other firms. Part of this trend toward innovation and efficiency is achieving excellence in using global resources to best serve a global marketplace. Like the manufacturing sector of computer

Personal computers shown in a shopping center (GETTY IMAGES)

hardware, and many other manufacturing areas, a significant number of jobs have been sent overseas. In recent years, global outsourcing has become increasingly common with U.S.-based information technology (IT) firms in programming and IT services.

See also WATSON, THOMAS J.

Further reading

Campbell-Kelly, Martin. *From Airline Reservations to Sonic the Hedgehog: A History of the Software Industry.* Cambridge, Mass.: MIT Press, 2003.

Campbell-Kelly, Martin, and William Aspray. *Computer: A History of the Information Machine.* New York: Basic Books, 1996.

Chandler, Alfred Dupont, Takashi Hikino, and Andrew Von Nordenflycht. *Inventing the Electronic Century: The Epic Story of the Consumer Electronics and Computer Industries.* New York: Free Press, 2001.

Hiltzik, Michael A. *Dealers of Lightning: Xerox PARC and the Dawn of the Computer Age.* New York: HarperBusiness, 1999.

Jeffrey R. Yost

Conestoga wagon   The Conestoga wagon, also called the "ship of inland commerce" and the "Dutch wagon," was a heavy horse-drawn vehicle that, prior to the extension of the RAILROADS across the Allegheny Mountains in the 1850s, became the primary method of transporting freight to the interior regions of the United States.

In the early 18th century, German and Swiss immigrants in the Conestoga Creek region of Lancaster County, Pennsylvania, developed the wagon, which was used to haul furs to Philadelphia. Following the Revolutionary War, farmers depended on Conestogas to transport produce to market, and manufacturers on the East Coast used the wagons to carry finished goods to frontier regions of the Ohio Valley west of the Allegheny Mountains. Conestoga wagons, usually drawn by six horses, could carry loads of up to six tons.

The floor of the wagon was lower in the middle than at the front and rear so that freight would be less likely to shift while traveling over rough terrain. The white covering, supported by eight bows and made of homespun hemp and later of canvas, was curved to conform to the wagon bed. At the front and back, the top of the covering extended farther than the bottom, thus offering protection from sun and rain. The wagon's wheels were especially broad in order to navigate the ruts and mud of primitive dirt roads. The Conestoga wagon anticipated the development of the prairie schooner, so called because from a distance this white canvas-covered wagon resembled a sailing ship. Compared to the Conestoga, the schooner was lighter, simpler, and less expensive and had lower sides and a flat floor. It usually required no more than four horses, mules, or oxen. The wagon had an oval opening at each end to allow for ventilation and to let light into the interior. The prairie schooner was a major mode of transportation for pioneers traveling to Oregon, Utah, and California. It is estimated that during the 1849 California gold rush more than 12,000 schooners headed west.

Further reading
Shumway, George. *The Conestoga Wagon, 1750–1850: Freight Carrier for 100 Years of America's Westward Expansion.* Williamsburg, Va.: Early American Industries Association, 1964.

Glenn H. Utter

conglomerates Large, diversified holding companies that buy operating companies to form corporations with a wide array of interests. As a form of industrial organization, conglomerates diversify their activities to make themselves less susceptible to changes in the business cycle. This type of corporation dates from the end of World War II, when industrialists began buying companies and assembling them under the umbrella of a HOLDING COMPANY.

Often conglomerates are described as a form of merger, along with horizontal and vertical MERGERS. While horizontal mergers join two companies in similar businesses and vertical mergers join two in different parts of the supply or productive chain, conglomerates are described as bringing dissimilar businesses together. One of the by-products of this merging is that conglomerates often fall outside the traditional lines of ANTITRUST law. While horizontal and vertical mergers fall under the Sherman Antitrust Act and the CLAYTON ACT, conglomerate mergers tend to remain relatively free of antitrust action unless a conglomerate acquires more than one company in a highly concentrated business, behaving like a 19th-century trust.

After World War II, conglomerates began to appear and contributed to the merger and acquisition trend on Wall Street in the 1950s and 1960s. Companies such as International Telephone & Telegraph, Ling-Temco-Vaught, Litton Industries, and United Technologies all actively pursued conglomerate strategies. In 1950, Congress passed the Celler-Kefauver Act, which was aimed at the conglomerates. The law blocked a company from purchasing the assets of another if the combination created threatened a monopoly. But if it did not, as was the case of most conglomerates, then the law was powerless to prevent conglomerate formation.

As a form of merger between two companies with no apparent common interests or common markets, conglomerates seemed immune to antitrust laws. One criticism of conglomerates in the past was that although there were no apparent common interests between many of the companies assembled by a holding company, there were often illegal arrangements between them that violated antitrust laws. For instance, the parent company could require that subsidiaries do business exclusively with each other, eroding competition in the marketplace. In a well-diversified conglomerate, that may have been possible, but it was also difficult to prove by antitrust regulators.

The conglomerates became the target of antitrust efforts by the Nixon administration in the late 1960s after fears that they were poised to begin buying established older companies. Their growth was slowed by a stock market downturn in the early 1970s. In the 1980s, their diversification principles were adopted by other multinational companies, and today the distinction between conglomerates, diversified for their own sake, and other well-diversified companies is less pronounced than in the past. While many of the older conglomerates established in the 1960s began to fade from view, others such as GENERAL ELECTRIC were highly successful, and their stocks remained as investor favorites.

Further reading

Fortune Magazine. *The Conglomerate Commotion.* New York: Viking Press, 1970.

Sobel, Robert. *The Rise and Fall of the Conglomerate Kings.* New York: Stein & Day, 1984.

Winslow, John F. *Conglomerates Unlimited: The Failure of Regulation.* Bloomington: Indiana University Press, 1973.

consumer movement A movement that began developing in the early 20th century, dedicated to protecting the rights of consumers against big business. The study of consumers became more important after the 1920s, when it became clear that 67 percent of the American economy was driven by consumption. Since that time, the study of consumer behavior and attitudes and their effect on the economy has evolved into a systematic and rigorous discipline, and many laws have been written to protect what are considered fundamental consumer rights.

The consumer movement began during the Progressive Era, tracing its intellectual origins to the writings of the MUCKRAKERS. At the time, the emphasis was on the nature of big business and the apparent disregard that it displayed toward ordinary citizens. The writings of Ida Tarbell, Louis BRANDEIS, Frank Norris, Gustavus Myers, and others cut across different literary genres,

displaying the nature of various businesses ranging from Standard Oil to the meatpacking industry and illustrating the helplessness of the individual in the face of corporate power. One of the first organizations to emphasize the link between consumers and workers was Florence Kelley's National Consumers' League, founded in 1899. The social writings of the Progressives also helped the labor movement establish better working conditions, which were organizing during the same period.

After World War I, the movement took a back seat to the bull market of the 1920s. After the 1929 crash, it was resurrected in the securities and banking laws of the NEW DEAL, which sought to offer protection to bank depositors and investors. The clear lack of social institutions capable of offering basic services during the early years of the Great Depression was the impetus behind many New Deal laws passed during the first administration of Franklin D. Roosevelt. The purpose of the National Industrial Recovery Act of 1933 was to help stimulate economic activity by forging links between labor and management, taking some of the impetus out of the labor and consumer movements. The act was declared unconstitutional in 1935. Throughout this period, the spirit of the consumer movement was closely related to the ANTITRUST movement. The ROBINSON-PATMAN ACT was passed in 1937 to protect small storekeepers and consumers from the corporate power of the new retail CHAIN STORES being created nationwide, although the law proved relatively ineffective. During the Depression and World War II the movement was mostly quiet, with most political and economic forces galvanized to the recovery and war efforts.

In 1936, the Consumers Union was founded. The private organization began testing consumer products for quality and safety and published the magazine *Consumer Reports.* The magazine was dedicated to protecting the consumer from deceit and low quality; the slogan "let the buyer beware" was in vogue at the time and underscored the importance of intelligent consumer behavior. The movement picked up considerable emphasis with the publication of Ralph NADER's *Unsafe at Any Speed* in 1965, an expose of the safety faults of the Chevrolet Corvair. Nader later successfully sued GENERAL MOTORS for invasion of privacy after the company investigated him because of the book. He later founded several consumer groups. Following in his footsteps, several consumer organizations were established, including the Consumer Federation of America (1968) and the Consumer Product Safety Commission (1972).

One manufacturing process that caused serious problems stimulated the consumer movement in the 1950s and 1960s. Planned obsolescence became an operational manufacturing concept, designed to stimulate the demand for manufactured goods. It began with the marketing of automobiles in the 1920s. Alfred SLOAN introduced the practice at General Motors. The concept was later adopted by many manufacturers, who used it as a marketing tool to convey the impression that their new products were different, and better, than previous models. Changing models frequently also placed considerable pressure on smaller competitors to convey the same message to their customers and could often be extremely expensive for them.

The practice came under considerable scrutiny when Vance Packard exposed the concept in his book *The Waste Makers* in 1960. In it, he described how manufacturers purposely designed many products to deteriorate prematurely so that customers would replace them. Many industries, including the automobile industry, changed models every year, mostly in design rather than substantive improvements, requiring a great deal of capital investment by the manufacturers. Smaller manufacturers, unable to raise funds for design improvements, were often faced with declining market share and eventual BANKRUPTCY because they were not able to compete.

Planned obsolescence also became an issue in some antitrust actions for many of the same reasons. Were manufacturers conspiring to change models, forcing smaller competitors out of business, or were they simply introducing periodic changes in their products to stimulate sales when the new product was essentially no better than its predecessor?

The consumer movement became very successful and helped change the old slogan "let the buyer beware" to "let the seller beware." The state and federal laws that were passed during the 1970s also helped give rise to the use of the class action lawsuit as a weapon against large companies producing inferior or dangerous products.

See also BETTER BUSINESS BUREAUS; NATIONAL RECOVERY ADMINISTRATION.

Further reading
Cohen, Lizabeth. *A Consumer's Republic: The Politics of Mass Consumption in Postwar America*. New York: Knopf, 2003.

Packard, Vance. *The Waste Makers*. New York: David McKay, 1960.

Pertschuk, Michael. *Revolt against Regulation: The Rise and Pause of the Consumer Movement*. Berkeley: University of California Press, 1984.

Satterthwaite, Ann. *Going Shopping: Consumer Choices and Community Consequences*. New Haven, Conn.: Yale University Press, 2001.

Strasser, Susan. *Satisfaction Guaranteed: The Making of the American Mass Market*. New York: Pantheon, 1989.

Cooke, Jay (1821–1905) *financier* Born in Sandusky, Ohio, Cooke's father was a lawyer who also sat in Congress. After finishing school, Jay took a job in St. Louis, but his employer was ruined in the Panic of 1837. He moved to Philadelphia. Two years later, he went to work for the banking firm of E. W. Clarke & Co. (later, CLARK DODGE & CO.) in Philadelphia while still in his teens.

After the Panic of 1857, he withdrew from the firm and then in 1861 founded his own firm, Jay Cooke & Co., as the Civil War was beginning. His first notable deal came when he raised an issue of war bonds for Pennsylvania, which needed the money to defend its southern border against possible attack from the Confederacy.

Further success soon followed. Cooke was introduced to Secretary of the Treasury Salmon Chase by his brother, who was also a partner in the new firm. He undertook to sell several large issues of war bonds. The best known were dubbed the 5–20s, allowing the Treasury to issue GREENBACKS during the war.

Cooke employed novel methods of selling the war bonds. Rather than sell them to other banking firms who would then sell them overseas, Cooke employed a vast network of salesmen and sales offices around the country, which distributed the bonds to retail buyers. They were sold in small denominations so that the average citizen could buy them. Subsequently, he also sold additional issues and was responsible for ensuring the Union's success through his successful fund raising. He sold more than $500 million of the 5–20s alone as fiscal agent for the U.S. Treasury. He sold bonds to more than 600,000 individual investors while working as the Treasury's agent.

After the war, Cooke led the refunding of the 5–20s after they were eligible to be redeemed (after five years). In order to do so, he arranged the first modern underwriters' syndicate, consisting of banks that all subscribed to a portion of the deal. By that time, however, his attentions had turned to other pursuits.

In the late 1860s, Cooke's firm began to engage in railroad financing on a large scale. An issue of bonds sold on behalf of the Pennsylvania Railroad was the first to use a syndicate of other bankers to distribute the bonds to investors and became the first underwritten securities issue in the United States. Cooke also became interested in railroad operations, especially with the Northern Pacific Railroad. His firm became a major shareholder in the unfinished railroad, which was planned to run from the Great Lakes to the Pacific Northwest. But he had difficulty finding financing for the project because investors recognized that his costs were among the highest in the industry. When the Panic of 1873 developed, his railroad problems made investors uneasy, and his bank suffered a liquidity crisis, effectively putting an end to his career as a financier and

railroad builder. His firm was liquidated in 1873, and Cooke retired to a quiet life.

Cooke's firm was resurrected by his son-in-law, Charles D. Barney, and resumed operations as Charles D. Barney & Co. The firm eventually became Smith Barney & Co. and today is a part of Citigroup. Cooke is best remembered as the major financier of the Union during the Civil War, while his bond distribution techniques became standard practice in financing long after he retired from INVESTMENT BANKING.

Further reading

Larson, Henrietta. *Jay Cooke: Private Banker.* Cambridge, Mass.: Harvard University Press, 1936.

Oberholtzer, Ellis Paxson. *Jay Cooke: Financier of the Civil War.* Philadelphia: George W. Jacobs, 1907.

Cooper, Peter (1791–1883) *businessman, inventor, and manufacturer* Cooper was born in New York City to a family that had resided in the area since the mid-17th century. He had little formal education and went to work at an early age with his father making hats. He then tried his hand at various other endeavors such as brewing and brick making before turning to the cloth business. After opening a shop for making cloth and prospering during the War of 1812, he turned his attention to furniture making and then the grocery business. Using his earnings, he invested in a glass manufacturing business before finally opening the Canton Iron Works in Baltimore in 1828. But it was his experience with the Baltimore & Ohio Railway that was to make him his fortune and fame.

The railroad crossed his property, and Cooper became interested in steam locomotion. As a result of the proximity and his interests in steam, Cooper designed the first steam locomotive built in the United States for the Baltimore & Ohio, nicknamed the "Tom Thumb." Another similar engine was called the "Teakettle." The small engine proved to be only a prototype but earned him a reputation nevertheless. He then sold his Baltimore operations for several times what he paid for them and opened iron mills in New York and New Jersey.

In 1856, the Bessemer process was first attempted in the United States at his plant in Trenton, New Jersey. Other foundries followed in New Jersey and Pennsylvania. He also became involved with Cyrus Field in laying the first transatlantic cable and became president of the New York, Newfoundland & London Telegraph Co. Later, he became president of the North American Telegraph Co., which controlled more than half the telegraph lines in the country.

Cooper was also an inventor who invented washing machines and ferry boats that were propelled by compressed air. He was active politically and supported emancipation. He served as an alderman in New York City and advocated full-time, paid fire and police departments for the city, as well as public schools. In New York, he is best remembered for establishing Cooper Union, a well-known college devoted to engineering and science, offering free tuition to successful applicants.

He was also the presidential candidate of the Greenback Party after the Civil War in 1876 but received less than 1 percent of the votes cast. He died in New York City in 1883. Only one of his six children, Edward, survived until adulthood. Edward was a partner with his father in some business ventures and also active politically in New York City.

See also FIELD, CYRUS W.; RAILROADS.

Further reading

Nevins, Alan. *Abram S. Hewitt with Some Account of Peter Cooper.* New York: Harper & Bros., 1935.

Raymond, Rossiter W. *Peter Cooper.* Boston: Houghton Mifflin, 1901.

corporation   A form of business organization in which the capital of the firm is supplied by shareholders. As owners of the company, shareholders are liable only for the amount of their investment. Unlike partnerships, shareholders have no further risk or obligation beyond the percentage that their investment represents of the firm's total equity. The proportion that a shareholding represents in the ownership of a corporation is determined by dividing the number of shares owned by the total amount of outstanding stock in the company.

Before corporations came into common use, partnerships were the traditional form of business organization. A partnership is a form of company ownership whereby the equity of a firm is privately held by two or more individuals. Each individual shares in the profits or losses of the partnership equally unless some other arrangement has been made limiting the share of a partner. In that case, an individual may be a limited partner rather than full partner. Partners also share any liabilities the partnership may incur in the course of business. Each partner may act as agent for others. As a result, partners bear the full risk of the business.

Partnerships were the first form of business organization beyond the sole proprietorship. Traditionally, new partners cannot be admitted to a partnership unless the partners agree. Admitting new partners is the method used to enlarge the financial base of the partnership or gain new expertise. But the form has had its drawbacks. Any capital that the business accumulates as a result of its activities is shared equally and, as a result, may be transient. When a partner retires or dies, he or she is entitled to withdraw capital. As a result, the equity of the organization diminishes unless a new source can be found to replace it.

As the economy grew larger in the 19th and early 20th centuries, many firms decided to incorporate rather than continue as partnerships. By doing so, they had access to more capital and also limited the shareholders' liability in the firm to the amount of their equity holding. Regulations from the state and federal level also made partnerships somewhat dated in some industries, since capital requirements for banks and securities firms (for example) were raised, and firms were required to have access to capital markets in order to raise fresh funds. Partnerships generally are too small to be able to access funds from the markets and traditionally rely upon new investment from newly admitted partners or retained earnings from continuing operations.

The first corporations traced their history to the mercantilist trading companies established in Britain and Holland in the 17th and 18th centuries. Incorporating on a smaller business scale occurred later in the 18th century. Firms began incorporating in the United States after independence, but the process was slow. At the end of the 18th century, some banks and insurance companies began selling stock in order to expand their operations. One of the early stock companies was the government-chartered BANK OF THE UNITED STATES. The movement continued into the 1830s, and the early canal companies and RAILROADS were incorporated in order to raise capital. As the country grew, raising capital became a primary concern because many of the early industries, such as the railroads, were capital intensive and required funds beyond the financial capacity of partnerships or sole proprietorships.

The trend toward incorporation was aided by developments in the stock exchanges. Many exchanges originally were local markets, located in the major eastern cities. In order to list a company on an exchange, thus helping to market its name, incorporation was necessary, so the process went hand-in-hand with stock exchange trading. As more investor money found its way to the exchanges, more also became available to bring new companies public.

After the Civil War, business entered the phase of MANAGERIAL CAPITALISM, and the modern corporation, run by a professional managerial class, was born. Companies could now be ensured a viable succession that did not depend upon the founder or the founder's family to run the business. At the turn of the 20th century, the U.S. STEEL CORP. was formed by J. P. Morgan in 1901. It was the first company to have more than a billion dollars of assets on its balance sheet and was the most widely held company of the day. Many more giant companies followed in its wake, including AT&T and GENERAL ELECTRIC,

became widely held, and remained so for decades.

Business expansion was rapid after the Civil War, and many new companies were incorporated. An obstacle to the largest companies was the antitrust movement that emerged as business consolidation increased after 1870. Companies purchasing others were organized into trusts and became the predecessors of the modern HOLDING COMPANY. Often, the stock in these new forms of organization was held by relatively few shareholders. After the consolidation of many oil producers into the Standard Oil Company, the trusts were required to find states where local laws were friendly to companies that did much of their business out-of-state. As a result, many companies were incorporated in Delaware and New Jersey.

During the 1920s, a record number of corporations emerged, many in states of convenience. The post–World War I period witnessed the greatest growth in corporations registered since the 1880s and 1890s, and the trend lasted until the stock market crash of 1929 and the Great Depression. Studies subsequently appeared examining the ownership of many corporations, including the demographics surrounding their shareholders, but the number of incorporated companies continued to grow. Listings on the stock exchanges increased in the post–World War II period, along with a record number of MERGERS that continued to reduce the number of corporations at the same time that many new ones were being registered.

Business corporations are the most common types of corporation, but other types do exist, including single-person corporations, government-owned corporations, nonprofit corporations, and municipal corporations. The major advantage that corporations, especially business corporations, have over partnerships or sole proprietorships is that they are potentially able to raise significant amounts of capital. In addition to selling stock, they may also borrow bonds and COMMERCIAL PAPER and sell preferred stock.

In the 1980s and 1990s, variations on the single stock company emerged, with many corporations establishing subsidiaries that stood alone and had their own stock structures, with shareholder profits depending on the revenue of the subsidiary rather than the parent company, as had been the case in the past. As business risks increased over the years, the number of incorporations increased in order to shield principal owners from risk while at the same time increasing the total number of shares outstanding.

See also ANTITRUST; BANKRUPTCY; MORGAN, JOHN PIERPONT; MULTINATIONAL CORPORATION.

Further reading
Beatty, Jack. *Colossus: How the Corporation Changed America.* New York: Broadway Books, 2001.
Berle, Adolph, and Gardiner Means. *The Modern Corporation and Private Property.* Rev. ed. New York: Harcourt Brace, 1968.
Chandler, Alfred D., Jr. *The Visible Hand: The Managerial Revolution in American Business.* Cambridge, Mass.: Harvard University Press, 1977.
Micklethwait, John, and Adrian Wooldridge. *The Company: A Short History of a Revolutionary Idea.* New York: Modern Library, 2003.
Nohria, Nitin, Davis Dyer, and Frederick A. B. Dalzell. *Changing Fortunes: Remaking the Industrial Corporation.* New York: John Wiley, 2002.

cotton industry Cotton has played an important role in the growth and development of U.S. agriculture, industry, and trade almost from the birth of the nation. The invention of the cotton gin (which reduced the time needed to remove cottonseed from the cotton fiber) by Eli Whitney in 1793 set off an almost continuous increase in production that did not cease until the 1930s. From 10,000 bales produced in 1793, cotton production expanded to almost 4 million bales in 1860, the largest commercial crop in the South and the mainstay of its entire economy and of SLAVERY.

The slave plantations had been managed centrally. Although following the Civil War farmers who owned small amounts of land produced some cotton, most of the crop would again be grown by large-scale landlords who now organized tenant plantations, renting parcels of land to families who worked with varying degrees of supervision. Until the 1940s, cotton dominated life from the Carolinas through Texas, an area referred to as the "Cotton Belt," at the center of which were cotton tenant plantations.

Since World War I, wide year-to-year fluctuations but no discernible trend had occurred in total U.S. cotton production due to governmental programs and yield variability. Only following World War II did the tractor and mechanical cotton harvester sweep away the 19th-century production methods of lots of labor, a mule, and a plow. U.S. farmers now produce the same quantity of cotton with about one-third less land than in the 1920s. Rising yields have resulted from the rapid substitution of new and improved production practices, industrial inputs (e.g., pesticides, varieties, and fertilizers), and capital (i.e., mechanization and irrigation) for land and labor. Accordingly, cotton production has shifted to land well suited to mechanization and from production under rainfall conditions to irrigation. These shifts have been both within and between major producing areas in the Southeast and the newer areas in the West. Thus, cotton farmers are now important producers from California to the Carolinas but comprise a broken, instead of continuous, Cotton Belt.

Millions of cotton farmers and workers, primarily African Americans, left the South during the post–World War II years, settling primarily in northern and western cities. Although many of them were displaced by machines and chemicals, most abandoned the cotton fields for what they hoped would be a life of greater freedom and opportunity.

See also WHITNEY, ELI.

Further reading
Andrews, Mildred G. *The Men and the Mills: A History of the Southern Textile Industry.* Macon, Ga.: Mercer University Press, 1989.

Lemann, Nicholas. *The Promised Land: The Great Black Migration and How It Changed America.* New York: Macmillan, 1991.

Wright, Gavin. *Old South, New South: Revolutions in the Southern Economy Since the Civil War.* New York: Basic Books, 1986.

Wayne Grove

crashes Precipitous stock market price drops. There is no precise definition of the term, although the most serious crashes of the 19th and early 20th centuries caused serious collateral damage in the banking system as well as in the STOCK MARKETS.

In the 19th century, crashes were referred to as "panics." Before much was known about the interrelationship of different sectors of the economy, panic implied that investors lost confidence in the market and began to sell at the same time, causing serious deterioration in stock prices. Panics occurred in 1837, 1857, 1869, 1873, and 1893, as well as in 1907. When the market fell in October 1929, the term *crash* became widely used. In all of the panics prior to 1929, dozens of banks were forced to close their doors, especially when the United States was still on a gold standard. The U.S. banking system was seriously affected after the 1929 crash, and many savers withdrew their funds from banks, fearful that banks would close, leaving them penniless. The most serious banking collapse after the crash came in 1930 when the BANK OF UNITED STATES was forced to close its doors.

In the post–World War II era, the term *crash* has been used more liberally, connoting any serious price drop on the stock exchange in which recovery was not imminent. But a crash is materially different from a bear market, in which prices fall and stay depressed for a period of time before recovering. In the past, a crash was acknowledged to have occurred when a market's precipitous drop had serious effects for the economy rather than simply being a price correction from inflated stock values. Since the development of the safety net of banking and securities laws during the

1930s, crashes have not been so unexpected or dramatic as in the pre-1929 period, although they have occurred in one form or other in 1987 and in the post–Internet bubble period after 2000.

See also NEW YORK STOCK EXCHANGE.

Further reading
Galbraith, John Kenneth. *The Great Crash 1929.* New York: Penguin, 1954.
Collman, Charles Albert. *Our Mysterious Panics, 1830–1930.* New York: William Morrow, 1931.
Kindleberger, Charles P. *Manias, Panics, and Crashes: A History of Financial Crises.* 4th ed. New York: John Wiley & Sons, 2000.

credit cards Plastic cards that pay for financial transactions by extending credit to the user when the purchase or transaction is complete. The company issuing the credit card then collects the balance due from the customer upon demand or over time by extending revolving credit, for which a rate of interest is charged.

The general idea for credit cards originated in the 19th century as a vision of a utopian future society. In *Looking Backward, 2000–1887,* published in 1888, Edward Bellamy accurately foresaw the introduction of credit cards in the 20th century when he predicted that many transactions would be cashless, using a form of identification card. The actual mechanism by which payments would be collected was a more difficult issue and would have to await developments in computer technology.

The first credit card was developed by Diners Club after the Second World War, and it required the balance to be paid in full when due. In the mid-1960s, a new card was developed by the BANK OF AMERICA—the Visa card—and it enabled the customer, for the first time, to pay outstanding balances over time. It was soon followed by MasterCard, another franchise operation that sold its name and facilities to banks and finance companies that used a card with its generic logo. Bank of America divested itself of the card business several years after introduc-

Montage of credit card images, 1960 (Library of Congress)

tion, and the operation became franchised, with the card being offered by many banks that paid the licensor a fee. By the late 1960s, credit cards began revolutionizing the way in which payments were made for purchases, replacing cash and checks in many instances. The use of cards grew exponentially over the next four decades and by 2000 represented the major form of consumer debt outstanding.

The growth of credit cards was made possible by the rapid growth of the COMMERCIAL PAPER market. Bank holding companies and finance companies were able to borrow for short terms in the market and use the proceeds to buy receivables from merchants at a small discount from the customer's purchase price. The growth in the commercial paper market paralleled the growth of credit cards, allowing nonbanks to offer the services as well. Today credit cards are offered by banks and financial companies having access to the commercial paper market as a source of low-cost funding.

The outstanding amount of credit card debt has become a closely watched statistic in order to determine the condition of consumers in general, since two-thirds of the U.S. economy is generated by consumer spending.

Further reading

Calder, Lendol. *Financing the American Dream*. Princeton, N.J.: Princeton University Press, 1999.

Evans, David S., and Richard Schmalensee. *Paying with Plastic: The Digital Revolution in Buying and Borrowing*. Cambridge, Mass.: MIT Press, 1999.

Mandell, Lewis. *The Credit Card Industry: A History*. Boston: Twayne Publishers, 1990.

credit-rating agencies Ratings of the creditworthiness of business borrowers were provided historically in the United States by two types of firms: credit-reporting agencies and credit-rating agencies. Although they performed broadly similar functions, they provided different services and are discussed separately. Early credit-reporting agencies provided information that influenced the type and amount of trade credit offered by wholesalers and manufacturers to small retailers. Credit-rating agencies, on the other hand, provide standardized ratings of large borrowers who issue bonds and other marketed debt instruments.

When the Mercantile Agency was founded in New York City in 1841 by Lewis Tappan, it offered a new service to American businessmen. Before then, wholesalers, jobbers, and others seeking information about the creditworthiness of potential borrowers occasionally hired agents or sought assistance from distant correspondents who may have known something about the potential borrower's business and personal habits. The Mercantile Agency was the first organized effort to systematically collect and collate information about thousands of scattered small businesses and provide that information to lenders in useful form. The Mercantile Agency's efforts were novel in the mid-19th century but became a mainstay of modern business practice by the beginning of the 20th century. Despite some early legal and political concerns, the firm provided a vital economic function and became a widely accepted, nearly indispensable, enterprise. In time the Mercantile Agency faced a number of competitors—some such as Bradstreet's represented a real competitive threat; most others did not and quickly closed.

It is generally believed that the formation of the Mercantile Agency in 1841 was a consequence of a realization on the part of many wholesalers and jobbers that the existing system was woefully inadequate. Relying on informal reports and recommendations from correspondents, wholesalers suffered significant losses as small retailers went bankrupt by the thousands during the economic downturn of the late 1830s and early 1840s. Such rapid change in the financial condition of so many businesses impressed upon merchants, especially Tappan, the need for more accurate and time information.

Tappan collected information on merchants and retailers in New York and elsewhere from reports provided by unpaid correspondents—mostly local attorneys—who ostensibly had some insights into the character and business practices of neighbors. After receiving a solicited report on the personal and business habits of merchants, clerks at the agency recorded the information in longhand in large ledgers. Subscribers to the agency's services, considering whether to offer a small-town retailer goods on credit, could then receive the agency's most recent report on the retailer by calling the office, where a clerk would read the report to the subscriber. The agency generated revenue by charging subscribers fees commensurate with the scale of the subscriber's business on the assumption that larger enterprises would make more use of the service than smaller ones. Correspondents provided reports without charge because Tappan encouraged subscribers to use his correspondents as collection agents when borrowers fell into arrears.

Although Tappan may have had larger aspirations, under his leadership the Mercantile Agency principally served New York City merchants despite agreements and copartnerships with comparable firms in other cities. His partner and successor, Benjamin Douglass (1849–58), envisioned a more centralized firm providing services on a national scale. He expanded the group of correspondents to include banks, insurance companies, manufacturers, and commission merchants. Douglass also centralized direction and made branches part of the New York operation rather than semiautonomous entities. Under Douglass, the firm expanded coverage into the southern and western United States, provided some collection and direct-mail advertising services, and introduced a rating system provided in published form instead of descriptive reports available for inspection.

The last innovation was forced on the Mercantile Agency by the Bradstreet Agency, founded in 1849 by John M. Bradstreet, who in 1851 was the first to publish standardized firm ratings. Douglass and his successor, Robert G. Dun (1858–1900), initially resisted publishing the agency's ratings, but competition by Bradstreet's forced its hand. Dun published his first *Reference Book* in 1859, a practice continued long afterward. Published volumes of both firms organized rated businesses by city or town, name of businessman, type of business, and reported two code letters or numbers with one signifying the rated firm's invested capital—the other its general creditworthiness. Dun's earliest books rated about 20,000 businesses. By 1880, his firm rated about 800,000 and by 1900 about 1.3 million.

After 1875, credit-reporting firms matured. Routines and procedures were formalized, flow charts detailing information flows were developed, accounting practices were standardized, control was more fully centralized, pricing policies were rationalized, and new technologies were utilized. Two important innovations that significantly increased the scope and efficiency of credit-reporting agencies were the telegraph and the typewriter. The telegraph lowered the cost of collecting and disseminating information; the typewriter in collating and distributing it among branch offices. Typewriters and carbon paper quickly replaced hundreds of clerks hand-copying information longhand into bound ledgers.

Relatively little is known about the operation of either major credit-reporting firm after 1900, as no detailed history has yet emerged. Dun & Company grew increasingly international following Robert G. Dun's death, opening 77 overseas offices. Dun's firm merged with Bradstreet's in 1933 to form Dun & Bradstreet. In 1962, it acquired Moody's Investors Service and subsequently acquired a number of other firms. In 2000, Moody's Investors Service was spun off, and the firm changed its name to D&B in 2001.

Modern credit-rating agencies play an important role in modern financial markets. Credit-rating agencies assess the default risks of corporate and governmental borrowers and issuers of other fixed-income securities, such as commercial paper, preferred stocks, bank certificates of deposit, mortgage-backed securities, and several other financial derivatives. Agencies sift through and make sense of enormous amounts of quantitative and qualitative information about borrowers to provide lenders and investors accurate and timely assessments of the risks involved in purchasing a borrower's securities. Like the previously discussed credit-reporting agencies that

developed alphanumeric codes to summarize a borrower's likely ability to repay its obligations, credit-rating agencies developed codes to distinguish between investment-grade and lesser-grade issues.

There are currently four full-service credit-rating agencies in the United States, in addition to several agencies that provide credit ratings for specific industries, such as banks and insurance companies. The earliest full-service rating agency was Moody's Investors Service, established by John Moody in 1909. Poors Publishing Company opened in 1916; Standard Statistics Company and Fitch Investors Service in 1922. Duff & Phelps Credit Rating Agency opened in 1932 but focused on public utilities until 1982, when it expanded its ratings and became a full-service rating agency. McCarthy, Crisanti, and Maffei opened in 1975 but was acquired by Duff & Phelps in 1991. Two prominent specialized rating agencies are Thomson BankWatch, founded in 1974, which rates only financial firms, and A. M. Best, which rates the claims-paying abilities of insurance companies. Relatively little is known about the internal operations of these firms because no large-scale history has been written about any of them. Nevertheless, it is possible to piece together a basic chronology of the industry.

John Moody & Company published *Moody's Manual of Industrial and Miscellaneous Securities* in 1900. Moody's manual provided information about stocks and bonds and became quite popular. The company failed during the financial panic of 1907, but Moody formed a new business in 1909 with a new objective. Instead of collecting and publishing businesses' accounting statistics and managerial data, his new company published a manual that analyzed each firm's relative investment quality. He borrowed the alphanumeric rating system then in use by credit-reporting firms and became the first to offer systematic ratings. Moody' 1909 manual concentrated on railroads, but by 1913, he included industrials and utilities. In 1914, he began including ratings of municipal bonds. By 1924, Moody's rated nearly every outstanding corporate and municipal bond. In the 1970s, it started rating commercial paper and bank certificates of deposit. Moody's published its first ratings of international bonds in 1981 and ratings of over-the-counter securities in 1986. The Financial Information Services division was acquired by Mergent, Inc. in 1999, which currently delivers financial services to Internet subscribers.

Although Moody's provided the first formal credit ratings of railroads, Henry Varnum Poor was among the first to collect and publish information about the financial condition and managerial structure of railroads. H. V. and H. W. Poor's was founded in 1867 and by 1868 was publishing, to wide acclaim, the *Manual of Railroads in the United States.* This and subsequent manuals provided four types of information on each U.S. railroad: line of road, rolling stock, operations and general balances, and officers and directors. In providing this information, the Poor's provided bankers, lenders, and investors with a portrait of each railroad's current operations and financial condition. The Poor's company faced some early competition but had the field to itself until Moody's published its first manual in 1909. Poor's Publishing Company changed from simple reporting to rating in 1916. Standard Statistics Company entered in 1922, offering ratings of corporate bonds. The firms merged to form Standard & Poor's in 1941, which was itself acquired by the publisher McGraw-Hill Companies, Inc. in 1966.

Fitch Ratings was founded by John K. Fitch in 1913 and, like Poor's, initially published financial statistics in such volumes as the *Fitch Bond Book* and the *Fitch Stock and Bond Manual.* Between 1922 and 1924, Fitch moved into credit rating and is sometimes credited with having developed the now familiar "AAA" to "D" ratings.

Four notable factors led to the establishment and success of credit-rating agencies. The first was the growing use of the corporate form of organization and the issuance of bonded debt by railroads, public utilities, manufacturing firms, as well as state and local governments. Second, growing wealth among the middle class increased the demand for information about the riskiness of different investments. Third, existing investment banks came under fire for conflicts of inter-

est and became less reputable certifiers of bond quality. And fourth, the First World War and the mass marketing of government bonds introduced middle America to war bonds, which increased interest in and the demand for public and private debt. With this massive growth in both the supply and demand for bonds, investors needed some way to differentiate between alternative investments by risk and return. Rating agencies provided this sorting mechanism.

Credit-rating agencies historically provided ratings of issuers without charge and generated revenues by selling publications reporting the ratings. Because the materials were easily copied, however, potential revenues were lost. An opening for changing the revenue source presented itself following the default of the Penn Central Railroad in 1970. Penn Central defaulted on its outstanding commercial paper, and concerned investors refused to roll over their holdings of other firm's commercial paper, forcing many others into default. To assure nervous investors, issuers of commercial paper sought out and paid for objective ratings of their commercial paper issues. This new practice quickly took hold for other securities and is now standard practice in the industry.

Further reading
Cantor, Richard, and Frank Packer. "The Credit Rating Industry." Federal Reserve Bank of New York *Quarterly Review* (1994): pp. 1–26.

Chandler, Alfred D., Jr. *Henry Varnum Poor: Business Editor, Analyst, and Reformer.* Cambridge, Mass.: Harvard University Press, 1956.

Madison, James H. "The Evolution of Commercial Credit Reporting Agencies in Nineteenth-Century America." *Business History Review* (1974): pp. 164–186.

Norris, James D. *R. G. Dun & Co., 1841–1900: The Development of Credit-Reporting in the Nineteenth Century.* Westport, Conn.: Greenwood Press, 1978.

Sylla, Richard. "An Historical Primer on the Business of Credit Ratings," in Richard M. Levich, Giovanni Majnoni, and Carmen Reinhart, eds., *Ratings, Rating Agencies, and the Global Financial System.* Boston: Kluwer Academic Publishers, 2002.

Howard Bodenhorn

D

Dawes, Charles G. (1865–1951) *financier and politician* Born in Ohio, Dawes's family traced its origins to the *Mayflower.* After graduating from Marietta College and studying law, he moved to Lincoln, Nebraska, where he engaged in several successful businesses, including real estate, meat packing, and banking. It was only after he and his brothers acquired extensive holdings in two utility companies that he began to amass a sizable fortune. The brothers would eventually control 28 companies in 10 states. Then in 1902, Charles turned his attention to banking, founding the Central Trust Co. of Illinois.

He entered politics about the same time. After working for William McKinley's presidential campaign, he was named comptroller of the currency in 1898. He enlisted in the army as a major in 1917 and rose to brigadier general within two years. He served on General John Pershing's staff and was in charge of supply procurement and disbursement for the American Expeditionary Force. Dawes also became one of the few Republicans to support the League of Nations. The nickname "Hell and Maria" for Dawes began to be used after he appeared at a congressional hearing investigating budgetary waste during the war.

When asked whether he paid excessive prices for mules, he replied, "Hell, Maria, I would have paid horse prices for sheep if the sheep could have pulled artillery to the front."

He was appointed the first director of the budget in 1920 and proceeded to introduce efficiency measures into government accounting, many for the first time. The League of Nations invited him to write a report on German war reparations in 1923; the Dawes Report was published in 1924, suggesting reparations be made on a sliding scale. The report was so popular and powerful in political and diplomatic circles that he was awarded the Nobel Peace Prize, which he shared with Austen Chamberlain of Britain for his efforts in 1925. He then became Calvin Coolidge's vice president in 1925, ambassador to Great Britain in 1929, and American delegate to the Disarmament Conference in 1932 but resigned to become chairman of the RECONSTRUCTION FINANCE CORP. (RFC) in the same year. The government agency was developed to make loans to distressed companies during the early days of the Great Depression. Controversy erupted when the RFC's first loan was made to Dawes's bank in Chicago.

During his life, he also found time to write nine books and become an accomplished musician, playing both flute and piano. He died in Evanston, Illinois, in 1951.

Further reading

Dawes, Charles G. *The First Year of the Budget of the United States.* New York: Harper & Row, 1923.

Timmons, Bascom N. *Portrait of an American: Charles G. Dawes.* New York: Henry Holt, 1953.

Debs, Eugene V. (1855–1926) *labor organizer* Eugene Victor Debs was born in Terre Haute, Indiana, on November 5, 1855, the son of French immigrant parents. At 14 he quit school to join the RAILROADS and spent several years employed as a paint scraper. Through dedication and hard work, Debs eventually rose to become a locomotive fireman, although he ultimately lost

Eugene V. Debs, 1921 (LIBRARY OF CONGRESS)

his job during the depression of the 1870s. He found new work as a grocery clerk but nonetheless maintained close contact with the railroad industry, and in 1874, he joined the Brotherhood of Locomotive Firemen. By now a committed labor activist, he became editor of the *Firemen's Magazine,* in which he promoted social harmony through labor reform and peaceful means. In 1880, Debs's popularity was parlayed into politics, and he was elected city clerk of Terre Haute and also briefly held a seat in the Indiana legislature. However, he remained disillusioned by railroad workers who were often bitterly divided along trade lines and sought to consolidate them to present a unified face to management. Therefore, in 1893, he helped to organize the American Railway Union (ARU) and was roundly elected its first president. Debs continued arguing for change through peaceful means, but in 1894 he was unable to prevent union members from participating in the unsuccessful Pullman strike. As the strike spread and nearly paralyzed rail commerce in the West, federal troops were eventually dispatched to put down the strike. Debs was subsequently arrested for contempt of court, and, while serving out his six-month sentence, he became exposed to the writings of Karl Marx. This proved a turning point in his political fortunes, for he formally converted to socialism. In 1898 he established the Social Democratic Party and its more famous successor, the Socialist Party of America, in 1901. Based on his own experiences, Debs also added prison reform to his progressive social agenda.

Like most socialists, Debs felt that ingrained competition between capital and labor ensured class struggle and social inequity. To him no single union could protect worker's rights, and he argued that a cooperative commonwealth would better serve the workers than the profit system. Debs nonetheless couched his radicalism in terms of peaceful political change. In fact, he strenuously maintained that America's traditional political values, which he strongly endorsed, were threatened by the unwillingness or inability of capitalism to promote economic democracy. He was nonetheless a fiery orator and highly popular with the rank and file, who nominated him five times to run for the presidency. In 1900, 1904, 1908, 1912, and 1920, Debs ran unsuccessfully for high office, ultimately receiving only 6 percent of votes cast; as a political movement, the Socialists failed to gain broad electoral acceptance. Part of this failure was Debs's continual struggle to unite moderate factions of the party with more revolutionary elements. However, after 1917 his reputation as a moderate was reaffirmed when he was repelled by the antidemocratic nature of the Russian Revolution and refused to join the newly emerging Communist Party.

In 1916, Debs vocally criticized the neutralist policies of President Woodrow Wilson and predicted that they would culminate in war. When the United States formally entered World War I in 1917, he was arrested for sedition under the Espionage Act and received a 10-year prison sentence the following year. He thus ran for president in 1920 from his prison cell and received nearly 1 million votes, but his political impact began to wane. Debs was released from prison under an amnesty program in December 1921, and, although in poor health, he labored to bring the discredited Socialists back to prominence. But despite large, enthusiastic crowds, the party had lost its previous appeal. He died in Elmhurst, Illinois, on December 20, 1926, a successful labor leader, a failed politician, and a forceful advocate for social change. Curiously, many of the radical positions he enunciated, such as abolition of child labor, woman suffrage, and a graduated INCOME TAX, were eventually co-opted by the political mainstream.

Further reading

Carey, Charles W. *Eugene V. Debs: Outspoken Labor Leader and Socialist.* Berkeley Heights, N.J.: Enslow Publishers, 2003.
Constantine, J. Robert, ed. *Letters of Eugene V. Debs, 3 vols.* Urbana: University of Illinois Press, 1990.
Debs, Eugene V. *Walls and Bars: Prisons and Prison Life in the "Land of the Free."* Chicago: C. H. Kerr, 2000.
Papke, David R. *The Pullman Case: The Clash of Labor and Capital in Industrial America.* Lawrence: University Press of Kansas, 1999.
Young, Marguerite. *Harp Song for a Radical: The Life and Times of Eugene Victor Debs.* New York: Alfred Knopf, 1999.

John C. Fredriksen

Deere, John (1804–1886) *inventor and businessman* Born in Vermont in 1804, Deere's father was British, and his mother was the daughter of a British army officer who served during the American Revolution. At age 17, Deere became a blacksmith's apprentice and then worked as a blacksmith until 1837. He moved to Grand Detour, Illinois, where he began designing plows with a partner, Leonard Andruss. His first inventions used steel cut from an old sawmill blade and bent into shape. The invention was much more effective than plows currently in use by farmers, and within 10 years they were selling more than 1,000 per year.

Deere sold his interest in the company to Andruss and started his own business in Moline, Illinois, in 1847, which initially used English steel as its main component because American steel at the time was inferior. He then commissioned the same sort of steel to be made in Pittsburgh to save on costs, and the plow he produced became the first steel plow manufactured in the United States. Within 10 years, he produced more than 10,000 annually. In 1858, Deere took his son Charles H. Deere into partnership and five years later took his son-in-law Stephen Velie in as well. In 1868, the company was incorporated as Deere & Co., with John Deere as president, Charles Deere as vice president, and Velie as secretary. It introduced the first successful riding plow in 1875. John Deere died in Moline in 1886. Charles succeeded him as president of the company.

Charles Deere expanded the company's distribution as president and also added new lines of

Deere products, including corn planters, plows, and harrows. Over the next century, Deere & Co. again added other lines to its product mix, including tractors, lawn care products, forestry equipment, and other types of farm equipment. The company name became a household word in the Midwest, especially after it offered very liberal lines of credit to farmers during the Great Depression so they could remain in business. By 1958, Deere surpassed INTERNATIONAL HARVESTER as the country's largest manufacturer of agricultural equipment. Five years later it became the largest in the world, selling more than $3.5 billion worth of its products.

Despite its growth, the company remained headed by a family member until the early 1980s. Many of its tractors and plows were painted green, and the color became the company's hallmark. The name Deere and the image of a green tractor became synonymous with American farm equipment manufacturing.

See also FARMING.

Further reading

Broehl, Wayne G. *John Deere's Company: A History of Deere & Company and Its Times.* New York: Doubleday, 1984.

Burlingame, Roger. *March of the Iron Men.* New York: Charles Scribner's Sons, 1938.

Sanders, Ralph W. *Ultimate John Deere: The History of the Big Green Machines.* Stillwater, Okla.: Voyageur Press, 2001.

Depository Institutions Act (1982) Also known as the Garn–St. Germain Act, named after its two congressional sponsors, Senator Jake Garn of Utah and Representative Fernand St. Germain of Rhode Island, the act was passed to aid thrift institutions. In the mid- to late 1970s and early 1980s, many thrift institutions (SAVINGS AND LOANS and savings banks) were disintermediated as savers withdrew their deposits in favor of higher yields offered by money market mutual funds. Savings deposits at thrifts, like commercial banks, were regulated by Regulation Q of the FEDERAL RESERVE, which allowed the central bank to cap the amount of interest paid. As a result, the outflow from the thrifts caused many to begin recording losses, and the entire industry recorded a net loss between 1980 and 1982.

The act allowed the thrifts to liberalize their balance sheets in favor of an expanded array of assets that could potentially yield more than a conventional mortgage. They were allowed to offer commercial loans and consumer loans in limited amounts and to acquire insurance underwriting operations. Interest rate restrictions on accounts were lifted, and they were also allowed to purchase corporate bonds, again as a specific maximum percent of their total assets. They were also allowed to invest in computer networks that provided automated teller machine facilities across state lines.

Unfortunately, in their rush to regain profits, many of the thrifts made ill-advised investments, including poor nonresidential mortgages and JUNK BONDS. Within six years, the industry again was in financial trouble, caused by defaults in the junk bond market and a weakening in the commercial real estate market. As a result, Congress passed the Financial Institutions Return, Recovery and Enforcement Act (FIRREA) in 1989, which reformed the industry and forced many of the marginal thrifts out of business. On balance, the act only temporarily saved the industry before its more liberal provisions caused the industry to fail again.

The greatest legacy of the act was to help spark the interest in junk bonds during the early and mid-1980s. The thrifts became major investors in the bonds, many of which were sold by the investment banking house DREXEL BURNHAM LAMBERT. The act remains as one of the least successful efforts at DEREGULATION in financial services passed in the 1980s.

See also DEPOSITORY INSTITUTIONS DEREGULATION AND MONETARY CONTROL ACT; FINANCIAL INSTITUTIONS REFORM, RECOVERY AND ENFORCEMENT ACT.

Further reading

Barth, James R. *The Great Savings and Loan Debacle.* Washington, D.C.: American Enterprise Institute, 1991.

White, Lawrence J. *The S&L Debacle*. New York: Oxford University Press, 1991.

Depository Institutions Deregulation and Monetary Control Act

(1980)   Better known by its acronym, DIDMCA, the act was passed by Congress in 1980. It was the first major bank deregulatory legislation since strict regulations were passed during the NEW DEAL. The act had two sides. On one side, it deregulated some activities of banks, while on the other it gave the FEDERAL RESERVE more power to cope with all depository institutions in the new deregulated environment.

DIDMCA began the phasing out of Regulation Q, which allowed the Federal Reserve to cap interest paid on savings accounts. The original plan was to phase out the ceiling over a six-year period, with the actual mechanics controlled by a committee of federal officials. When the DEPOSITORY INSTITUTIONS ACT was passed in 1982, the phaseout was completed earlier than originally anticipated. Deposit insurance offered by the FEDERAL DEPOSIT INSURANCE CORPORATION was also increased to $100,000 per account at insured banks and in authorized NOW accounts (negotiated orders of withdrawal), a checking account that paid interest. NOW accounts had been offered for several years by a small group of banks, but they were legal only after the law was passed.

The Federal Reserve was given widened powers to deal with the high interest rate environment caused by oil-driven inflation. The Fed now set reserve requirements for all depository institutions in the country, not just for its member banks. This measure was designed to stop banks from withdrawing from membership in the Fed system and shore up the central bank's authority in the marketplace. Banks had been withdrawing since the 1960s because the Fed traditionally paid no interest on the reserve balances it held, and many banks wanted to revert to a state charter in order to earn interest on their reserves. The new law substituted a mandatory requirement on all depository institutions, regardless of type or charter. It also shortened the time for check clearing. All banks in the country were now also allowed access to the Fed's discount window, not just members as in the past.

Before the act was passed, the Fed's authority extended only to banks that were members of one of the regional Federal Reserve Banks. Now, by allowing all banks access to the lender of last resort facilities at the discount window and imposing standard reserve requirements, the Fed's authority was more uniform, extending to state-chartered banks and thrifts and the agricultural cooperatives as well. The act, along with the Eccles Act passed in 1935 and the BANK HOLDING COMPANY ACT passed in 1956, became a major building block in shoring up the authority of the Federal Reserve while liberalizing interest rates at the same time.

Further reading

Timberlake, Richard H. "Legislation Construction of the Monetary Control Act." *American Economic Review* 75 (May 1985): 97.

West, Robert Craig. "The Depository Institutions Deregulation Act of 1980: A Historical Perspective Economic Review." Federal Reserve Bank of Kansas City, Mo., February 1982.

deregulation   The process of lifting governmental restrictions that had been placed on certain industries since the Great Depression. Beginning in the 1970s and given further impetus by the Reagan administration in the 1980s, a new attitude toward business led Congress to begin passing legislation allowing various industries greater latitude in the sorts of activities they could engage in. Not all industries were involved, and the new environment was not put into place at once but phased in over a number of years.

REGULATION of industry began in the 19th century, when several states established regulatory commissions to monitor RAILROADS operating within their borders. Congress created the INTER-STATE COMMERCE COMMISSION in 1887 in order to regulate the railroads from Washington. But regulation became stalled until the stock market crash of 1929 and the early 1930s. During the Depression, restrictions were placed upon the securities and banking industries as well as on the UTILITIES. Since the early 1920s, AT&T had a virtual monopoly over telephone service that seriously restricted competition in telecommunications. During and after World War II, restrictions were placed upon other industries as well, including the airlines, defense contractors, and other forms of transportation. Many of these regulations defined the scope of an industry and sometimes prohibited companies within select businesses, such as banking, from branching across state lines. During the post–World War II period, many industries were regulated over rates that they could charge the public. Others were limited to domestic investors so that foreigners could not gain control over industries considered vital to the national defense.

A great deal of regulation was passed during the NEW DEAL, restricting the activities of many different businesses, among them the securities industry, banking, and public utility companies. The general theory behind these regulations was that any business serving the public interest needed to be regulated by government so that it would not violate its basic purpose of providing a public service at a reasonable price. After the Korean War in the 1950s, these regulations became less popular as a strengthening and growing economy often caused conflicts in regulated industries. Thus a slow drive toward deregulation was begun.

Deregulation can be interpreted in different ways depending upon the industry under consideration. Often, patterns in the regulation of industries paralleled developments in antitrust law. At other times, it was more closely related to trends in FOREIGN INVESTMENT. Conversely, changes in ANTITRUST signaled changes in regulation, especially in the case of AT&T, which lost its government-granted monopoly after a challenge to its dominance in the 1970s. The deregulation movement gained strength in the 1970s. Transportation was one of the first sectors of the economy to experience deregulation. One of the first industries to be deregulated was the airlines, and the STAGGERS RAIL ACT of 1980 allowed railroads greater flexibility in pricing. During the Reagan years in the 1980s, deregulation picked up considerable momentum and was advocated by the administration as a way of reducing the role of government in business.

Deregulation continued during the Clinton administration, and significant new laws were passed allowing previously regulated businesses greater flexibility, if not total freedom. The Energy Policy Act of 1992 allowed utility companies greater flexibility in pricing and eventually paved the way for many MERGERS between them later in the decade. The Telecommunications Act of 1996 broke down the barriers existing between AT&T and the local Bell companies, while the Surface Transportation Board, created in 1996, abolished the Interstate Commerce Commission, the first regulatory agency created in 1887. The Financial Services Modernization Act of 1999 abolished many of the regulations found in the BANKING ACT OF 1933, and the Interstate Banking Act of 1994 replaced the restrictive branching provisions of the MCFADDEN ACT of 1927.

The deregulation trend in the 1990s and the 21st century also owed much of its impetus to the increasing globalization of the world's markets. In order to be as competitive as possible, many regulated industries argued for greater freedom in order to maintain a competitive edge in the global marketplace, especially if they had to compete with foreign companies that had no restrictions on their activities.

Further reading

Geisst, Charles R. *Deals of the Century: Wall Street, Mergers, & the Making of Modern America.* New York: John Wiley & Sons, 2003.

McCraw, Thomas. *Prophets of Regulation.* Cambridge, Mass.: Harvard University Press, 1984.

Rose-Ackerman, Susan. *Rethinking the Progressive Agenda: The Reform of the American Regulatory State.* New York: Free Press, 1992.

Dillon Read & Co. An investment banking house founded by William Read in 1905. Its predecessor, Vermilye & Co., was founded in 1832. Over the years, Vermilye developed as a conservative bond house, and when Read joined in 1886, he specialized in fixed income securities, mainly bonds and preferred stocks. He helped develop many early bond valuation techniques that later became standard calculations on Wall Street. When Vermilye dissolved, Read founded his own firm that continued to specialize in bonds.

Read remained a small, specialized securities firm until 1913, when Clarence Dillon joined the firm. Beginning as a bond salesman, Dillon soon helped revamp the firm, making it more aggressive. He also introduced it to the mergers business, whereby the firm's reputation would be made in the following years. The first major deal for Read came in 1920, when Dillon helped refinance the Goodyear Tire & Rubber Co. The size of the $90 million transaction established the firm's reputation on Wall Street, and its name was officially changed to Dillon Read in the same year.

Dillon's best-known deal came later in the 1920s, when he won the mandate to arrange the sale of Dodge Brothers, the third-largest automobile manufacturer in the country. After the death of the two brothers, the company was put up for sale by the Dodge family, and Dillon bid for it, intending to run the company himself. He competed with J. P. Morgan Jr., who bid for the company on behalf of GENERAL MOTORS. Dillon won the bidding with an offer that was less than Morgan's but was all cash versus a cash and securities offer by Morgan. Dillon's method of estimating the company's future cash flows and then discounting their value to arrive at his bid price was one of the first deals employing that method, which has been commonly used on Wall Street since that time. The deal established the firm's reputation as a merger and acquisitions specialist.

Within a few years, Dillon realized that he was unable to run Dodge successfully and in 1928 sold the company to Walter CHRYSLER of Chrysler Motors for $170 million, $24 million more than the purchase price. The deal made Chrysler the second-largest manufacturer in the country at the time. Dillon withdrew from the firm at the end of the 1920s to pursue other interests. The firm continued as a small merger specialist with other limited product lines, including underwriting. In 1971, it chose Nicholas Brady as its senior partner. Brady later became secretary of the Treasury under Ronald Reagan. Clarence Dillon died in 1979.

Dillon Read survived as a partnership until BARING BROTHERS of Britain bought a 40 percent stake in the mid-1990s. A scandal at the British bank caused Dillon Read to buy back the share, and the bank remained independent until it was purchased by the Swiss Bank Corp. in 1997 and merged with another subsidiary, S. G. Warburg & Co. After the purchase, it operated as Warburg Dillon Read.

See also INVESTMENT BANKING; MORGAN, JOHN PIERPONT, JR.

Further reading

Geisst, Charles R. *The Last Partnerships: Inside the Great Wall Street Money Dynasties.* New York: McGraw-Hill, 2002.

Perez, Robert C., and Edward F. Willett. *Clarence Dillon: Wall Street Enigma.* Lanham, Md.: Madison Books, 1995.

Sobel, Robert. *The Life and Times of Dillon Read.* New York: Dutton, 1991.

Disney, Walt (1901–1966) *animator and businessman* Born in Chicago, Disney studied drawing informally as a youth. After a series of odd jobs, he studied art in the evening at the

Chicago Academy of Fine Arts. In 1918, he served as an ambulance driver for the Red Cross in France. Upon his return to the United States, he became an apprentice cartoonist for the magazine *Film Advertising.* Deciding to pursue his interest in cartooning, he opened a small production company in Kansas City that produced animated shorts, which ran before feature films at cinemas.

After a short period, he moved his operation to Hollywood in 1923 and opened a movie studio dedicated solely to cartoons. In collaboration with his brother Roy Disney (1893–1971), the Disney brothers' studio began producing cartoons featuring a heroine named Alice. These early cartoons became known as the Alice movies. By 1926, they had produced more than 50 short films.

The next cartoon character he created was Oswald the Rabbit, under contract with Universal Studios, and his cartoons became very successful. But he lost the Oswald copyright and had

Walt Disney (LIBRARY OF CONGRESS)

to create a new character. He developed Mickey Mouse after watching mice scurry around his studios. Originally, the character was called Mortimer. After a couple of short films, Mickey Mouse starred in his first hit, *Steamboat Willie.* It was the first cartoon with a sound track that Disney produced, and the film became very successful. By 1934, the company was producing more than 20 pictures per year, and profits were almost $700,000 per year. Part of the profits was from merchandise tie-ins that Disney helped pioneer along with manufacturers of consumer goods, a practice that the company continues today.

Success followed upon success. Disney produced *Snow White and the Seven Dwarfs,* Hollywood's first feature-length animated film, in 1937. It won a special Academy Award that year. Other successful full-length films followed, among them *Pinocchio, Fantasia,* and *Bambi.* When television made its breakthrough after World War II, Disney quickly embraced the medium. In 1950, his first television show was produced, and by 1954, he introduced his first television series, called *Disneyland.* The name of the program was also the name of the company's first amusement park, opened in Anaheim, California, in 1955. The theme park became one of the most popular attractions in the country and prompted the opening of another in 1971 in Florida, called Disney World. This park, along with the EPCOT center, was planned from the mid-1960s. Disney himself did not live to see the opening. He died in 1966 in Los Angeles.

By the 1990s, under the leadership of Michael Eisner, Disney had become the world's largest media company, with annual sales exceeding $20 billion. A Disney theme park was opened in Europe and another planned for Japan, and the company continued to engage in movie production, publishing, and television production in addition to the signature cartoons and entertainment parks. In 1996, the company expanded its operations, buying broadcaster Capital Cities/ABC for $19 billion, giving it access to broadcasting and television stations across the country.

Further reading

Eliot, Marc. *Walt Disney: Hollywood's Dark Prince.* New York: HarperCollins, 1994.

Schickel, Richard. *The Disney Version: The Life, Times, Art and Commerce of Walt Disney.* New York: Simon & Schuster, 1968.

Watts, Steven. *The Magic Kingdom: Walt Disney and the American Way of Life.* Boston: Houghton Mifflin, 1997.

Dow Chemical Company   Founded by Herbert H. Dow (1866–1930), chemist and horticulturist, in Midland, Michigan, in 1897, the company is the second-largest chemical company in the United States. Dow was born in Belleville, Ontario, Canada, but grew up in Cleveland, where he studied chemistry at Case School of Applied Science (now Case-Western Reserve University). He invented a process for extracting bromine from brine while still a student, and after several failed ventures founded the Dow Chemical Company at Midland, Michigan, in 1897.

Dow continued his chemical research activities throughout his life, amassing 107 patents while simultaneously directing a growing chemical company. Among his developments was Dowmetal, a magnesium metal extracted from underground brines. At the time of his death he was working on the extraction of magnesium from seawater, a development completed under the direction of his son and successor, Willard H. Dow. He died at Rochester, Minnesota, in 1930. His avocation, horticulture, gave birth to his company's agricultural chemicals division and to the Dow Gardens, now a major Michigan tourist attraction.

The company continued to flourish after his death and inaugurated a plant where magnesium was extracted from seawater in 1939 in Freeport, Texas. The process was considered an engineering triumph and a major contribution to the Allied victory in World War II. The company also was a pioneer in the plastics field during the 1930s, developing polystyrene, saran, and Styrofoam, among other products. Its styrene was a key component of styrene-butadiene rubber, which replaced natural rubber during the war. In the postwar era the company again expanded rapidly to become a global force in the CHEMICAL INDUSTRY, manufacturing some 2,000 products. These range from metals to agricultural chemicals, among them Dursban, the world's largest-selling insecticide. In the 1960s, the company became a favorite target of students protesting the war in Vietnam because of its production of napalm for the military forces. During the 1990s the company reorganized, selling its pharmaceutical branch, Marion Merrell Dow, to the Hoechst Company of Germany, disposing of several smaller ventures, and streamlining its workforce from about 55,000 to 40,000. In 1999, it announced plans to merge with Union Carbide Corporation of New York City.

See also DuPont de Nemours & Co., E. I.

Further reading

Brandt, E. N. *Growth Company, Dow Chemical's First Century.* East Lansing: Michigan State University Press, 1997.

Campbell, Murray, and Harrison Hatton. *Herbert H. Dow, Pioneer in Creative Chemistry.* New York: Appleton-Century-Crofts, 1951.

Whitehead, Don. *The Dow Story: A History of the Dow Chemical Company.* New York: McGraw-Hill, 1968.

E. N. Brandt

Dow Jones Industrial Average   The first stock market index devised and widely used in the United States. It was created by Charles H. Dow (1851–1902), cofounder of Dow Jones & Co. and editor of the *Wall Street Journal*. Dow began his career in journalism as a reporter for the *Springfield* (Mass.) *Daily Republican*. Eventually he moved to New York to work for the Kiernan News Agency, and in 1882 he and Edward Jones founded Dow Jones & Co. They specialized in financial news, originally distributed to

Wall Street by messengers until the *Wall Street Journal* was founded in 1889. Dow remained active at the newspaper until 1902, when he sold the company to Clarence BARRON.

Dow's index was first devised in 1896 in order to act as an accurate gauge of the market and became regularly reported in the *Wall Street Journal*. The Dow Jones Industrial Average, first published in the newspaper on May 26, 1896, originally contained 12 industrial stocks—Lachlede Gas & Light, GENERAL ELECTRIC, American Cotton Oil, American Sugar, Chicago Gas, AMERICAN TOBACCO, Distilling & Cattle Feeding, National Lead, North American Co., Tennessee Iron & Coal, U.S. Leather Preferred, and U.S. Rubber. Later in the same year, a railroad average was also introduced, which became the Dow Jones Transportation Average when it was renamed in 1970. In 1929, the utilities average was also introduced to monitor the performance of the energy sector.

The original index was increased gradually over the years to its present 30 stocks. New stocks are added and old stocks dropped from the averages in an attempt to keep the indexes closely attuned to developments in the sectors they represent. Other Dow indexes were introduced over the years, but the original index remains as the best-known and most widely reported of the Dow Jones statistics.

Further reading

Prestbo, John, ed. *The Market's Measure: An Illustrated History of America Told Through the Dow Jones Industrial Average.* New York: Dow Jones & Co., 1999.

Drew, Daniel (1797–1879) *stock trader and speculator* Born in Carmel, New York, Drew became the best-known and most feared stock trader of his era. Possessing no formal education, he joined the army to serve in the War of 1812 in order to receive a $100 payment for those who enlisted. He took the money and became a cattle drover and horse trader. He developed a reputation for delivering cattle that had been fed excessive amounts of water to make them look fat. The term *watered stock* was used to describe the condition, and the term carried over to the stock market to mean stock that had been seriously diluted.

Using money supplied by Henry Astor, Drew expanded his operations to the west and became one of the first drovers to herd cattle across the Allegheny Mountains. In 1834, he entered the steamboat business and became a competitor of Cornelius VANDERBILT, with whom he would battle again in later years. In 1844, he moved to Wall Street, opening the firm of Drew, Robinson, & Co., where he began a career of stock manipulation and speculation. In 1853, he became involved with the ERIE RAILROAD. By 1857, he had become a director of the Erie and was widely known for manipulating its stock. But he was a loser in a classic confrontation with Cornelius Vanderbilt in the manipulation of shares of the Harlem Railroad in 1864.

One of the first traders to use public deception to his own advantage, Drew became famous for his notorious "handkerchief trick," whereby he "accidentally" dropped a handkerchief in a New York club with stock tips contained inside. Traders picked it up and read them, thinking they had become privy to his trading secrets when they were actually being manipulated by him.

Drew engaged in the infamous "Erie Wars" with Jay GOULD and Jim FISK against Cornelius Vanderbilt to gain control of the railroad between 1866 and 1868. Along with his two allies, he managed to swindle Vanderbilt out of several million dollars by dumping newly printed shares of the Erie on the market despite a court order. After 1870, his luck failed him after being duped by Gould and Fisk, who sold Erie stock in England in a plan to foil him; he lost more than a million dollars. As a result, he became bankrupt in 1876.

Although widely reputed to be a curmudgeon and barely literate, Drew donated money for a seminary in New Jersey, which subsequently became Drew University. He died in 1879, still remembered as one of the most feared stock traders and manipulators of his era.

Further reading
Adams, Charles F., and Henry Adams. *Chapters of Erie and other Essays.* Boston: James R. Osgood, 1871.
Browder, Clifford. *The Money Game in Old New York: Daniel Drew and His Times.* Lexington: University Press of Kentucky, 1986.
White, Brouck. *The Book of Daniel Drew.* New York: Citadel Press, 1980.

Drexel, Anthony J. (1826–1893) *banker*
Born in Philadelphia, Drexel's father was Francis M. Drexel, a prominent city banker from a well-known Catholic family. Anthony joined the family firm at age 13 as an apprentice and was made a partner in 1847. Although lacking a university education, Drexel was well versed in several languages and became one of the best-known bankers of his generation.

The Drexel firm was upstaged by Jay Cooke & Co. during the Civil War as the major distributor of TREASURY BONDS, and a rivalry developed between the two firms until the collapse of Cooke in 1871. Drexel's career was somewhat overshadowed by his partnership with John Pierpont Morgan. Drexel & Co. joined in a partnership with Morgan in 1871 at the suggestion of Junius S. Morgan, and Drexel Morgan & Co. opened for business and became the American agent for J. S. Morgan & Co. of London. In addition to doing substantial domestic investment banking business by underwriting securities issues for the U.S. Treasury and many RAILROADS, Drexel Morgan also engaged in international banking. When his older brother Joseph William Drexel died in 1888, Anthony became the sole head of the firm. After the formation of J. P. Morgan & Co. in 1895, Drexel & Co. faded into the background and for all intents and purposes became a subsidiary of the Morgan bank.

Drexel also became the guardian of his niece, Katherine Drexel (1858–1955), the daughter of his brother Francis. She became active in the Catholic Church and founded numerous institutions with her inheritance, among them the Sisters of the Blessed Sacrament. She was later canonized by the church in 2000.

Drexel was also involved in philanthropic activities, the best known being the founding of the Drexel Institute in Philadelphia in 1892, today known as Drexel University. Originally, he gave the institution $3 million. He died in Bohemia in 1893. After the 1933 separation of commercial and INVESTMENT BANKING by the Glass-Steagall Act, Drexel & Co. continued as an independent partnership until it merged several times, first to become Drexel Harriman, Ripley & Co., then Drexel Firestone, and finally DREXEL BURNHAM LAMBERT in 1973. The firm was finally dissolved after the insider trading scandals of the late 1980s.

See also MORGAN, JOHN PIERPONT; MORGAN, JUNIUS SPENCER.

Further reading
Carosso, Vincent. *Investment Banking in America: A History.* Cambridge, Mass.: Harvard University Press, 1970.
Rottenberg, Dan. *The Made Who Made Wall Street: Anthony J. Drexel and the Rise of Modern Finance.* Philadelphia: University of Pennsylvania Press, 2001.

Drexel Burnham Lambert A major securities dealer and underwriter in the 1980s, best known for introducing, underwriting, and trading high-yield, or junk, bonds. The activities of the firm centered around Michael Milken, who developed the market during the 1970s as a means of providing capital for companies with less than investment-grade credit ratings.

Drexel Burnham was the product of the merger of two smaller Wall Street securities houses. Burnham & Co. was founded by I. W. Burnham in 1935, while Drexel & Co. was older, dating back to the 19th century. Before the Glass-Steagall Act was passed in 1933, Drexel was an affiliate of J. P. Morgan & Co. but was separated from the bank after the act became law. Burnham and Drexel merged in 1971, but a continuing shortage of capital forced another merger with broker William D. Witter & Co. in 1976. Banque Brussels Lambert, a shareholder in Witter, became an owner in the merged entity, and the firm became known as Drexel Burnham Lambert.

Drexel became known for underwriting and selling high-yield, or junk, bonds in the 1970s due to the presence of Michael Milken, a young bond trader hired from business school by the original Drexel & Co. By 1980, the firm emerged as the sole leader in junk bonds on Wall Street. By the mid-1980s, the firm stood among the top five Wall Street underwriters, mainly because of its continued success. The firm also sponsored the famous Predator's Balls, lavish parties given at a Hollywood hotel to promote investment in high-yield bonds.

Drexel Burnham became active in MERGERS and acquisitions because of its junk bond expertise but also ran into regulatory problems as a result. Because of the firm's involvement in the insider trading scandal of the 1980s, Milken and several associates from outside the firm were charged with securities violations and sent to prison. Throughout its short history, Drexel Burnham was never a publicly traded corporation but one that was privately held by both shareholders and some employees. The firm settled charges against it by the Securities and Exchange Commission (SEC), but the $600-million fine imposed wiped out its capital base. The firm was forced to file for BANKRUPTCY in 1990. It reorganized several years later under a different name but remained a small Wall Street house. Its failure remains the largest failure in modern investment banking history and the only one to be caused by the direct actions of the SEC.

See also DREXEL, ANTHONY J.; INVESTMENT BANKING.

Further reading

Bruck, Connie. *The Predators' Ball: The Inside Story of Drexel Burnham and the Rise of the Junk Bond Raiders.* New York: Penguin Books, 1989.

Ehrlich, Judith Ramsey, and Barry J. Rehfeld. *The New Crowd: The Changing of the Jewish Guard on Wall Street.* New York: Harper Perennial, 1989.

Drucker, Peter (1909–2005) *economist* Peter Ferdinand Drucker was born in Vienna, Austria-Hungary, on November 19, 1909, the son of a prominent lawyer and civil servant. After receiving his secondary education in 1927, he pursued advanced studies at the Universities of Hamburg and Frankfurt, Germany. Because neither institution offered courses at night and Drucker was obliged to work by day, he completed his courses and passed his exams solely by reading texts on his own. Drucker ultimately received his doctorate in public and international law but opted to dabble in economics as an editor and financial writer. As such, he observed closely the failure of economic democracy in the Weimar Republic and the concomitant rise of political extremism. However, when Adolph Hitler became German chancellor in 1933, Drucker was offered a lucrative position within the Ministry of Information. He responded by composing a scathing pamphlet condemning Nazi excesses and fled the country for England. There he worked with an insurance firm as a securities analyst and also encountered the noted economist John Maynard KEYNES at a Cambridge University seminar. At this juncture Drucker decided to shift his expertise from economics to management. In 1937, he arrived in the United States as an economic correspondent for British financial newspapers. Two years later, he published his first book, *The End of Economic Man*, which was well received—and the first of 30 tomes to follow. Drucker decided to remain in the United States while World War II raged, and in 1943, he became a naturalized citizen.

It was as an observer at GENERAL MOTORS during the war years that Drucker made an indelible impact upon American managerial practices. His experiences there culminated in his most influential book, *The Concept of a Corporation* (1946). Here Drucker broke new ground intellectually by viewing the corporation as less of a business entity than a social one. He also posited that a new concept of management was necessary for the expanding corporate world and insisted that greater cooperation between labor and management was essential to extract maximum efficiency from the system. Most radical for its time was his notion that the assembly line was obsolete and that workers should receive greater autonomy and influence over daily routines. By virtue of challenging traditional tenets of managerial authority, his book became one of the most popular texts in business history. But Drucker nonetheless remained closely identified with the conservative school of economics, and he stridently defended profit making as the key ingredient of economic success. Moreover, he maintained that large profits were a better guarantor of full employment than the best-intended government planning. Corporations agreed with him wholeheartedly, and at one point he was on the payroll of more than 50 companies, advising them how to improve their management and business oversight.

Throughout the rest of his long career, Drucker became a much sought-after lecturer and instructor. By turns he held important economic chairs at Sarah Lawrence University, Bennington College, New York University, and the Claremont Graduate School. But Drucker always saw himself as more of a business philosopher than a practitioner, and he repeatedly declined invitations to head large corporations. In addition to business and management, he turned his eclectic interests to teaching such diverse topics as government, statistics, religion, and literature. He also became celebrated for invariably changing his teaching interests every three to four years and is further regarded as something of an authority on Japanese art. Even after his death on November 11, 2005, Drucker is still considered the most important managerial theorist of the 20th century and was a mentor to several generations of business leaders. Many of his 30 books have been translated into several languages and successfully sold around the world. He has also published long-running economic columns in numerous respected newspapers such as the *Wall Street Journal, Forbes, Inc.,* and the *Harvard Business Review.* But, most importantly, he is viewed as the single most important philosophical force behind modern management.

Further reading

Beatty, Jack. *The World according to Peter Drucker.* New York: Free Press, 1998.

Drucker, Peter. *Adventures of a Bystander.* New York: Harper & Row, 1979.

———. *The Essential Drucker.* New York: HarperCollins, 2001.

Flaherty, John E. *Peter Drucker: Shaping the Managerial Mind.* San Francisco: Jossey-Bass, 1999.

Schwartz, Michael D. "Peter Drucker's Weimar Experience: Moral Management as a Perception of the Past." *Journal of Business Ethics* (December 2002): 51–69.

Tarrant, John J. *Drucker: The Man Who Invented Corporate Society.* Boston: Cahners Books, 1976.

John C. Fredriksen

Duer, William (1747–1799) *merchant and speculator*   Born in Devonshire, England, to a prominent family with landed interests in the West Indies, Duer was educated at Eton College and commissioned as an ensign in the British army. After serving in India and visiting the family holdings in the Caribbean, he visited New York in 1768 and purchased land in northern New York. He immigrated to America permanently in 1773.

Sympathetic to the colonists' grievances against Britain, he remained in the United States and became influential in New York City. He became a member of the Continental Congress from New York and a judge and was a signer of the Articles of Confederation. He resigned from Congress in 1779 to attend to his commercial interests. He was also instrumental in establishing the BANK OF NEW YORK along with Alexander HAMILTON.

His influence increased in the 1780s, when he became secretary to the Board of the Treasury in

1786 and assistant secretary of the Treasury under Alexander Hamilton between 1789 and 1790. In 1787, he became involved in the Scioto land speculation and was later charged by the Treasury for using his government posts inappropriately. In order to finance his land speculations, he borrowed heavily from the existing New York banks and then was unable to repay. He also speculated heavily in stock of the first BANK OF THE UNITED STATES and the Bank of New York using borrowed money.

Duer's default reverberated through the New York stock market, which was conducted out-of-doors at the time. News of the BANKRUPTCY caused the market to drop precipitously. His total losses were reputed to be worth more than the total value of New York City real estate at the time. As a result, the outdoor traders banded together and signed the Buttonwood Agreement that became the first organized foundation for the NEW YORK STOCK EXCHANGE, founded two decades later.

Duer was convicted and sent to debtors' prison. The harsh sentence imposed on him reflected in part anti-British feeling in New York during the 1790s. His friend Alexander Hamilton intervened on his behalf, and he was freed for a time in 1797 but was finally returned to prison, where he died in 1799. His death also prompted bankruptcy laws to be written by Congress. He retains the distinction of being the first fallen financier after Independence to create a panic in the stock market.

Further reading

Jones, Robert F. *The King of the Alley: William Duer, Politician, Entrepreneur, & Speculator.* Philadelphia: American Philosophical Society, 1992.

Mason, Bernard. "Entrepreneurial Activity in New York During the Revolution." *Business History Review* (summer 1966): 180–212.

Duke, James Buchanan (1856–1925) *tobacco magnate, power developer, and philanthropist*

Duke was born near Durham, North Carolina, to Washington and Artelia Roney Duke. He received his basic education in local academies and attended the Eastman Business College in Poughkeepsie, New York. His primary education, however, was in the family's business: the farming, hand manufacture, and marketing of tobacco products.

In 1884, at the age of 28, Buck, as he was called, opened a branch of the family firm, W. Duke, Sons & Company, in New York City. Within five years the business was furnishing half the country's production of cigarettes. After a "tobacco war" among the five principal manufacturers, Duke emerged as president of the AMERICAN TOBACCO CO., a tribute to his organizational skills. Through foreign and domestic combinations, this trust controlled the manufacture of a majority of tobacco products. The U.S. Supreme Court dissolved the enterprise under provisions of the SHERMAN ACT in 1911.

By 1892, however, Duke had begun to diversify his interests. His older brother, Benjamin, had launched the family into textiles. As this enterprise grew, a need for economical waterpower led the Dukes into hydroelectric power generation. In 1905, they founded the Southern Power Company. Within two decades, this was supplying electricity through a system of power grids to more than 300 mills, factories, and cities and towns in the Carolinas. It is now Duke Power Company, a part of Duke Energy.

A lifelong Methodist, Duke practiced the financial stewardship encouraged by his church. The family, ardent Republicans and sympathetic to the downtrodden, gave individually and collectively to many causes. Beginning in 1892, Washington Duke had aided a small Methodist-related institution, Trinity College, and from 1887 Benjamin Duke had been a member of its board of trustees. Continuing the family's pattern of giving, James B. Duke, its most financially successful member, established the Duke Endowment in 1924. Its primary beneficiary was a university organized around Trinity College. At the urging of the college's president, William Preston Few, the school was rechartered as Duke

University in honor of the family that had long supported it.

In addition, Duke designated income from the endowment to be distributed to nonprofit hospitals and child care institutions for blacks and whites in the Carolinas; to rural Methodist churches and retired Methodist preachers in North Carolina; and to three other educational institutions: Furman University (Greenville, South Carolina), Johnson C. Smith University (Charlotte, North Carolina), and Davidson College (Davidson, North Carolina). Now one of the largest foundations in the United States, the Duke Endowment, with offices in Charlotte, North Carolina, has distributed more than $1.5 billion to its beneficiaries.

After a brief first marriage that ended in divorce, James B. Duke married a widow from Atlanta, Nanaline Holt Inman, in 1907. One daughter, Doris, was born to the couple. James B. Duke died in New York City on October 10, 1925. He is interred with his father and brother Ben in the chapel on the campus of Duke University.

See also UTILITIES.

Further reading

Durden, Robert F. *The Dukes of Durham, 1865–1929.* Durham, N.C.: Duke University Press, 1987.
———. *Electrifying the Piedmont Carolinas: The Duke Power Company, 1904–1997.* Durham, N.C.: Duke University Press, 2001.
———. *Bold Entrepreneur: A Life of James B. Duke.* Durham, N.C.: Carolina Academic Press, 2003.

Thomas F. Harkins

DuPont de Nemours & Co., E. I.   Founded by Eleuthère Irénée du Pont de Nemours (1771–1834) in 1802, the company began as a manufacturer of gunpowder. Born into an aristocratic French family, du Pont immigrated to the United States in 1800 with the intention of establishing a utopian community in Virginia. The venture failed, and du Pont took up the manufacturing of gunpowder instead, having learned chemistry from the French chemist Antoine LAVOISIER. The concept proved successful in the United States because American facilities for making gunpowder were poor.

He established a powder manufacturing facility in Delaware. Hearing of his reputation, Thomas Jefferson commissioned him to produce gunpowder. While demand for du Pont's product increased rapidly, he was in financial difficulties until the War of 1812. When he died, the company had assets of around $320,000, and his factories were producing more than a million pounds of powder per year. During his lifetime, du Pont constantly heard criticisms about him being a merchant of death, especially since he originally had intended to start a model community.

During the Civil War, the company built a plant in New Jersey to manufacture dynamite, and for the remainder of the 19th century, the company continued to manufacture powders. In 1902, at the beginning of the 20th century, the DuPont Company was purchased by three great-grandsons of the founder—Thomas Coleman DuPont, Alfred Irénée DuPont and Pierre S. DuPont—and the company was given a new direction. Alfred DuPont (1864–1935) in particular was credited with saving the company from falling into outside hands in 1902. Known as an inventor and gunpowder specialist, he helped incorporate the company. The three renamed the company after the founder and established several research centers in order to develop new and improved products. The company also diversified into new businesses, including nonexplosives such as lacquer.

New ownership also provided the opportunity for the DuPonts to introduce new management techniques and a new structure for the company. They discarded the old company organizational structure and integrated it vertically in order to avoid waste and duplication. Following the new structure, the company began to manufacture many of its own supplies rather than purchase from outside vendors. Pierre DuPont also introduced many changes in accounting and financial planning that became the standard for years to come. The company emphasized its cost of capital when calculating returns on investment and introduced a financial ratio, now called the DuPont ratio, that measured return on investment differently from standard practice at the time. By World War I, it was producing one-half the dynamite needs of the United States.

Toward the end of the war, the company began investing in the chemical and dye industry and in 1923 acquired the rights to manufacture cellophane. Pierre DuPont (1870–1954) left the company in 1920 to help rescue the GENERAL MOTORS CORP. from the prospect of BANKRUPTCY. Previously, the company had been persuaded by John RASKOB, a former DuPont treasurer, to invest $25 million in the auto manufacturer, and Pierre was persuaded to join the company to resuscitate its fortunes after the company had been wrestled from William C. Durant, its founder. In the 1920s and 1930s, the company continued its expansion into other chemicals, including resins and synthetic rubber. In 1935, two of its researchers developed nylon, described originally as a synthetic silk. During World War II, the company built and operated two plants that were part of the highly secret Manhattan Project that developed the first atomic bomb.

During the 1950s and 1960s, DuPont continued to develop a host of synthetic fibers and materials. In 1957, the company was found to be in violation of the CLAYTON ACT through its investment in GM, and it divested its holdings by 1961. In 1981, it acquired Conoco, an oil company, in what was the largest acquisition at the time. The acquisition almost doubled the size of the company and its revenues. Conoco was sold in 1999. DuPont also made investments in the biotechnology and pharmaceutical industries and became one of the leading producers of soy protein additives that were sold to other companies.

Further reading

Chandler, Alfred D. *Pierre S. DuPont and the Making of the Modern Corporation*. New York: Harper & Row, 1971.
Dutton, William S. *DuPont–One Hundred and Forty Years*. New York: Charles Scribner's Sons, 1942.
James, Marquis. *Alfred I. DuPont: The Family Rebel*. Indianapolis: Bobbs-Merrill, 1941.
Kinnane, Adrian. *DuPont: From the Banks of the Brandywine to Miracles of Science*. Baltimore: Johns Hopkins University Press, 2002.
Taylor, Graham D., and Patricia E. Sudnik. *Du Pont and the International Chemical Industry*. Boston: Twayne, 1984.

Durant, William Crapo (1861–1947) *automobile executive and investor* Born in Flint, Michigan, in 1861, Durant left high school before graduating to become a traveling cigar salesman. After other jobs selling, he purchased a carriage manufacturer after being impressed with the smooth ride of its carriages, which were supported by coil spring suspension. At age 25, Durant and a partner, Josiah Dallas Dort, purchased the Coldwater Road Cart Co., a manufacturer of carriages, with $1,500 borrowed from a bank. Within several years, the company was the nation's largest of its type, producing more than 150,000 units per year, and was the largest employer in Flint.

After making his first million manufacturing carriages and wagons, he entered the automobile business in 1904 when he became chief executive and treasurer of the Buick Motor Company at the behest of James Whiting, the company's president. Buick soon acquired the Cadillac Motor Company, and the two companies produced highly regarded touring cars. Within several years, Durant proposed that the four leading auto manufacturers of the time combine to form a giant company to be called the International Motor Car Co. But two of the four, Ford and REO, demurred, and Durant founded GENERAL MOTORS (GM) instead. In 1908, GM was incorporated and sold stock initially worth $12 million. Within two years, it acquired Oldsmobile and Pontiac. But after an internal dispute, Durant lost control of the company in 1910 to a bankers' group, which provided financing. He remained as a vice president of GM.

Before World War I, Durant opened several new companies, including the Chevrolet Motor Co. and the Republic Motor Co. He regained control of GM after acquiring a majority of its stock in the market but lost it again in 1920, after falling out with the company's primary bankers at J. P. Morgan. In 1921, he founded Durant Motors and became a major speculator in the stock market. His investment activities overshadowed his car company, and he became heavily leveraged by borrowing money on margin to buy stocks. He became known as one of the most celebrated investors in the stock market prior to 1929. He tried to convince President Herbert Hoover about the dangers of a crash prior to October 1929, blaming the FEDERAL RESERVE for the market's problems. When the 1929 crash occurred, he lost most of his fortune.

Later in his life, Durant left the auto industry and investing and operated several bowling alleys near his home in Flint, Michigan. He never again had the capital for successful business ventures. He died in obscurity in 1947. His major legacy remains the initial organization of General Motors, which overtook Ford as the

William C. Durant (LIBRARY OF CONGRESS)

major auto producer in the United States in the mid-1920s.

See also AUTOMOTIVE INDUSTRY.

Further reading

Madsen, Axel. *The Deal Maker: How William C. Durant Made General Motors.* New York: John Wiley, 1999.

Seltzer, Lawrence H. *A Financial History of the American Automobile Industry.* Boston: Houghton Mifflin, 1928.

Weisberger, Bernard A. *The Dream Maker: William C. Durant, Founder of General Motors.* Boston: Little, Brown, 1979.

E

Eastern Airlines The company, originally Pitcairn Aviation, began in the early 1920s when civil aviation consisted mainly of barnstorming and stunt flying. Founded by Harold Pitcairn, who shocked his wealthy family by announcing his intention of making a business out of airplanes, the young company entered the marketplace as a contract mail carrier.

In a surprise move, Pitcairn sold the airline in 1930 to Clement Keys, who moved the airline's headquarters to Brooklyn, New York, and changed its name to Eastern Air Transport. As a promotional gimmick, 22 women were selected as cabin attendants—among them Mildred Aldrin, whose nephew Buzz found fame as an astronaut.

The company remained relatively healthy throughout the depression years until Keys took an extended trip to Europe. In his absence, his business associates diverted funds into the still-plunging stock market, leaving Keys to face financial ruin. Keys saved the airline through negotiation, in exchange for his resignation. On January 1, 1935, a new general manager was named to (then called) Eastern Air Lines whose name would forever be associated with the company. His name was Edward Vernon Rickenbacker.

Rickenbacker, a World War I flying ace, ruled the company with an iron fist for a quarter of a century and left a glittering record of 26 consecutive years of profit to his successors. When Rickenbacker turned over the leadership of Eastern to Malcolm MacIntyre in 1959, the airline served 128 cities in 27 states, encompassing almost three-fourths of the American population. MacIntyre was an accomplished lawyer but had virtually no experience in the rough-and-tumble game of running a major airline. When he left office in 1963, Eastern was headed for financial oblivion. MacIntyre will be remembered for two bright spots in the company's history—the introduction of the Boeing 727 and the development of the Shuttle.

The former became a workhorse of the industry, and the latter involved a brilliant customer relations strategy. Shuttle flights between New York, Washington, and Boston required no reservations and guaranteed a seat to anyone who showed up. The Shuttle immediately became a way of life for people moving along the heavily traveled Washington–New York–Boston corridor.

In 1975, Eastern's fortunes were entrusted to a man who was called the real inheritor of Captain

Eddie's leadership mantle—former astronaut Colonel Frank Borman. As president and CEO, Borman brought a familiar military ethic back to Eastern. He negotiated wage concessions from the employees in an attempt to save the company from disaster, but failed to compensate for the exorbitant cost of the new airplanes he had ordered or the costly effects of DEREGULATION. Borman and Eastern's machinist unions clashed furiously and frequently.

Industry analysts blamed Eastern's troubles partly on poor management and partly on the company's uncooperative labor unions, but the root of Eastern's troubles lay in a poor route structure and huge debt. As a result of these seemingly incurable financial distresses, Eastern succumbed to a takeover bid by Frank Lorenzo and his Texas Air empire. The conflict over Texas Air's acquisition extended to several employee groups and proved to be the beginning of the end for Eastern.

A period of severe employee unrest followed. In March 1989, a strike against the airline was called by the machinists and supported by the flight attendants and the pilots. A week later, Eastern filed for BANKRUPTCY, and its management fought to retain control over Eastern in the face of furious resistance from labor and rapidly diminishing confidence among its investors. In April 1990, bankruptcy court judge Burton Lifland ruled that Frank Lorenzo, the brash corporate raider who had acquired Eastern, was unfit to run the company and appointed a trustee for the airline. A last-ditch effort for order failed, and on January 18, 1991, the company folded its wings for good.

See also AIRLINE INDUSTRY; PAN AMERICAN AIRWAYS.

Further reading
Bernstein, Aaron. *Grounded: Frank Lorenzo and the Destruction of Eastern Airlines.* New York: Simon & Schuster, 1990.
Saunders, Martha Dunagin. *Eastern's Armageddon: Labor Conflict and the Destruction of Eastern Airlines.* New York: Greenwood Press, 1992.
Serling, Robert J. *From the Captain to the Colonel: An Informal History of Eastern Airlines.* New York: Doubleday, 1980.

Martha Dunagin Saunders

Eastman, George (1854–1932) *businessman*
Born in Waterville, New York, Eastman moved to Rochester with his family as a young boy. The death of his father forced him to leave school at age 14 and find work as a messenger. While working in that capacity, he studied accounting in the evenings and gradually worked his way up to the position of clerk in a Rochester bank. But it was not until his first planned vacation that he became interested in photography.

He bought his first camera for a vacation that was never to take place. The large, cumbersome camera he purchased intrigued him, however, and he decided to improve upon the design of the photographic plates that were until that time covered with gelatin. By 1880, he had devised a process for dry plates and opened up shop in Rochester to manufacture them for sale to other camera manufacturers, initially operating as a partnership called the Eastman Dry Plate Co. After manufacturing plates for several years, he hit upon the idea of producing film on a roll, which in turn would help make cameras smaller. He began producing film in 1885. Three years later, he produced the first Kodak camera, which was unique for being able to be operated with the click of a simple button. The trademark name was registered and quickly became synonymous with photography itself.

The original camera had film installed capable of taking 100 pictures. The price was $25. When the customer used the entire roll of film, it was returned to the factory, where the film was developed and the camera reloaded before being returned to its owner. Previous partnerships gave way to the Eastman Co. in 1889 and finally the Eastman Kodak Co. in 1892. Eastman served as chairman of the company's board from 1925 to 1932.

From the beginning, Eastman emphasized MASS PRODUCTION combined with low costs so that he could reach as wide a market as possible. He was also much more generous to his employees than many other industrialists of the period. As early as 1899, he began distributing a portion of his own profit to his employees. He later established a program called the "wage dividend" that paid each employee a percentage equivalent to the common stock dividends above his or her salary. After World War I, he gave one-third of his stock holdings to his employees. The gift was worth about $110 million.

Eastman Kodak Company became the largest American producer of cameras and film until challenged by the Polaroid Co., founded by Edwin LAND, and later by imports, mostly from Japan. Eastman remained a generous philanthropist throughout his life. He was a major benefactor to the University of Rochester, M.I.T., Hampton Institute, and Tuskegee Institute. The University of Rochester was the main beneficiary, especially its Eastman School of Music. He died in 1932.

Further reading

Brayer, Elizabeth. *George Eastman: A Biography.* Baltimore: Johns Hopkins University Press, 1996.

Swasy, Alecia. *Changing Focus: Kodak and the Battle to Save a Great American Company.* New York: Random House, 1997.

Tedlow, Richard S. *Giants of Enterprise: Seven Business Innovators and the Empires They Built.* New York: HarperBusiness, 2001.

Eaton,   Cyrus (1883–1979) *financier and industrialist*   Born in Nova Scotia, Eaton was a member of an established New England family that moved to Canada in 1760. He graduated from Amherst Academy in Ontario and decided to become a Baptist minister. After graduation, he visited an uncle who was a Baptist minister in Cleveland, where he was introduced to John D. Rockefeller, a member of his uncle's congrega-

tion. After working at a summer job for Rockefeller, he was persuaded to attend McMaster University and study business. He graduated in 1905 and went to work for Rockefeller after a brief series of odd jobs.

Eaton began working for Rockefeller in Manitoba in 1907. He was put in charge of acquiring franchises for power plants in Canada, although the Panic of 1907 intervened, and Rockefeller was unwilling to pursue the enterprise. Eaton then assumed part of the project himself, borrowed money, and built a power plant in Manitoba. He soon followed this success by building other plants, and he eventually established the Continental Gas and Electric Company with holdings in the United States and Canada.

In 1913, he returned to Cleveland and established a partnership in the investment banking firm Otis & Company. Over the next 10 years, Eaton became one of the major investors in the UTILITIES industry, which was expanding rapidly in the 1920s. He merged Continental Gas and Electric with the Kansas City Power and Light Co. and the Columbia Power and Light Co. to form United Light and Power, a giant utility that served more than 5 million people in a dozen midwestern states.

During the late 1920s, Eaton was best remembered for engaging in a takeover battle with Samuel INSULL for Insull's holdings in the Commonwealth Edison Company. In order to fend off Eaton's unwanted advances, Insull was forced to seek the help of New York bankers, who forced his downfall and the notable bankruptcy filing that followed in the early 1930s. He also entered the STEEL INDUSTRY in the 1920s and merged several smaller companies into the Republic Steel Corporation, destined to become one of the country's largest producers. The same year that he created Republic, he also took control of the Goodyear Tire and Rubber Company.

The stock market crash of 1929 reputedly cost Eaton more than $100 million in losses. Three years later, he became associated with Harold Stuart of the Chicago investment banking firm Halsey Stuart & Co. Halsey Stuart was the former financier of much of Insull's utilities empire. One of the firm's major contributions to finance during this period was the introduction of competitive bids for underwriting mandates for new securities issues, especially in the railroad industry, which was later made standard by the Securities and Exchange Commission.

In his later years, Eaton remained active in industry by becoming the chairman of the Chesapeake & Ohio Railroad and the Kaiser-Frazer Automobile Co. after World War II. He also developed a close relationship with the Soviet Union and organized a series of meetings at his home in Nova Scotia between American and Soviet scientists designed to ease world tensions. These meetings became known as the Pugwash Conferences. He also helped develop the St. Lawrence Seaway.

Further reading

Allen, Frederick Lewis. *The Lords of Creation.* New York: Harper & Brothers, 1935.
Gleisser, Marcus. *The World of Cyrus Eaton.* New York: A. S. Barnes, 1965.

Eccles, Marriner S. (1890–1977) *businessman and banker*

Born in Logan, Utah, Eccles was the oldest of nine children. After attending Brigham Young College, he became familiar with investments and established an investment company that acquired many of his father's successful business enterprises. In 1924, he and his brother joined with a prominent banking family in Utah to form the Eccles-Browning Affiliated Banks, which rapidly began to expand by acquiring banks in Utah and Wyoming. In 1928, he and several partners organized the First Security Corporation, a HOLDING COMPANY that managed the acquired banks. The company was one of the first multibank holding companies in the United States.

Eccles's banks survived the Great Depression without serious disruption, and he became the most prominent banker in the West during the 1930s. A Republican until the early 1930s, he shared many of the Roosevelt administration's goals and became an avid supporter of the Democrats. He helped the administration draft the Emergency Banking Act of 1933, the Federal Housing Act of 1934, and the BANKING ACT OF 1933 (Glass-Steagall Act). As a result of his public service, Eccles was named chairman of the Federal Reserve System in 1934 and assumed the position in 1935 after being confirmed.

He was also the principal force behind the Banking Act of 1935, which reorganized the Federal Reserve System. Since its inception, the central bank had been criticized in many quarters as being elitist, but it lacked power in many crucial areas that would allow it to maintain control of the creation of money and credit. The central bank was restructured by the 1935 act and given specific powers that were lacking during the 1920s and were widely blamed for contributing to the 1929 crash. The Fed was now allowed to perform system repurchase agreements. Prior to the law, the branches could perform open market operations, undoing board policy as the New York Federal Reserve Bank had done in 1929. The Fed's membership also was redesigned so that members of the board would be full-time employees.

After World War II, Eccles helped work on the agreements drawn up at Bretton Woods, New Hampshire, that created the World Bank and International Monetary Fund. In 1948, President Truman did not reappoint him chairman of the Fed, but he remained as vice chairman until 1951, when he resigned. He died in Salt Lake City in 1977.

Eccles is widely remembered as a successful banker with wide practical experience, which eventually contributed to the most significant reforms of the FEDERAL RESERVE since it was founded. The Federal Reserve building in Washington, D.C., is named in his honor.

Further reading

Eccles, Marriner S. *Beckoning Frontiers: Public and Personal Recollections.* New York: Knopf, 1951.

Hyman, Sidney. *Marriner S. Eccles: Private Entrepreneur and Public Servant.* Palo Alto, Calif.: Stanford University School of Business, 1976.

Edison, Thomas A. (1847–1931) *inventor*

Born in Milan, Ohio, to Samuel and Nancy Elliott Edison, Edison began experimenting while still a child. Not academically talented as a child, his mother often instructed him at home, and he developed an early interest in chemistry. He sold sundries on trains to earn money and suffered an accident that caused lifetime deafness. After learning how to telegraph messages from a railway agent, he took a job as a telegraph agent in Canada before returning to the United States. After working at a series of jobs as a telegraph operator, he began inventing and patented a stock TICKER TAPE machine. While working in New York City, he made improvements for a stock ticker while working for the Gold Indicator Company. The patents he registered were sold to his employer for $40,000, and he promptly took the proceeds and opened a workshop in Newark, New Jersey.

While in Newark, Edison improved the stock ticker and also made substantial improvements for the TYPEWRITER. Both developments helped increase business efficiency once the devices were put into use. Shortly thereafter, he moved his headquarters to Menlo Park, New Jersey, where he made improvements on the telephone. His most important invention to date was the phonograph, which he invented as a way to record telegraph messages, but it was the electric incandescent bulb that earned him the nickname "The Wizard of Menlo Park." In 1879, he succeeded in placing a filament in a bulb that burned for many hours before going out. He was also one of the first developers of the electric chair, bringing him into direct competition with George WESTINGHOUSE. Edison's version of the electrocution device used direct current (DC), while Westinghouse's used alternating current (AC) and eventually became the standard model used.

Thomas Edison and his original dynamo, Orange, New Jersey, 1906 (LIBRARY OF CONGRESS)

In 1887, Edison moved his laboratories to West Orange, New Jersey, and continued to invent while perfecting his older inventions. He also spent considerable time marketing his ideas. The electric lightbulb was only a part of the process of electric generation, and Edison spent considerable time organizing power stations to support his invention. The first power station in New York City was at Pearl Street, near Wall Street, and J. P. Morgan was the first user of the power that it generated. Morgan later bought Edison's operation, freeing the inventor from business matters, and used it as the basis for the GENERAL ELECTRIC CO. Edison's assistant at the time was Samuel INSULL, who would later build a massive UTILITIES empire in Chicago.

Using research first developed by George EASTMAN, Edison also invented the motion picture camera. He connected the phonograph and the camera in order to produce talking pictures but was less interested in this development than others. During his lifetime, he also was responsible for developing the dictaphone, allowing secretaries to transcribe messages from a machine that recorded voices, and a duplicating machine, among many other inventions.

Edison's original company, the Edison General Electric Company, was later consolidated by J. P. Morgan with the Thompson-Houston Company to become the General Electric Company. During World War I, Edison was president of the Naval Consulting Board and conducted research on torpedoes and submarine periscopes. As a result of his research, he was awarded the Distinguished Service Medal. He died in West Orange in 1931, the most prolific and celebrated inventor of modern times.

See also MORGAN, JOHN PIERPONT.

Further reading

Baldwin, Neil. *Edison: Inventing the Century.* New York: Hyperion, 1995.

Israel, Paul. *Edison: A Life of Invention.* New York: John Wiley & Sons, 1998.

Jonnes, Jill. *Empires of Light: Edison, Tesla, Westinghouse, and the Race to Electrify the World.* New York: Random House, 2003.

Enron Corporation   An energy company created in 1985 with the merger of the Houston Natural Gas Co. and InterNorth Corp. of Omaha, integrating several pipeline companies to create the first nationwide natural gas pipeline system. A year later, Kenneth Lay became the chief executive officer, and the company officially chose Enron as its name.

In 1987, the company began developing risk reduction techniques to protect itself against the fluctuating prices of gas and oil. It also began offering customers the ability to buy long-term gas contracts at fixed prices and began diversifying itself internationally, especially in Britain and South America. In 1994, it entered the electricity trading market after the DEREGULATION caused by the Energy Policy Act of 1992. As a direct result, throughout the 1990s the company continued to acquire UTILITIES companies, including the Dabhol power plant in India and Wessex Water in Britain. It also expanded into the domestic utilities business by purchasing the Portland General Electric Corp. in 1997 in a much-contested acquisition pitting the company against Oregon's utilities board.

Jeffrey Skilling joined the company in 1989 and was elected president and chief operating officer in 1996. The company continued to make acquisitions during the later 1990s as a deliberate strategy of growing through merger. In 1999, the company initiated a broadband services group and began trading energy through an on-line Web site, which quickly became the largest e-business site in the world. By 2000, annual revenues had reached $100 billion, much of it provided by energy trading. Within a year, the company was reported to be the sixth-largest energy company in the world and ranked in the top 10 largest U.S. companies measured by assets.

In the fall of 2001, fortunes began to change at Enron when it announced more than $1 billion in charges for the third quarter and the Securities and Exchange Commission began an inquiry into its affairs, including special investment partnerships Enron had created over the preceding years. Then it announced that it would have to restate its earnings for the previous four years. It was subsequently discovered that the company had engaged in massive fraud regarding its earnings. Its stock price plummeted in the market. Its bankruptcy filing following these discoveries was the largest in U.S. history at the time and prompted the SARBANES-OXLEY ACT, passed by Congress to monitor the activities of accountants and directors of public companies. The company's accountant, Arthur Andersen & Co., was also sued by the Justice Department and was subsequently disbanded for its role in helping Enron shred documents deemed vital for the investigation ordered by the Securities and Exchange Commission.

Further reading

Fox, Loren. *Enron: The Rise and Fall.* New York: John Wiley & Sons, 2002.

Swartz, Mimi, and Sherron Watkins. *Power Failure: The Inside Story of the Collapse of Enron.* New York: Doubleday, 2003.

Erie Canal The first major inland waterway built in the United States. Canals became the first commonly used method of transporting goods in America, especially from areas that were located between two bodies of water. They quickly replaced the TURNPIKES that had been built decades before but proved expensive to build and maintain. The Erie crossed New York State from Buffalo to the Hudson River, covering 363 miles. It was completed in 1825 at a cost of $7.1 million and completely funded by New York. Some other smaller canals were funded by private investors, such as the Morris Canal in New Jersey. Originally, the Erie Canal charged tolls of about a cent and a half per mile, but tolls finally were abandoned in 1882.

The canal opened New York State to commerce from the Hudson River to Lake Erie and helped develop it into a major commercial and financial center. This was just as vital to the area's commerce as the St. Lawrence Seaway would be in the 20th century. Although the idea had circulated for years in New York, DeWitt Clinton (1769–1828) was responsible for planning and developing the canal. Originally, he and Gouverneur Morris petitioned Washington for help in building the canal but were denied. Then he petitioned New York, which was much more amenable to the proposal. Clinton was appointed the head of a canal commission. The canal received substantially more support when Clinton was elected governor in 1817, and ground was finally broken for construction. The canal was completed eight years later, and Clinton was aboard the first boat to navigate it, taking nine days to make the journey. The opening of the canal was a national event, and news of its opening traveled quickly throughout the country. The stocks of canals also became popular investments on the stock exchanges.

Canals were quickly overtaken by RAILROADS before the Civil War as a means of transportation but nevertheless remained popular throughout most of the 19th century, remaining as a symbol of economic growth and bringing goods to market as quickly as possible. The Erie was enlarged several times in order to make it more accommodating for increased trade and larger barges. New York finally incorporated the Erie into the New York State Barge Canal System in 1918, merging it with several other smaller canals connecting many of the lakes in the interior of the state.

In addition to building the canal and serving as governor (1817–22 and 1825–28), Clinton was also a state assemblyman, state senator, and mayor of New York City (1803–15). While mayor, he established the New York City school system. The Erie Canal remains his most noteworthy achievement.

Further reading

Cornog, Evan. *The Birth of Empire: DeWitt Clinton and the American Experience, 1769–1828.* New York: Oxford University Press, 1998.

Shaw, Ronald E. *Erie Water West.* Lexington: University Press of Kentucky, 1966.

Sheriff, Carol. *The Artificial River: The Erie Canal and the Paradox of Progress, 1817–1862.* New York: Hill & Wang, 1996.

Erie Railroad Company In 1851, the first unit of the later Erie Railway System opened under the corporate banner of the New-York & Erie Railway Company. At the time, this 447-mile, broad-gauge (six feet) line between the "ocean and the lake" was touted as the "technological marvel of the age." Specifically, the Erie built across the rugged "Southern Tier" of New York counties from the village of Piermont, located on the Hudson River about 25 miles north of New York City, to Dunkirk, a small community on Lake

Erie southwest of Buffalo. While likely a routing mistake, the company subsequently strengthened its position with entry to the Port of New York at Jersey City, New Jersey, and also at Buffalo. Because of bad management and other factors, the "first" Erie fell into BANKRUPTCY in 1859. The reorganized company, the Erie Railway, never became the profitable property that its leaders had expected, and this led to a battle for control among speculator Daniel DREW, "Commodore" Cornelius VANDERBILT of the New York Central & Hudson River Railroad, and the stock traders "Jim" FISK and Jay GOULD. The so-called Great Erie War, which erupted in 1867, created additional financial problems, but when the victorious Gould took control, he made it a much better property. "[Before Gould] its iron was worn and its roadbed in bad order," reported the *Railroad Gazette* in 1871. "There is now no better track in America. Then it was scarcely safe to run twenty miles an hour; now the road is as safe at forty-five miles as human precaution can make it."

Unfortunately for both the Erie and Gould, the "scarlet woman of Wall Street" image forever haunted them. In the early 1870s the talented Gould left the Erie, and the road limped along under ineffectual leadership until entering its second bankruptcy. The widespread depression triggered by the Panic of 1873 caused the property to experience serious financial woes. By the end of the decade a better day had dawned for the Erie, reorganized in 1878 as the New York, Lake Erie & Western Railroad. Modernization of rail and rolling stock, standardization of gauge at four feet 8.5 inches, and creation of an expanded albeit patchwork system that featured a nearly 1,000-mile mainline between Jersey City and Chicago, Illinois, encouraged investors, employees, and customers. But hard times returned in the wake of the catastrophic Panic of 1893, and once again the Erie stumbled. A third bankruptcy followed.

Then in 1895 a "new" Erie emerged. The New York, Lake Erie & Western moniker gave way to simply the Erie Railroad. Even though the road experienced a relatively rapid reorganization, the reconcentrated firm lacked a financial structure that would have truly enhanced its chances of avoiding future difficulties. By the early 20th century the Erie had become a "Morgan property," controlled by the giant J. P. Morgan & Company. Generally, this relationship with the "House of Morgan" worked to the advantage of the Erie. Its debt sold well, making possible a substantial upgrading of its physical plant. Perhaps the capstone of this rehabilitation work was an impressive line relocation in southern New York. And the Erie acquired modern steam locomotive and freight and passenger equipment. The old vaudevillian wheeze, "I want to go to Chicago the worst way. . . . Take the Erie!" seemed less apropos than ever. The Morgan connection brought to the presidency a "manly man," Frederick Underwood, who did yeoman service for the company during much of his 26-year tenure. "He sparked growth and confidence in the Erie," observed a latter-day official.

But in the 1920s the Erie underwent a major change of ownership and management. Beginning in 1923 the emerging rail titans from Cleveland, Ohio, O. P. Van Sweringen and M. J. Van Sweringen, two reserved bachelor brothers who already controlled the Nickel Plate Road, began buying large blocs of Erie stock. The "Vans" particularly liked the Erie's low-grade, double-tracked speedway between Ohio and Chicago. As they "collected" other RAILROADS through clever stock arrangements, the brothers attempted to receive regulatory approval to unite their properties into a great system. Twice, however, the INTERSTATE COMMERCE COMMISSION refused to bring the Erie under control of their Chesapeake & Ohio Railroad. The Great Depression of the 1930s sent the Vans' empire into disarray, resulting in still another receivership for the Erie.

Yet at the end of 1941 the railroad emerged from court protection and prospered from heavy wartime traffic. Reduced interest payments and robust wartime earnings prompted the Erie Railroad (its name after the reorganization remained the same) to declare a modest dividend in 1942,

This cartoon shows Cornelius Vanderbilt and James Fisk in a race for control of the Erie Railroad, 1870. (LIBRARY OF CONGRESS)

the first in 69 years and a proud moment for management. The press release, orchestrated by its image-conscious president (1941–49) Robert Woodruff, said in part: ". . . Wall Street tradition was shattered and Brokers were dazedly groping for reliable replacements for the immemorial dictums—When Erie Common pays a dividend, there'll be icicles in hell—and three things are certain—Death, Taxes, and no dividends for Erie Common." Paying dividends did not mean that the Erie was splurging; it was "a penny-pinching property." Early on the company correctly recognized that substantial savings could be derived from dieselization. Even before the war ended, powerful General Motors road units pulled long trains over the hilly main line between Marion, Ohio, and Meadville, Pennsylvania.

Yet savings derived from this replacement technology could not "save" the Erie. By the late 1950s a variety of factors, including increased highway competition, steep property taxation, high labor costs caused by union "featherbedding," and unprofitable commuter trains in the metropolitan New York City area prompted the road to seek a merger partner. After numerous studies and negotiations, the Erie found a mate, the faltering "Road of Anthracite," the 940-mile Delaware, Lackawanna & Western Railroad. On October 17, 1960, the new couple met the corporate world as the 3,188-mile Erie-Lackawanna Railroad (EL). But by the early 1970s the EL had become the "Erie-Lack-of-money," and failed. In 1976, portions of the property entered the quasi-public Consolidation Railroad

Corporation (Conrail), and by the early 1990s, the remaining assets were liquidated.

Further reading

Gordon, John Steele. *Scarlet Woman of Wall Street: Jay Gould, Jim Fisk, Cornelius Vanderbilt, the Erie Railway Wars and the Birth of Wall Street.* New York: Grove/Atlantic, 1988.

Grant, H. Roger. *Erie Lackawanna: Death of an American Railroad, 1938–1992.* Stanford, Calif.: Stanford University Press, 1994.

Hungerford, Edward. *Men of Erie.* New York: Random House, 1946.

H. Roger Grant

euro   A basket or composite currency developed by the European Economic Community (EEC) in the 1970s and 1980s as the community's accounting currency. The currency then became used in commercial transactions, although it did not exist in note or currency form. It was used by members of the community to offset the often volatile effects of the U.S. dollar, the world's major reserve currency. As the EEC became larger, the need for currency stability against the dollar and for a common transaction currency prompted the development of the contemporary euro.

The common currency of the members of the European Union was created on January 1, 1999, not only to provide the European Union with a common currency, but also to provide some insulation against movements in the U.S. dollar, which had caused distortions in the past against the individual currencies of its members. It included Austria, Belgium, Finland, France, Germany, Ireland, Italy, Luxembourg, the Netherlands, Portugal, and Spain. Greece joined in 2001, while the United Kingdom and Sweden have kept open their option to join. In a fall 2000 referendum, Denmark decided not to join.

Since 1999, the exchange rates of the participating countries are fixed. Capital market transactions (including the bond and equity markets, the foreign exchange markets, and the interbank market) were run exclusively in euro, while retail transactions with notes and coins were conducted in national currencies. In the first two months of 2002, national currencies disappeared completely, replaced by euro notes and coins.

With the introduction of the euro, the national central banks became part of the European System of Central Banks (ESCB). The European System of Central Banks comprises a European Central Bank (ECB) located in Frankfurt (Germany) and the national central banks of each country participating in the euro. The governing council of the ESCB formulates the monetary policy. It is made up of the governors of each central bank participating in the euro and of the members of the executive board of the European Central Bank. The executive board implements the monetary policy, giving the necessary instructions to the national central banks.

The creation of the euro cannot be separated from the Single Market Program, another part of the February 1992 Maastricht Treaty on the European Union. The 1992 program provides for the free flow of goods, capital, and persons. Resistance to the creation of the single market was reduced by the single currency as it prevents "beggar-thy-neighbor" type of competitive devaluations. The European Monetary Union (EMU) is therefore the cement of the single market, which by integrating previously fragmented markets allows firms to realize gains in productivity and competitiveness.

Four major benefits of a single currency were identified: reduction in transaction costs (estimated at 0.4 percent of gross domestic product), reduction in foreign exchange risk, increased competition in a more transparent market, and emergence of an international currency competing with the U.S. dollar. A potential cost of the EMU mentioned by several economists, is the sacrifice of national monetary autonomy and the possibility of controlling interest rates or adjusting exchange rates to restore competitiveness.

In its first year of existence, the replacement of national currencies by the euro had a significant impact on financial institutions. Firms or governments of a particular country were accustomed to turn to domestic banks to issue bonds or shares since, being denominated in local currency, these securities would be distributed and sold primarily to local investors. This is the well-known home bias according to which investors have a preference for securities denominated in their own currency. Moreover, issuers had difficulty in raising very large amounts as domestic financial markets were fragmented. With the euro in place, the dynamics of underwriting and placement changed completely. As a consequence, domestic banks lost one source of competitive advantage: a captive home investor base. Moreover, the liquidity of the market driven by a larger pool of investors increased very rapidly. Euro-denominated bonds amounted to euro 812 billion in 1999, exceeding by 49 percent the amount of U.S. dollar–denominated international bonds. Very large issues exceeding euro 5 billion are frequently observed. The consolidation of the banking industry followed rapidly.

The creation of the euro has raised concerns about the functioning of the international monetary system with three major currencies—the euro, the dollar, and the yen. There has been a fear that the absence of a political will to anchor the exchange rates would lead to excessive volatility. In the early years of the euro, economic growth differential in favor of the United States has induced a large appreciation of the U.S. dollar. However, the new currency served a serious integrative function by eliminating the need for businesses to constantly turn to the FOREIGN EXCHANGE MARKET, using the euro as a common currency instead.

See also BRETTON WOODS SYSTEM.

Further reading
Dermine, Jean, and Pierre Hillion, eds. *European Capital Markets with a Single Currency*. London: Oxford University Press, 1999.
Duff, Andrew, ed. *Understanding the Euro*. London: Kogan Page, 1998.

Jean Dermine

Export-Import Bank of the United States

Commonly known as the Eximbank, the Export-Import Bank was created in 1934 by the Roosevelt administration to promote trade with the United States. Specifically, the bank is designed to promote exports by offering favorable financial terms to importers of American goods. It is managed by a five-person board of directors, which is appointed by the president and confirmed by the Senate.

The Eximbank was created during the Great Depression in order to stimulate trade through exports. After the passage of the Hawley-Smoot tariff in 1930, world economic conditions worsened, and the creation of the bank was seen as a way of improving trade and returning the international economy to some order while promoting American exports at the same time. The bank normally guarantees financing to a buyer of American products by offering to guarantee the transaction to the American exporters' bank. These guarantees are known as export credits and form a significant part of American trade. All developed countries have such export guarantee operations falling under a variety of names. Usually, the terms and conditions of the credits are subject to international convention, specifying the length of loans and amounts extended.

The activities of the Eximbank are also combined with other forms of export guarantees in order to generate export activity. Export insurance is provided by the Foreign Credit Insurance Association, which guarantees exports of American sellers. The combination of the two, along with other forms of credits and guarantees, is part of American trade policy and can significantly affect the balance of payments.

The Eximbank has come under severe criticism, especially during the 1980s when the United States ran large trade imbalances. Many studies showed that the foreign buyers of American goods supported by the bank were the customers of a handful of the largest manufacturing exporters, usually those that produced big-ticket items that would provide the largest foreign orders for American producers. Despite the criticism, the bank remains the premier government agency designed to promote trade and competes with similar institutions in other industrialized countries, all designed to stimulate their home country's exports.

See also FOREIGN CORRUPT PRACTICES ACT; HAWLEY-SMOOT TARIFF ACT.

Further reading

Adams, Frederick C. *Economic Diplomacy: The Export-Import Bank and American Foreign Policy 1934–1939*. Columbia: University of Missouri Press, 1976.

Becker, William H., and William McClenahan. *The Market, the State, and the Export-Import Bank of the United States, 1934–2000*. New York: Cambridge University Press, 2003.

Feinberg, Richard E. *Subsidizing Success: The Export-Import Bank in the United States Economy*. New York: Cambridge University Press, 1981.

F

Farm Credit System The first federal agency founded after the Federal Reserve Board, dedicated to providing credit for a specific sector of the American economy. The system evolved from a need to make credit for farmers more easily available and provide a mechanism by which credit could be allocated on a national scale. As a result, a system of federal farm banks was designed that closely resembled the model originally used for the FEDERAL RESERVE.

The original legislation creating what would become known as the Farm Credit System was the Federal Farm Loan Act of 1916. At the time, private farm credit ranged from 7 to 12 percent per annum, depending upon the source, and was widely recognized to depend to a great degree on the nature and reliability of the lender. The act provided for the creation of 12 federal land banks, organized under the aegis of a Federal Farm Loan Board (FFLB), located in Washington, D.C. The board had five members. Private banks were given the opportunity to sign up and become members of the system, and the banks rushed to join, since as members of a regional land bank they would be eligible for loans. The FFLB was authorized to borrow on the bond markets, and the proceeds were used to provide funds for the local banks.

The Farm Credit System was enhanced by several pieces of legislation. The first came in 1923, when Congress passed the Agricultural Credit Act, creating 12 intermediate credit banks to be supervised by the federal land banks. During the Depression, the Farm Credit Act of 1933 was passed, establishing another layer of credit institutions standing between the land banks and the intermediate credit banks. This also created the Farm Credit Administration. In 1939, President Roosevelt ended its agency status by issuing an executive order that passed its jurisdiction to the Department of Agriculture. It remained there until 1953. Then it was returned to agency status so that it could become farmer-owned as quickly as possible. It remains responsible for the REGULATION and examination of the banks, associations, and related entities that collectively comprise what is known as the Farm Credit System.

Congress passed another Farm Credit Act in 1971 that was designed to streamline the agency. By this time, the system consisted of the land banks, intermediate credit banks, production associations, and cooperative banks. The system funded itself by borrowing in the bond markets and passing the funds to its constituent banks. In the 1970s and 1980s, several farm crises put the system under severe financial strain. Most significant was the rise of the dollar in the early 1980s that reduced farm exports. By 1986, the system recorded losses of almost $2 billion, and within a year the losses swelled to $4.6 billion. The credit markets looked unfavorably upon the agency's bonds, and Congress passed the Agricultural Adjustment Act of 1987 in order to shore up the system. As a result, the entire system was restructured, and a specialized agency, the Federal Agricultural Mortgage Corp. (Farmer Mac), was created to borrow money to make up for the loss.

After restructuring, the Farm Credit System remains the major source of loans and mortgages for farmers. Like other GOVERNMENT-SPONSORED ENTERPRISES, its credit carries the implicit guarantee of the U.S. Treasury in the case of default, and the interest rates at which it borrows are passed to the banks within the system, producing a relatively cheap cost of funds for farm credit.

Further reading

Farm Credit System. *The Federal Land Bank System, 1917–1967.* Washington, D.C.: Farm Credit System, 1967.

Jones, Lawrence, and David Durand. *Mortgage Lending Experience in Agriculture.* Princeton, N.J.: Princeton University Press, 1954.

farming   Farming is at the same time a vocation, a necessity, and an industry. It provides the essentials for life but can also function like any other business using capital investment, technology, political lobbying, and marketing strategies to maximize profit. Until the last part of the 20th century, subsistence farming and production for market have always existed simultaneously in the United States. Thus, a survey of American farming does not offer a simple trend toward capitalistic agriculture. Instead it presents a complex interaction between the need for food and the desire for profit, influenced at all times by cultural and political realities, scientific and technical change, and the potentials and limitations of the natural environment.

Most of the early colonists of North America came to improve their financial situation. They were in search of a way to make money, and, for many, agriculture proved the answer. So, from the very beginning of white settlement, both subsistence and capitalist agriculture coexisted. Commercial agriculture was especially strong in the southern colonies, with tobacco, rice, and indigo dominating profit-export crops until the 1793 invention of the cotton gin. The northern and middle colonies also produced crops for export, especially wheat, and farms in these colonies also supplied the growing local and urban markets.

During the 50 or so years from the American Revolution to the 1830s, agriculture in the new United States continued some trends established in the colonial era, while simultaneously undergoing dramatic changes sparked by technological developments and the creation of the public domain.

Most agriculture remained a mix of subsistence and commercial, and as many as 96 percent of the people lived in rural areas. Farms, with the exception of southern plantations, tended to be small (80–120 acres or so), and they generally produced a wide range of crops and livestock, supplying the farm family's needs as much as possible. Once the needs of subsistence were met, farmers used additional land to produce a surplus to sell or trade at market for goods that they could not grow themselves—for example, iron, salt, and coffee.

On these farms, most of the labor was provided by the farm family. The homeplace was the workplace, and everyone except the very young contributed their labor. The women and children were responsible for the farm garden and the smaller livestock, as well as such food production as brewing, baking, and preserving, while the men farmed the field crops and took care of the stock animals. At harvest time, all hands were needed in the fields, and other chores were postponed until the crops were in. Although farm labor was gender-differentiated, most labor during this period was unpaid, with the only income generated through barter or sale of produce. Farmers marketed most of their surplus production locally and were limited by the distance they could travel—either by foot or wagon—before their product spoiled. Thus, farmers who had settled on the frontier—over the Appalachian ridge—tended to produce for market only items that were durable, transportable, and had a high value for a small bulk, such as hogs and whiskey, while farmers nearer urban centers produced grain and truck crops.

The main exception to these small-scale farms were the plantations of the slave South. These farms were very large, ranging upward of 500 acres; produced mainly cash crops (although they aimed at self-sufficiency); and operated with slave labor. The farm family on the plantations did not labor manually, but rather both men and women adopted a managerial role. Plantation owners largely produced crops for the export market. Although the market for indigo had ended after the American Revolution removed British subsidies from the crop, the United Kingdom provided a growing market for the South's new main crop—cotton. Other key staples in the South included tobacco, sugar, rice, and hemp. These crops were generally sent directly to Europe in the care of factors, who would supervise the sales and then purchase luxuries for the plantation family with the profits. Thus, without much local trade or production, town growth in the American South during this period was slow and politically driven.

While the family farm and the plantation had existed in colonial times, the period of the new republic did see some dramatic shifts. One of the most significant decisions for the agricultural future of the United States was the creation of the public domain in 1781, when states that held lands west of the Appalachians ceded them to the confederation government. This public domain was considerably expanded in 1803 with the Louisiana Purchase and again in 1848 in the Treaty of Guadalupe Hidalgo that ended the Mexican-American War. Theoretically, the public domain was intended to benefit all citizens by giving them access to cheap land, something that no longer existed in Europe. Between its creation and the Homestead Act of 1862, the government experimented with various land laws that sold the public domain to citizens relatively inexpensively.

The other main change in this period that had an impact on agricultural development was the improvement of transportation systems. In the early 19th century, the invention of the steamboat and the proliferation of canals in the Northeast revolutionized the movement of both people and products. The steamboat made traveling up rivers such as the Mississippi and the Ohio as easy as traveling down them. Therefore, goods could be hauled to the settled markets of the East from western farms and likewise supplies hauled to frontier farms. In conjunction with canals, the steamboats made it easier and quicker for families to move west, take advantage of the public domain, and farm the frontier. In 1830, the first RAILROADS were constructed in the United States to haul agricultural produce from hinterlands to urban markets. This development increased the marketing range of farms, allowing them to ship heavier goods farther with little loss of profit.

The middle part of the 19th century was marked by expansion, innovation, and violence, much of which affected agriculture on American farms. Over the course of 50 years, the farm population expanded to meet the food needs of a growing nation. At the same time, as the Industrial Revolution took a firm hand on the country's economy, farmers believed, somewhat justifiably, that their income and their status were declining. To counter this problem, farmers adopted new techniques and machines to increase production, they appealed to the federal government for help, and they organized themselves into both nonpartisan and political groups to force the changes they saw as necessary for survival.

One of the main characteristics of this period was the continuation of westward expansion. The initial movement leapfrogged the Great Plains, which were seen as infertile, and thousands of people trekked overland to Oregon and California. Here they sold their agricultural surpluses to miners and lumbermen and local urban centers. As the transcontinental railroads were completed, more and more of the farmers of the West were able to tap into the large markets of the East.

Toward the end of the century, after the federal government had confined many of the native plains people on reservations and enacted the Homestead Act (1862), awarding a free 160 acres to anyone willing to improve it, many settlers flocked to the central regions of the country. Because of the distances involved on the Great Plains, these farmers were the first in the nation to be completely dependent on railroads. Largely producing wheat, their markets were in the big midwestern cities—Chicago, Kansas City, Minneapolis, and Omaha. This dependency on railroads created resentment, as farmers saw their profits fade, while railroad income seemed to remain strong.

Northern farmers during the 19th century became dependent on other technologies, along with railroads. Various innovations such as McCormick's reaper (1834), the steel plow (1837), and artificial fertilizers (1849) made farming easier and more efficient. Farmers could increase acreage and production with the same amount of labor. However, the farmers did not

Corn harvester in action, 2004 (LIBRARY OF CONGRESS)

benefit as much as they hoped. Overproduction and other factors caused crop prices to fall in the 1880s and 1890s. In addition, many farmers assumed debt to purchase new machinery, and these liens could not be repaid with their ever-decreasing income. The initial response of many farmers was to produce still more, but this just compounded the problem, and so they searched for other solutions.

In the Reconstruction South, planters faced the problem of no cash and no labor. Meanwhile, freedmen needed work but had limited skills. Sharecropping was initially seen as a solution mutually beneficial to both groups. Land owners would provide a freed family with land, seed, a house, and mules. The family would farm the land and pay the landlord with a share of the crop. This sharecropping system degenerated over time, as white landlords and shopkeepers took advantage of black illiteracy to reduce them to a state of crop peonage. Poor whites, too, were increasingly trapped in sharecropping, losing their land to the massive cotton plantations that dominated the South far more than they ever had before the war.

Faced with marginalization in an increasingly industrialized society and with declining profits, farmers in both North and South started to organize. Starting with the Patrons of Husbandry, or the Grange, in 1867, farmers came together for socialization, economic well-being through cooperatives, and political leverage. As the century progressed and the farming community did not see economic improvements, these organizations became politicized, culminating with the formation of the People's Party. This partisan organization, aimed to free farmers from the oppression of middlemen, first ran a candidate for the presidency in 1892. In the election of 1896, however, the party found its issues subsumed by the major parties, and, although it continued to exist for 20-some more years, it never had any substantial political clout.

Along with the creation of independent organizations and political parties, farmers in the second half of the 19th century looked to the federal government to solve their problems. This started in 1862, with the passage of both the Homestead Act and the Morrill Land Grant Act that established a system whereby every state could have its own school devoted to teaching scientific agriculture and mechanical arts. Farm organizations also looked to government on a state and local level to legislate on their behalf. Thus, the 1870s saw the Granger laws, regulating railroad charges and culminating in the 1887 establishment of the INTERSTATE COMMERCE COMMISSION that regulated railroads on a national level. After the failure of the People's Party, farmers increasingly saw the federal government and its legislation as their only source of protection and promotion.

The new century began well, with some of the best years ever for American agriculture. However, a combination of overproduction, debt, and drought made the 1920s and 1930s difficult years, and many families abandoned agriculture altogether. The New Deal's response to the farm crisis altered national farm policy profoundly, making the federal government ultimately responsible for farm income. Despite this, it took World War II to revive the flagging agricultural economy.

Farmer protests dried up in the early 20th century as good weather and World War I provided an optimum economic situation for agriculture: high production, high demand, and high prices. The situation was so good, in fact, that the period from 1909 to 1914 was seen as the golden age of farming, when the purchasing power of farmers was equal or better than that of other workers. Until 1976, when "parity" became determined by a complex formula of production costs, farmers strove for parity, or the same purchasing power as in the golden age. During this boom, farmers moved on to the northern Great Plains, plowing up the land and producing bumper crops on soils previously deemed barren to meet the seemingly endless demand for agricultural produce. On the flat, treeless plains, machinery, either steam or gasoline driven, was particularly useful.

Continued mechanization in the early 20th century reduced the labor needed on farms while increasing the cost of farming. Especially important was the spread of the tractor. These gasoline-driven engines were introduced around the turn of the century and quickly replaced steam-driven machinery. Labor shortages engendered by World War I made tractors even more attractive to farmers, but many stuck to horse or mule power, often out of a preference for the animals. During the 1920s manufacturers developed lighter, cheaper tractors that sped the shift toward mechanical power in agriculture.

Mechanization of agriculture, along with developments in chemical fertilizers, pesticides, and herbicides, reduced the need for labor on farms. Since the advent of the INDUSTRIAL REVOLUTION in the United States, more and more rural people had migrated to towns, and this migration sped up in the 20th century. By the census of 1920 the United States had officially become an urban nation, with more of its population residing in towns and cities than in rural areas.

The 1920s saw a downturn in agricultural prosperity. Foreshadowing the national depression of the 1930s, the decade saw farm prices plummet after the end of the war. Farmers, in debt for their new machinery and new land, found themselves unable to maintain their prosperity, and foreclosures skyrocketed. Once again farm organizations prospered. From the more conservative Farm Bureau (1919) to the radical Nonpartisan League (1916), these organizations tried to stop foreclosures and force up farm prices. All of them believed in self-help through cooperation among farmers. However, they saw the ultimate solution as political: They believed that the government, either on a state or national level, had to regulate costs and prices to ensure that farmers could maintain a reasonable standard of living. Governments, with the exception of that in North Dakota under the Nonpartisan League until 1921, did not agree until the onset of the Great Depression.

The Crash of 1929 did not greatly affect the farming population, which generally had little money to invest. What did hurt farmers, especially on the Great Plains, was the drought that started in 1931 and lasted most of the decade, and the complete collapse of food prices. Not able to get back the price of production, farmers left crops to rot in the fields or burned them for fuel, while throughout American cities people suffered starvation. Government loans, work programs, and credit arrangements helped the nation's farmers. The main solution devised by the federal government for agriculture, and implemented in 1933 in the form of the Agricultural Adjustment Act, was to reduce farm production and thereby force up prices by paying farmers not to produce. This act, along with the second Agricultural Adjustment Act of 1938, generally benefited farmers in direct proportion to the amount of land that they could not farm. Thus, the larger the land holdings, the greater the government payments. The two main consequences of this were that as less land was being cultivated, sharecroppers and farm laborers were dismissed and displaced, becoming part of the large transient population of the decade and made famous as "Okies"; large landowners received substantial government funds, enabling them to mechanize their operations, thus decreasing still further the need for labor. The onset of World War II finally rescued America from the Great Depression. Large landowners, who had capitalized on the New Deal policies, were well-placed to meet and profit from the increased demand for agricultural produce that the war generated.

The second half of the 20th century, in many ways, continued the trends in agriculture that were established during the previous half century: consolidation, technological influence, and government involvement. However, all of these trends were to reach new heights by the start of the third millennium.

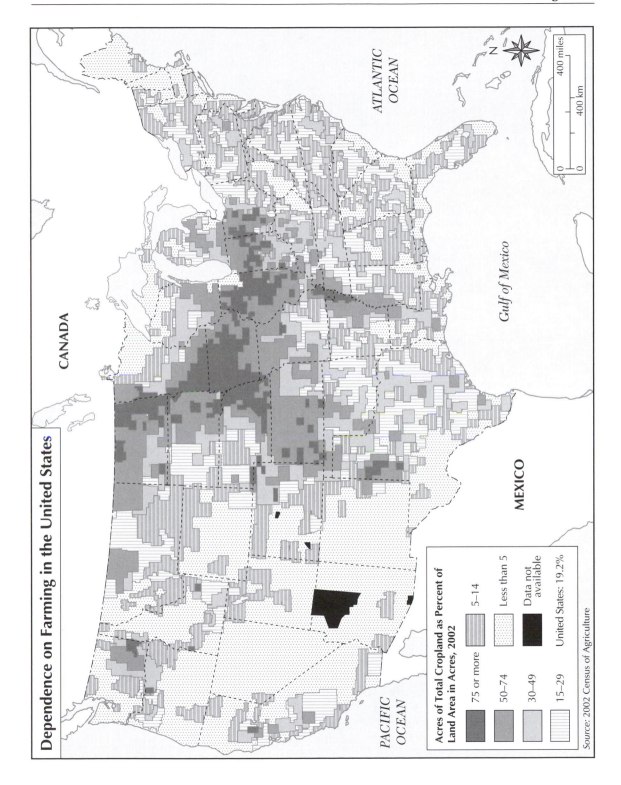

Dependence on Farming in the United States

N

400 miles

400 km

CANADA

ATLANTIC OCEAN

Gulf of Mexico

MEXICO

PACIFIC OCEAN

Acres of Total Cropland as Percent of Land Area in Acres, 2002

75 or more

50–74

30–49

15–29

5–14

Less than 5

Data not available

United States: 19.2%

Source: 2002 Census of Agriculture

After World War II, large-scale commercial farmers steadily increased their share of the country's agricultural wealth. Continuing to receive more in government subsidies than small-scale farmers, they were able to adopt new machinery, seed, fertilizer, and computers to maximize their production. At the same time, agribusinesses flourished. These large, vertically integrated operations, sometimes owned by farmer cooperatives, as in the case of Crystal Sugar, controlled food production literally from the ground to the store. The main thing that distinguished agribusinesses from the large commercial farms was that the owners of the land not only did not work it, but also did not even have to see it.

With huge amounts of money thrust at agricultural improvements, American farmers and landowners embarked on introducing technology to agriculture with a new, aggressive efficiency. From pumping water from the Ogallala aquifer to aerial spraying of crops with herbicides and pesticides, from hybridizing soft fruits and vegetables to endure the rigors of travel to genetically modifying crops to make them disease and chemical resistant, success in farming became more removed from nature and more dependent on science and technology than ever before. This ensured that American farmlands were more productive than ever, while overproduction and consequent low farm prices continue to be a national problem today. However, an increasing number of people are questioning the validity, sustainability, and healthfulness of such artificial farming. This is reflected in the growing interest, both here and abroad, in organic farming and in rescuing traditional, heritage varieties of plants and animals from extinction.

The federal government continued and increased its support of agriculture. Having made the decision to subsidize food production in the nation rather than letting prices find their own, perhaps much higher levels, the government consistently responded to the farm lobby by pro-viding payments for everything from set-aside land to price supports on commodities. Additional subsidies are often hidden in the form of large grants to agricultural research designed to increase the production that is already keeping prices low.

Farmer organizations remained active in the postwar period, although, as the average farm size grew, they split into two camps. On the one hand, a number of farm workers' unions emerged, trying to improve the status of the laborer in the field. The most colorful, famous, and successful of these was the United Farm Workers of America led by Cesar Chavez. Active in the 1960s and 1970s, the organization did achieve some benefits for its migrant members, but these were paltry in comparison with continued company profits. On the other hand, commercial farmers have had considerable success with their farm lobby in maintaining government price supports and the imbalance in favor of larger landowners.

Finally, the late 20th century saw a globalization of agriculture on a tremendous scale. Increasingly, farmland in America, as well as elsewhere, is held by multinational companies. This facilitates the flow of money and sometimes disease around the world, but does not seem to have had much of an impact on the movement of food from regions of plenty to areas of scarcity.

Further reading

Danbom, David B. *"Born in the Country"*: A History of Rural America. Baltimore: Johns Hopkins University Press, 1995.

Drache, Hiram M. *History of U.S. Agriculture and Its Relevance Today*. Danville, Ill.: Interstate Publishing, 1996.

Lauck, Jon. *American Agriculture and the Problem of Monopoly: The Political Economy of Grain Belt Farming, 1953–1980*. Lincoln: University of Nebraska Press, 2000.

McMath, Robert C., Jr. *American Populism: A Social History, 1877–1898*. New York: Hill & Wang, 1993.

Shover, John L. *First Majority, Last Minority: The Transforming of Rural Life in America*. DeKalb: Northern Illinois University Press, 1976.

Claire Strom

Federal Communications Commission (FCC)

A federal agency created by Congress in the Federal Communications Act of 1934 to regulate the communications industry. At the time, the FCC assumed regulatory authority for broadcasting, TELEGRAPH, and telephone services. Originally, the commission consisted of seven commissioners, appointed by the president. In 1982, the number was reduced to five. Its main objective was to ensure communications at reasonable prices to the public.

The FCC is empowered to grant broadcasting licenses. During the 1940s, it also began insisting that stations to which it granted licenses also begin introducing public service programming. Over the years, the FCC helped AT&T maintain its effective monopoly over the telephone industry, a monopoly established in 1921 with the Willis-Graham bill, which allowed AT&T to purchase rival exchanges. Originally, AT&T was aided when the commission refused to entertain licenses from smaller companies that wanted to break into the telephone business. Eventually, the FCC began entertaining complaints from potential telephone competitors, and AT&T's monopoly was officially broken in 1982 in a landmark agreement with the Justice Department. The FCC also took a similar stance in the TELEVISION INDUSTRY, which helped the large networks maintain their dominance over the industry at the expense of smaller stations until the advent of cable television in the 1970s.

The agency's basic powers include approving rate increases for interstate telephone and telegraph services, assigning new frequencies for radio and television, and issuing licenses to station operators. More recently, it also assumed regulatory authority over satellite communications. In addition to radio, TV, telegraph, and cable TV, the agency also has authority over transmitters that are used by police and fire departments and the national medical emergency service. Its administration of the various services has not always been consistent over its 70-year history, but the FCC remains the chief regulator of communications in the country. It often responds to trends in the communications industry by passing rules addressing communications issues of the moment, such as the level of competitiveness within the broadcast industry and matters of public taste.

Often, its position on communications issues, especially concerning competition within the communications industry, can have far-reaching ANTITRUST and trade ramifications. Its decisions may be overridden by Congress in special circumstances.

Further reading

Emery, Walter B. *Broadcasting and Government: Responsibilities and Regulations*. East Lansing: Michigan State University Press, 1961.

Fleissner, Jennifer. *The Federal Communications Commission*. New York: Chelsea House, 1992.

Federal Deposit Insurance Corporation (FDIC)

An agency created by Congress to provide insurance against customer deposits at banks and other banking institutions. The concept of deposit insurance was introduced during the banking crisis of 1932 as a means of attracting customers back to banks, from which they had been withdrawing their money. The "money hoard" exemplified the loss of confidence by the public in the banking system and also was reducing credit creation by banks at a particularly vulnerable time during the Great Depression. Although the concept was not universally popular, it was seen as a measure that could help restore confidence in the banking system.

There had been more than a dozen experiments with deposit insurance within the states prior to the creation of the FDIC, several of which were mandatory and the rest voluntary. Federal deposit insurance was provided by the BANKING ACT OF 1933. The law created the FDIC, a private government-sponsored agency that provided insurance for deposits at member banks for a maximum of $2,500 per account. The amount was raised to $5,000 a year later, $10,000 in the 1950s, and $20,000 in 1969. All banks that were members of the FEDERAL RESERVE were required to join, and state banks had the option to join. Premiums were charged to member banks, and these funds provided the money needed to insure deposits at failed banks. A similar fund called the Federal Savings & Loan Insurance Corp. (FSLIC) was created in 1934 to provide similar insurance to savings institutions not technically classified as commercial banks.

Insurance was increased to $100,000 per account by the DEPOSITORY INSTITUTIONS DEREGULATION AND MONETARY CONTROL ACT (DIDMCA) in 1980. In the late 1980s, a banking crisis forced a reform of the FDIC, and the Federal Deposit Insurance Corporation Improvement Act (FDICIA) was passed in 1991. The act provided more stringent requirements concerning bank capital, calculated the insurance premium on the banks' risk activities, and gave the FDIC the right to borrow from the U.S. Treasury to cover bank failures in the event that the Bank Insurance Fund became depleted. Today, the Bank Insurance Fund, the actual fund itself, technically covers the bailout of a failed member.

The thrift crisis of the 1980s also caused the failure of the FSLIC, which was dissolved in 1989 by the FINANCIAL INSTITUTIONS REFORM, RECOVERY AND ENFORCEMENT ACT (FIRREA). The thrifts' fund became the Savings Association Insurance Fund, administered along with the bank fund by the FDIC. It too charges premiums to its members so that it can provide assistance to failing thrift institutions if required.

The amount of premiums charged to participating banks in deposit insurance funds has always been contentious, with many larger banks claiming that they were being penalized for the mismanagement of smaller banks that required assistance. In the largest bailout ever provided by the FDIC, that of the Continental Illinois Bank in 1984, the amount of insured deposits at the bank was greater than the fund's ability to guarantee all deposits, so a special bailout arrangement with other large banks had to be arranged to provide cash to depositors if requested.

Further reading

Barth, James, and R. Dan Brumbaugh. *The Reform of Federal Deposit Insurance: Disciplining the Government and Protecting Taxpayers.* New York: HarperBusiness, 1992.

Kennedy, Susan Estabrook. *The Banking Crisis of 1933.* Lexington: University Press of Kentucky, 1973.

Federal Home Loan Bank Board (FHLBB)

Founded in 1932 during the Hoover administration, the FHLBB was the first federal agency designed to oversee SAVINGS AND LOANS institutions (S&Ls). Following the pattern of the FEDERAL RESERVE, founded in 1913, the FHLBB was created to supply credit to the S&Ls on a nationwide basis. During the early years of the Depression, the health of the S&Ls was critical to the economy since they were the major providers of home mortgages.

The Federal Home Loan Bank Act created 12 Federal Home Loan Banks around the country. The individual banks raised the cash they needed initially by selling stock to the S&Ls in their districts, enabling those that did so to call themselves federally chartered. The districts were similar to those of the Federal Reserve, but the geographical lines were somewhat different. Shortly thereafter, Congress created two federal agencies designed to provide assistance to the mortgage market: the Home Owner's Loan Association in 1933 and the Federal Housing Administration in 1934. Both institutions were designed to further assist the residential housing market and, when combined with the credit supplying ability of the FHLBB, helped stabilize the residential housing sector throughout the 1930s.

The FHLBB was authorized to fund itself by borrowing in the bond markets. Its activities were aided by the creation of the Federal Home Loan Mortgage Corporation, or Freddie Mac, created by Congress in 1970 as a federal agency designed to purchase approved mortgage loans from thrift institutions, helping to create more liquidity among the thrifts. Despite the assistance provided, in the 1980s problems began to appear among the S&Ls due to high interest rates and net withdrawals by customers while interest rates were still regulated.

Despite the DEPOSITORY INSTITUTIONS ACT passed in 1982, the problem was only temporarily remedied, and the industry again suffered a serious crisis in 1988–89. Many junk bond investments made by the S&Ls as a result of the 1982 act declined in value, and many commercial real estate ventures, also authorized by the act, also went bad, forcing the S&Ls to write off many assets. As a result of the inability of the board to effectively monitor the mortgage-granting banks, Congress passed the FINANCIAL INSTITUTIONS REFORM, RECOVERY AND ENFORCEMENT ACT in 1989 in order to bail out the thrift industry. The act created the Office of Thrift Supervision (OTS), which assumed the regulatory powers of the FHLBB. Congress also passed the FINANCIAL SERVICES MODERNIZATION ACT 10 years later, reforming the structure of the banking system. As part of that legislative package, the Federal Home Loan Bank System Modernization Act reorganized the system again.

Further reading

White, Laurence. *The Savings and Loan Debacle.* New York: Oxford University Press, 1991.

Woerheide, Walter. *The Savings and Loan Industry.* Westport, Conn.: Quorum Books, 1984.

Federal National Mortgage Association (FNMA)

Better known as Fannie Mae, the FNMA was created by an act of Congress in 1938 in order to further stabilize the market for residential mortgages during the Great Depression. The association was created as a wholly owned federal agency dedicated to purchasing federally guaranteed mortgages from lenders. As a result, the lenders would be free to loan more mortgages to potential homeowners.

Fannie Mae performs a wholesale function in the market. Originally, it was designed to buy mortgages guaranteed by the Federal Housing Administration and, later, veterans' mortgages. During World War II, its functions were somewhat limited, but it began to increase its activities during the housing boom following the war. The agency was substantially revamped in 1954, when a housing act passed Congress. Although owned by the U.S. Treasury, Fannie Mae raised substantial funds on the bond markets, its traditional source of long-term funds.

The agency was privatized in 1968, when Congress passed the Housing and Urban Development Act. A new government agency was created at the same time—the Government National Mortgage Association, or Ginnie Mae. After this time, Fannie Mae operated as a private company, and its stock eventually was listed on the NEW YORK STOCK EXCHANGE. It expanded the scope of its operations, adding new mortgages to the list of qualified obligations it could purchase from lenders. Its function began to shift to the secondary market, while Ginnie Mae continued to buy guaranteed mortgages from lenders.

Fannie Mae also helped develop different types of mortgage-backed bonds that have come to dominate the mortgage market. Since its privatization, it has become known as a GOVERNMENT-SPONSORED ENTERPRISE, or GSE—an agency originally founded by Congress and subsequently privatized but still bearing what is known as the implicit guarantee of the Treasury. In other words, if the agency should fail, the government ultimately would be forced to guarantee Fannie Mae's obligations to its investors.

Fannie Mae's activities dominate the residential mortgage market along with those of its smaller counterpart, the Federal Home Loan

Mortgage Corporation, or Freddie Mac. Between them, they purchase about 60 percent of all new residential mortgages created. They have also become two of the largest users of interest rate derivatives among financial institutions. In 2003, the agency had to restate its earnings from previous years under criticism from Congress and accounting regulators.

While the value of the implicit guarantee has been widely debated, the agency remains one of the two largest guarantors and traders of mortgages, at times holding as much as 40 percent of all conforming residential mortgages.

See also FEDERAL HOME LOAN BANK BOARD.

Further reading

Break, George, and Jack Guttentag. *Federal Credit Agencies*. Englewood Cliffs, N.J.: Prentice Hall, 1963.

Stanton, Thomas H. *A State of Risk*. New York: Harper-Business, 1991.

———. *Government-Sponsored Enterprise: Mercantilist Companies in the Modern World*. Washington, D.C.: American Enterprise Institute, 2002.

Weicher, John. *Housing: Federal Policies and Programs*. Washington, D.C.: American Enterprise Institute, 1980.

Federal Reserve   In 1913, Congress passed the Federal Reserve Act, creating the Federal Reserve System (Fed) in response to several banking panics in the late 1800s and early 1900s. Its main purpose was to act as a lender of last resort, or supplier of liquidity when banks faced temporary financial problems. Since the early 1900s the role of the Fed in the U.S. economy has grown to one of chief economic watchdog.

There are three main parts of the Federal Reserve System: the board of governors in Washington, D.C., 12 regional Federal Reserve banks, and the Federal Open Market Committee (FOMC). The board of governors is made up of seven individuals nominated by the president and confirmed by the Senate to formulate mone-

tary policy, supervise and regulate member banks, and oversee the smooth functioning of the payment system in the economy.

The most powerful member of the board of governors is the chairman. The 12 regional banks act as the operating branches of the Fed. They can be thought of as a banker's bank, managing reserve accounts and currency levels in their regions.

The most well-known part of the Fed is the FOMC. The FOMC meets regularly during the year to set monetary policy. The board of governors and five of the 12 regional bank presidents make up the voting members of the FOMC. The FOMC meetings have became some of the most watched and anticipated events by financial markets. At each meeting, the FOMC now sets a target for the federal funds rate, a key overnight interest rate that affects the cost of borrowing throughout the economy. For this reason, financial market participants closely scrutinize the motives of the FOMC.

There are several key moments in the history of the Fed. Prior to 1929, the Federal Reserve had no clear notion of its role in responding to cyclical forces. This resulted in a policy that allowed the money supply to contract dramatically over the first few years of the Great Depression. After the election of President Roosevelt in 1932, the Federal Reserve System was reorganized to resemble the structure we observe today. The Eccles Act was passed in 1935, enlarging some of the powers of the Fed and giving it greater control over the system of 12 branch banks.

During World War II, the Fed pegged interest rates, lasting until the end of the Korean War, in order to manage the wartime economy. Banks were also allowed to hold TREASURY BONDS in exchange for a relaxation of reserve requirements. During the 1940s, the Federal Reserve moved from keeping Treasury borrowing costs low toward seeking to achieve full employment. The latter of these goals was in response to the Employment Act of 1946, which set as a responsibility of the federal government the stabilization of employment at near-full employment levels. These goals of low borrowing costs and stable employment at near-full employment levels sometimes clashed, until March 1951, when an "Accord" was reached between the Treasury and the Federal Reserve System in which the Fed could actively and independently set monetary policy.

The 1950s and 1960s were an era of relatively good economic outcomes for the U.S. economy. During the 1950s, the Fed developed open market operations (the buying and selling of U.S. government securities on the open market) as the main policy tool used to affect interest rates. The next major challenge for the Federal Reserve was the "Great Inflation" of the 1970s. The inflation rate in the United States rose to 12.5 percent in 1974 and was 11 percent in 1980.

In 1979, in response to the spiraling inflation rate, Federal Reserve chairman Paul VOLCKER instituted an era of "tight money" in which the growth rate of the money supply was reduced.

This policy was intended to slow the growth of output and reduce the inflation rate. It succeeded very well. In the early 1980s, the United States suffered a severe RECESSION that many economists credit (or blame) the Federal Reserve for creating. By 1984, inflation was less than 4 percent.

The final years of Paul Volcker's term as chairman and the appointment of Alan Greenspan to replace him in 1987 mark the beginning of a very successful period of monetary policy. The main goal of inflation stability initiated during the 1979 monetary policy tightening resulted in historically high interest rates until 1984 but has since been reinforced with the additional goal of stabilizing the growth of output.

Currently the Federal Reserve actively uses open market operations as its main tool in meeting its goals. Also at the disposal of monetary policy makers are two additional tools: the discount rate (the rate at which banks can borrow from the Federal Reserve) and the required reserve ratio (the proportion of bank deposits that must be held as reserve against possible withdrawals). By far the most often used tool is open market operations. In accordance to directions given by the FOMC, the Federal Reserve Bank of New York actively enters the market for U.S. government securities as a buyer or seller in an effort to influence the level of interest rates.

The main target of the Federal Reserve is the federal funds rate, an overnight rate directly affected by open market operations. The New York bank either buys or sells securities to move the Federal Funds rate to the target level set by the FOMC. The power of monetary policy is then transmitted to the economy by the changes in interest rates. An increase (or decrease) in interest rates reduces (increases) the level of consumer and business expenditures that require borrowing. This in turn decreases (increases) the level of output in the economy, reducing (increasing) pressure on prices to rise (fall).

The FOMC sets the target Federal Funds rate in accordance with its feelings as to the direction of the U.S. economy. If the FOMC believes inflation is on the upswing, it will raise interest rates to slow the economy. If it believes unemployment is too high (reducing pressure on inflation), it will lower interest rates to increase economic activity. For this reason, financial market participants pay very close attention to economic activity to gain some insight into the future actions of the Federal Reserve in setting interest rates. The Fed also acts as agent for the U.S. Treasury in the marketplace. It intervenes in the FOREIGN EXCHANGE MARKET when requested and also auctions Treasury securities for the government.

The Federal Reserve has a long history of intervening in the U.S. economy. From overseeing a dramatic decrease in the money supply during the early years of the Great Depression, to participating in producing monetary growth rates that allowed the Great Inflation to continue, to engineering a dramatic recession to lower inflation rates in the early 1980s, the Federal Reserve has been instrumental in the evolution of economic activity in the United States.

Much of the expertise used by the Federal Reserve has been developed over its long history. This has culminated in perhaps the greatest period of economic expansion in U.S. history. From 1983 to 2000, gross domestic product grew steadily with only a slight interruption in the early 1990s, and inflation steadily fell.

See also COMMERCIAL BANKING; ECCLES, MARRINER S.

Further reading

Beckner, Steven. *Back from the Brink: The Greenspan Years.* New York: John Wiley & Sons, 1996.

Greider, William. *Secrets of the Temple: How the Federal Reserve Runs the Country.* New York: Simon & Schuster, 1987.

Meltzer, Allan H. *A History of the Federal Reserve, 1913–1951.* Chicago: University of Chicago Press, 2003.

Meulendyke, Ann-Marie. *U.S. Monetary Policy and Financial Markets.* New York: Federal Reserve Bank of New York, 1989.

Steve Perez

Federal Trade Commission (FTC)   The Federal Trade Commission Act of 1914 established the Federal Trade Commission (FTC). Originally part of Woodrow Wilson's effort to "bust the trusts," the FTC is an independent government agency responsible for ensuring free and fair competition in the economy and protecting consumers from unfair or misleading practices.

The FTC is composed of five members. These members are appointed to seven-year terms by the president, subject to Senate approval, and report directly to Congress. The president chooses one commissioner to act as chairman. No more than three members can be of the same political party, thus ensuring the commission's bipartisanship. Over the years, the FTC has become increasingly involved in ANTITRUST enforcement. Since 1914, Congress has given the FTC increasingly greater authority to police anticompetitive practices by passing additional laws.

Originally, the SECURITIES ACT OF 1933 required the registration of securities with the FTC before the FTC was created. Today, the FTC enforces federal antitrust and consumer protection laws, maintains truth in advertising, and enforces consumer protection laws that prevent fraud, deception, and unfair business practices.

The FTC works to prevent unfair and anticompetitive business practices by enforcing federal antitrust laws. It does so by preventing unlawful business practices such as those prohibited by the Clayton Antitrust Act, including certain MERGERS and other practices that have the potential to inhibit competition. In the post–World War II years, the FTC and the Antitrust Division of the Department of Justice both brought antitrust actions. While the Antitrust Division investigates and prosecutes businesses that violate antitrust regulations, the FTC has the power to order a company to stop unfair competition methods. In the 1990s especially, several notable antitrust cases were brought by the FTC, including an action against Intel and intense scrutiny of the McDonnell Douglas–Boeing merger.

The FTC also enforces federal consumer protection laws. It does so by investigating complaints initiated by individual consumers, businesses, and reports in the media. The FTC and the Consumer Product Safety Commission are the government agencies chiefly responsible for enforcing these consumer protection laws. However, it is not only large companies that have come under scrutiny by consumer advocates. In the 1960s, the FTC itself also came under heavy criticism for its alleged indifferent approach to antitrust action during the conglomerate era. During this era many large companies looked to mergers as a way of diversifying their bases and maintaining their markets in the face of rising costs. However, this activity quickly swamped the Antitrust Division and the FTC. The result was that only the biggest cases with the most potential impact were pursued. Beginning in the 1970s there was a considerable reduction in the number of antitrust cases being brought by the

Department of Justice and the FTC. In 1976, Congress passed the Hart-Scott-Rodino Act, requiring companies desiring to merge to file notification so that the FTC and the Justice Department have time to review the consequences of the proposed corporate marriage.

Another important facet of consumerism—advertising—is also regulated by the FTC. It monitors advertising, and if it determines an ad to be false or misleading, the commission has the power to impose fines and order corrective advertising or withdrawal. Along with the Federal Drug Administration, the FTC regulates labeling and packaging of consumer products. When a consumer refers to care labels in clothes, product warranties, or performance claims for computers and other high-tech products, that consumer is consulting information required by the FTC. In addition, the commission's Division of Financial Practices enforces many of the nation's other consumer credit statutes, including the Truth in Lending Act, which requires creditors to disclose in writing certain information such as the annual percentage rate, and the Consumer Leasing Act, requiring lessors to disclose certain information to their potential customers. Since it was established, the commission has been empowered to administer a variety of other consumer protection laws, including the Equal Credit Opportunity Act and the Telemarketing Sales Rule.

Although given power to regulate the nation's businesses, it is important to note that the FTC has no authority over common carriers and banks, which are supervised separately. The FEDERAL RESERVE and INTERSTATE COMMERCE COMMISSION (now the Surface Transportation Board) traditionally had jurisdiction over those two respective areas. In 2003, the FTC established the National Do Not Call Registry, which requires most telemarketers to remove the listed numbers in order to limit the number of unwanted telemarketing calls.

Further reading

Holt, William Stull. *The Federal Trade Commission: Its History, Activities, and Organization.* New York: AMS Press, 1974.

Kanwit, Stephanie. *Federal Trade Commission.* Colorado Springs, Colo.: Shepard's/McGraw-Hill, 1979.

Labaree, Robert. *The Federal Trade Commission: A Guide to Sources.* New York: Garland, 2000.

Margaret A. Geisst

Field, Cyrus W. (1819–1892) *businessman*
Born in Stockbridge, Massachusetts, Field was the son of a prominent Congregational clergyman. His family had lived in New England since 1629, and several other members also distinguished themselves. An older brother, Stephen J. Field, became a member of the U.S. Supreme Court, and another, David Dudley Field, was well known as a jurist and legal reformer. Cyrus did not receive a college education, however, and left home at age 15 to travel to New York to become a clerk in a dry goods store.

Several years later he returned to Massachusetts and entered the paper business, but the firm he joined failed. He reorganized it, within nine years accumulated a personal fortune of more than $250,000, and then retired at age 34. After trips to Europe and South America, he became interested in the idea of a transatlantic cable that could carry messages between the United States and Europe. He wanted a cable capable of transmitting Samuel F. B. MORSE's telegraph messages from New York to London and beyond. He organized a company for the purpose of laying cable across the North Atlantic and obtained permission to use two naval ships, one British and the other American, to lay the cable. Field raised the money necessary for the project in London, while the American company formed to promote the project included several wealthy New Yorkers, among them Peter COOPER.

The first attempt at laying cable failed in 1857, breaking some 400 miles from America's shore. Another attempt the following year also failed. In the summer of 1858, Field was successful in laying cable between Newfoundland and

Allegorical scene showing the lion of Great Britain holding one end of the Atlantic cable and the eagle of the United States holding the other end. Includes a portrait of Cyrus Field at top center. (LIBRARY OF CONGRESS)

Ireland. The first transcontinental telegraph message was sent by Queen Victoria to President James Buchanan, and the feat was lauded on both sides of the Atlantic, although the cable broke a month later. Because of these failures, Field had to find new financing for the project. In 1866, the *Great Eastern* finally succeeded in laying a full transatlantic cable, with repairs to the existing cables, and Field, who was once derided as something of a madman, became universally admired for the scope and technical difficulty of the project.

Field also sponsored other projects, such as a cable between Hawaii and Australia, but the project never materialized successfully. He also helped revive and promote the New York City elevated railway system. During the latter part of his career, he was a partner of Jay GOULD in the Wabash Railroad and was also the principal owner of the *Mail & Express,* a New York newspaper. In 1887, he became bankrupt after a battle with Gould for control of the Manhattan Railroad. He died five years later, spending his last years in Stockbridge, Massachusetts.

The cable remained his most notable achievement, however, and it opened a new era of commerce between the United States, Britain, and the rest of Europe. The new form of communications aided the commodities markets and the securities markets especially and promoted investment in the United States as well as speculation in American stocks, bonds, and futures contracts.

Further reading

Carter, Samuel. *Cyrus Field: Man of Two Worlds.* New York: G. P. Putnam, 1968.

Gordon, John Steele. *A Thread across the Ocean: The Heroic Story of the Transatlantic Cable.* New York: HarperCollins, 2002.

Hearn, Chester G. *Circuits in the Sea: The Men, the Ships, and the Atlantic Cable.* Westport, Conn.: Greenwood Press, 2004.

Field, Marshall (1834–1906) *merchant* Marshall Field was born near Conway, Massachusetts, on August 18, 1834, the son of small farmers. At 17 he began clerking in a local dry goods store and gained a reputation for hard work and courtesy. In 1856, the ambitious young Field relocated to Chicago, Illinois, where he soon found employment with the retail firm of Cooley, Wadsworth, and Company, the city's largest dry goods operation. He again distinguished himself by his business acumen, and by 1860, he functioned as a junior partner. In 1862, when Field rose to full partner, the company was renamed Farwell, Field, and Company. Three years later, Field bought out his partner and joined forces with Potter Palmer and Levi Z. Leitner to found the new dry goods firm of Field, Palmer, and Leitner. With competent direction, the company flourished and posted sales of $8 million by 1867. At that time Field and Leitner bought out Palmer, renamed their firm after themselves, and continued to achieve great prosperity. Disaster struck during the Great Chicago Fire of 1871 and again in a second conflagration of 1877, but Field rebuilt his firm at new locations and continued flourishing. Throughout the 1880s, he was largely responsible for its impressive success, and in 1881 Leitner was finally bought out. The new establishment, renamed Marshall Field and Company, had yet to achieve its pinnacle of success.

During his tenure as company head, Field pioneered many business practices that were innovative and revolutionary in their day. He was one of the first American retailers to purchase high-quality goods from both domestic and foreign sources, and in 1871, he opened his first buying office in England. From a consumer standpoint, he introduced the practice of selling goods at a marked price, proffered generous credit, and initiated the policy of offering customers full refunds for returned merchandise. He was also quite possibly the first merchant to recognize the growing purchasing power of women and established company policies to win and keep their loyalty. Employees were instructed to be prompt and courteous, and the store was usually stocked full of high-quality yet moderately priced shawls, furs, perfumes, and other items of interest to female buyers. Fields was also quite adept at consumer psychology. He erected an immense store that ultimately covered 36 acres of Chicago's city center and opulently stocked it with exotic goods, but then included such amenities as a bargain basement and a tea room. It became the largest retail operation in the world and was highly successful. He also pioneered the practice of buying goods in volume and creating a demand for them at a later date, which forced potential competitors to buy and subsequently offer the same objects at higher prices. He further manufactured goods at his own factories and sold them only through his own outlets. Field proved so adept at promoting customer satisfaction and retaining customer loyalty that by the turn of the century he was among the 10 wealthiest Americans. In 1906 alone, his annual sales brought in $86 million.

For all his success, Field himself was something of a quiet, elusive individual, rather flinty in outlook and not given to ostentatious display. He invariably worked long hours, spent money frugally, and declined to participate in social activities usually associated with the upper classes. Field was nonetheless quite generous in terms of philanthropy and indelibly altered the cultural and intellectual landscape of Chicago by subsidizing several of its most famous landmarks. These included the University of Chicago, the Academy of Fine Arts, and the Field Museum of Natural History. When he died of pneumonia on January 16, 1906, Field left behind an estate valued at $150 million. His legacy continues in the family owned Marshal Field stores that have survived in the Midwest and Texas. More important, his twin pillars of quality goods and customer satisfaction have become the lynchpin of the retail business everywhere.

Further reading

Becker, Stephen D. *Marshal Field III: A Biography*. New York: Simon & Schuster, 1964.

Madsen, Axel. *The Marshal Fields: The Evolution of an American Business Dynasty*. New York: John Wiley, 2002.

Palmer, James L. *The Origin, Growth, and Transformation of Marshall Field & Company*. New York: Newcomen Society in North America, 1963.

Tebbel, John W. *Marshall Field: A Study in Wealth*. New York: E. P. Dutton, 1947.

John C. Fredriksen

Financial Accounting Standards Board (FASB)

The organization in the private sector that sets standards of financial accounting and reporting in the United States. The FASB establishes GENERALLY ACCEPTED ACCOUNTING PRINCIPLES (GAAP), which govern the preparation of financial reports. Accounting standards are necessary for the efficient functioning of the economy. Financial reports based on accounting standards help investors, lenders, and the public efficiently to make decisions on allocating their resources to business organizations.

The FASB receives its authority to set accounting standards from the U.S. Securities and Exchange Commission (SEC). The SECURITIES EXCHANGE ACT OF 1934 gives the SEC statutory authority to establish financial accounting and reporting standards for publicly held companies. In 1938, the SEC adopted a policy of relying on existing accounting principles with significant authoritative support in the private sector, in Accounting Series Release No. 4. This action effectively shifted authority to the American Institute of Certified Public Accountants (AICPA), through its Committee on Accounting Procedure (CAP, 1936–59) and its Accounting Principles Board (APB, 1959–73). The FASB was founded in 1972 and began operations in 1973 to provide an equal opportunity for all interested groups to participate in the standards-setting process. In contrast, independent auditors dominated its two predecessors.

The FASB is the operating arm of a three-part organizational structure that also includes the Financial Accounting Foundation (FAF) and the Financial Accounting Standards Advisory Council (FASAC). The FAF is the nonprofit parent organization, administered by 16 trustees with an executive vice president. Its trustees raise funds for the FASB but do not advise it. The FAF trustees appoint members of the FASB and the FASAC. The FASAC advises the FASB on the priorities of accounting issues and the suitability of its tentative resolutions. The FASAC has a minimum of 20 members, which includes financial statement users, auditors, preparers, and the public.

The FASB has seven board members who work full time to resolve financial accounting issues, communicate with constituents, and serve as a focal point for research. Members preserve their independence as standard setters by severing ties with their previous employers. They are appointed to a five-year term, with the possibility of reappointment for a second term. The FAF attempts to appoint knowledgeable board members from diverse accounting backgrounds to represent its various constituents. In February 2001, three board members were auditors, two were corporate financial officers, one was a securities analyst, and one an academic immediately before their appointments to the FASB. The FASB has a research and technical activities staff to support its members.

To establish generally accepted accounting principles (GAAP), the FASB first endorsed the standards of its predecessors, the CAP Accounting Research Bulletins and the APB *Opinions*. It has continued to establish GAAP through three types of pronouncement: statements of financial accounting standards (SFAS), interpretations, and technical bulletins. The board follows an orderly public process before issuing any pronouncement. Due process includes preliminary evaluation of the problem, admission of the problem to the FASB agenda, early deliberations, tentative resolution, further deliberations, and final resolutions. Statements of financial accounting standards consist of principles at the highest level, approved by a two-thirds majority of board members. As of February 2001, the FASB issued 140 SFAS, although many amend previous standards or delay implementation of new standards. The board issued 44 interpretations by February 2001 to explain, clarify, or expand on an existing SFAS, an APB opinion, or a CAP accounting research bulletin. The research and technical activities staff of the FASB issued 50 technical bulletins through February 2001 to address less controversial and pervasive problems. In addition, the FASB has issued seven general statements of financial accounting concepts as a framework to guide its standard setting, to help practicing accountants, and to educate nonaccountants.

Further reading

Miller, Paul B. W., Rodney J. Redding, and Paul R. Bahnson. *The FASB: The People, the Process and the Politics.* Homewood, Ill.: Irwin, 1994.
Previts, Gary John, Barbara Dubis Merino. *A History of Accountancy in the United States: The Cultural Significance of Accounting.* Columbus: Ohio State University Press, 1998.

Mary Michel

Financial Institutions Reform, Recovery and Enforcement Act (FIRREA) Better known by its short name, the FIRREA was enacted

on August 9, 1989—one of the most significant laws to affect the savings and loan industry since the 1930s. The industry had been devastated by high interest rates in the early 1980s and by deterioration in asset quality in the middle to late 1980s. The major impetus behind FIRREA was to provide funds to resolve failed SAVINGS AND LOANS. But it also fundamentally changed the regulatory structure of the industry and reversed the trend toward liberalizing the powers of institutions.

FIRREA dissolved the Federal Savings and Loan Insurance Corp. (FSLIC), making the FEDERAL DEPOSIT INSURANCE CORPORATION (FDIC) the administrator of two separate insurance funds: the Savings Association Insurance Fund (SAIF), which replaced the FSLIC, and the Bank Insurance Fund (BIF). The independent FEDERAL HOME LOAN BANK BOARD (FHLBB) was replaced by the Office of Thrift Supervision (OTS), a bureau within the Treasury Department, as the regulator of savings and loans.

FIRREA established the RESOLUTION TRUST CORPORATION (RTC) to resolve failed savings and loans with funding provided primarily by taxpayers. The RTC was charged with selling assets of failed thrifts to the private sector, many sales occurring at a substantial loss from book value. To replenish SAIF, deposit insurance premiums were raised. The type and extent of activities in which savings and loans could engage was restricted, reversing federal and state legislation of the early 1980s. State-chartered institutions were restricted to those activities permitted to federally chartered institutions. Savings and loans were prohibited from purchasing JUNK BONDS and had to divest themselves of any such holdings. Commercial real estate loans were significantly restricted, as were loans to one borrower. Savings and loans were also required to hold at least 70 percent—up from 60 percent—of their assets primarily in housing-related investments.

FIRREA strengthened capital requirements for savings and loans in three regards. First, tangible capital was to be at least 1.5 percent of assets. Second, a core capital ratio of 3 percent was required. Third, an institution's capital requirement was to be based on the risk of its portfolio.

FIRREA also substantially enhanced the enforcement powers of savings and loan regulators. They were authorized to restrict the asset growth of institutions and to order institutions to stop engaging in specific activities. Regulators were given the power to remove individuals from savings and loans for cause and to impose an industry-wide ban on their employment. Civil money penalties could also be imposed of up to $1 million a day.

FIRREA enhanced the environment in which savings and loans operated by facilitating the removal of failed institutions. However, restrictions mandating that savings and loans be more specialized home mortgage lenders impaired their ability to diversify and to participate in potentially profitable activities. The new capital requirements, moreover, were a continuation of the practice of relying and acting on the basis of accounting measures of capital rather than on market measures. Nonetheless, FIRREA has continued to have a lasting affect on the shrinking savings and loans industry.

See also DEPOSITORY INSTITUTIONS ACT.

Further reading
Barth, James R. *The Great Savings and Loan Debacle.* Washington, D.C.: American Enterprise Institute, 1991.

Barth, James R., George J. Benston, and Philip R. Wiest. "The Financial Institutions Reform, Recovery and Enforcement Act of 1989: Description, Effects and Implications." *Issues in Bank Regulation* (Winter 1990): 3–11.

White, Lawrence J. *The S&L Debacle.* New York: Oxford University Press, 1991.

James R. Barth

Financial Services Modernization Act

(1999)   Also known as the Gramm-Leach-Bliley Act; legislation passed in late 1999 reforming the structure of American banking. Since the late 1980s, the FEDERAL RESERVE had allowed commercial banks greater leeway in such previously proscribed activities as INVESTMENT BANKING and insurance underwriting. The Fed did so under the authority of the BANK HOLDING COMPANY ACT, the law that gave it the authority to govern a bank holding company's activities. But the Fed's ability to liberalize a bank's activities fell short of allowing a complete return to investment banking and insurance.

Commercial banks had been pressing Congress for years to abolish the BANKING ACT OF 1933 (Glass-Steagall Act). They argued that the securities business was a natural complement to their overall banking activities and that being able to deal and underwrite securities was vital to their health in an increasingly global economic environment. As a result, the 1999 act repealed the existing limitations on a bank's ability to own or merge with securities firms and insurance companies. It also created a new form of HOLDING COMPANY called the financial holding company. Subsidiaries of this new holding company that did not engage in banking would be able to engage in securities and insurance underwriting.

Banks possessing a federal charter can also engage in the same activities but must do so in financial subsidiaries, allowing them to do virtually the same activities as a bank holding company. These provisions allow banks to engage in activities not permitted since the 1930s, but the old separation of securities and banking activities within the same unit of the bank is still followed.

In addition, the act provided for fuller disclosure of ATM fees and use of plain language from federal banking regulators, beginning in 2000. Another law affected by the new bill, the COMMUNITY REINVESTMENT ACT of 1977, was protected under the new law, which did change procedures in how the banks were to be examined under the 1999 act in the future. The net effect of the organizational part of the bill was to allow banks to create financial supermarkets—financial institutions where all sorts of financial services could be found under one roof.

The law was passed after CITIBANK agreed to be acquired by the Traveler's Group, an insurance company. Under the existing banking laws, the merger would not have been allowed, but the Federal Reserve Board permitted the merger provided that certain conditions were met. As part of the merger deal, the new Citigroup was given two years to comply with the existing banking laws. But within a year, the new law was passed, allowing the merger to stand. The new banking law allowed American banks to behave more like European banks by owning other types of financial service companies without serious restriction.

Further reading
Federal Reserve Bank of Minneapolis. *The Financial Services Modernization Act of 1999*. Minneapolis: Federal Reserve Bank of Minneapolis, 2000.

Fisk, James, Jr. (Jim) (1834–1872) *businessman and speculator*   Born in Bennington, Vermont, to a YANKEE PEDDLER, Fisk quit school at 12 and joined his father in selling wares from his wagon around New England. After buying his father's business, he enjoyed great success and was soon hired by a dry goods firm with which he had done business. His first great success as a wholesaler of dry goods came when the Civil War began, and he sold various dry goods to the U.S. Army from a base he established in Washington, D.C. He was so successful that he was made a partner.

After spending most of the Civil War buying dry goods for his firm, Fisk sold his partnership back to the firm and, with the money he made, ventured to Wall Street. He became a protégé of the noted speculator Daniel DREW, who helped him establish a brokerage called Fisk, Belden & Co. Through his Wall Street connections, he became acquainted with Jay GOULD, and the two obtained seats on the board of the ERIE RAILROAD.

While sitting on its board, they became involved in what became known as the Erie Wars, fighting Cornelius VANDERBILT for control of the line. Along with Drew and Gould, he personally seized 50,000 shares of Erie stock and fled with his two compatriots to Jersey City, New Jersey, to avoid Vanderbilt. Emerging victorious, they ran the railroad in lavish fashion from its New York headquarters. The operations made him a wealthy man, and he spent his money amply. Fisk bought Pike's Opera House in New York City, refurbished it, and threw lavish productions until the costs eventually caused him to stop funding the operation.

Fisk also gained notoriety when he participated in the gold corner with Jay Gould in 1869, when they were suspected of forcing up the price of gold to unsustainable heights with the purported and unwitting support of President Ulysses Grant. The corner created what became known as Black Friday in 1869 and led to a depressed stock market and a subsequent RECESSION that hit New York City especially hard. Combined with his relationships with Tammany Hall leaders, the gold corner made him, like Gould, one of the most despised men of the era. But his flamboyant manner also endeared him to many New Yorkers. He ran the largest steamboat on the Hudson River, aptly named the *James Fisk*.

Fisk met an untimely end when he was shot by a suitor of his mistress at New York's Grand Central Hotel in 1872. He died the day after the shooting. He was widely mourned in New York City and remains one of the period's most colorful characters.

Further reading

Ackerman, Kenneth D. *The Gold Ring: Jim Fisk, Jay Gould, and Black Friday 1869*. New York: Dodd Mead, 1988.

Fuller, Robert H. *Jubilee Jim: From Circus Traveler to Wall Street Rogue*. New York: Texere, 2001.

Swanberg, W. A. *Jim Fisk: The Career of an Improbable Rascal*. New York: Charles Scribner's, 1959.

Flagler, Henry M. (1830–1913) *oil executive*

Born in Canandaigua, New York, to a Presbyterian minister of modest means, Flagler attended local schools until he was 14. Leaving home while still in his teens, he traveled to Sandusky, Ohio, where he became a grain merchant. He established a business, and one of his clients was John D. ROCKEFELLER, who was then in the produce business. After switching to the salt business, he lost most of his money and had to start over again in the grain business in Cleveland.

Flagler joined forces with Rockefeller in the firm of Rockefeller, Andrews, and Flagler in Cleveland in 1867. The new firm was not a grain firm but one that produced oil, a new commodity showing much promise. Three years later, the firm was incorporated as the Standard Oil Company. Throughout the 1870s, Flagler and Rockefeller split duties at the company, with Rockefeller handling personnel and logistics while Flagler concentrated on legal matters. He also negotiated the rates railroads charged for shipping oil and oil products, often striking advantageous deals for the new company.

As the public outcry against large corporations grew louder in the 1880s, Flagler developed the first trust agreement for the company and in 1882 designed the Standard Oil Trust, which proved to be a revolutionary industrial organization. Under the agreement, Flagler, Rockefeller, and Andrews effectively held the stock of the company in trust for other shareholders, keeping control of Standard Oil while still proclaiming it to be a public company. The agreement served its purpose well, for it was another 30 years before Standard Oil was ordered broken up by a Supreme Court decision.

His interests after 1880 are those for which he is best remembered. Flagler began developing an interest in railroads and in land development in Florida. He developed the first railroad line to serve the east coast of Florida—the Florida East Coast Railroad—stretching from Daytona to Miami, and also built luxury hotels along the line to serve passengers. The rail line was extended to

Key West in 1912 despite significant technical difficulties. The various projects helped contribute significantly to the state's rapid development in the 20th century as the country's premier resort area.

Flagler also developed land in south Florida. His companies dredged the Miami harbor, and he also established steamship companies connecting Florida to the Bahamas as well as to Key West. Among the hotels he developed, the Breakers in Palm Beach is perhaps the best known. The area around St. Augustine also benefited from his business activities, while Flagler College in that city enjoyed his family's largesse over the years.

Further reading

Akin, Edward N. *Flagler, Rockefeller Partner and Florida Baron.* Kent, Ohio: Kent State University Press, 1988.

Martin, Sidney Walter. *Florida's Flagler.* Athens: University of Georgia Press, 1949.

Standiford, Les. *Last Train to Paradise: Henry Flagler and the Spectacular Rise and Fall of the Railroad that Crossed an Ocean.* New York: Crown, 2002.

Tarbell, Ida. *A History of the Standard Oil Company.* Reprint, 1904. Gloucester, Mass.: Peter Smith, 1963.

Forbes, Malcolm (1919–1990) *publisher* Malcolm Stevenson Forbes was born in New York City on August 19, 1919, the son of Scottish emigre Bertie C. Forbes. In 1919 his father established *Forbes Magazine* as a business journal; its moderate success enabled the younger Forbes to enjoy the benefits of an upper-middle-class upbringing. He was educated privately in New York and New Jersey and passed through Princeton University in 1941 with a degree in political science. Like his father, Forbes intended to pursue journalism, and he established several small-town newspapers in the Midwest before enlisting in the U.S. Army during World War II. Forbes served with distinction as an infantry sergeant in Europe, was severely wounded in combat, and

was awarded the Bronze Star. Afterward he returned home and joined the family magazine as an associate publisher. Over the years, he rose to positions of increasing responsibility within the business. After 1947, Forbes developed an interest in local politics and within two years gained election to a New Jersey council. In 1952, he won election to the state senate as a Republican, where he served until 1958. Forbes subsequently failed to win the gubernatorial election that year and retired from politics to pursue publishing full time.

After his father died in 1954 Forbes assumed control of the magazine as editor, while his elder brother Bruce handled financial matters. By 1964, Forbes had became president of the family business, and the tempo of success rapidly quickened. It was in this capacity that Forbes made a name for himself in both the business and journalistic communities. Capitalizing on his own brash, flamboyant personality, he transformed the magazine into a prosperous enterprise by combining accurate business information with dry and humorous commentary. More than anything else, Forbes saw himself as a cheerleader for American-style capitalism, and his magazine consciously reflected his exuberance for business. He was determined to portray making money as fun and to celebrate financial success with all its attendant wealth. Furthermore, all this information was relayed in a breezy, easily digested style conducive to mass readership. The fact that *Forbes Magazine* now touted itself as a "capitalist tool" underscored the editor's personal philosophy in bold relief. This approach was a refreshing change to the usually staid world of business publishing, and within a decade the circulation of *Forbes* rose from 400,000 to 625,000. With annual earnings of $65 million, it became one of the most influential mass publications in American business history—and an icon of popular culture.

A conspicuous factor in the magazine's mounting popularity was Forbes's own extravagant lifestyle. Being partial to ostentatious displays of wealth, he embarked on high-profile publicity stunts such as motorcycle races and lavish business parties at his New York mansion and on his 150-foot yacht. Forbes also became a serious devotee of hot-air ballooning and broke an unprecedented six aeronautical records. In 1973 he became the first person to successfully cross the United States nonstop via hot air balloon, and his efforts garnered both the prestigious Harmon Trophy and a slot in the Aviation Hall of Fame. He was also a world-class art collector specializing in the jeweled eggs of Russian sculptor Peter Carl Faberge and in various toy soldiers. Forbes further enhanced his reputation for extravagance through the acquisition of numerous ranches, farms, castles in Europe, and a palace in Morocco. In return, his rakish celebration of entrepreneurial success only drove the circulation of *Forbes* higher. His most outlandish endeavor was a $2-million extravaganza held in Morocco to celebrate his own 70th birthday.

When not conspicuously flaunting his wealth, Forbes found the time to pen several humorous and well-received memoirs. He died in Far Hills, New Jersey, on February 24, 1990, with a personal worth estimated at between $400 million and $1 billion. His talent for self-indulgence notwithstanding, Forbes possessed an uncanny business mind coupled with a flair for splashy public relations. Not surprisingly, his funeral was copiously attended by several former presidents, Hollywood celebrities, and—most appropriately—50 bikers from the Hell's Angels motorcycle gang. In light of his panache and gratuitous flamboyance, Forbes remains celebrated as the world's "happiest millionaire."

Further reading

Forbes, Malcolm S. *Around the World on Hot Air and Two Wheels*. New York: Simon & Schuster, 1985.
———. *More than I Dreamed*. New York: Simon & Schuster, 1989.
Jones, Arthur. *Malcolm Forbes: Peripatetic Millionaire*. New York: Harper & Row, 1977.
Winans, Christopher. *Malcolm Forbes: The Man Who Had Everything*. New York: St. Martin's Press, 1990.

John C. Fredriksen

Ford, Henry (1863–1947) *businessman and automaker* Born near Dearborn, Michigan, Ford attended school for eight years before becoming an apprentice in a Detroit machine shop at age 16. He first learned about power plants while working for the Detroit Drydock Company, a shipbuilding firm. In 1891, he moved to Detroit permanently and became an engineer with the Edison Illuminating Company, and two years later he became its chief engineer. During his spare time, he experimented with gasoline engines at a small shop at his home.

After working for others until he was 33, Ford introduced his first automobile in 1896 after years of development. He dubbed it the

Henry Ford (LIBRARY OF CONGRESS)

"Quadricycle." He received $200 for the car and used the money to build another. After a humble start, he formed the Henry Ford Co. in 1903. From the beginning, Ford decided to manufacture automobiles that could be bought by the average citizen, as cheaply as possible. This was a radical departure in the early automobile industry because most cars were priced higher and aimed at a more well-heeled customer.

The competition in the early motor industry was intense. Michigan alone was home to 15 different manufacturers, and more than 80 existed in the United States. Ford incorporated the FORD MOTOR COMPANY in 1903 with capital of $150,000, mostly from outside investors. After an internal battle about what sort of car to produce, Ford won the day with his concept of an inexpensive car that could be sold to the general population. Ford bought the closely held shares of his opponents in the firm and emerged as president, free to produce his concept car. His first attempt at a car for the masses was the Model N, which sold originally for $700. The car was very popular, and the company's earnings soared to $1 million.

In 1908, Ford introduced what would become his best-selling car, the Model T. The original price was $825, and the car could be ordered only in black. It became an immediate hit with the public and reached almost a quarter of a million units in 1914. In order to facilitate production, Ford introduced the moving assembly line at his Highland Park, Michigan, plant. Within two years, the 1-millionth car rolled off the assembly line, and the plant was producing 2,000 units per day. And the price continued to fall in both real and absolute terms. The price of a Model T in 1916 was in the mid-$300s, $500 less than the originals in 1908. He also introduced innovations on the shop floor that made him a legend among his workers. Worker rotation, year-end bonuses, a profit-sharing plan, and the introduction of the $5 day made his workers extremely loyal, especially since the wage was twice the industry average at the time. By the

early 1920s, more than 5 million Model Ts had been produced.

During World War I, Ford emerged as an opponent of the war, although he did put his factories at the government's disposal after hostilities began. The company made all sorts of vehicles necessary to the war cause, and Ford was a strong supporter of Woodrow Wilson, although he had been a Republican most of his life. He became a candidate for the Senate in the election of 1918 with the support of Wilson but lost. He soon blamed Jews for his defeat, and the result set off a torrent of anti-Semitic remarks that would plague him for the rest of his life.

After the election defeat, Ford subsequently purchased a newspaper, the *Dearborn Independent,* which reflected his extremely conservative political views and became best known for a series of anti-Semitic articles that it ran in continuing installments. He also made an unsuccessful bid for the Muscle Shoals power plant in Alabama, which the government was thinking of selling to the private sector. The facility later became the base for the TENNESSEE VALLEY AUTHORITY.

Although the Model T was the most popular car of its day, Ford held only about 56 percent of the American market for new cars and in the 1920s faced increased competition from the newly reorganized GENERAL MOTORS and Chrysler. In the 1930s, Ford spent less time with the company and more on outside projects such as the Greenfield Village, a museum in Dearborn. He suffered a stroke in 1938, removing him from the company even more and helping senior executives and his only son, Edsel, to greater positions of power. He assumed the presidency of the company again after Edsel Ford died in 1943.

Ford and his wife, Clara Bryant Ford, established the Ford Foundation in 1936, mainly to maintain family control of the company after Ford's death. The foundation held 95 percent of Ford stock, with family members holding the remaining 5 percent. The foundation became a major benefactor of social causes around the world and one of the major forces in philanthropy. Ford died in 1947.

See also CHRYSLER, WALTER PERCY; CHRYSLER CORP.; DURANT, WILLIAM CRAPO.

Further reading

Bak, Richard. *Henry and Edsel: The Creation of the Ford Empire.* Hoboken, N.J.: John Wiley, 2003.
Brinkley, Douglas. *Wheels for the World: Henry Ford, His Company, and a Century of Progress, 1903–2003.* New York: Viking Press, 2003.

Ford Motor Company   An automobile manufacturer founded by Henry FORD and incorporated in 1903. The company originally began as the Detroit Automobile Company in 1899. The company subsequently was reorganized as the Henry Ford Company in 1901. Needing additional capital, the company again was reorganized in 1903 as the Ford Motor Company when Ford and 11 associates went into business with only $28,000 in cash. It sold its first car to a Detroit physician in 1903.

After initial success producing Model N autos, Ford introduced the Model T in 1908. The car was an immediate success, also inspiring Ford to began a new type of production that would revolutionize manufacturing. In 1913, Ford introduced the moving assembly line at the Highland Park plant in Michigan. The line allowed workers to remain in one place and perform the same task as cars moved by their workstations. Within 20 years, the results were phenomenal. Ford sold more than 15 million cars and became a household name. The assembly line also proved that economies of scale could be achieved in mass manufacturing because the cost of the Model T fell over the years.

The Ford Motor Company began to lose market share during the 1920s in the face of intense competition. The original Model T was available only in black and, despite its low price tag, began to lose its appeal for many motorists. In 1925, Ford acquired the Lincoln Motor Company, a maker of high-end luxury cars, in order to diversify its line. In 1927, when the last Model T came off the assembly line, more than 15 million of the model had been produced. It was succeeded by the Model A, which was more refined and offered a choice of colors. The Mercury brand was established 10 years later to cater to mid-market customers. In 1931, the company produced its 20 millionth car.

In the same year, Ford began production in England, building cars for the European market. It also maintained a large manufacturing operation in Germany. Ford founded the Ford Foundation in 1936. The Lincoln Continental model was introduced in 1939. After years of eschewing unions, Ford finally agreed to unionization at its plants in 1941. After Edsel Ford, Henry's son, died in 1943, Henry again assumed the presidency. He resigned after World War II and was succeeded by his grandson Henry Ford II in 1945. The company resumed producing civilian automobiles in July 1945 after several years of devoting its production to military vehicles.

Henry Ford died in 1947, but the family tradition would continue. The postwar period brought expansion, and new models were added in the 1950s, including the Thunderbird in 1954 and the Edsel. Only the former was successful. The Thunderbird, like the Ford and Lincoln Continental, would become one of the company's most enduring models. The Ford Motor Company remained in family hands until an initial public offering in 1956, when Henry Ford II sold some of the family holdings to raise additional capital for expansion.

The company introduced the ill-fated Edsel in 1957, but the car did not remain in production past 1959. In that year, the company created Ford Motor Credit to help provide financing for its cars. Robert McNamara was named president in 1960 but quit a year later in order to join the Kennedy administration as defense secretary. In 1964, the company introduced another model that would be phenomenally successful. The

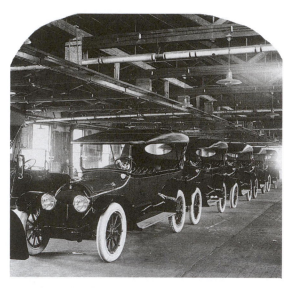

Row of completed "Tin Lizzys," or Model Ts, coming off the Ford assembly line, 1917 (LIBRARY OF CONGRESS)

Mustang sold more than 2 million units in the first two years of production. Ford Motor continued to expand its operations in Europe in 1967 and became the largest manufacturer of cars in Britain and one of the largest in Germany.

In 1970, Lee IACOCCA was named president of the company and remained in the job for eight years. Henry Ford II remained with the company until 1980 and then served on its finance committee until his death in 1987. William Clay Ford Jr., Henry's great-grandson, joined the company in 1979 and was named president in 1999. After poor financial performance in the 1970s and 1980s, Ford produced a new model called the Taurus that helped turn around the company's performance and became the best-selling car in the United States by the mid-1990s. In 1997, Ford celebrated production of its 250-millionth vehicle. The company acquired foreign manufacturers in the 1990s, as a result of its success, purchasing Volvo of Sweden and Jaguar, Rover, and Aston Martin of Britain.

See also CHRYSLER, WALTER PERCY; CHRYSLER CORP.; DURANT, WILLIAM CRAPO; GENERAL MOTORS.

Further reading
Barry, James P. *Henry Ford and Mass Production.* New York: Franklin Watts, 1973.
Brinkley, Douglas. *Wheels for the World: Henry Ford, His Company, and a Century of Progress, 1903–2003.* New York: Viking Press, 2003.
Shook, Robert L. *Turnaround: The New Ford Motor Company.* Englewood Cliffs, N.J.: Prentice Hall, 1990.

Foreign Corrupt Practices Act (FCPA)

Passed by Congress in 1977, the FCPA makes it illegal for Americans to bribe foreign business contacts in order to do business with them. Enforcement of the act is shared by the Department of Justice and the Securities and Exchange Commission (SEC).

In the 1970s, the SEC discovered that hundreds of American companies doing business abroad regularly bribed foreign officials in return for contracts or other favors. The payments often were made to government officials in order to facilitate business. After the act was passed, several companies accused of bribery were found guilty, fined, and subsequently barred from bidding on federal contracts in the United States.

The law was not totally effective, however. It put many firms at a disadvantage since bribing foreign officials is not illegal in many other countries. Some firms even allowed the deduction of the bribes as business expenses. As a result, the law made the playing field overseas more uneven for American companies attempting to compete. In 1988, the United States began a concerted effort to convince other countries that such a law should be passed among all developed countries in order to create a level playing field for all. As a result, the United States and 33 other countries signed the OECD Convention on Combating Bribery of Foreign Public Officials in International Business Transactions.

The FCPA has required companies to establish compliance departments to monitor their overseas activities in much the same way that securities firms maintain compliance departments to ensure they remain within securities guidelines. The act also requires companies with securities listed in one of the U.S. stock markets to meet American accounting standards. Detractors have claimed that the law ties their hands when dealing with foreign companies and governments, many of which expect off-the-record payments as part of the expense of doing business.

See also GENERALLY ACCEPTED ACCOUNTING PRINCIPLES; SECURITIES EXCHANGE ACT OF 1934.

Further reading

Prasad, Jyoti N. *The Impact of the Foreign Corrupt Practices Act of 1977 on U.S. Exports.* New York: Garland, 1993.

foreign exchange market The market for currencies, conducted mainly through bank dealers around the world. Although the market has existed since ancient times, developments since World War II have changed the modern market that is conducted in the United States by money center banks in the major financial centers.

The market is divided into two compartments—the spot market and the forward market. The spot market trades currencies for immediate delivery, while the forward market trades for delayed delivery for periods up to one year. Spot prices for the dollar against most other currencies can be obtained daily, although the forward market is limited to prices between the major trading currencies only. Banks in the United States quote the dollar against other currencies, and the dollar also is quoted against the same currencies by banks in other countries. In such a manner, the market has developed into a 24-hour exchange that is constantly quoting prices in the major trading currencies around the world. When a dollar is traded in another country against a currency that is not native to the country in which it is being quoted, the rate is called a cross-rate.

Until the early 1930s, the market was based upon the dollar and the gold bullion standard.

Most major trading currencies were stated in gold terms. When Britain and the United States abandoned the GOLD STANDARD in the early 1930s, the system did not return to normal until after World War II. After the BRETTON WOODS SYSTEM was implemented, the dollar was the major currency in the system, quoted at $35 per ounce of gold. Many currencies were protected in some form or other by exchange controls. Their respective central banks controlled their international flows to ensure stability of the exchange rate and their own reserves.

The Bretton Woods system effectively was abandoned in August 1971, when President Nixon pulled the United States off the convertibility standard. The old system was temporarily replaced by the Smithsonian Agreement, but it lasted only a short time. The foreign exchange markets were in turmoil until a new regime emerged. Within a year the major trading, or hard, currencies were floating against each other. Rather than be stated in gold terms and have a fixed parity in the market, the currencies floated freely against each other and continue to do so today. Smaller currencies continue to be linked to larger currencies, normally to that of their major trading partner.

The international monetary system has undergone other changes in addition to the adoption of floating currencies. The European Union adopted the EURO, a composite currency representing a weighted value of its members, in January 1999 to ensure stability of the European Union's imports and exports in light of competition from the dollar and the yen. Within that system, currencies do not float against each other but have stable values that may require adjustment from time to time.

In the 1980s, the foreign exchange market began developing new financial products for use by its large institutional customers. New currency-related products such as options, caps, and collars were developed so that customers could limit foreign exchange exposure rather than use traditional forward contracts.

In the 1990s, many countries with historically weak currencies tried linking them to the U.S. dollar. There were several ways of doing this, with some countries adopting the direct peg and a currency board. These techniques were usually attempts by a country to link its currency directly to the fortunes of the dollar, although the results were mixed at best.

See also FOREIGN INVESTMENT.

Further reading

Einzig, Paul. *The History of Foreign Exchange.* London: Macmillan, 1970.

McKinnon, Ronald I. *The Rules of the Game: International Money and Exchange Rates.* Cambridge, Mass.: MIT Press, 1996.

Solomon, Robert. *The International Monetary System.* New York: Harper & Row, 1977.

foreign investment   Investments made in a country by a foreign investor, usually a corporation. Foreign investment differs from foreign trade, which is selling goods from a domestic base to foreign customers. In the case of foreign investment, a company invests money to produce and/or distribute goods overseas in order to be closer to the foreign market.

Foreign investment is divided into two types—direct and portfolio. Direct investment occurs when a foreign investor acquires tangible assets, or what is considered to be a dominant shareholding, in an American company. The size of the investment does not necessarily have to be a majority shareholding. Traditionally, a foreign investment in the United States has been considered to be any shareholding in an American company of 10 to 15 percent, but certainly less than a 51 percent majority holding. Exactly how much of a foreign investment in an American company constitutes foreign investment has changed periodically and traditionally is defined by the U.S. Department of Commerce.

Portfolio investment involves a foreign investor buying intangible assets in the United States, namely stocks, bonds, and other financial instruments, or holding copyrights and patents. Portfolio, or indirect, investment is considered to be the less stable of the two since foreign investors can liquidate their holdings and withdraw their capital from the markets at short notice. Direct investment, on the other hand, is assumed to be more stable since it represents a "brick and mortar" investment that is long-term in nature.

The American experience with foreign investment has fallen into two broad historical periods. From the 18th century to the end of World War I, the United States was a net importer of long-term capital. The traditional suppliers of funds were the Dutch and the British, along with other European countries. Private banking firms such as BARING BROTHERS and the House of ROTHSCHILD provided much-needed foreign investment during the 19th century, especially before the Civil War. American banks such as August Belmont & Co. and Drexel Morgan & Co. also helped bring in foreign investment, as did Drexel Morgan's successor, J. P. Morgan & Co.

After World War I, the United States became a supplier of investment funds to the rest of the world, reversing its earlier reliance on foreign investment. The trend accelerated after World War II. Then in the 1970s, as the United States began experiencing balance of payment problems, the situation changed. In the late 1970s and 1980s, the Japanese became one of the largest foreign investors in the United States. European investors also supplied substantial funds, including the British, Germans, and Swiss. These traditional sources supplied money for both direct and portfolio investments, often on a large scale.

In the late 1970s and early 1980s, many foreign companies, notably Japanese, began opening operations in the United States to produce goods and sell them locally. Often these operations were prompted by changes in TARIFFS, especially in the case of automobiles. The Reagan administration urged Japanese auto manufacturers to agree to a voluntary quota on the number of compact autos sold each year in the United States. While they did agree, the agreement did not prohibit production within the United States, and, as a result, several Japanese companies opened manufacturing facilities to build the cars domestically.

A major accounting change for valuing overseas assets and liabilities in the early 1980s helped American firms operating abroad and softened the blow of major currency changes on the FOREIGN EXCHANGE MARKETS that could affect the value of those investments. American foreign investment has centered mostly on Britain and western Europe, but American investments are spread around the globe. Britain traditionally is the major recipient of American investment along with Canada. The United States remains the largest foreign investor in the world and has also attracted the largest amount of foreign investment from abroad. With the emergence of China and South Korea as major trading nations in the 1990s, both have become investors in American assets, notably Treasury securities and other indirect investments.

See also BELMONT, AUGUST.

Further reading

Geisst, Charles R. *Entrepot Capitalism: Foreign Investment and the American Dream in the Twentieth Century.* New York: Praeger, 1992.

Graham, Edward M., and Paul Krugman. *Foreign Direct Investment in the United States.* Washington, D.C.: Institute for International Economics, 1989.

Wilkins, Mira. *A History of Foreign Investment in the United States to 1914.* Cambridge, Mass.: Harvard University Press, 1989.

free agency   A labor concept that allows a member of a professional sports team to sign with a team of his or her choice rather than be tied to a specific team under contract terms that do not allow freedom to move. The practice is now used by all professional athletes, although the practice originated in baseball.

Until 1976, baseball management maintained a "reserve clause" that tied players to a franchise for the duration of their careers unless traded, sold, or given an outright release. The reserve clause of player contracts had been a part of the game dating back to 1879 and the 1880s, and management sold player contracts at will. Management had sought ways to limit the movement of players from team to team. Initially, the leagues instituted rules that prohibited players from changing teams during the course of the season, but in 1879 the National League team management instituted a "gentleman's agreement" to recognize five players on each team who would be reserved from negotiations with other teams, and thus through informal collusion kept player salaries down. In 1887, National League management represented by Albert Spalding agreed to a uniform contract, but included the "reserve clause" in the contract. Two years later, National League players issued a manifesto challenging the recent actions of management and in 1890 set out to form the Players League under player control. Spalding orchestrated the fall of the Players League after one year and allowed the players to return to the original franchises.

Major league baseball also enjoyed an exemption from antitrust legislation granted by Congress in 1922. This exemption made it possible for franchise owners to exercise a monopoly over the talent of players. As early as 1946, players presented legal challenges to the "reserve clause," but the system would remain in place until the early 1970s. In 1968, player representative Marvin Miller negotiated a contract with management that raised minimum player salary to $10,000, and recognized a grievance procedure and the right of players to have representatives during salary negotiations. In 1969, a dispute over pension payments resulted in players not signing their contracts and a boycott of training camps by 391 players.

The first major legal challenge to the reserve clause came in 1969, when St. Louis Cardinals player Curt Flood attempted to block his off-season trade to the Philadelphia Phillies franchise. Flood's major league career began in 1956, and he had spent 11 seasons with the Cardinals. Flood sued in federal court to overturn the reserve clause, and his lawyers argued that the restrictive contract measure violated the Thirteenth Amendment, which prohibits slavery and indentured servitude. Flood's suit failed, but while the suit was still pending during the 1970 season, Flood refused to play for the Phillies. Instead, Flood agreed to a trade to the Washington Senators for the 1971 season, but only with the understanding that the trade in no way would impair the pending legal action.

The federal district court and appeals court rendered negative decisions on Flood's suit, and on June 18, 1972, the U.S. Supreme Court also ruled against him. Flood's career ended with these legal decisions. He saw limited playing time with the Senators in 1971 (13 games) and did not play again after the 1971 season. The majority of active major league players failed to support Flood's suit, but some retired players such as Jackie Robinson testified on his behalf.

The next challenge came in 1973 as a consequence of terms agreed upon pursuant to a new collective bargaining agreement. Salary disputes could be submitted to impartial binding arbitration, and after 10 years with a team a player could veto a trade. In 1974, eight Oakland Athletics players submitted salary disputes to arbitration. The arbitrator rendered favorable decisions for Rollie Fingers, Ken Holtzman, Darold Knowles, Sal Bando, and Reggie Jackson, and unfavorable decisions for Gene Tenace, Joe Rudi, and Ted Kubiak. Owner Charles Finley suffered a major reverse with the loss of Jim "Catfish" Hunter. Hunter won free agent status because Finley had failed to fulfill the terms of his contract with Hunter. As an unrestricted free agent Hunter signed a contract with the New York Yankees franchise.

Two years later, in 1976, the reserve clause fell. The impartial arbitrator Peter Seitz ruled that at the end of a contract the team could exercise its option to retain the player for one year, but after the option year the player became a free agent. Management fired Seitz and challenged his decision in court, but the courts upheld Seitz's ruling. This decision effectively ended the reserve clause. A collective bargaining agreement negotiated in 1976 contained the provision that a player became a free agent after six years. The Seitz ruling and 1976 collective bargaining agreement gave players greater control over their careers and dramatically altered the personnel of some franchises, as seen in the case of the Oakland Athletics. In 1976, 24 veteran players were on the Oakland roster; when a number of them left, they broke up a squad that had won three consecutive World Series championships.

Free agency resulted in an increase in salaries for star players, who would command salaries in the six and seven figures. Jim Hunter, for example, received $2.5 million a year to move to the Yankees franchise. The salaries of selected star players came close to the value of franchises created only a few years earlier with expansion in 1969. For example, a group headed by William Daley paid $5.25 million for the new Seattle Pilots franchise when it was created in 1969. The franchise sold for $10.8 million in 1970 to a group headed by Bud Selig, which moved the franchise to Milwaukee. As the salaries of star players increased, so too did the value of franchises.

Over the next 14 years, management attempted to limit the gains made by players through free agency. Players initiated a strike in 1981 in response to an effort by management to gain compensation for free agents. After seven weeks, management backed down. Arbitration decisions in 1987 and 1990 ruled that management had colluded to not hire free agents, thus violating the collective bargaining agreement. The 1987 ruling was the most serious, since it ruled that there was evidence of collusion in 1985 and 1986. A strike during spring training in

1990 was ended before the beginning of the season. The strike that ended the 1994 season in early August came in response to new management initiatives to limit player rights, including the imposition of a salary cap. Spring training for the 1995 season began with replacement players in camp, but management and players eventually resolved the dispute. During the last dispute, management emphasized the high salaries of the minority of elite players as a public relations ploy to undermine potential public support for the players' cause.

The 1995 players' strike ended after a New York federal judge issued an injunction against the team owners to prevent them from using replacement players, and for them to resume normal labor relations under the previous collective bargaining agreement. Following the issuance of the injunction, players agreed to suspend the strike, and a reduced-schedule season with regular players began on April 25. The end of the strike also found a number of free agents without teams, but the bidding for their talents began immediately after the final agreement to resume the season had been worked out. Those teams with deep pockets paid high salaries to acquire skilled free agents.

Further reading

Markusen, Bruce. *Baseball's Last Dynasty: Charlie Finley's Oakland A's.* Indianapolis: Masters Press, 1998.

Neft, David, and Richard Cohen. *The Sports Encyclopedia: Baseball.* New York: Grosset & Dunlap, 1993.

Rader, Benjamin. *Baseball: A History of America's Game.* Urbana: University of Illinois Press, 1994.

Robert H. Jackson

Frick, Henry Clay (1849–1919) *industrialist and steel executive* Frick was born in Westmoreland County, Pennsylvania, and worked on his father's farm as a boy, receiving only sporadic education. He worked for his uncle, Abraham Overholt, who manufactured Old Overholt

Whiskey, as a clerk and worked his way to becoming bookkeeper. He also developed an interest in steel and soon began developing steel and coke ovens in western Pennsylvania.

Finding steel more to his liking, he opened H. C. Frick Coke Co. in 1871 to operate coke ovens in the local coal district. After the Panic of 1873, Frick used the economic crisis to his advantage by buying out several competitors. Borrowing money from Thomas Mellon of the Pittsburgh banking family, he began buying coal-producing land while prices were depressed. By 1880, he had made a sizable return and was worth more than $1 million. Like John D. Rockefeller in the oil business, he began to consolidate his operations after the panic, assuming correctly that the economy would soon right itself.

In 1881, Andrew CARNEGIE acquired substantial holdings in Frick's company, and Frick was paid with a large block of Carnegie stock. After being named chairman of Carnegie Steel in 1892, Frick continued to consolidate the STEEL INDUSTRY and expanded into RAILROADS as well. He acquired Duquesne Steel Company in 1890. A black mark appeared on his management record shortly thereafter. While chairman of Carnegie Steel, Frick dealt with strikers at the company's Homestead plant in Pennsylvania who were protesting low wages. While Carnegie was in Europe, Frick called in private Pinkerton security guards to calm the workers, and a riot ensued, claiming casualties on both sides. An attempt was also made on his life. Although the strike was broken when the governor of Pennsylvania sent in 8,000 National Guard troops, the incident became a national sensation and helped to underscore the plight of the poverty-stricken steel workers in the region.

In 1899, Frick resigned his position at Carnegie Steel after a disagreement with Carnegie. Subsequently, he served as intermediary between Carnegie and J. P. Morgan, who wanted to buy Carnegie Steel. After the transaction was complete in 1901, he became a director of the newly organized U.S. STEEL CORP. He also was intermediary between Morgan and John D. Rockefeller, obtaining some of Rockefeller's mineral resources for the new company. He helped reorganize the Equitable Life Assurance Company in 1905 and acquired large tracts of land in his native Pittsburgh.

Frick was known as a patron of the arts. His art collection and New York mansion were left to the public as the Frick Museum. He also made several notable contributions to Princeton University as well as donations of parkland in Pittsburgh.

See also MORGAN, JOHN PIERPONT.

Further reading

Sanger, Martha. *Henry Clay Frick: An Intimate Portrait.* New York: Abbeville Press, 1998.

Warren, Kenneth. *Triumphant Capitalism: Henry Clay Frick and the Industrial Transformation of America.* Pittsburgh: University of Pittsburgh Press, 1996.

Fulton, Robert (1765–1815) *engineer and inventor*   Born in Lancaster County, Pennsylvania, to Irish immigrant parents, Fulton spent his early years designing little paddleboats and sketching. At age 17, he moved to Philadelphia, where he was apprenticed to a jeweler, beginning a long career of design and invention. Then in 1786, he moved to Britain, where he studied with the well-known American artist Benjamin West and became an illustrator and essayist as well.

Fulton also became interested in canals and canal boats in the 1790s and spent a considerable number of years in Britain and France designing marine vessels and torpedoes. Shortly thereafter, he began to expand his interests, learned several languages, and became interested in design. He began to design canal boats first, before turning his attention to submarines. He developed the first submarine capable of diving and surfacing, but propulsion was a problem he could never successfully solve.

After becoming acquainted with Robert LIVINGSTON, then the U.S. minister to France, he turned his attention to steamboats. After meeting

with some initial success, he returned to the United States and began building a steamboat in New York that would become known as the *Clermont.* The boat became the first successful steamboat and in 1807 began a service between New York City and Albany. The trip took 32 hours. Other similar boats followed, and the New York legislature granted him and Livingston a monopoly on steamboat transportation in New York harbor. The monopoly would later be challenged by a rival company operating between New York, New Jersey, and Philadelphia and headed by Thomas Gibbons and his captain, Cornelius VANDERBILT. The case was decided in the Supreme Court of the United States in favor of Gibbons. One of Fulton's last achievements was the design of a steam warship to defend New York harbor

Robert Fulton, a wood engraving (LIBRARY OF CONGRESS)

against the British in the War of 1812; Congress ordered the boat built in 1814, but Fulton died before its completion.

In addition to his designs, Fulton was also known as an artist, although few of his original works remain. Along with John STEVENS, he is remembered as the father of the steamboat that revolutionized transportation after the War of 1812.

Further reading

Hill, Ralph Nading. *Robert Fulton and the Steamboat.* New York: Random House, 1954.

Philip, Cynthia Owen. *Robert Fulton: A Biography.* New York: Franklin Watts, 1985.

Sale, Kirkpatrick. *Fire of His Genius: Robert Fulton and the American Dream.* New York: Free Press, 2001.

futures markets Or commodity futures markets—the term given to financial markets in which contracts for future delivery are traded rather than the actual commodities or financial instruments that they represent. These markets originally were established so that farmers could sell their crops to buyers at prices determined in the present but for delivery at some future date. This was called "when-arrived" trading.

In these markets, traders buy and sell futures contracts in a pit environment, where traders congregate solely to trade in that particular futures contract. Orders from customers are relayed to the pit, where the actual transactions takes place. The system, known as "open outcry," has been employed since the futures exchanges were founded in the 19th century. Open outcry is still employed, although proposals are underway at certain exchanges to replace it with computerized trading that would take place away from the trading floor.

The futures markets began before the Civil War in Chicago and New York, trading agricultural commodities contracts. The CHICAGO BOARD OF TRADE was established in 1848, becoming that city's first established futures market, although it took several decades for futures trading to become well established. Markets were opened in other midwestern cities, including St. Louis and Kansas City, as well as in New York. Other exchanges include the Kansas City Board of Trade (founded 1856), the New York Mercantile Exchange (1898), and the Chicago Mercantile Exchange (1872). Exchanges tended to specialize in certain types of contracts. Originally, the exchanges in the Midwest specialized in home-grown agricultural commodities, while those in New York specialized in commodities related to international trade, including agriculturals such as coffee and sugar, as well as precious metals. Over the years, contracts on a wide array of commodities were added, including precious metals, building supplies, livestock, agricultural by-products, heating oil, fuel oil, and financial instruments, among others. The clear-cut lines of demarcation between exchanges no longer exist, and today all of the futures exchanges trade financial futures on financial instruments such as stock indexes, bonds, and foreign currencies. Contracts traded on one exchange are not interchangeable with those traded on another.

Congress passed legislation in the 1920s and 1930s in an attempt to control the futures markets. In 1922, Congress passed the Grain Futures Act, an attempt to control speculation in the grain futures markets. The legislation was not successful, and in 1936 Congress responded by passing the Commodity Exchange Act. This law made price manipulation on the exchanges illegal and sought to curb excessive speculation and fraud. Further legislation was necessary because the markets still did not have a regulatory body. Today, they are regulated by the COMMODITY FUTURES TRADING COMMISSION, established in 1974. This five-person regulatory commission is responsible for overseeing trading on the various exchanges in much the same way that the SEC oversees securities trading on the stock exchanges. In the futures markets, margin is set by the individual exchanges and, when securities derivatives products are involved, by the SEC and the

Commodities Futures Trading Commission through powers delegated by the FEDERAL RESERVE since 2002.

One of the major issues concerning the relationship between stock, futures, and OPTIONS MARKETS is program trading, also referred to as portfolio insurance. Program trading involves the use of computer programs assessing the value of individual stocks, futures, and option prices and then buying and selling each accordingly. It became a major issue during the stock market collapse in October 1987 and was blamed for much of the market's fall. Stock traders blamed computer programs for selling stocks based upon derivatives valuations, adding significant downside selling pressure to stocks at a vulnerable time.

This interrelationship also becomes especially critical at what is known as triple witching hour, the day when options and futures related to stocks expire. Many of these instruments' prices have an effect on each other, and when triple witching hour occurs, usually at the end of a particular business day, individual stocks and the market indexes may experience sudden price changes due to arbitrage between them. For instance, a stock that is included in a major market index and has options listed on it may experience volatility in the last hours of trading as traders adjust their positions in index futures, individual stock options, and in the stock itself. Usually, the adjustments are made by computer through program trading whereby programs react to price discrepancies and automatically enter buy and sell orders in the various markets as a result.

See also BLACK-SCHOLES MODEL.

Further reading

Cowing, Cedric. *Populists, Plungers and Progressives: A Social History of Stock and Commodity Speculation, 1890–1936.* Princeton, N.J.: Princeton University Press, 1965.

Geisst, Charles R. *Wheels of Fortune: The History of Speculation from Scandal to Respectability.* New York: John Wiley & Sons, 2002.

G

Gallatin, Albert (1761–1849) *banker and politician* Born into a prominent Swiss family in Geneva in 1761, Gallatin attended the prestigious Academy of Geneva, where he displayed considerable academic promise. Against his family's wishes, he immigrated to the United States in 1780 after refusing a commission in the Hessian army. After arriving in Boston, he began various business ventures, most of which were not successful. As a result, he also lectured in French at Harvard College in order to help support himself. He took the oath of allegiance in Virginia in 1785 and then moved to Pennsylvania, where his political career began.

Gallatin was elected to the state legislature in 1790 from a constituency in western Pennsylvania and then to the U.S. Senate in 1793 but was rejected by that body because his citizenship was in doubt. He left the Senate after only three months in office and after infuriating Alexander HAMILTON, secretary of the Treasury, by asking him for an itemized statement of the national debt as of January 1, 1794. In the same year, his constituents led the Whiskey Rebellion in Pennsylvania over the matter of a tax on spirits produced in the area. In 1795 he returned to Congress as a member of the House of Representatives, which then was meeting in Philadelphia. He became a member of the Standing Committee of Business, one of that body's first finance committees.

After the hotly contested presidential election of 1800, new president Thomas Jefferson appointed Gallatin secretary of the Treasury. In the same year, Gallatin produced a famous tract entitled "Views of the Public Debt, Receipts & Expenditures of the United States," a report critical of U.S. financial policy over the previous decade. He took office pledging to reduce the national debt and actually did so, reducing federal indebtedness by almost $14 million. He produced a plan to pay down the federal debt by 1817, but the Louisiana Purchase and the War of 1812 intervened. In 1813, he was part of the delegation that negotiated peace with Great Britain. He served as secretary until 1814 but declined reappointment to the job when it was offered by James Madison. In 1826, he served as ambassador to Britain.

At John Jacob Astor's request, Gallatin was named president of the newly formed National Bank of New York in 1831. In the same year he wrote another famous tract, "Considerations on the Currency and Banking System of the United States." He was a strong supporter of the Second BANK OF THE UNITED STATES, advocating hard money policies and free trade. Later, the National Bank of New York was renamed the Gallatin National Bank.

Gallatin was also a founder of New York University in 1830 and president of the New-York Historical Society in 1842. He died on Long Island in 1849. He is best remembered for his views on the soundness of government finances, opposing Hamilton and the Federalists, and serving in government during a critical period of American history, especially at the time of the Louisiana Purchase.

Further reading

Adams, Henry. *The Life of Albert Gallatin.* 1879. Reprint, New York: Peter Smith, 1943.

Stevens, John Austin. *Albert Gallatin.* Boston: Houghton Mifflin, 1895.

Walters, Raymond. *Albert Gallatin: Jeffersonian Financier and Diplomat.* New York: Macmillan, 1957.

Gary, Elbert H. (1846–1927) *lawyer and industrialist* Born in Illinois, Gary worked on his father's farm and served in the Union Army during the Civil War. He then worked briefly as a teacher before deciding to study law. Gary graduated from Union College of Law in Chicago and served as a court clerk for three years before beginning his career as a corporate lawyer. He entered politics when he was elected mayor of Wheaton, Illinois, and later served as a county judge in DuPage County. From that time, he acquired the title Judge Gary, which he used throughout his professional life.

His work with corporate clients piqued an interest in the STEEL INDUSTRY, and he organized the American Steel and Wire Co. Coming to the attention of J. P. Morgan, he joined the Federal Steel Company in 1898 and moved to New York. He was asked to organize the U.S. STEEL CORP. in 1901 after Morgan purchased Carnegie Steel. He

became chairman of the board of directors and personally directed the expansion of the company into the largest steel producer in the world, a position he would keep for the next two years. He also helped develop the steel-producing town of Gary, Indiana, which was named after him. As chairman of the company, he organized the famous Gary dinners at which steel executives from other companies were invited to discuss matters of mutual interest and concern. The first was held at the Waldorf Astoria in New York City in 1907 and was attended by 49 steel company executives who were invited to achieve gentleman's agreements about prices and production, not price fixing, as Gary always maintained. The dinners later became evidence in Justice Department antitrust suits against the industry as examples of collusion among steel executives to fix prices and control production.

Gary's reputation within the industry was one of a fair employer who paid high wages and promoted safety for his employees. He also was a proponent of employees owning stock in their employers' companies, although he was opposed to labor unions. His greatest coup was a favorable ruling by the Supreme Court in 1920 adjudging that U.S. Steel did not violate the SHERMAN ACT, as the Justice Department had contended in a suit filed years before. The ruling was favorable in part because he had always been forthcoming about the company's policies, dating back to the Roosevelt administration when the president tacitly agreed not to prosecute the company for its part in many potential antitrust problems caused by the Panic of 1907 and J. P. Morgan's activities. He remained active in the company until his death in 1927.

Further reading

Allen, Frederick Lewis. *The Lords of Creation.* New York: Harper & Brothers, 1935.

Tarbell, Ida. *The Life of Elbert H. Gary: The Story of Steel.* 1925. Reprint, New York: Greenwood Press, 1965.

Gates, Bill (1955–   ) *computer software pioneer* Gates was a cofounder of the Microsoft Corporation. Born in Seattle, Gates began programming while in his teens. He teamed with schoolmate Paul Allen and began taking on freelance projects while still in high school and before enrolling at Harvard. He left Harvard after only a year and, with Allen as his partner, founded a small software company in 1974 that would later become the Microsoft Corporation.

Originally, their company was located in Albuquerque, New Mexico, and developed programs based upon the BASIC computer language. It was not until the advent of the small, or personal, computer (PC) that the company got its initial break. When IBM introduced the first PCs in 1980, Microsoft was given a contract to develop an operating system for the computer hardware. Gates and Allen had moved their company back to Seattle, where a small competitor, Seattle Computer Products, had developed an operating system called the Quick and Dirty Operating System. Gates changed the name to disk operating system, or DOS. After making improvements, DOS was licensed to IBM. From that point, Microsoft operating systems and software became the standard for PCs around the world, with the exception of the products of its smaller competitor, Apple Computer.

Because of the ease and user friendliness of the Apple operating system, Microsoft announced its Windows operating system in 1983. Unlike its older DOS system, Windows employed a graphical interface that allowed users to access the system as easily as they could the Apple system. Allen retired from the company in the same year. However, Windows was not released for another two years, and Microsoft soon was sued by Apple for copyright infringement. Although the suit continued into the 1990s, Windows became extremely popular and helped solidify Microsoft's hold on the PC market. Subsequently, the company launched a successful IPO in 1986, which made Gates extremely wealthy and provided the capital Microsoft needed to develop new prod-

Microsoft chairman Bill Gates (GETTY IMAGES)

ucts and buy out smaller competitors, a strategy the company successfully employed as it grew larger.

In 1990, Windows 3.0 was introduced and provided further competition for Apple software. Eventually, Apple's suit against Microsoft was dismissed. Microsoft continued to introduce software products based upon the Windows system. By the 1990s, the company held a virtual monopoly over the operating systems of PCs, with an estimated 80 percent of the world's PCs using either DOS or Windows. Microsoft's agreements with manufacturers also called for a fee to be paid to the company for each PC sold, a practice that, critics contended, illustrated its virtual dominance of the industry.

In 1998, the Antitrust Division of the Justice Department filed suit against Microsoft, charging it with violations of the Sherman Antitrust Act. The company vigorously defended itself against the charges, although the initial trial judge found against Microsoft and ordered the company broken into two parts. Gates continued to maintain the company's innocence against the charges and filed an appeal. During the bull market of the late 1990s, the advance in the company's stock price easily made Gates the wealthiest man in the world, with an estimated fortune valued somewhere between $70 and $90 billion. He also became actively involved in philanthropy.

See also COMPUTER INDUSTRY.

Further reading

Heller, Robert. *Bill Gates.* New York: Dorling Kindersley, 2000.

Manes, Stephen. *Gates: How Microsoft Reinvented an Industry.* New York: Touchstone Books, 1993.

Wallace, James. *Hard Drive: Bill Gates and the Making of the Microsoft Empire.* New York: HarperBusiness, 1993.

Geneen, Harold S. (1910–1997) *conglomerate executive* Born in Bournemouth, England, Geneen immigrated to the United States with his parents in his infancy. He studied accounting at New York University and, to help pay his expenses, worked as a runner on the NEW YORK STOCK EXCHANGE. In the 1930s, he worked as an accountant for several companies before accepting the top accounting job at the American Can Company during World War II.

Geneen then worked briefly for camera maker Bell & Howell and steelmaker Jones & Laughlin before accepting a job in 1956 with Raytheon, an electronics company that did much defense-related work for the government in the postwar years. The company was run by Charles Francis Adams, who allowed Geneen to reorganize the company substantially. Although he quadrupled the amount of Raytheon's earnings, he was still not given the top job at the company, so in 1959 he left to accept the presidency of

International Telephone & Telegraph, a company founded in the early 1920s.

Geneen became convinced that many companies could benefit from diversification of their operations in order to protect themselves against swings in the economic cycle. Part of the strategy was an aggressive acquisitions program. After 1963, he began acquiring specialty manufacturing companies producing things such as industrial pumps, air conditioning units, and control devices used in domestic appliances. In 1964, true diversification began when he acquired Aetna Finance, a consumer finance company, and a British insurance company, creating the foundation of ITT Financial Services.

By 1965, ITT's revenues had doubled, reaching $1.5 billion. Geneen began pursuing Avis, the car rental company. ITT also made a bid for ABC, the television broadcast company, but there was much regulatory concern about the acquisition. ITT ultimately abandoned it. The company also acquired the Sheraton group of hotels in 1967 and the Hartford Fire Insurance Company. The Hartford acquisition aroused the interest of the Nixon administration and would be allowed only when ITT agreed to divest itself of Avis and two other companies. At the height of its acquisitions program, ITT was adding a company per day, accumulating 250 companies with more than 2,000 operating units.

By the late 1960s and early 1970s, ITT moved into the top 20 largest American corporations measured by assets. Geneen came under severe pressure in the early 1970s, being accused of meddling in the affairs of Chile, where ITT had a substantial presence. He and ITT were also accused of buying political influence from the Republican Party during the 1972 presidential election, although none of the charges were ever proved irrefutably. Geneen served his last full year at ITT in 1977 and was succeeded by Rand Araskog as chairman.

See also CONGLOMERATES; LAZARD FRERES; MERGERS.

Further reading

Geneen, Harold. *The Synergy Myth*. New York: St. Martin's Press, 1997.

Schoenberg, Robert. *Geneen*. New York: Norton, 1985.

Sobel, Robert. *ITT: The Management of Opportunity*. New York: Times Books, 1982.

General Electric Co.   Founded as the Edison Electric Co. by Thomas EDISON in 1878, the company is one of the few American companies to retain its original corporate name, later adopted in 1892. Under Edison's guidance, the firm developed the incandescent lightbulb before merging with the Thomson-Houston Electric Co. in 1892. For the first 20 years of its life, the company was run by Charles Coffin, a former shoe company executive. Its technological developments were overseen by Charles Steinmetz, its chief electrical engineer, who was responsible for steering the company's development.

The company then branched out into electric transformers and locomotives, although Edison himself ended his involvement with the company several years after the merger. When Charles Dow initiated his stock market average in 1896, GE was one of the first stocks included. Today it is the only original member remaining in the Dow Jones Industrial Average.

During World War I, the company did research work for the U.S. Navy. When the war ended, it was attracted to the market for radios and the nascent broadcasting industry. It manufactured radio receivers and also helped organize an early radio station, WGY, in Schenectady, New York, the home of its research division. GE also produced a wide array of small appliances, which made it a household name with consumers. During World War II, the company produced airplane engines, including the first jet engine produced in the United States.

After the war, the company continued to expand its line of household electronic devices while also moving into more sophisticated areas such as jet propulsion, medical technology, and financial services. In 1981, John WELCH was named head of the company, and he overhauled its operating divisions, adding new ones and cutting others. He also began an aggressive acquisitions program, helping the company to become a successful conglomerate. Among GE's continued interests were broadcasting (including NBC), appliances, electrical distribution, power systems, medical systems, and INVESTMENT BANKING. GE acquired Kidder Peabody, an investment banking firm, before divesting it in 1995. Many divisions were subsequently sold and others bought in a relentless quest to maintain profitability.

In 1997, GE became the world's largest company in terms of stock market capitalization. One of its divisions, GE Capital, became one of the country's largest nonbank financial service companies, offering CREDIT CARDS, insurance, MUTUAL FUNDS, and wholesale lending. General Electric continues as one of the most successful, highly diversified companies into the 21st century.

See also CONGLOMERATES; MORGAN, JOHN PIERPONT.

Further reading

Carlson, W. Bernard. *Innovation as a Social Process*. Cambridge: Cambridge University Press, 1992.

O'Boyle, Thomas F. *At Any Cost: Jack Welch, General Electric and the Pursuit of Profit*. New York: Knopf, 1998.

Generally Accepted Accounting Principles (GAAP)   A body of accounting rules that consists of agreed-upon standards, conventions, and procedures that define financial accounting and reporting in a society. Accounting standards are necessary for the economy to function efficiently. Financial reports prepared according to GAAP help investors and lenders to allocate their resources among business organizations.

The SECURITIES EXCHANGE ACT OF 1934 gives the Securities and Exchange Commission (SEC) the legal authority to establish GAAP for companies that issue securities to the public in the United States. Throughout its history, the SEC has relied upon the private sector to establish GAAP, as long as it performs this function in the public interest. From 1936 to 1959, the Committee on Accounting Procedures (CAP) of the American Institute of Certified Public Accountants (AICPA) issued 51 accounting research bulletins (ARBs) on various subjects to establish GAAP. In 1953, the CAP issued ARB 43, which codified preceding research bulletins and remains widely influential. From 1959 to 1973, the Accounting Principles Board (APB) of the AICPA established GAAP through its 31 opinions. Unlike the CAP, the APB had a full-time research staff.

The FINANCIAL ACCOUNTING STANDARDS BOARD (FASB) began operations in 1973 to provide an equal opportunity for all interested groups to participate in the standards-setting process. In contrast, independent auditors dominated the CAP and the APB. The FASB has seven board members who work full time to resolve financial accounting issues, communicate with constituents, and serve as a focal point for research. Members preserve their independence as standard setters by severing ties with their previous employers, unlike the part-time members of the CAP and APB. The FASB endorsed the pronouncements of the CAP and APB as GAAP, unless superseded or amended by its own pronouncements. The FASB creates GAAP through three types of pronouncement: statements of financial accounting standards (SFAS), interpretations, and technical bulletins. The board follows due process publicly before issuing any pronouncement.

Statements of financial accounting standards (SFAS) consist of principles at the highest level, approved by a two-thirds majority of board members. As of February 2001, the FASB had issued 140 SFAS, although many amend or rescind prior standards. Among the topics covered by SFAS are accounting for leases, income taxes, pensions, derivative financial instruments, not-for-profit organizations, segments of an enterprise, motion picture films, oil and gas producing activities,

insurance enterprises, foreign currency translation, research and development costs, earnings per share, and contingencies. The development of an SFAS often involves controversy. Employers fought against SFAS 106, which caused them to recognize a liability for postretirement benefits other than pensions. The business community vigorously criticized a proposed standard to charge executive stock options against earnings. The relevant standard, SFAS 123, required disclosure of the cost of most stock options in footnotes, rather than on the income statement.

Unlike its predecessors, the FASB issued seven statements of financial accounting concepts (SFACs) as a framework for standard setting. The SFACs, while not GAAP, have significant implications for the development of GAAP. The seven existing SFACs describe objectives for financial reporting, qualitative characteristics of accounting information, elements of financial statements, recognition and measurement in financial statements, and use of cash flow information and present value in accounting measurements.

See also SARBANES-OXLEY ACT; SECURITIES ACT OF 1933.

Further reading

Baskin, Jonathan B., and Paul Miranti. *A History of Corporate Finance.* Cambridge: Cambridge University Press, 1997.

Previts, Gary, and Barbara Merino. *A History of Accountancy in the United States: The Cultural Significance of Accounting.* Columbus: Ohio State University Press, 1998.

Mary Michel

General Motors Corp. Founded in 1908 by William Crapo DURANT, General Motors became the world's largest car maker and largest corporation after World War II. In the early years, it was created by consolidating several car companies and other specialty companies under one umbrella. The company captured almost 50 percent of the domestic market for cars and trucks before losing some of its market share in the 1980s.

Durant, a former cigar salesman, got his start in transportation by building the Durant–Dort Carriage Company into the country's largest carriage manufacturer before turning his attention to automobiles. He began by purchasing the Buick Motor Company in 1904 and sold stock to finance its operations. By 1908, Buick had become the largest producer of cars in the country. The same year he founded General Motors in order to diversify his product line. Within a year, GM had sold more than cars and trucks on sales of $29 million. But Durant's management was poor, and he lost control of his company in 1910. He regained control in 1918, after having created Chevrolet in the interim. The new GM included Chevrolet, and he soon purchased Fisher Body, which was to become the standard carriage designer for the company. The General Motors Acceptance Corp. was also founded in 1919 to act as the finance arm of the company.

Durant lost control of GM again in 1920. One of his former appointments was Alfred SLOAN, and in the 1920s Sloan began introducing a series of then-radical management changes that led to a more efficient and productive company. In 1923, Sloan was named president. Another of his innovations was changing models slightly from year to year so that the public would sell its older models in favor of the new. During World War II, the company was heavily involved in war-time production of military vehicles. In the 1950s, the company recorded its first billion-dollar profit year. Sloan retired in 1956, and its new chairman, George Wilson, was on the cover of *Time* magazine, having made headlines by stating before a congressional committee that "what is good for General Motors is good for the country." The company managed to hold its grip on the worldwide auto market for another 20 years before encountering serious competition from overseas automakers in Japan and Europe.

In the 1980s, domestic market share continued to drop to about 35 percent. The company remained as the world's largest automaker, but its market dominance was about 12 percentage points below what it had been during Sloan's administration. The company also began an aggressive campaign of adding other nonauto divisions. It bought Electronic Data Systems (EDS) from Ross Perot in 1984 and Hughes Aircraft in 1986. It also launched ventures with foreign automakers, especially Toyota, and purchased Saab of Sweden in 1989.

In 1990, GM launched Saturn, its first new line of cars in decades, as an independent operating subsidiary. Jack Smith was named chairman in 1991, and the company began a turnaround. It experienced its best net income ever in 1995. But the company's market share continued to drop and was only about 28 percent in the late 1990s. EDS was sold in 1996 as the company sought to streamline its operations. By the late 1990s, its sales were slightly less than $200 billion per year.

Further reading

Farber, David R. *Sloan Rules: Alfred P. Sloan and the Triumph of General Motors.* Chicago: University of Chicago Press; 2002.

Freeland, Robert F. *The Struggle for Control of the Modern Corporation: Organizational Change at General Motors, 1924–1970.* New York: Cambridge University Press, 2001.

Jacobs, Timothy. *A History of General Motors.* New York: Smithmark, 1992.

Madsen, Axel. *The Deal Maker: How William C. Durant Made General Motors.* New York: John Wiley & Sons, 2000.

Sloan, Alfred. *My Years with General Motors.* 1964. Reprint, New York: Doubleday, 1996.

Getty, J. Paul (1892–1976) *oil magnate* Jean Paul Getty was born in Minneapolis, Minnesota, on December 15, 1892, the son of an insurance lawyer. In 1903, his father relocated the family to Oklahoma to engage in the nascent oil industry. The endeavor proved successful, and young Getty gradually acquired an intimate knowledge of wildcat oil practices. After working on his father's rigs for several years, he briefly attended college in California and Oxford, England, but failed to graduate. Instead, Getty came home to concentrate his energies on starting a business of his own. In 1916, he acquired his first lease in Oklahoma, struck oil, and gradually acquired a small fortune. However, Getty's profligate lifestyle gradually alienated him from his father; after his father's death in 1930 he was also on increasingly strained terms with his mother. The source of trouble was Getty's single-minded determination to become rich: He exhibited real flair and intelligence as a businessman but proved utterly ruthless in the pursuit of lucre. He was also apparently incapable of sustaining long-term relationships. Over the course of his long life, he was married and divorced no less than five times and was on less than salubrious terms with his three surviving sons. Nonetheless, by 1929 Getty was well on the way to becoming a multimillionaire, and the onset of the Great Depression only accelerated that trend. As the national malaise increased, he quickly bought up millions of dollars in stocks at a fraction of their costs, confident—and correctly so—that their value would increase with time. By 1936, his success spurred him to acquire Pacific Western, the largest oil concern in California. That same year, he also engaged in an internecine struggle with Standard Oil of New Jersey to gain control of the Tidewater Associated Oil Company, another large and lucrative business. In 1936, he had to settle for controlling 40 percent of company stock, but in 1950, he had finally consolidated his hold.

By 1939, Getty was one of the world's richest men, and he frequently visited Europe to acquire rare art, his lifelong passion. He also socialized with many of Nazi dictator Adolf Hitler's circle, which made the American government suspect his loyalties. Accordingly, when the United States entered World War II in 1941, Getty applied for a naval commission but was denied. He neverthe-

less acquired control of the Spartan Aircraft Company and produced training aircraft for the armed forces. After the war, Getty took his interest in oil exploration overseas. In 1949, he paid the kingdom of Saudi Arabia $30 million for rights to explore the Neutral Zone between that nation and Kuwait. After many unsuccessful years of drilling, Getty tapped into the fabulous oil reserves of the Middle East. By 1956, he was touted as the world's richest man and its first acknowledged billionaire. Getty himself simply shrugged off celebrity and concentrated on what he did best—making money. By 1957, he had consolidated control over the three pillars of his commercial empire—Tidewater, Mission, and Skelly Oil—which were subsequently amalgamated into the new Getty Oil Company. Thanks to Getty's foresight, this functioned as a completely self-contained entity managing its own exploration, refining, marketing, and distribution of petroleum products. Its dramatic success further demonstrated Getty's business acumen and his indomitable will to prevail.

With time, Getty also acquired a reputation, deservedly or not, for a degree of eccentricity rivaling that of his great contemporary, Howard HUGHES. He deliberately cultivated a miserly, grasping persona, reinforced by stories of his rumpled outfits, his refusal to leave tips at restaurants, and the installation of payphones on his lavish European estate. Most stories, in fact, were exaggerated, but Getty did little to disown them. He also gained renown as a serious art collector who built a world-class institution, the J. Paul Getty Museum, to house and display his treasures. When he died at his mansion in Sutton, England, on June 6, 1976, he endowed the museum with $2 billion, rendering it the world's richest. Getty may have been a curmudgeon by nature and difficult to influence on a personal level, but his spectacular career in the unpredictable oil industry underscores his reputation as the 20th century's foremost oilman.

See also PETROLEUM INDUSTRY.

Further reading

De Chair, Somerset S. *Getty on Getty: A Man in a Bil-lion.* New York: Sterling Pub., 1989.

Getty, Jean Paul. *As I See It: The Autobiography of J. Paul Getty.* Englewood Cliffs, N.J.: Prentice Hall, 1996.

Lenzer, Robert. *The Great Getty: The Life and Loves of J. Paul Getty, Richest Man in the World.* New York: Crown, 1986.

Miller, Russell. *The House of Getty.* New York: Henry Holt, 1986.

Pearson, John. *Painfully Rich: The Outrageous Fortune and Misfortunes of the Heirs of J. Paul Getty.* New York: St. Martin's Press, 1995.

John C. Fredriksen

Girard, Stephen (1750–1831) *businessman and entrepreneur* Born in Bordeaux, France, Girard came to America in 1776. Leaving school at an early age, he became a cabin boy on a ship when he was 14. At age 20, he became a seaman and owner of several merchant ships. After an unsuccessful venture as a commercial seaman, he settled in Britain's American colonies, working for the firm of Thomas Randall & Son. A rough voyage from Europe caused his ship to drop anchor in Philadelphia as the Revolutionary War broke out. When the British departed the city, he took an oath of allegiance to Pennsylvania. During the war, Girard became a merchant in Mt. Holly, New Jersey, outside Philadelphia. He became a citizen in 1778 and settled in the United States permanently. When the war ended, he moved to Philadelphia and continued his career as a merchant and owner of a small fleet of ships.

Using money he made in his ventures, he established an office in Philadelphia and began trading sugar with Santo Domingo and financing American privateers against the British. He eventually developed his own fleet of 18 ships, many of which were named after French philosophers. Using his profits, he then branched into banking and real estate. He became an avid supporter of the BANK OF THE UNITED STATES. When the first bank was closed after Congress refused to renew its charter, he bought the premises and turned it into the Bank of Stephen Girard, which had capital of more than $1.3 million, one of the few banks in the country so highly capitalized. Although initially he encountered resistance from other Philadelphia bankers, the bank became successful very quickly. By buying the bank, Girard quickly became Philadelphia's best-known banker.

In his role as banker he became one of the major subscribers to a war loan to the U.S. Treasury in 1812 that helped raise desperately needed cash to fight the war against the British. In 1813, he joined with John Jacob ASTOR and David Parrish and subscribed to $10 million of the $16 million loan at a sharp discount. The support helped to arouse public opinion during the war, helping to contribute to eventual victory.

Later in life, Girard invested in coal mining lands in Pennsylvania and the early RAILROADS. He gave generously to Philadelphia to establish a trust for the education of orphans. He died in 1831. His legacy was that of banker and lender to the Treasury at a particularly difficult time in relations with Great Britain.

See also BARING BROTHERS.

Further reading

Adams, Donald R. *Finance and Enterprise in Early America: A Study of Stephen Girard's Bank, 1812–1831.* Philadelphia: University of Pennsylvania Press, 1978.

Arey, Henry. *The Girard College and Its Founder.* Philadelphia: C. Sherman, 1856.

Wildes, Henry Emerson. *Lonely Midas: The Story of Stephen Girard.* New York: Farrar & Rinehart, 1943.

Glass-Steagall Act   See BANKING ACT OF 1933.

Goldman Sachs & Co.   An INVESTMENT BANK-ING company founded by Marcus Goldman immediately after the Civil War. Goldman arrived in the United States from Bavaria in 1848 and became an itinerant merchant. He opened a small finance house 20 years later near Wall Street and began trading in commercial bills, which later would become known as COMMERCIAL PAPER.

In 1880, Goldman took his son-in-law Sam Sachs as a partner, and in 1885, the firm was renamed Goldman Sachs & Co. Before World War I, the firm entered into an agreement with LEHMAN BROTHERS that allowed the two firms to share underwritings for new stock issues. One of their first joint ventures was the underwriting for a common stock issue of SEARS ROEBUCK & CO., the large retailer. Over the next 20 years, the two shared more than a hundred underwritings, many for retailers, which catapulted Goldman to prominence on Wall Street. In the 1920s, prior to the crash, of 1929, the firm embarked upon marketing its own investment trusts. The trusts did not fare well in the aftermath of the crash, and the firm's reputation was tarnished as a result. The chairmanship then passed to Sidney Weinberg, who had joined the firm originally as a janitor's assistant before the war. Under his leadership the firm continued to grow and severed its relationship with Lehman.

Goldman's most notable success in the years following World War II was the initial public offering of Ford Motor Co. The firm had never sold shares under Henry Ford's leadership, but his grandson brought the company to market with Weinberg's help. The deal secured the firm's position as one of Wall Street's notable equity houses, and by the time Weinberg died in 1969 its reputation was secure. Commercial paper continued to be one of its specialties in addition to a full array of investment banking services.

In the 1970s and 1980s, the firm began to expand internationally but remained a partnership. Many of its senior members also served in several administrations in Washington, in various capacities ranging from economic advisers to Treasury secretary. Robert Rubin, a partner, served in the Clinton administration as secretary of the Treasury.

Continual pressures to expand and a few isolated poor financial years led the firm to consider a public offering. The issue was planned for 1998 but was postponed because of the troubles in the marketplace created by the downfall of LONG-TERM CAPITAL MANAGEMENT. It finally was brought to market in 1999, making Goldman the last major Wall Street investment bank to go public.

Further reading

Endlich, Lisa. *Goldman Sachs: The Culture of Success.* New York: Knopf, 1999.

Geisst, Charles R. *The Last Partnerships: Inside the Great Wall Street Money Dynasties.* New York: McGraw-Hill, 2002.

gold standard   The term used to describe a national currency that is backed by gold. There are two types of gold standard: the gold bullion standard and the gold exchange standard. The gold bullion standard is the type that the United States maintained in the years following the Civil War, while the gold exchange standard traditionally has been used by smaller countries whose currency is tied to another that uses the bullion standard.

Under the bullion standard, a country establishes an official price for gold using a fixed value of its own currency. Banknotes and other paper money are then declared convertible into gold at the fixed rate. Most advanced industrial nations used this standard from about 1870 to the beginning of World War I. In 1890, the Sherman Silver Act temporarily introduced silver as part of a bimetallic standard, but there was little widespread support for the metal. It was officially dropped as part of the standard. The United States officially joined the gold standard with the Gold Standard Act of 1900, which unequivocally stated that only one metal would be the standard, thereby demoting silver to obscurity. Unstable conditions in the world economy after the Great War led to the demise of the classic standard in the 1920s. The chaotic international trading conditions caused by the Depression in the 1930s led to the inauguration of the bullion standard. Under the Gold Reserve Act of 1934, all monetary gold in the United States was nationalized, and citizens were not allowed to hold gold except for industrial purposes. The prohibition lasted almost 50 years.

Adhering to the gold standard helped many countries maintain the discipline demanded by the official rate, although clearly there was more demand for gold reserves at the world's central banks than there was supply. In the Bretton Woods era, after the end of World War II, the United States officially maintained gold at $35 per ounce, and other currencies were given a value in U.S. dollars, extending the gold exchange standard for smaller countries' currencies. The system lasted until 1971, when the United States officially pulled the dollar off the standard by devaluing the currency unilaterally. Foreign central banks held more dollars than the United States could redeem, and the currency was devalued as a result. Within a year and a half, the major currencies began to float freely against each other in the FOREIGN EXCHANGE MARKET, and the last vestiges of the gold standard vanished in a move toward easier and more flexible money and monetary policies.

See also BRETTON WOODS SYSTEM.

Further reading

Bernstein, Peter. *The Power of Gold.* New York: John Wiley & Sons, 2000.

Eichengreen, Barry. *Golden Fetters: The Gold Standard and the Great Depression, 1919–1939.* New York: Oxford University Press, 1995.

Laughlin, J. Laurence. *The History of Bimetallism in the United States.* New York: Appleton, 1900.

Gompers, Samuel (1850–1924) *labor leader*

Gompers was born in London and moved to the United States with his family when he was 13. He began rolling cigars with his father at an early age and became involved with labor unions when he was 14, becoming the first member of the Cigar Makers International Union. Soon he became a skilled cigarmaker, in demand by many companies that manufactured tobacco products.

Although he received a scant education, Gompers nevertheless studied socialism while in his 20s, and he participated in meetings of the International Workingmen's Association and the Workingmen's Party of the United States. In 1875, he became the president of a local union. In 1881, he helped organize the Federation of Organized Trades and Labor Unions of the United States and Canada (FOTLU), a congress of national and local labor unions designed to educate the public on working-class issues and to lobby the U.S. Congress. As an officer of FOTLU, Gompers advocated compulsory school attendance laws, the regulation of child labor, and the eight-hour work day. He became president of the AMERICAN FEDERATION OF LABOR in 1886 and held the post for the next four decades.

Gompers believed that economic power preceded political power, and therefore unions should bargain and negotiate directly with employers so that their members could attain an economic status that they could then translate into political action. To this end, he constantly sought to protect the workingman from privations and what he called little tyrannies that could deprive workers of a better quality of life. He believed that government should refrain from becoming involved in the process and that political influences should also be excluded. He was a firm supporter of the CLAYTON ACT when it was passed in 1914, often hailing it as the Magna Carta of labor. The act exempted unions from some of its ANTITRUST provisions. He asserted that unions should be exempt from antitrust actions because there was a philosophical difference between a man's labor and the goods he produced, since the goods could be exploited by corporate management. He also championed a host of labor reforms, including higher wages, shorter working hours, and safe and clean working conditions.

After World War I, Gompers represented labor at the Versailles Peace Conference. He died in 1924 in San Antonio, Texas, and has been hailed as one of the giants of the American labor movement.

See also LEWIS, JOHN L.

Further reading

Chasan, Will. *Samuel Gompers: Leader of American Labor.* New York: Praeger Publishers, 1971.

Gompers, Samuel. *Seventy Years of Life and Labor.* New York: Dutton, 1957.

Kaufman, Stuart B. *Samuel Gompers and the Origins of the American Federation of Labor.* New York: Greenwood Press, 1973.

Livesay, Harold. *Samuel Gompers and Organized Labor in America.* Boston: Little, Brown, 1978.

Goodrich, Benjamin Franklin (1841–1888)
rubber goods manufacturer Goodrich was born in Ripley, New York, the son of farmers. Orphaned at an early age, he was brought up by his mother's brother. Attracted to medicine, Goodrich served as an assistant surgeon on the Union side during the Civil War. Goodrich sought success as a doctor immediately after the conflict, but failed.

Moving to New York City, he had some success in real estate ventures and, most importantly, became acquainted with America's nascent RUBBER INDUSTRY. With a friend, he invested in the Hudson River Rubber Company and, when that business had difficulties, became deeply involved in its affairs to protect his investment. Optimistic about the future, Goodrich married in 1869 and a year later moved his rubber business from New York to Ohio. Locating in Akron, Goodrich set up a partnership—in 1880 becoming a corporation, the B. F. Goodrich Company—to manufacture and sell rubber products. Relying on funds from friends, family, and Akron's business elite, Goodrich established the first rubber manufac-

turing venture west of the Appalachians. He did so to escape ruinous competition from well-established eastern firms. Following a policy of diversification, Goodrich's business turned out fire hoses, rubber belting, and many other items—in fact, just about everything made from rubber, except boots and shoes, which were made by the large eastern rubber concerns. By the time of Goodrich's death of exhaustion and tuberculosis in a Colorado sanatorium, his firm had become a regional powerhouse with assets of $564,000, profits of $107,000, and sales of $696,000. B. F. Goodrich—as the company was later known—went on to become one of America's "Big Four" rubber manufacturers in the mid-20th century and an important firm in the nation's aerospace and chemical industries in the late 20th century.

Further reading

Blackford, Mansel G., and K. Austin Kerr. *B. F. Goodrich: Traditions and Transformations, 1870–1995.* Columbus: Ohio State University Press, 1996.

Mansel G. Blackford

Gould, Jay (1836–1892)
businessman and financier Born in Delaware County, New York, Gould had a tumultuous childhood but showed promise in school. He taught himself surveying and wrote *A History of Delaware County* while still in his teens. But the lure of business would dominate his life. After leaving upstate New York, he worked in the leather tanning business in eastern Pennsylvania before finally moving to New York City, where he had been speculating in the futures market for leather hides.

In the Panic of 1857, Gould lost most of the money he had made speculating. He soon joined forces with Daniel DREW and James "Jubilee Jim" FISK and began speculating in the stock market. He established a sizable position in the stock of the ERIE RAILROAD and became a director of the company. During his tenure at the railroad, he was suspected of looting its books for his own use and was summoned to testify before a congressional committee investigating the railroad's management. Then in 1869 he engaged in his most famous market operation when he staged the "gold corner," in an attempt to drive up the price of gold in the market. Using borrowed money, he attempted to purchase most of the gold circulating in the New York market, forcing its price up and ruining his enemies in the process. The plan depended upon the reluctance of the U.S. Treasury to intervene. By selling its own supply of gold, the price would be forced down. Rumor abounded that Gould had made an unwitting ally of President Ulysses S. Grant by convincing him that intervention was not necessary. Eventually the Treasury did intervene, and the price of gold fell. Gould was already out of the market, having made his fortune.

The "gold corner" made Gould one of the most vilified men in the country. The fallout from the operation caused a stock market panic in 1869, dubbed "Black Friday," and dozens of investors and brokers were ruined in the process. The incident prompted hundreds of unfavorable newspaper accounts and books dedicated to exposing Gould and the Erie. Subsequently, Gould was forced out of the Erie Railroad but not before dueling with Cornelius VANDERBILT for control of the company and absconding across the Hudson River with a horde of cash and the company's books. His lieutenant at the time was Jim Fisk. He reentered the railroad business by assuming a large position in the stock of the Union Pacific and was granted a board seat in 1874. This marked something of a turnabout in his career. After assuming control of the company, he merged it with the Kansas Pacific in 1880 and strengthened the RAILROADS considerably. By the early 1880s, he controlled nearly 10,000 miles of railroad track in the country, including the Union Pacific and the Missouri Pacific.

Later in life, Gould began to diversify his interests. Becoming interested in communications as well as railroads, he purchased the *New York World*, one of the best-known New York newspapers, along with WESTERN UNION and the Manhattan Elevated Railway Co. He died of tuberculosis in 1892. Although he had a diversified career, Gould is best remembered as being one the country's most notorious ROBBER BARONS, due to his early reputation at the Erie Railroad, the gold corner, and association with Jim Fisk. His family became one of New York's most prominent and wealthy for 50 years after his death.

See also MUCKRAKERS.

Jay Gould (LIBRARY OF CONGRESS)

Further reading

Klein, Maury. *The Life and Legend of Jay Gould*. Baltimore: Johns Hopkins University Press, 1986.
O'Connor, Richard. *Gould's Millions*. New York: Doubleday, 1962.

government-sponsored enterprises GSEs are privately owned companies chartered by the federal government to serve public purposes in the financial markets. GSEs include some of the largest financial institutions in the United States, such as Fannie Mae (the FEDERAL NATIONAL MORTGAGE ASSOCIATION) and Freddie Mac (the Federal Home Loan Mortgage Corporation). Those two GSEs each fund more than a trillion dollars of home mortgages and dominate the U.S. housing finance system.

Government subsidizes the organizations by giving them exemptions from taxes and regulations that apply to other companies. The most important subsidy that government gives to GSEs is the ability to borrow money inexpensively, at rates close to those of the U.S. Treasury. The government does this by creating the perception that it will not permit GSEs to default on their financial obligations.

This so-called implied government guarantee means that taxpayers could be called upon to provide resources if a GSE ever fails. When one GSE, the FARM CREDIT SYSTEM, announced in 1985 that it could not meet its obligations, the government arranged for funding to allow the system to continue in business. The Wilson administration created the Farm Credit System (FCS) as the first GSE in 1916. The FCS was a borrower cooperative that helped farmers to obtain credit at a time when most financial institutions concentrated their lending in urban areas. In economic terms, the FCS helped to overcome a significant market imperfection.

Government established the second GSE, the Federal Home Loan Bank System, in 1932 to help the savings and loan (S&L) industry to deal with the financial devastation caused by the Great Depression. Savings and loan associations owned the Federal Home Loan Banks and used them to provide credit to help the S&Ls to fund home mortgages. As a result, some liquidity was preserved in the industry, and the market for residential mortgages was preserved in the face of bank failures, common during the depression.

The Reconstruction Finance Corporation, the giant New Deal federal agency, chartered the Federal National Mortgage Association in 1938 to help cope with the impact of the Great Depression on the home mortgage market. In 1968, the government divided the agency into two parts, the Government National Mortgage Association (Ginnie Mae), which remained within government, and a privately owned company called the Federal National Mortgage Association (Fannie Mae). Fannie Mae is an investor-owned company with shares that trade on the NEW YORK STOCK EXCHANGE.

In 1970, the savings and loan industry persuaded Congress to create the Federal Home Loan Mortgage Corporation (Freddie Mac), as a GSE with powers similar to those of Fannie Mae, but that would be owned by savings and loan associations. In 1989, after the collapse of much of the S&L industry, Congress changed the ownership structure so that it, too, was owned by private investors.

In their early years, Fannie Mae and Freddie Mac helped to standardize mortgage forms and to make the home mortgage market more efficient. Thanks to their implied government backing, the two GSEs are able to issue hundreds of billions of dollars of debt obligations and mortgage-backed securities that help to reduce the cost of homeownership by perhaps one-quarter of a percentage point, in terms of the interest rate that consumers pay on their mortgages. The two mortgage assistance agencies have purchased approximately 60 percent of residential, conforming mortgages from originators as a result.

The government has also created two other GSEs, Sallie Mae (the Student Loan Marketing Association) and a small struggling GSE known as Farmer Mac (the Federal Agricultural Mortgage Corporation). Sallie Mae supported legislation that in 1996 provided for a transition period for removing government sponsorship from the company. As a completely private company, Sallie Mae will be able to enter new lines of business that today are precluded by the terms of its federal charter.

Recently GSEs have become controversial as a tool of government. As the financial markets, and especially the home mortgage market, have become more efficient, the GSEs have lost much of their original ability to overcome the market imperfections that previously existed. Thus, when Fannie Mae and Freddie Mac deployed new automated mortgage underwriting systems in the 1990s, some large commercial banks and other competitors charged that the two GSEs were using their huge size and market power to dampen rather than promote innovation.

The two GSEs have evolved from providers of supplementary assistance to the home mortgage market to become predominant funders. Their government subsidies have permitted the two companies to double in size every five years since 1970. Because of the immense political influence that accompanies the market power of the GSEs, it is not clear whether government can devise an exit strategy so that they can give up their government sponsorship to become completely private competitors in today's efficient financial markets.

Further reading

Congressional Budget Office. *Controlling the Risks of Government-Sponsored Enterprises.* Washington, D.C.: April 1991.
———. *The Public Costs and Public Benefits of Fannie Mae and Freddie Mac.* Washington, D.C.: Congressional Budget Office, July 1996.
Stanton, Thomas H. *A State of Risk.* New York: Basic Books, 1991.
———. *Government Sponsored Enterprises: Mercantilist Companies in the Modern World.* Washington, D.C.: American Enterprise Institute, 2002.

Thomas H. Stanton

Great Atlantic & Pacific Tea Co. (A&P)

Better known as the A&P, the company was founded as the Great American Tea Company on Vesey Street in lower Manhattan in 1859 by George Huntington Hartford and George Gilman. It originally was a merchandiser of tea, coffee, and spices bought in bulk from suppliers. By purchasing tea directly from ships, the two discovered that they could lower the cost by two-thirds and still make a profit. They spent heavily on their marketing efforts, including advertising in magazines and newspapers and sponsoring a horse-drawn wagon with the company's name on it.

The store became so successful that they were able to open many more in surrounding areas. It was renamed the Great Atlantic & Pacific Tea Company in 1870. In the late 19th century, it began offering groceries in addition to tea. In 1880, the company introduced the first private label product—baking powder. Over the next 40 years, private manufacturing became an important aspect of its business, and by the end of World War I, A&P had opened its own factory and packing plant.

In 1912, John Hartford, a son of the founder, introduced the concept of "cash and carry" to retailing by allowing customers to come in to the store and take their purchased goods home with them rather than have them delivered, as was the norm. The idea was so successful that the company opened more than 1,600 new stores in the next two years.

By 1916, the stores' sales had increased to more than $76 million per year. The company continued to expand during the retailing revolution of the 1920s, reaching 10,000 stores in 1923. By 1925, the company had almost 14,000 stores and sales of almost $450 million. In the 1930s, many of the stores were converted to supermarkets. By the 1930s, A&P had become the top-grossing grocery store with almost 16,000 stores and sales of more than $1 billion.

The new stores reduced the number of old stores but increased volume and sales exponentially. By 1950, only GENERAL MOTORS had greater annual sales among American companies. During the 1960s and 1970s, sales slumped, and the company reorganized and began to expand by making new acquisitions. It continued to do so into the 1990s and reestablished itself as one of the country's leading supermarket chains. Today,

Front window of a Great Atlantic & Pacific Tea Co. store (NEW YORK PUBLIC LIBRARY)

the Great Atlantic & Pacific Tea Company comprises a group of supermarkets, including A&P, Waldbaum's, and the Food Emporium, among others.

See also CHAIN STORES.

Further reading

Humphrey, Kim. *Shelf Life: Supermarkets and the Changing Cultures of Consumption.* New York: Cambridge University Press, 1998.

Walsh, William I. *The Rise and Decline of the Great Atlantic & Pacific Tea Co.* Secaucus, N.J.: Carol Publishing, 1986.

greenbacks   Paper money first issued by the U.S. Treasury during the Civil War. Unlike other notes in circulation, issued by state banks, greenbacks did not have gold or silver backing. In the 19th century, this was called "nonredeemable into specie." As a result, greenbacks were originally viewed with great suspicion by critics who thought that the money was worthless. Unpopular when first issued in February 1862, they accounted for almost three-quarters of all notes in circulation within three years.

Opponents of greenbacks, technically nonconvertible paper money, saw their issuance as an unfair advantage to the federal government since most notes issued by banks in the individual states were required to be converted into specie (silver or gold) by the issuer. Opponents of big business and government in the 19th century, notably agrarian radicals, saw the issuance of money as a government monopoly that could be influenced by big business to serve its own ends. But the federal government was burdened with financing the Civil War and needed a way to issue money without potentially draining the Treasury. As a result, it issued the notes and at the same time borrowed large amounts of TREASURY BONDS, used to finance the war effort.

The bonds backing the notes paid their interest in gold coin to satisfy the fears of those who believed that the Treasury would bankrupt itself by issuing worthless money. At the same time, greenbacks could be used to buy Treasury bonds paying 6 percent interest, maturing in 20 years but redeemable after five years. These bonds were known as the 5–20s and became very popular due to the selling efforts of Jay Cooke & Co., which represented the Treasury in a nationwide sale of the bonds.

Greenbacks began to disappear from circulation in 1879, when the Treasury again began redeeming them with specie. The United States, along with Britain, then embarked on a GOLD STANDARD, which lasted until the 20th century, when nonconvertible paper money became the standard rather than the exception to the rule. The term has survived since the Civil War to denote paper money in general and American dollars in particular.

See also COOKE, JAY.

Further reading

Barrett, Don. *The Greenbacks and the Resumption of Specie Payments: 1862–1879.* Cambridge, Mass.: Harvard University Press, 1931.

Goodwin, Jason. *Greenback: The Almighty Dollar and the Invention of America.* New York: Henry Holt, 2003.

Ritter, Gretchen. *Gold Bugs and Greenbacks: The Antimonopoly Tradition and the Politics of Finance in America.* New York: Cambridge University Press, 1997.

Unger, Irwin. *The Greenback Era: A Social and Political History of American Finance, 1865–1879.* Princeton, N.J.: Princeton University Press, 1964.

Greenspan, Alan (1926–) *chairman of the Federal Reserve Board*   Alan Greenspan was born in New York City on March 6, 1926, the child of divorced parents. After attending public schools he briefly matriculated at the prestigious Juilliard School of Music but subsequently left to tour with a jazz band. Greenspan finally graduated from New York University with a master's degree in economics in 1950, but three years later, he failed to complete his doctorate at nearby Columbia University. However, he had become a disciple of business writer Ayn Rand, who championed the free market and discouraged government intervention in the economy. After befriending Alan Burns, a future economist of note, Greenspan hit upon the idea of formulating economic analyses and forecasting for senior executives. He then founded the consulting firm of Townsend-Greenspan and Company, which proved extremely successful and included such prestigious clients as Alcoa Aluminum, Capital Cities/ABC, J. P. Morgan, and the Mobil Corporation. Greenspan had by then become an extremely wealthy individual, and his success in business did not go unnoticed in the political realm. In 1968, presidential aspirant Richard Nixon proffered him a post as economic adviser, and in 1974 Arthur Burns, now head of the FEDERAL RESERVE, tendered him the position of chairman of the Council of Economic Advisors. The national economy was beset by rising inflation, and Greenspan accepted the challenge out of a sense of public duty. Under his tight-fisted tutelage, inflation dropped from 11 percent to 6 percent in three years, a considerable success. In 1977, Greenspan abandoned the public sector and returned to economic consulting. However, his expertise had indelibly impressed the political establishment, especially those adhering to Republican political philosophies. The turning point in his career occurred in 1987, when Treasury Secretary James Baker suggested him to replace outgoing Paul A. VOLCKER as chairman of the strategically important Federal Reserve. The nomination may have raised eyebrows considering Greenspan's inclination to avoid the limelight, but his rumpled, bespeckled persona belied a disciplined aptitude for economic policy.

Commencing in 1989, Greenspan enacted his trademark fiscal austerity programs to control the onset of inflation, but his main goal was to promote economic growth. Lending practices were subsequently tightened, but he occasionally allowed an infusion of cash into the economy to prevent it from sputtering. By 1992, he had managed to usher in a period of general prosperity, although it occurred too late to help the presidency of George H. W. Bush. During the first term of President Bill Clinton, inflation spiked upward again, but Greenspan steadfastly refused to inflate the money supply. In fact, he actually raised interest rates to cool off the otherwise bounding economy. This brought on a degree of tension with the White House, which was prepared to accept some inflation in return for fuller employment, but in 1996, President Clinton surprisingly nominated Greenspan for another four years as chairman. Consequently, unemployment for the remainder of Clinton's second term in office was only 4.7 percent, inflation dropped to only 2 percent, and the national economy boomed. It was a period of unprecedented prosperity and growth.

Such was Greenspan's reputation that in 2000 he was nominated for another term as chairman by Clinton. But halfway through George W. Bush's first term, the nation was beset by a serious downturn and unemployment rates exceeding 6 percent, so Greenspan continually adjusted interest rates lower to stimulate growth. He boldly and confidently predicted a return to better conditions within a few months, and few among the political establishment either confronted or questioned his sagacity. Unquestionably, Greenspan is one of the most influential chairmen of the Federal Reserve, and his tenure has been generally marked by unrivaled growth, low inflation, and prosperity.

Further reading

Chevallier, Francois X. *Greenspan's Taming of the Wave, or, a Golden Age Revisited.* New York: St. Martin's Press, 2000.

Martin, Justin. *Greenspan: The Man behind the Myth.* Cambridge, Mass.: Perseus Press, 2000.

Tuccille, Jerome. *Alan Shrugged: The Life and Times of Alan Greenspan, the World's Most Powerful Banker.* Hoboken, N.J.: Wiley, 2002.

Woodward, Bob. *Maestro: Greenspan's Fed and the American Boom.* New York: Simon & Schuster, 2000.

John C. Fredriksen

H

Hamilton, Alexander (ca. 1755–1804) *politician* Hamilton, an American politician and first secretary of the Treasury, was born on the island of Nevis in the West Indies in 1755. As a boy, he worked for a trading company in St. Croix before being sent to America for further education by his employer. He attended school in what is today Elizabeth, New Jersey, before further study at King's College in Manhattan (today Columbia University).

Hamilton served in the New York artillery during the Revolutionary War and was a secretary and assistant to George Washington from 1777 to 1781. He was admitted to the bar in New York in 1782 and also became a delegate to the Congress of the Confederation from New York in the same year. During the Constitutional Convention held in Philadelphia in 1787, he, John Jay, and James Madison wrote a series of letters to newspapers urging approval of the new Constitution. These letters were later collected and reprinted as *The Federalist*. He became secretary of the Treasury under Washington in 1789. Disputes with Madison and Jefferson in the early 1790s led to the development of the Federalist Party, which he led at a critical period in American political history.

As first secretary of the Treasury, Hamilton attempted to put the United States on a sound financial footing, especially since debt was consuming more than 50 percent of annual government revenues. He had a plan, as did a successor, Albert GALLATIN, to totally extricate the country from debt within 15 years, but the Louisiana Purchase would intervene.

Hamilton's main contributions to business were twofold. As Treasury secretary, he favored establishing a national bank and also opposed excessive government spending. He also supported businessmen, whom he believed were the lifeblood of the nation. His essay *The Report On Manufactures* (1791) strongly supported early forms of manufacturing as a way of developing a strong economy, less dependent upon agriculture and imports of finished goods from Britain. In his view, independence in manufacturing would guarantee economic and political independence in the future.

Hamilton resigned as Treasury secretary in 1795 but continued to be involved in politics, taking opportunity to criticize John Adams, a Federalist, as well as Aaron Burr, whom Hamilton opposed as a gubernatorial candidate in New

A wood engraving of Alexander Hamilton (LIBRARY OF CONGRESS)

York in 1804. His opposition to Burr led to their famous duel, in which Hamilton was severely wounded. He died a day later, in 1804.

See also DUER, WILLIAM.

Further reading

Brookhiser, Richard. *Alexander Hamilton, American.* New York: Free Press, 1999.

Chernow, Ron. *Alexander Hamilton.* New York: Penguin Books, 2004.

McDonald, Forrest. *Alexander Hamilton: A Biography.* New York: Norton, 1979.

Harriman, Edward Henry (1848–1909) *financier and railroad developer* Born in Hempstead, Long Island, New York, by age 14 Harriman was employed on Wall Street. In 1870,

Harriman became a member of the NEW YORK STOCK EXCHANGE, specializing in railroad securities. He married Mary Averell in 1879; one of their six children, William Averell Harriman, became a respected statesman and foreign policy expert.

Harriman's association with financier Stuyvesant Fish enabled him to modernize and reorganize the Illinois Central Railroad. Growing conflict with Fish led Harriman away from the Illinois Central and toward the UNION PACIFIC RAILROAD. Harriman realized that Union Pacific's performance could be improved by restructuring its debt and by making massive physical improvements to accommodate the traffic potential of a region that was beginning to emerge from the depression of the 1890s. Within 10 years, Harriman had orchestrated the expenditure of $160 million in capital improvements.

In addition to his commitment to modernization, Harriman understood the value of communities of interest—essentially, interlocking directorates—in the railroad industry in order to prevent overbuilding, guarantee equitable access to the traffic of connecting RAILROADS, and control competition. Harriman envisioned these communities of interest as the precursors of giant rail systems in the West. To that end, he acquired control of the Southern Pacific Railroad in 1901 and began to "Harrimanize" it in much the same manner as the Union Pacific. The Illinois Central, the UP, and the SP formed the core of the Harriman system—three technically separate corporations with similar organizational structures and philosophies, employing standardization to reduce the cost of purchasing, operations, and maintenance.

These communities of interest ran counter to the reformist impulses of the Progressive Era and won Harriman the personal displeasure of President Theodore Roosevelt. Harriman's public disagreements with former ally Stuyvesant Fish and his association with the financially ailing Equitable Life further tarnished his reputation. In

1907, the INTERSTATE COMMERCE COMMISSION launched an inquiry into Harriman's railroad and financial enterprises.

Harriman pledged his corporate and personal resources to a variety of public works. While Harriman never established a charitable trust, as did so many other philanthropists, he was instrumental in the creation of a state park near his New York home, sponsored a scientific expedition to Alaska, assisted victims of the 1906 San Francisco earthquake, and helped save California's Imperial Valley from flooding. Harriman succumbed to stomach cancer in 1909.

See also BROWN BROTHERS HARRIMAN.

Further reading
Hofsommer, Don L. *The Southern Pacific, 1901–1985.* College Station, Tex.: A & M University Press, 1986.
Klein, Maury. *The Life and Legend of E. H. Harriman.* Chapel Hill: University of North Carolina Press, 2000.

Albert Churella

Harvard Business School   Established in 1908, the school became the first postgraduate school of business to require an undergraduate degree for admission. The first dean was Edwin F. Gay, and the new graduate program lasted for two years, leading to the master of business administration, or MBA, degree. The original faculty numbered 15, with 33 regular students and 47 special students. According to an original school announcement, "the school does not pretend to graduate men who will begin at the top or high up in their several lines of business. It does aim to teach them how to work and how to apply powers of observation, analysis, and invention to practical business problems."

Among the first faculty members were Herbert Knox Smith, commissioner of corporations, James Jackson, ex-chairman of the Massachusetts Railroad Commission, and Frederick W. TAYLOR, the efficiency engineer. In 1912, the school used its first "case study," adopting an idea used widely in law whereby a particular case is studied both on its own merits and in the context of similar cases that have gone before. In 1924, it adopted case studies as its primary educational teaching technique. In the same year, George F. BAKER donated $5 million, and the school opened its own campus in Boston on the Charles River. Within a few years, it had more than 750 full-time students living on campus. The *Harvard Business Review,* a leading management journal, was begun in 1922.

In 1963, the school admitted women to the MBA program for the first time. The school expanded its offerings to both MBA and doctoral students over the years, and its publishing arm, the Harvard Business School Press, became a diversified publisher of management books after its inception in 1993. The institution continually ranks among the top graduate business schools in the country and is a leader in postgraduate management education. One of its graduates, George W. Bush, became the first MBA to be elected president.

See also WHARTON SCHOOL.

Further reading
Copeland, Melvin Thomas. *And Mark an Era: The Story of the Harvard Business School.* Boston: Little, Brown, 1958.
Cruickshank, Jeffrey L. *A Delicate Experiment: The Harvard Business School, 1908–1945.* Boston: Harvard Business School Press, 1987.

Hawley-Smoot Tariff Act   A protective tariff introduced in Congress by Representative Willis Hawley and Senator Reed Smoot in 1930. At the time, it became the highest tariff ever introduced in the United States. Widespread disaffection plagued the tariff when it was introduced, but Congress passed it. President Hoover signed it into law in June 1930.

The law was passed in the aftermath of the Crash of 1929, at a time when international trade was beginning to decline and domestic unemployment was rising. It was similar in many respects to the Fordney-McCumber Tariff Act in 1922. Hoover favored a tariff that would moderately increase duties levied on farm products and select manufactured goods. However, the House and Senate versions of the bill contained a long list of items subject to the tax, and the final product emerging from both versions was harsh and extensive.

More than 900 items could be found in the bill. Disputed items were sent to a Tariff Commission, which had the power to investigate inequities in trade and make recommendations to the president. The chief executive had the power to set TARIFFS that would equalize the price of an import so that it did not unfairly compete with American-produced goods. Several hundred economists sent the president a letter protesting the tariff, but Hoover decided to employ it when he believed conditions warranted.

The tariff was so severe that it caused an international reaction; many other countries enacted protective tariffs in retaliation. The result was a slowdown in world trade, which exacerbated the Depression and led to problems in the FOREIGN EXCHANGE MARKET that were addressed later in the 1930s when the United States and Britain both abandoned the GOLD STANDARD.

Another repercussion of the act was the new monetary system constructed after World War II at Bretton Woods, New Hampshire. Part of the reason for establishing the International Monetary Fund was to dissuade countries from acting unilaterally in the future when considering devaluations of their currencies, which in the immediate past had been tied to tariff decisions.

See also BRETTON WOODS SYSTEM; FOREIGN INVESTMENT.

Further reading

Eckes, Alfred E. *Opening America's Markets: U.S. Foreign Trade Policy Since 1776*. Chapel Hill: University of North Carolina Press, 1995.

Jones, Joseph M. *Tariff Retaliation: Repercussions of the Hawley-Smoot Bill*. New York: Garland, 1983.

Hill, James J. (1838–1916) *railroad builder*
Hill was born in Ontario and moved to St. Paul, Minnesota, at age 16 after the death of his father. He found work with a steamboat line and soon became a partner in the company. After several other ventures in transportation, he bought, along with two partners, the St. Paul & Pacific Railroad. The line became the basis for the Great Northern Railway Company that would earn him the name "Empire Builder."

Hill envisaged this railroad as reaching the West Coast and set about building the line through the northern tier of states. From Minnesota, he reached Montana by 1887 and Seattle in 1893. The railroad was notable for being built without any federal government assistance, and, unlike many of the earlier RAILROADS, it suffered no financial scandals or setbacks. The completed line ran from Lake Superior to the Pacific. While a masterful piece of engineering, the line competed with the Northern Pacific Railroad, which had been bankrupted in the Panic of 1893. Hill helped reorganize the line, but the courts would not allow a merger between the two rivals. The Northern Pacific was taken over by interests led by J. P. Morgan, a Hill ally. The two again joined forces to attempt to purchase the Chicago, Burlington & Quincy line serving Chicago, in an attempt to prevent E. H. HARRIMAN from buying the line. The battle spilled over to the stock market, causing the Panic of 1901.

As a result, Morgan, Harriman, and Hill established the Northern Securities Company to act as a HOLDING COMPANY for the Great Northern and Northern Pacific. But the company was held in violation of the Sherman Antitrust Act in a Supreme Court decision, the *United States v. Northern Securities Co.*, in 1904. Hill retired as president of the Great Northern in 1907. He also helped construct the Canadian Pacific Railroad and was the author of *Highways and Progress*, published in 1910. He financed and built a library named after him in St. Paul. Unlike many other railroad tycoons of the 19th century, Hill's reputation was built upon the soundness of his ideas, lack of government assistance, and the absence of financial scandal surrounding his operations.

See also MORGAN, JOHN PIERPONT.

Further reading
Malone, Michael P. *James J. Hill: Empire Builder of the Northwest*. Norman: University of Oklahoma Press, 1996.
Martin, Albro. *James J. Hill and the Opening of the Northwest*. New York: Oxford University Press, 1997.

holding company   A form of industrial organization designed to hold the stock of other companies. In a typical holding company, the parent company is not an operating unit but simply an administrative one, with the subsidiary companies producing actual goods or services. The use of holding companies is quite common and crosses a wide range of business sectors. The first holding company was organized by John D. Rockefeller as a trust in Ohio, the Standard Oil Trust. The term *trust* was the immediate predecessor of the term *holding company* although its aims were the same. In a trust, a company holds the stock of other companies in trust. The original Standard Oil Trust did not have stock as such but trust certificates. The purpose of organizing a wide group of businesses into a trust was to control production and prices. Usually, the trust certificates were held by a small group of directors who effectively controlled large sections of an industry. After Standard Oil was moved to New Jersey in 1899, the holding company began to supplant the trusts.

Ordinarily, holding companies are organized as acquisition vehicles so that other companies may be brought under the same control. They began to grow after World War I as many companies began to expand, often establishing themselves in friendly political or tax jurisdictions. Holding companies may also be organized in order to relocate tax liabilities in friendly jurisdictions or to avoid unfriendly legal jurisdic-

tions. The Standard Oil Company moved its headquarters from Ohio to New Jersey when its charter was challenged by Ohio after incorporation in that state.

In certain industries, holding companies have been regulated. The PUBLIC UTILITY HOLDING COMPANY ACT (1935) and the BANK HOLDING COMPANY ACT (1956) both sought to curtail holding companies in those industries so that they did not circumvent other legislation specifically designed to restrict their expansion activities. Subsequent DEREGULATION eased the original restrictions on many companies established during the NEW DEAL.

After World War II, the CONGLOMERATES also employed holding companies effectively as a means of establishing a portfolio of diverse companies under the same roof. By the 1960s, the holding company was the predominant form of industrial organization used by large companies, since many were multinational, and the holding company was used to establish foreign subsidiaries and other international operations.

See also ANTITRUST; GENEEN, HAROLD S.; GENERAL ELECTRIC; SECURITIES EXCHANGE ACT OF 1934.

Further reading
Federal Bar Association, Securities Law Committee. *Federal Securities Laws: Legislative History, 1933–1982*. Washington, D.C.: Bureau of National Affairs, 1983.
Stevens, William S. *Industrial Combinations and Trusts*. New York: Macmillan, 1913.

Hudson's Bay Company   The Hudson's Bay Company is one of the longest-lived business organizations in history. It was chartered by the British Crown in 1670 to trade for furs in the drainage basin of Hudson Bay. Indeed, for much of its life, it was primarily a fur-trading company, purchasing a wide variety of furs, but mainly beaver pelts, at posts along the coast of Hudson Bay and inland and transporting them by ship directly from the bay to Britain. Despite the company's prominence in the fur trade literature, it was in the early years a relatively minor player in the fur market, accounting for less than 10 percent of North American exports. Instead, the trade was dominated first by French and then by Scottish traders operating out of Montreal and farther south.

In 1821, after a long and often bitter rivalry, the Hudson's Bay Company absorbed the North West Company and thereby established a monopoly over much of the fur-trading hinterland. By that time, however, the intense competition had led to severe depletion of animal populations, and, to allow stocks to recover, the company introduced strict conservation measures. These measures were generally successful, but by the mid-19th century the fur industry had become a minor part of Canada's economic life. Shortly after confederation in 1867, the Hudson's Bay Company surrendered its charter to the Crown, thus giving up its claim to the region. In return the company was paid £300,000 and was permitted to keep a 20th of the fertile land as well as land in the vicinity of its trading posts.

The relationship between the Hudson's Bay Company and the Indians with whom it traded has become an area of special interest to economic, business, and social historians, as well as to geographers and anthropologists. This is due partly to the extensive company records, which were meticulously kept and, happily, have been preserved. These records offer a great insight into how a company with a head office thousands of miles from its main operations—and faced with premodern communication—was able to manage a complex and, in many ways, unfamiliar industry.

Central to the company's approach, especially during the 18th century when trade was almost entirely through barter, was a system of accounts based on the Made Beaver (MB). This unit of accounts established prices for every type of fur and every type of European goods traded. For example, at its largest post, York Factory, a prime beaver pelt had a price of 1 MB, and a gun had a price of 14 MB. Thus, at the official rate, guns and beaver pelts traded at a ratio of 14 to 1. Post traders, however, were given flexibility and so actual exchanges depended on a variety of factors, among them how strong was the market for furs in Europe, how severe was the competition from the French and others, and how plentiful were the beaver stocks. Indeed, the company and its traders appear to have responded to these market conditions in a way that preserved the company's long-run profitability.

In the 20th century, the company moved into retailing. Beginning with small outlets in Winnipeg and Vancouver in the late 19th century, the Hudson's Bay Company expanded to the point that it now operates a large chain of department stores (The Bay/La Baie) located throughout much of Canada. The company also has a mining arm; it closed its fur trading division in 1996.

See also ASTOR, JOHN JACOB.

Further reading

Newman, Peter C. *Company of Adventurers, 3 vols.* Markham, Ontario: Viking Penguin, 1985–1991.
Rich, E. E. *The History of the Hudson's Bay Company, 1670–1870, 2 vols.* London: Hudson's Bay Record Society, 1958–1959.

Ann M. Carlos and Frank D. Lewis

Hughes, Howard, Jr. (1905–1976) *businessman and entrepreneur* Born in Houston, Hughes's family was in the oil drilling business. His father developed an oil bit capable of drilling to previously unreachable areas, and the company became the Hughes Tool Co. Howard Jr. was a tinkerer as a youth and attended several colleges, including Rice Institute, but never graduated. When he was 19, his father died and the company passed to him. His newfound wealth became the basis for the wide array of entrepreneurial enterprises he undertook beginning while he was in his early 20s.

After inheriting Hughes Tool, he embarked upon a career in Hollywood, directing several movies that achieved notable success. He also continued to develop an interest in flying. In 1932, he became interested in the aviation industry and formed the Hughes Aircraft Corp., which developed a plane called the H-1. He also flew a twin-engine plane around the world, a trip that helped prove that passenger air travel was the wave of the future. Subsequently, he bought TWA in 1937 and financed the Lockheed Constellation, an advanced-design passenger airplane.

During World War II, Hughes took up defense contracting, but his projects did not materialize before the war ended. One was a reconnaissance plane and the other a huge wooden plane, nicknamed the Spruce Goose. Like many of his projects, they never fully succeeded while he was personally involved with them. Hughes acquired a reputation as an eccentric whose close personal involvement with a project often spelled its demise. His personal involvement in test piloting was not always successful, either. On a test flight of his reconnaissance plane, the XF-11, in 1946, it crash-landed in California, and he was seriously injured, spending nine months in the hospital recuperating.

The Spruce Goose also proved a failure, being unable to carry the large number of military equipment and soldiers as originally planned because war was over. Hughes Aircraft began to succeed after the war as Hughes distanced himself from the company. He also lost control of TWA when the airline needed to purchase its first generation of jet liners, and Hughes could not finance the purchase from company resources. But he still managed to earn more than $500 million when he divested. He also continued to produce the occasional Hollywood movie, but none of the later films achieved the success of his earlier ones.

Howard Hughes (LIBRARY OF CONGRESS)

In later life, Hughes became extremely reclusive and never appeared in public. Much speculation about his private life ensued. He made a substantial investment in several Las Vegas resorts, which were eventually sold. One of his few ventures into the public light came just before his death when he called the press to state that a recent biography of him was a fake. He died in 1976 and was buried in Houston.

See also AIRPLANE INDUSTRY.

Further reading

Barlett, Donald, and James B. Steele. *Empire: The Life, Legend, and Madness of Howard Hughes.* New York: W. W. Norton, 1979.

Drosnin, Michael. *Citizen Hughes.* New York: Holt, Rinehart & Winston, 1985.

Phelan, James. *Howard Hughes: The Hidden Years.* New York: Random House, 1976.

I

Iacocca, Lee (1924–) *automobile executive* Lido (Lee) Anthony Iacocca was born in Allentown, Pennsylvania, on October 15, 1924, to Italian immigrants. His father was a successful businessman who lost most of his wealth during the Great Depression, but imparted a love of automobiles to his son. Iacocca graduated from Lehigh University in 1945 intent upon becoming an automotive engineer, and he relocated to Dearborn, Michigan, as an executive trainee with the Ford Corporation. After a brief period with the company Iacocca departed for Princeton University, where he obtained a master's degree in industrial engineering. Back at Ford he decided that he was better at selling cars than designing them and switched his career over to sales. Iacocca possessed an uncanny knack for persuasion, and he rose quickly through Ford's promotional department. By 1960, as he confidently predicted during his undergraduate years, Iacocca had become vice president of the automotive division of Ford at the age of 36. In this capacity, he convinced a reluctant company president, Robert S. MacNamara, that a new, sporty car design was needed to attract the growing youth market. In 1964, Iacocca's suggestion came to fruition in the form of the Mustang, a low-cost sports vehicle that broke all existing sales records for Ford products. His success resulted in promotion to executive vice president in 1967 and president of the company three years later. Iacocca, now an internationally recognized corporate celebrity, continued serving Ford successfully until he ran afoul of company chairman Henry Ford II, who dismissed him in June 1978 for reasons that have never been explained.

Iacocca rebounded from this reversal with typical panache when he was installed as president of the CHRYSLER CORP., one of the automotive "Big Three." The company had been hit by sagging sales, unimaginative engineering, and a debt approaching $6 billion. Iacocca threw himself into the task of rescuing the ailing giant by personally visiting all Chrysler plants, talking with workers about the need for sacrifice, and streamlining overall operations. His drastic strategy included selling off profitable parts of the company, such as its army tank division, and tooling up for new and better products. To better ensure union harmony and support during this austerity period, Chrysler became the first-ever American manufacturer to place the head of the auto worker's union on the corporate board. Moreover, he managed to win an unprecedented loan from the federal government totaling $1 billion. Iacocca then took his offensive to the airwaves and became Chrysler's best-known salesman through a series of tough-talking commercials. Invariably he assured the public of the company's impending return to solvency and offered revolutionary incentives such as an unconditional refund within 30 days. Within a few years, he dramatically turned around Chrysler's fortunes, paid off all its debts, and began posting record profits. Iacocca was also personally responsible for creation of the new K-car and the minivan, which he felt would be attractive to struggling young families. His sagacity and ingenuity again paid dividends, and by 1985, Chrysler was positioned to acquire new properties such as the Gulfstream Aerospace Corporation and the E. F. Hutton Credit Corporation. Iacocca's rescue of the company—and the thousands of jobs it represented—again catapulted him into the ranks of national celebrity. His reputation was further abetted through his numerous ads, public appearances, and a highly regarded set of memoirs.

Iacocca remained at the helm of Chrysler until 1992, when the American auto industry was again buffeted by stiff competition from efficient Japanese imports. That year he concluded 30 years of distinguished service as an AUTOMOTIVE INDUSTRY executive by retiring from the board, although he received the sinecure of a major stockholder. In 1995, Iacocca became embroiled in a controversial and unsuccessful attempt to take control of Chrysler in concert with Las Vegas financier Kirk Kerkorian. He has since withdrawn from the public sector, although as late as 1998 Iacocca was pursuing the idea of mass-produced electric cars. His bravura and timely rescue of Chrysler remain the stuff of legend.

Further reading

Gordon, Maynard M. *The Iacocca Management Technique.* New York: Dodd, Mead, 1985.

Iacocca, Lee A. *Talking Straight.* New York: Bantam Press, 1988.

———. *Iacocca: An Autobiography.* Boston: G.K. Hall, 1984.

———. *I Gotta Tell You: Speeches of Lee Iacocca.* Detroit: Wayne State University Press, 1994.

Jeffreys, Steve. *Management and Managed: Fifty Years of Crisis at Chrysler.* New York: Cambridge University Press, 1986.

Levin, Doron P. *Behind the Wheel at Chrsyler: The Iacocca Legacy.* New York: Harcourt Brace, 1995.

Wyden, Peter. *The Unknown Iacocca.* New York: Morrow, 1987.

John C. Fredriksen

income tax   While a number of states and municipalities experimented with an income tax throughout the 18th and 19th centuries, the first federal income tax in the United States was not instituted until the Civil War, as a direct response to the national war emergency. A low flat rate of 3 percent on incomes above $800 was established in 1861; subsequent amendments to the tax laws during the war years reduced the exemption level and introduced modestly graduated rates, with a maximum rate of 10 percent on incomes above $10,000 established in 1864.

Although the Civil War income tax generated significant federal revenue, financing nearly 20 percent of Union Army costs, it affected only a small percentage of affluent Americans. Since the tax was instituted under the guise of a war emergency, nationalistic sentiment ensured relatively high rates of individual compliance. By the end of the war, 10 percent of all Union households had paid some form of income tax. But once the wartime and Reconstruction emergencies were over, many of the constituents affected by the income tax lobbied to have it removed. By 1872, America's first experiment with a federal income tax came to an end when Congress allowed the existing tax legislation to expire without renewal.

Throughout the 1870s and 1880s, federal policy makers neglected the income tax and returned to a regime of high indirect consumption taxes that included the tariff and sales taxes on items such as tobacco and alcohol. During the depression of the early 1890s, however, criticism of the regressive nature of the high tariff regime began to mount. The rise of corporate consolidation, together with the economic downturn, led Populists and disciples of Henry George's "single tax" to call for a more equal distribution of the burdens of financing a modern, regulatory state. Organized political parties such as the Greenbacks and the Populists inserted calls for a graduated income tax in their platforms, and federal politicians from the South and West introduced numerous income tax bills.

Congressional Democrats responding to this clamor for tariff reform reinstituted the income tax in the 1894 Wilson-Gorman Tariff Bill. Like the Civil War income tax, the 1894 law affected only a small percentage of the population, taxing all incomes above the exemption level of $4,000 at the modest rate of 2 percent. Nevertheless, the 1894 income tax law was a poignant symbol of the federal government's attempt to address the growing disparity of wealth and power in a modern industrial society. Instituted during peacetime, the 1894 law demonstrated that the income tax was not simply a tool for raising revenue, but could also be a viable vehicle of social justice.

The 1894 income tax did not last long, however. One year later the U.S. Supreme Court, in a controversial 5 to 4 decision in *Pollock v. Farmers' Loan & Trust Co.*, declared the new law unconstitutional. Many commentators at the time viewed the Court's decision as an example of judicial adherence to laissez-faire constitutionalism. But the Pollock decision helped galvanize the forces in favor of an income tax. In an effort to overcome the Court's decision, a movement for a constitutional amendment legalizing a federal income tax soon gained momentum, and by 1913 the Sixteenth Amendment made the income tax a permanent part of the U.S. tax system. Even with a constitutional amendment political leaders proceeded cautiously in passing

an income tax law in 1913. Enacted as part of the Underwood-Simmons Tariff Act, the new income tax was even more moderate than its Civil War predecessor. It taxed incomes above $3,000 at 1 percent and had a graduated rate reaching up to 6 percent for incomes above $20,000.

The income tax may have remained anemic had it not been for the national emergencies created by the two world wars and the Great Depression. During the First World War, the demand for government revenues combined with nationalistic sentiment not only to create a tax system that had steeply progressive rates reaching as high as 77 percent, but also to institute an "excess-profits" tax on corporate income. The first corporate income tax had been instituted in 1909, preceding the Sixteenth Amendment and the 1913 tax law, but it remained insignificant until the war emergencies.

After World War I, the income tax, like other aspects of economic policy making, returned to a period of normalcy. With the economic prosperity of the 1920s, income tax rates returned to their more modest prewar levels, and new sets of exemptions and deductions were introduced benefiting wealthy and corporate taxpayers. This philosophy of limiting tax rates and creating particular loopholes continued for the most part through the Hoover administration and the early phases of Roosevelt's NEW DEAL.

In 1935, as the Great Depression continued to drag on, the Roosevelt administration sought to change the course of federal tax policy. Treasury Secretary Henry Morgenthau worked with the Democratic leadership in Congress to enact a "soak the rich" tax law in 1935 that included a graduated corporation tax ranging from 12.5 to 15 percent; an intercorporate dividends tax that inhibited popular tax avoidance schemes; an increased estate and gift tax; and a surtax on incomes more than $50,000 that had a top rate of 75 percent on all incomes more than $500,000. The 1935 law did not reach many taxpayers, but the symbolism was significant, especially considering that FDR and the New Deal were coming under increased attack from the political left by such figures as Senator Huey Long of Louisiana and his radical "Share the Wealth" tax program.

With the onset of World War II federal income tax underwent dramatic change. The fiscal demands of war mobilization transformed a class-based income tax that affected only the wealthy few into a mass-based tax that touched a significant portion of the U.S. population. Whereas in 1939 only 4 million Americans were required to pay an income tax, that number had escalated to approximately 43 million by 1945. The collection of these revenues was facilitated by the introduction of a withholding system of taxation in 1943. The World War II tax regime also raised the marginal tax rates to a new high of 91 percent, allowing the federal government to collect an unprecedented amount of revenue. In fact, personal income tax revenues, which had never exceeded 2 percent of GDP between 1913 and 1940, had by the end of the war increased dramatically, reaching roughly 8 percent of GDP. Federal personal income tax revenues have remained close to 8 percent of GDP ever since World War II.

The postwar period ushered in a new era of public finance, whereby relatively high rates of taxation remained, but the aim of tax policies was focused more on economic growth rather than progressive equity. Keynesianism had convinced leaders on both the political right and left that countercyclical government policies were the key to economic stability, and this entailed tax cuts during economic downturns and tax increases during times of prosperity.

Postwar tax policy remained relatively stable until the "Reagan Revolution" of the 1980s. As the stagflation of the late 1970s continued to plague the country, Ronald Reagan embarked upon the presidency with an ideology and policy known as "supply-side economics." A key component of this economic thinking was a massive set of tax cuts instituted by the passage of the Economic Recovery Act of 1981. With this law, and the subsequent enactment of the TAX REFORM ACT of 1986, the American system of public finance dramatically diminished the role of the income tax, as both individual and corporate rates were severely slashed. Although succeeding political leaders have altered the tax structure at the margins, the fundamental concept of Reagan's low rates and relatively abundant deductions and exemptions remains a part of today's U.S. tax system. Indeed, despite political rhetoric to the contrary, the income tax appears to be a permanent part of the U.S. system of taxation.

Further reading

Brownlee, W. Elliot. *Federal Taxation in America: A Short History.* New York: Cambridge University Press, 1996.

Stein, Herbert. *The Fiscal Revolution in America.* Chicago: University of Chicago Press, 1969.

Weisman, Steven R. *The Great Tax Wars: Lincoln to Wilson: The Fierce Battles over Money and Power That Transformed the Nation.* New York: Simon & Schuster, 2002.

Witte, John F. *The Politics and Development of the Income Tax.* Madison: University of Wisconsin Press, 1985.

Ajay K. Mehrotra

Industrial Revolution in the United States

Manufacture is the process of physically transforming raw materials, semifinished goods, or subassemblies into product(s) with higher value. The Industrial Revolution in America saw activities traditionally performed in or close to the home migrate to shops, mills, and factories employing specialized workers and selling output commercially.

This entailed the application of new manufacturing processes and ultimately the development of new products, and was fostered by technical change in the transportation and communication sectors, in the extractive sectors producing raw materials (agriculture, fisheries, forestry, and mining), and by the growth and increased density of population. All of these factors, along with the availability of improved techniques within manufacture itself, affected the economic viability of specialized industrial production and the forms it took. So too did war, tariff policy, and the development of a financial infrastructure capable of facilitating the assemblage of large amounts of capital.

Most of the American economy during the colonial period consisted of subsistence agriculture. Overlaid upon this were commercial agricultural activities specific to particular regions (grain in the middle colonies, tobacco in the Chesapeake, and rice and indigo in the South), shipbuilding, fishing, and maritime trade. Most manufacturing was done at home and, if not at home, tended to be small-scale and located in the countryside. Aside from shipbuilding, the colonial period witnessed commercial manufacturing activity in the tanning of leather, milling of lumber, smelting of iron ore and forging of iron products, and grinding of grain. Most of this activity served local markets. High-value items were typically imported, usually from England.

Although British navigation laws, which governed trade within the Empire, were biased against the development of colonial industry, their architects intended the colonies to serve as a source of intermediate goods. Thus, some early-stage manufacture was actually fostered by the system. The refining and further manufacture of iron products was discouraged in the colonies and banned outright after 1750, but smelting was not so encumbered. This was partly a matter of weight: It was prohibitively expensive to ship unsmelted iron ore as opposed to pig iron to England.

The big money in the colonial period lay in export activities: sending tobacco, dried fish, naval stores, and ships to Europe, trading guns and rum for slaves on the West African coast, and provisioning the colonies with manufactures from England and the sugar islands of the Caribbean with slaves, foodstuffs, horses, and lumber. The vast bulk of imports to the colonies came from England, and most of these were man-

ufactured goods. At the time of the American Declaration of Independence, the radical transformation of the textile and iron industries generally identified as the Industrial Revolution in England was only just beginning, with many of the necessary preconditions, technological and other, already established. Still, the English were far ahead of the Americans and, even adding in the cost of transportation, could deliver finished textile and iron goods to the colonies more cheaply than the colonies could make such goods themselves.

During the Revolutionary War, trade with Europe was disrupted, creating pressures for self-sufficiency that provided some protection and stimulus to American manufactures. As a consequence of the peace settlement of 1783, the newly independent states again had access to cheap imports of British manufactured goods, a boon for consumers but bad news for import-competing domestic industries. The return of world war in 1793 (Britain and France were engaged in hostilities almost continuously through 1815) created bonanza opportunities for U.S. maritime interests. As a neutral party, U.S. vessels could trade with combatants on both sides of the struggle.

This mutually advantageous arrangement began to break down in 1805 with Britain's Essex decision and Napoleon's retaliation with the Berlin decree; soon more than a thousand U.S. ships had been seized by the warring parties, who claimed the ships were in violation of their newly declared and more restrictive rules. Wary of being drawn further into conflict with the European combatants, Jefferson initiated passage of the Embargo Act in 1807, prohibiting U.S. ships from trading in all foreign ports. Disastrous for U.S. shipping, the legislation created hothouse conditions for U.S. manufacturing, providing the equivalent of almost unlimited protection. The number of textile mills in the country jumped sixfold in the space of a year.

With the return of peace in 1815, U.S. industry again faced a flood of cheap imports from

England. Tariff protection then provided some substitute for the protection for American manufacturing that war had previously offered. Under a tariff umbrella, the U.S. textile industry became the first, and prior to the Civil War the only, industry to shift into large factories employing power-driven machinery to serve national markets. Centered initially in New England, the industry benefited from the immigration of mechanics such as Samuel Slater who carried with them designs for some of the water frames they had worked with in England. The American Francis Lowell, who designed a power-driven loom, also benefited from firsthand exposure to English designs.

Harnessing the new spinning machines and power looms in integrated water power–driven mills, the first large-scale factories in the United States arose on greenfields along the Merrimac River in Manchester, New Hampshire, in Lowell and Lawrence, Massachusetts, and along the Connecticut River in western Massachusetts. Until the 1840s, when large-scale Irish immigration began, much of the workforce consisted of unmarried Yankee farmgirls housed in company operated dormitories.

For the boot and shoe industry in antebellum New England, cheap imports and therefore the tariff were lesser issues. The sector nevertheless underwent substantial change, transitioning from a form of organization in which workers assembled in small shops overseen by bosses, although most continued to work with hand rather than power-driven tools until after the Civil War. Nevertheless, boots and shoes were the other major industry, along with textiles, that developed a clear national orientation before 1860, supplying cheap footwear, for example, to southern slave plantations.

Flour milling and the reduction of felled trees to lumber were other important water power–driven antebellum industries, although with few exceptions they remained rural and highly localized in terms of the markets they served. The iron industry also remained predominantly rural,

based until the 1840s on charcoal smelting and refining as opposed to the coal-fueled industry that had come to dominate England.

Finally, a subsector of manufacturing assembled small parts into such products as clocks, sewing machines, and small arms. Prior to the Civil War, Americans developed proficiency in organizing systems of assembly relying on more or less interchangeable parts, and the "American System of Manufacture" deeply impressed British observers at the 1850 Crystal Palace Exhibition in England. This expertise laid the groundwork for such late 19th- and early 20th-century growth sectors as TYPEWRITERS, bicycles, and automobiles.

The third triad of the Industrial Revolution in England was the use of steam power in mining, manufacture, and transportation. The steam engine, developed initially to deal with the problem of water encroachment in mines located near the ocean and used in early versions to pump water to the upper floors of English country houses, played less of a role initially in U.S. manufacturing than in Britain because of the abundance of exploitable water power on America's eastern seaboard. But applications in transportation (for which water power was obviously unsuitable) were a different matter, and beginning in 1808, on water, and in the late 1820s, on land, steam-powered vehicles contributed to the movement of goods and people. Americans innovated in the development of high-pressure steam engines, which initially were more dangerous and wasteful of fuel but were particularly suited for moving applications because they could be constructed compactly. Improvements in the internal infrastructure for moving freight made it increasingly feasible for some pioneering manufacturing sectors, in particular textiles and boots and shoes, to supply a national market in the antebellum period.

Although American manufacturing made great progress in the first part of the 19th century, on the eve of the Civil War the textile industry was the only manufacturing sector organized in power-driven factories producing for a national market. Thousands of sawmills and grist mills for grinding flour were, it is true, power-driven, but they produced almost exclusively for local markets. Boots and shoes were manufactured for national markets, but the factories were largely unmechanized, with sewing machines just beginning to appear. Building on advances pioneered in government arsenals, a small sector assembled sewing machines, clocks, and small arms using interchangeable parts, but the key innovations here were organizational, rather than the application of powered machinery that is typically seen as the hallmark of the Industrial Revolution.

Between the end of the Civil War and the beginning of World War 1, American industry decisively entered the 20th century in a variety of ways. In the 18th and the first part of the 19th century, commerce dominated manufacture. By 1910, manufacturing more than held its own. Its share of the labor force and value added had grown at the expense of agriculture. The United States had surpassed Great Britain as a manufacturing powerhouse and now stood first in the world, having also forged ahead of Germany, which had become its closest competitor. A wave of consolidations and MERGERS driven by a hunger for monopoly power complemented tendencies toward larger scale brought about by technological factors alone. Industrial firms became much larger on average, and size became a political as well as an economic issue, spawning largely quixotic attempts to tame it through antitrust policy.

Manufacturing has been declining among workers in the United States, but between roughly 1940 and 1960 the sector employed more than one in four U.S. workers. The second half of the 19th century in the United States witnessed a transformation in parts of U.S. manufacturing that brought it into the modern world, both in turns of the types of technology used and in terms of the organizational structures needed to coordinate and manage them. It laid the groundwork for the efflorescence of American manufacturing in the 1920s, a sector that experienced very high labor productivity growth as it built out the automobile and electrical machinery industries.

Key preconditions for this move into the modern age were the roughly simultaneous mid-19th-century transformation of technologies for moving both goods and information. The RAIL-ROADS, although far more expensive to construct per mile than canals, moved goods more quickly, were not subject to service outages because of inadequate water flow in the summer, or ice for as much as five months of the winter, and could be built over a much wider range of routes than those for which canals were suitable or economic. The railroad provided fast, reliable, around-the-clock transportation solutions in a way that had never before been possible.

The railroad's key complementary technology, the TELEGRAPH, also represented a qualitative breakthrough in speed and reliability, in this case in the movement of information. Prior to the telegraph, the speed of moving data was pretty much limited to how rapidly a horse could carry a rider, or how fast a ship could travel. With the telegraph, data could now move orders of magnitude faster, and in a relatively reliable fashion not subject to the vagaries of weather or season.

These two technologies made possible and required for their own operation the development of what business historian Alfred Chandler called Modern Business Enterprise. An MBE was a multidivisional firm administered by a staff of salaried managers. It arose first in the transportation sector as a means of coordinating railway traffic so as to reduce the number of collisions in a largely single-tracked system, and in communication (WESTERN UNION) to coordinate the operation of a national system. Railroad corporations, such as the Pennsylvania Railroad, which at its peak employed more than 100,000 people, dominated the U.S. economy in a way no business organizations have before or since.

The railroad and the telegraph enabled the development of mass distribution in the form of the urban department store such as R. H. Macy's

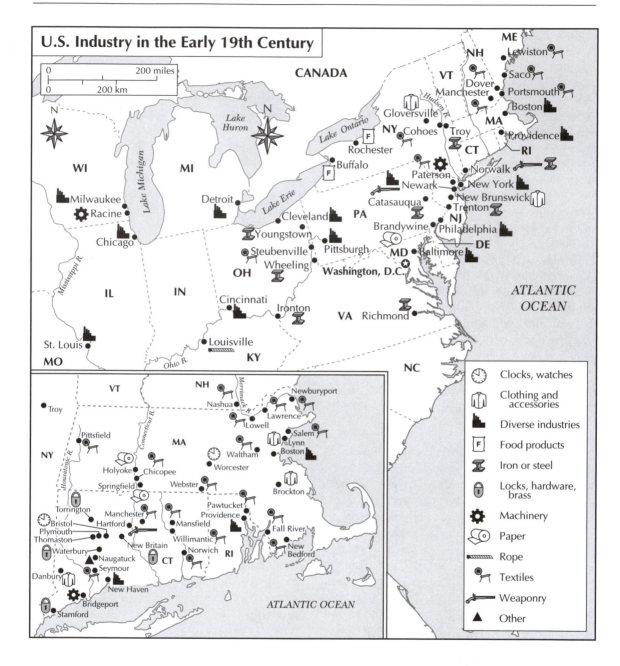

U.S. Industry in the Early 19th Century

Legend:

- Clocks, watches
- Clothing and accessories
- Diverse industries
- Food products
- Iron or steel
- Locks, hardware, brass
- Machinery
- Paper
- Rope
- Textiles
- Weaponry
- Other

as well as the mail order house such as SEARS, ROEBUCK and Montgomery Ward. Finally, MBE emerged in a few but ultimately important subsectors of manufacturing where the nature of technologies or customer service requirements made it particularly suitable. The pairing of reliable all-weather transportation and communication increased the rate of inventory turnover and made possible high-capacity utilization rates for fixed capital, necessary to make economically feasible the implementation of some of the new technologies in manufacturing, which had substantially higher minimum efficient scales. For the first time large-scale industry began to figure heavily within the economy of the United States.

One such sector was steel. Technological innovations, in particular the Bessemer converter and the Siemens-Martin open hearth, made possible drastic reductions in the price of steel, and in conjunction with the exploitation of the railroad and the telegraph by such entrepreneurs as Andrew CARNEGIE, enabled the real price of steel to drop by 90 percent over a three-decade period. In 1850, steel was an expensive alloy suitable only for surgical blades or military swords. By the end of the century it had become a structural material out of which rails, steamships, and ultimately SKYSCRAPERS could be constructed.

A blast furnace smelts iron ore and produces cast or pig iron with about 4 percent carbon content. A blacksmith can easily refine this down to wrought or malleable iron with almost no carbon. If, before the 1850s, one wanted steel (about 2 percent carbon), which combines the plasticity of wrought iron with the rigidity of cast iron, one had to laboriously add back some of the carbon in a fuel and labor intensive process that did not always produce a homogeneous product. The mid-century innovations made it technically possible to produce large batches of homogeneous steel cheaply, but it took entrepreneurs such as Carnegie to figure out how to use the telegraph and the railroad to coordinate raw material deliveries and develop the markets in such a way that a continuous flow of production could be sustained, thus warranting the heavy investment in physical capital that the new techniques required. Integration of smelting, refining, and rolling operations in one facility also saved tremendously on fuel and labor costs and was key to Carnegie's success.

Cigarettes were another case in point. The Bonsack cigarette making machine could produce thousands of cigarettes per hour. But it took James B. DUKE to exploit the new transport and communications industries, as well as mass market advertising, to coordinate the inflow of tobacco and outflow of cigarettes in a fashion that could keep these machines "fed" and avoid bottlenecks on either the input or the output side.

John D. ROCKEFELLER's success in building a business based on the refining and distribution of petroleum products was based again on the exploitation of the railroad and telegraph. Here the central engineering dynamic had to do with the economics of refineries, particularly the square-cubed relationship: The materials cost of building a refinery vessel with double the volume are not necessarily twice as much, so a firm that builds and controls larger vessels will be able to outcompete other entrants, provided the output from the refineries can be sold.

Toward the end of the century the assembly techniques that Henry FORD would pioneer in building automobiles were anticipated in the disassembly lines where meatpackers such as Swift and Armour revolutionized the production of dressed beef and pork. Again, these large-scale operations depended critically on the railroad and the telegraph to bring the animals to centralized slaughterhouses and rapidly to move the butchered meat in refrigerated railroad cars to markets.

In spite of these examples of dramatic increase in firm size, the coexistence of large- and small-scale manufacturing remained a feature of the economy at the end of the 19th century, as it does today.

American industry in the 1880s was abandoning its earlier dependence on water power for the more reliable but fuel-hungry steam engine. Although a steam-powered mill did not need to concern itself with lack of rainfall in the summer or freezing in the winter, it imposed essentially the same constraints as did water power on the industrial design of the factory. In either instance power was delivered through systems of rods, gears, and belts to the individual parts of the factory, and the enterprise relied on gas lighting for shift work after sunset.

Thomas EDISON inaugurated the first commercial provision of DC power in 1882 at his Pearl Street station in New York. But the initial market for his incandescent light bulbs and the power to energize them was residential space lighting for the well-to-do. It would be several decades—in some instances well into the 1920s—before electric power in conjunction with small electric motors led to a revolution in factory organization as power was distributed to work stations on an as-needed basis.

The idea of an industrial revolution as a sharp break with the past has come under increasing criticism insofar as it applies to Britain. If we wish to use the term for the United States, we can perhaps speak of a gradual transformation spanning the years from the early national period to those just before the First World War. By 1910 large-scale power-driven factories producing for a national market characterized a number of important manufacturing sectors.

Modern business enterprise had emerged and was well established in transportation, communication, distribution, and, by this point quite dramatically, in manufacturing. Commercial manufacture was no longer a localized, largely rural adjunct to activities performed in the home. And firms were no longer typically small sole proprietorships operating at a relatively leisurely pace. The railroads and the telegraph, supplemented eventually by the telephone, quickened the velocity of raw materials, semifinished goods, and wholesale and retail inventories as they passed among business entities toward their final user. At the commanding heights of American industry, armies of salaried managers and white-collar clerical and sales workers supported those engaged in basic production. And one had begun to see the routinization of research and development activities, such as those pioneered by Edison in his Menlo Park laboratories.

Although manufacturing today employs no more people than it did in 1950, its output is much higher and more efficient, reflecting continued high rates of productivity growth. Even as U.S. companies continue to transfer some production operations overseas, a U.S. manufacturing sector will persist into the future, its foundations established in the 12 decades following the ratification of the U.S. Constitution.

See also CORPORATION.

Further reading

Atack, Jeremy, and Peter Passell. *A New Economic View of American History, 2nd ed.* New York: W. W. Norton, 1994.

Chandler, Alfred. *The Visible Hand: The Managerial Revolution in American Business.* Cambridge, Mass.: Harvard University Press, 1977.

Field, Alexander J. "Modern Business Enterprise as a Capital Saving Innovation," *Journal of Economic History* 47 (June 1987): 473–485.

Walton, Gary M., and Hugh Rockoff. *History of the American Economy, 9th ed.* Stamford, Conn.: Thomson Learning, 2002.

Alexander Field

Insull, Samuel (1859–1938) *utilities executive* Born in London, Insull served as secretary for the London agent of Thomas A. EDISON until 1881. He was hired as Edison's private secretary in that year and began a long career in the American power industry that helped develop his reputation, and later his vilification, after the Crash of 1929.

Insull became Edison's general manager when the manufacturing operations of Edison's electrical company were moved to Schenectady, New York. In the five years that the operation was under Insull's control, it expanded substantially. In 1892, Edison Electric merged with another electrical equipment manufacturer, the Thompson-Houston Co., to form the GENERAL ELECTRIC CO., a J. P. Morgan creation. Insull realized that his future with the company was limited since Edison was no longer in effective control of the company. He resigned his position with GE and moved west to become president of the Chicago Edison Co.

Like many other industrialists of his era, Insull proved to be a master consolidator, and within 15 years the entire electrical business in Chicago was controlled by Insull through the Commonwealth Edison Co. Throughout the war years and the 1920s, he continued to expand operations, and by 1930, the company provided 10 percent of the nation's electricity in 32 states. He was a generous benefactor of Chicago and many of its local institutions. His company also was highly leveraged, resembling a pyramid, in which a handful of executives effectively controlled the HOLDING COMPANY and all of its subsidiaries. In order to accomplish this, Insull borrowed heavily from banks. When the stock market crash occurred in 1929, the stock fell dramatically, and many of his midwestern bankers were unable to support the company and called in New York banks as well. After negotiating with the bankers for months, many of his companies were declared bankrupt in 1932, and millions were lost, including many small investors' funds. The focus of increasing public hostility, Insull left the country for Paris and then fled France for Greece to avoid extradition.

Insull finally returned to the United States to face the charges against him, including mail fraud, embezzlement, and violation of federal bankruptcy laws. He finally was acquitted on all counts and returned to Paris, where he died of a heart attack in 1938. He is best remembered for bringing the consolidation trend to the production of electricity in the 1920s and creating one of the several large electrical utility combines, dubbed the "power trust," that produced more than half of the country's power and led to the passing of the Public Utility Holding Co. Act in 1935.

See also UTILITIES.

Further reading

McDonald, Forrest. *Insull.* Chicago: University of Chicago Press, 1962.

Ramsay, M. L. *Pyramids of Power: The Story of Roosevelt, Insull, and the Utilities Wars.* Indianapolis: Bobbs-Merrill, 1937.

insurance industry Insurance is a means of spreading risk across a large group of people. The uncertain risk—such as loss of life, property, or employment—is replaced by the predictable cost of an insurance premium. The two basic categories of insurance are the property and casualty industry and the life and health industry. The property and casualty industry comprises numerous different insurance lines, including automobile, homeowners' (a "multiple peril" type of insurance that covers fire, weather, and accidents), commercial multiple peril, general liability (to protect companies or professionals from damage claims), medical malpractice, fire, reinsurance (the selling of a portion of large policies to other insurance companies), ocean and inland marine, and surety (for professionals who require bonding). Additionally, state and federal governments offer various types of insurance not fully provided by the private sector, including protection for bank deposits, crops, property in flood-prone areas, and workers' compensation.

Although most 19th-century companies already specialized in one line of insurance, in 1865 New York specifically banned the provision of more than one line by the same company. After the Chicago fire of 1871 and the Boston fire of 1873, most other states similarly prohibited multiple-line insurance companies and continued to do so until the late 1940s. Due to space constraints, this article will cover only marine, fire, automobile, life, and health insurance.

The first form of insurance in the United States was on seagoing vessels and their cargo. As early as 1682, ships trading between England and the colonies were often protected against the hazards of the voyage by British insurance companies. During the 18th century, wealthy individuals or partnerships in Philadelphia and New York began establishing offices to underwrite marine risks, but English firms continued to dominate this field. The first American corporation to sell marine insurance was the Insurance Company of North America, chartered by Pennsylvania in 1794. The stability and longevity of incorporated insurance firms quickly spread to cities throughout the eastern seaboard including New York, Boston, New Haven, and Charleston, where numerous marine companies received charters over the next decade.

Despite their initial success, marine companies encountered a series of obstacles to their growth during the 19th century. Beginning in 1803 with the Napoleonic Wars between Britain and France, neutral American ships were continuously harassed by the two warring nations. While this hostile seagoing environment increased demand for marine insurance, the conditions of war likewise increased the risk of loss, placing the companies in a precarious financial condition. Between 1803 and 1812, the secretary of state reported 1,600 American vessels captured by the British, French, Neapolitans, or Danes. In contrast, the Embargo Act of 1807 brought all American trade to a virtual standstill and eliminated the business of marine insurance companies during most of 1808.

With the restoration of peace in 1815, marine insurance companies proliferated rapidly. The industry entered a period of intense competition during which rate wars forced many companies into BANKRUPTCY. A rash of fraudulent insurance claims during the 1820s further weakened the industry. One early historian estimated that one-third of all marine insurance claims from 1820 to 1840 were dishonest. The industry finally reached a period of stability and prosperity during the 1840s and 1850s, only to be disrupted again by the Civil War. The suspension of the cotton trade, heavy marine losses, and high wartime taxes all proved disastrous to the industry. Foreign competitors—the British in particular—capitalized on this weakened condition to regain dominance in both shipping and marine insurance. By the 1920s, only three major American marine companies were active in New York compared with 15 foreign companies. By the year 2000, only 3 percent of property and casualty premiums were for marine insurance.

Modern fire insurance originated as a direct result of the great London fire of 1666. In the colonies, attempts were made during the early 18th century to regulate the construction of buildings and to form organizations to extinguish fires. America's first fire company, the Friendly Society of Mutual Insuring of Homes Against Fire, was established in Charleston, South Carolina, in 1735, but a major fire in 1741 put the association out of business. It would be more than a decade before the next company, the Philadelphia Contributorship for Insuring Houses from Loss by Fire, opened in 1752. The first known New York company—the Mutual Insurance Company (renamed the Knickerbocker Fire in 1846)—was not chartered until 1787. During the late 18th and early 19th centuries, marine insurance companies also commonly underwrote fire risks, but marine insurance remained the main focus of these early firms.

Most early fire companies were set up as assessment companies serving one town, city, county, or neighborhood, where members would pay a fee only when another member suffered a property loss. During a period when fire-fighting equipment was inadequate and buildings were highly flammable, small fires quickly spread; this exposed a small group of people to a high risk of heavy loss, and many fire insurance companies were wiped out by a single conflagration. For example, the disastrous 1835 fire in New York bankrupted 23 of that city's 26 companies. As a result, mutual companies—in which members paid a regular fee with any annual surplus being redistributed to the policyholders—gained in popularity.

In 1837, Massachusetts began requiring fire insurers to maintain a reserve fund for the purpose of paying higher-than-predicted claims. New York enacted the nation's first comprehensive insurance code in 1849, followed four years later with its own reserve requirement for fire companies. In response to revelations of insolvency and fraudulent organization among several fire insurance companies, state insurance departments were created to supervise all types of insurance. Beginning with New Hampshire in 1851, Massachusetts in 1855, and New York in 1859, most other states followed suit with their own supervisory departments during the post-bellum period.

During the 1850s and 1860s, many states enacted protectionist legislation in order to promote local business interests or to raise revenues. Out-of-state companies in all lines of insurance were often charged higher taxes, required to invest in local bonds as a security deposit, and forced to purchase various state, county, and municipal licenses for their agents. The industry orchestrated a test case to challenge the constitutionality of these state regulations when a fire insurance agent representing several New York firms refused to pay a Virginia licensing fee. Unfortunately for the insurance industry, the Supreme Court ruled in the 1869 case of *Paul v. Virginia* that insurance polices were not commerce and therefore fell outside of federal jurisdiction as defined by the Constitution.

One of the biggest problems faced by fire insurance companies during the 19th and early 20th centuries was rate-cutting. Low barriers to entry allowed numerous companies to flood the market, frequently setting low rates in order to undercut the existing competition. These rates often proved inadequate in the event of a fire, resulting in company insolvency and high loss rates for policyholders. For example, three-quarters of the involved companies were bankrupted by the 1871 Chicago fire and 1873 Boston fire. In response, companies banded together into organizations of fire underwriters for the purpose of setting industry rates. Ironically, fire companies would come to rely on the *Paul* decision to argue that since they were not engaged in interstate commerce, this rate-setting activity was not in violation of the Sherman Antitrust Act of 1890 or the CLAYTON ACT of 1914.

The San Francisco earthquake of 1906 again forced many companies into bankruptcy and the remainder to raise rates. In 1910, New York established the Merritt Committee to investigate the practice of rate-setting among fire insurance companies. The committee uncovered numerous abuses committed by the industry, including charging discriminatory rates, boycotting customers, and challenging claims without due cause. In the aftermath of the investigation, many states mandated the establishment of rating bureaus to pool company data and determine ideal rates. State-sanctioned rate-setting, free from the restraints of antitrust legislation, was perceived to be the only viable means of ensuring the solvency of fire insurance companies.

The 1869 *Paul v. Virginia* decision was finally overruled in the 1944 case of *United States v. South-Eastern Underwriters Association*. The case involved a group of multistate fire insurance underwriting bureaus that were charged with conspiring to fix prices and limit competition—in violation of the Sherman and Clayton Antitrust Acts—by bribing insurance commissioners. In a 4 to 3 decision, the Supreme Court ruled that multistate insurance companies did indeed engage in interstate commerce and that insurance companies could therefore be prosecuted under the antitrust acts. In response, Congress passed the McCarran-Ferguson Act of 1945, declaring state regulation and taxation of the insurance industry to be in the public's best interest. It also placed the industry specifically outside the purview of the SHERMAN ACT, the Clayton Act, and the FEDERAL TRADE COMMISSION Act as long as such business was regulated by state law. Congress recognized that the sharing of information actually facilitated competition and solvency. By the year 2000, only 3 percent of property and casualty premiums were for fire insurance.

Automobile insurance began early in the history of the AUTOMOTIVE INDUSTRY, but the first compulsory law was not passed until 1927 by Massachusetts. Since then, most states have passed laws requiring some minimum level of insurance for all automobiles. As with other types of liability insurance, the person claiming injuries or damage as the result of an automobile accident had to prove that the other party was at fault. Consequently, the process itself was long and inefficient, with legal fees consuming approximately one-quarter of all insurance premiums. During the 1960s, states began considering no-fault insurance in which property and injury claims would be paid by each person's own insurance company, regardless of who was at fault. By the early 1970s, several major insurance companies joined consumer groups in announcing their support for no-fault policies, believing that the change would result in considerable cost savings. Massachusetts first adopted no-fault in 1971, followed by 23 other states by 1976. On several occasions during the 1970s, the federal government even considered mandating no-fault insurance across the country.

Metropolitan Life Insurance Building, New York City
(Library of Congress)

The drive for nationwide no-fault insurance had died quickly by the late 1970s. In most states, trial lawyers managed to win concessions from legislatures that weakened the laws. For example, several states offered no-fault insurance while still permitting damage lawsuits. Other states allowed drivers to sue for damages above a stipulated amount. Only in New York, Michigan, and Pennsylvania was a relatively pure form of no-fault insurance attempted. During the 1980s and 1990s, several states repealed some or all of their no-fault provisions due to rising insurance costs. The prudence of no-fault insurance continues to be debated in the remaining states. In the year 2000 automotive insurance was the largest line within property and casualty insurance, accounting for 46 percent of premium income.

The first American life insurance enterprises can be traced back to the late colonial period. The Presbyterian Synods in Philadelphia and New York set up the Corporation for Relief of Poor and Distressed Widows and Children of Presbyterian Ministers in 1759; the Episcopalian ministers organized a similar fund in 1769. In the half-century from 1787 to 1837, 26 companies offering life insurance to the general public opened their doors, but they rarely survived more than a couple of years and sold few policies. The only early companies to experience any success in this line of business were the Pennsylvania Company for Insurances on Lives and Granting Annuities (chartered 1812), the Massachusetts Hospital Life (1818), the Baltimore Life (1830), the New York Life and Trust (1830), and the Girard Life, Annuity and Trust of Pennsylvania (1836).

Despite this tentative start, life insurance did make some significant strides beginning in the 1830s. Life insurance in force (the total death benefit payable on all existing policies) grew steadily from about $600,000 in 1830 to just under $5 million a decade later. By 1850, just under $100 million of life insurance was spread among 48 companies. The top three companies—the Mutual Life of New York (1842), the Mutual

Benefit Life of New Jersey (1845), and the Connecticut Mutual Life (1846)—accounted for more than half of this amount. The passage of laws permitting women to purchase life insurance on the lives of their husbands—free from the claims of creditors—and a change in the corporate structure of firms from stock to mutual companies accounts for much of the success during the 1840s.

The major boom period in life insurance sales occurred during and after the Civil War. Although the industry had no experience with mortality during war—particularly a war on American soil—and most policies contained clauses that forbade military service, almost all companies agreed to ensure war risks for an additional premium rate of from 2 percent to 5 percent. The goodwill and publicity engendered with the payment of each death claim, combined with a generally heightened awareness of mortality, greatly increased interest in life insurance. Whereas only 43 companies existed on the eve of the war, the newfound popularity of life insurance resulted in the establishment of 107 new companies between 1865 and 1870.

The success and profitability of life insurance companies bred stiff competition during the 1860s; the resulting market saturation and a general economic downtown combined to push the industry into a severe depression during the 1870s. For many postbellum companies, innovation into markets previously ignored by the larger life insurance organizations was the only means of avoiding failure. Beginning in the mid-1870s, companies such as the John Hancock (1862), the Metropolitan Life (1868), and the Prudential of America (1875) began issuing industrial life insurance. First sold in England in the late 1840s, industrial insurance targeted lower-income families by providing policies in amounts as small as $100. Premiums ranging from $0.05 to $0.65 were collected on a weekly basis, often by agents coming door to door. Additionally, medical examinations were often not required, and policies could be written to cover

all members of the family instead of just the main breadwinner. Industrial insurance remained only one-sixth of the amount of life insurance in force through 1929, but the number of policies written had skyrocketed to just under 90 million. By the eve of the Great Depression there existed more than 120 million ordinary and industrial life insurance policies—approximately equivalent to one policy for every American man, woman, and child.

In response to a series of newspaper articles during 1905 that portrayed extravagant spending and political payoffs by executives of the Equitable Life Assurance Society, the New York state legislature convened the Armstrong Committee to examine the conduct of all life insurance companies operating within the state. Among the abuses uncovered were interlocking directorates, the use of proxy voting to frustrate policyholder control of mutual companies, inappropriate investments, unlimited company expenses, rebating (the practice of returning to a new client a portion of the first premium payment as an incentive to take out a policy), policy forms that were biased against policyholders, the encouragement of policy lapses, and the condoning of "twisting" (a practice whereby agents misrepresented and libeled rival firms in order to convince a policyholder to sacrifice her existing policy and replace it with one from that agent). The legislature responded by enacting a wide array of reform measures, including strict regulations regarding acceptable investments, limitations on lobbying practices and campaign contributions, the elimination of proxy voting, standardization of policy forms, and a ban on rebating and twisting by agents. Eventually 19 other states followed New York's lead in adopting similar legislation.

Throughout the 20th century, life insurance has been the second-largest financial intermediary in the country. In the year 2000, there were 369 million life policies worth $16 trillion.

Although health insurance existed as early as 1847, it remained an extremely minor insurance line until the late 1920s, when the cost and demand for medical care began to rapidly increase. In 1929, a group of Dallas teachers entered into a prepaid hospitalization plan with Baylor University Hospital. As incomes fell during the Great Depression, prepaid hospital plans began to spread among employee groups. In order to control competition between hospitals, the American Hospital Association eventually affiliated these plans under the name Blue Cross. Believing that such plans were in the public's best interest, states passed special legislation designating the Blue Cross plans as nonprofit corporations free from state insurance regulations. This nonprofit status required that they charge uniform rates regardless of health status.

As the popularity of Blue Cross plans spread, physicians began to fear that hospitals would use these plans to restrict their services. Additionally, the federal government began to consider the creation of national compulsory health insurance. In order to thwart these threats, in 1934 the American Medical Association began developing plans for prepaid insurance for physician's services, using Blue Cross as their model. The first such plan went into effect in California in 1939. By 1946, these plans affiliated under the name of Blue Shield.

With the success of Blue Cross and Blue Shield, for-profit insurance companies began entering the field. The major advantage enjoyed by the commercial companies was their ability to charge differential rates based on health status, enabling them to attract the healthiest groups away from the Blues with lower rates. Health insurance gained a further boost during World War II. As WAGE AND PRICE CONTROLS went into effect, companies began competing for scarce labor resources by providing better health benefit packages.

Although 75 percent of Americans were enrolled in some type of health insurance plan by the end of the 1950s, many groups were still excluded from this coverage. In 1965, Congress created Medicare to provide compulsory hospi-tal insurance and supplementary medical insurance to Americans 65 and over. Additionally, Medicaid was established to provide federally supported, state-level coverage for the poorest Americans. In the year 2000, with medical costs skyrocketing and 17 percent of people under the age of 65 lacking health coverage—including 12 percent of children under 18—politicians and consumer groups continue to debate the plausibility of establishing a national health insurance plan.

Further reading

Grant, H. Roger. *Insurance Reform: Consumer Action in the Progressive Era.* Ames: Iowa State University Press, 1979.

Meier, Kenneth J. *The Political Economy of Regulation: The Case of Insurance.* Albany: State University of New York Press, 1988.

Zartman, Lester W., and William H. Price. *Yale Readings in Insurance: Property Insurance—Marine and Fire.* New Haven, Conn.: Yale University Press, 1926.

Sharon Ann Murphy

International Business Machines (IBM)

IBM has been a worldwide leader in data processing for more than a century—first in electro-mechanical punched card tabulating machines, and then in digital computers and associated peripherals, software, and services. The firm had its origin in engineer and U.S. Patent Office employee Hermann Hollerith's invention of a punched card tabulator in the mid-1880s and the subsequent use of a refined version of this machine on the 1890 U.S. Census.

Hollerith's machine, which beat out others in a competition held by the Census Bureau to boost the tabulating efficiency over the prior census, greatly reduced the time and drudgery of this unparalled data processing task. Based on this success, in 1896 Hollerith formed the Tabulating Machine Company to market his machines to government and industry. Though there were some difficult periods in the firm's early years, it soon achieved steady success, and Hollerith retired to significant wealth in 1911, when he sold the firm to industrialist Charles Flint. Flint immediately combined the company with several other firms and renamed it the Computing Tabulating Recording Company (C-T-R). Though Hollerith continued to actively consult for C-T-R for a couple years, he took a less-active role as soon as the firm hired a powerful new leader, Thomas Watson Sr.

Thomas Watson Sr. was a gifted manager who had learned from one of the nation's best executives as a salesperson at National Cash Register (NCR) during the first decade of the 20th century. NCR president John Patterson was legendary for creating a world-class sales organization and building his firm's dominance as the international leader in cash registers. Watson moved up the ranks to become Patterson's top sales manager before conflict with the president led to Watson's forced departure. C-T-R soon hired Watson as general manager in 1914, and the following year he became president of the firm. Watson immediately instituted an unwritten, but very real, formal dress code of dark suits for managers, the use of team-building company songs, and a meritocracy of sales based on quotas and incentives. The latter was taken directly from his experience at NCR. Watson's long reign as the leader at International Business Machines (IBM), the firm's new name (to reflect its global reach and diversification of products) after 1924, helped the firm to surpass NCR, Remington Rand (formerly Remington Typewriter), and Burroughs as the world's leading office machine producer during the 1930s and early 1940s. IBM achieved this position through its domination of the tabulation field, its excellent marketing and service network, and its consistent revenue streams resulting from punched card sales and machine rentals (its competitors primarily sold rather than leased machines). These factors proved critical during the unprecedented decade-and-a-half downturn of the Great Depression, when few organizations could afford to buy new office equipment.

University of Pennsylvania Moore School researchers J. Presper Eckert and John Mauchly completed the first digital computer for the U.S. Department of Defense in 1946. While the future business possibilities for computers were uncertain at this time, IBM nevertheless began to position itself to potentially enter this emerging new trade by investing heavily in electronics research by the end of the 1940s. Remington Rand had established a commercial lead by taking over the two pioneering digital computer firms, the Eckert-Mauchly Computer Corporation (developer of the UNIVAC) and Engineering Research Associates. Unlike Remington Rand, which sold its expensive UNIVACs in very low volume, IBM's strategy was to continue to build on its capabilities in electronics, and enter the COMPUTER INDUSTRY only when it had either a major government contract or a commercial computer that could lease or sell in volume.

IBM, successfully implementing this strategy, entered the computer industry in the mid-1950s after receiving the primary computer contract on the Department of Defense Semi-Automatic Ground Environment project to create a computer-networked command and control air defense system. Over the next decade this brought in hundreds of millions of dollars in revenue to IBM. The firm also came out with a modest IBM 650 computer that rented, for several thousand dollars a month, in substantial volume. By the end of the 1950s, with Thomas Watson Jr. now president after his father's retirement, the firm announced its more powerful IBM 1401, a machine that took advantage of solid-state technology. Over the succeeding decade this machine would have more than 10,000 installations and establish IBM as the leading firm in the computer industry. Meanwhile, IBM's punched card tabulation machines continued to be very profitable in the 1950s and 1960s and greatly aided the company's computer business, as punched cards became the primary input-output device for early digital computers.

Despite IBM's success, by the beginning of the 1960s it faced a slow and steady challenge from competitors as a result of the lack of compatibility of its line of computers. IBM's customers had to invest substantially in purchasing custom software or developing programs internally, an investment that was lost each time they traded up to a new IBM computer. A special committee at IBM (the Spread Task Force) decided the best course of action was to develop an ambitious set of new computers, the IBM System/360 series. The series would cover a wide range of price points, and all would be compatible to run the same software. The number 360 was chosen to refer to 360 degrees, or the full circle of applications in science and business that the series would facilitate. IBM's investment in the project was massive, and its risk considerable. Thomas

Watson Jr.'s announcement referred to the System/360 series as the most significant event in IBM's history. The project included a major effort to program a new operating system, OS 360. Despite the operating system being late in delivery and having cost overruns, IBM System/360 series was a phenomenal success that led to the firm gaining 70 percent of the domestic computer market by 1970. Another part of the adopted Spread Task Force strategy, IBM's further integration into internally manufacturing components, was far less successful.

In the 1970s, IBM's growth led to even greater bureaucracy and slower reaction to market change—problems that were in part concealed, but would become increasingly apparent in computing's new era. During the 1970s, IBM successfully entered the minicomputing field and rose to

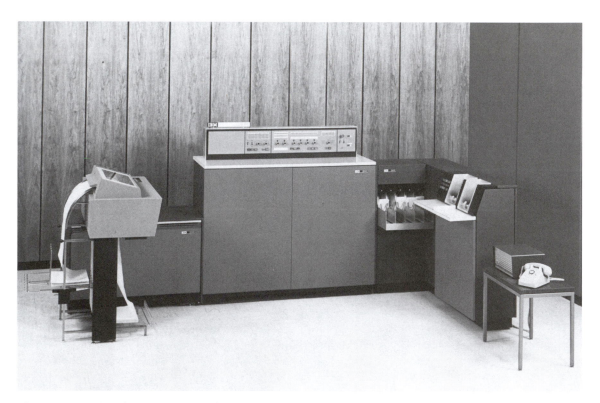

The IBM System/360 (IBM Corporation)

gain significant market share against industry segment leader Digital Equipment Corporation. Minicomputing, however, would soon give way to personal computing. The firm introduced a personal computer, the IBM PC, in 1981, several years later than Apple and others. While the IBM PC soon propelled the firm to the top of the personal computer sector, there were some inherent structural problems. First, even though IBM was the largest software producer in the world, the firm lacked the skills to quickly develop an operating system for the PC. The company initially approached Digital Research but soon went with Microsoft to design the system software. Second, IBM was highly integrated and had a history of internally producing most hardware components. This proved the wrong model in the fast-changing personal computer field, in which a number of computer assemblers quickly jumped into the market or switched from their own systems to sell IBM clones for less than the computer giant. While IBM's reputation and customer base led to the rapid legitimization and acceptance of the PC as standard office equipment in the business world, and the IBM platform remained dominant, the firm had inadvertently set up other companies to reap most of the longer-term profits from personal computers and associated software products. Apple was the only company that stuck with its own platform, adopting a differentiation strategy, rather than cost-leadership. Apple achieved its success by developing better systems software, particularly on its new Macintosh line of the early to mid-1980s.

Over the past decade, IBM has adopted a mixture of playing to traditional strengths and boldly changing its strategy. In 1993, IBM broke with tradition and named the first chief executive officer from outside the firm, hiring away RJR Nabisco CEO Louis Gerstner to turn around the struggling company. Rather than break up IBM into a number of pieces, as some analysts supported, Gerstner made strategic cuts in personnel and then focused on and enhanced the company's long-established ability to offer integrated solutions in numerous areas of data processing. In 1995, it acquired the Lotus Development Corporation, and the following year Tivoli Systems, Inc. With the growing importance of the World Wide Web by the 1990s IBM became committed to software and services to meet customers' e-business technological infrastructure and needs. This included competing in enterprise software fields against software powerhouses Oracle and BEA Systems. While IBM had built and extended its industry leadership by leasing and selling hardware and using strong after-sale services to further this primary goal, by the start of the 21st century, it was increasingly reversing this strategy to focus on selling high-margin software and services. IBM, long a firm with a major international presence, also extended its global services division, particularly in developing nations of the world.

See also WATSON, THOMAS J.

Further reading

Black, Edwin. *IBM and the Holocaust: The Strategic Alliance Between Nazi Germany and America's Most Powerful Corporation.* New York: Random House, 2001.

Cortada, James W. *Before the Computer.* Princeton, N.J.: Princeton University Press, 1993.

Pugh, Emerson. *Building IBM: Shaping an Industry and Its Technology.* Cambridge, Mass.: MIT Press, 1995.

Sobel, Robert. *Thomas Watson, Sr.: IBM and the Computer Revolution.* New York: Beard Books, 2000.

Jeffrey R. Yost

International Harvester Company Chicago-based manufacturer and distributor of agricultural machinery, trucks, and construction equipment. The company was formed in 1902 with the merger of five leading agricultural equipment companies: the McCormick Harvesting Machine Company, Deering Harvester Company, Milwaukee Harvester Company, Plano Manufacturing Company, and Warder, Bushnell and Glessner. The merger was the culmination of more than 10 years of negotiation between the McCormick and Deering families, and was made possible by the third-party intervention of George W. Perkins, a representative of J. P. Morgan. During its first 10 years, the company was governed by a voting trust of Cyrus MCCORMICK Jr., Charles Deering, and George W. Perkins. This trust expired in 1912, leaving Cyrus McCormick Jr. as president of the company and the other principals as vice presidents or directors.

Upon its formation the company controlled more than 80 percent of domestic production of the most important farm machines, binders, and mowers. Over the next 20 years, International Harvester greatly expanded its product line through the acquisition of existing companies and the creation of new production facilities in the United States and abroad. In 1917, it was the seventh-largest company in America. By 1920, the company had acquired the D. M. Osborne Company, Keystone Company, Weber Wagon Company, Kemp Manure Spreader Company, Chattanooga Plow Company, Minnie Harvester Company, and the Parlin and Orendorff Company. The company had also begun to manufacture construction equipment and trucks.

International Harvester's rapid growth continued during the 1920s, and its sales tripled to more than $300 million per year by 1929. One of the company's best-known and most important products, the Farmall tractor, contributed to this success. The Farmall was introduced in 1922 and by 1927 was the best-selling tractor in the industry. The company also continued to expand its overseas operations. By the end of the decade it had subsidiaries in Canada, France, Germany, Sweden, Argentina, Australia, Denmark, Great Britain, Italy, Latvia, New Zealand, Norway, South Africa, Spain, and Switzerland.

The growth of the company was interrupted by the onset of the Great Depression in 1929. The company suffered a drastic loss of income, and did not return to peak sales levels until the end of the 1930s. The company experienced renewed growth in the 1940s with the help of World War II government contracts and a postwar economic boom. In 1948, International Harvester was the world's leading manufacturer of farm machinery, America's largest heavy-duty truck manufacturer, and a major force in the construction equipment industry. The company also launched a major line of household refrigerators. Its total sales surpassed $900 million.

During the 1950s and 1960s, the company continued on a path of investment and expansion, but struggled to overcome labor strife and persistently weak profit margins. The company sold its refrigeration line to Whirlpool in 1955 and lost its lead in the farm machinery industry to John Deere & Co. in 1958. In addition, despite heavy investment in construction equipment, it failed to gain ground on Caterpillar, its chief rival in that industry. On the other hand, the company's truck business grew in importance, surpassing farm equipment in total sales in 1954. By 1961, the company controlled 33 percent of the heavy-duty truck market.

International Harvester made modest gains in profits in the early 1970s, particularly in its heavy-duty truck line. It continued to trail its competitors in the agricultural machinery and construction equipment industries, however. In 1980, the company experienced a six-month United Auto Workers strike, followed by a series of recessions in its prime markets. In serious financial trouble, the company sold its construction equipment line to Dresser Industries in 1982. Two years later it sold its agricultural equipment line to Tenneco, where it became part of the J. I. Case Corporation. In 1985, the company reorganized under the name Navistar International Transportation Corporation, and devoted itself to the manufacture and distribution of trucks and engines.

See also DEERE, JOHN; MORGAN, JOHN PIERPONT.

Further reading

Carstensen, Fred V. *American Enterprise in Foreign Markets: Singer and International Harvester in Imperial Russia*. Chapel Hill: University of North Carolina Press, 1984.

Marsh, Barbara. *A Corporate Tragedy: The Agony of International Harvester Company.* New York: Doubleday, 1985.

Ozanne, Robert. *A Century of Labor-Management Relations at McCormick and International Harvester.* Madison: University of Wisconsin Press, 1967.

Lee Grady

Internet A computer-based communications system allowing users to communicate quickly without relying upon telephone communication. The enabling technology of the Internet, packet switching, was invented in the early 1960s, but it took 30 years for the first primitive computer networks to evolve into today's ubiquitous information infrastructure.

Until the invention of packet switching, users could be connected to only one computer at a time, using a long-distance telephone line. This was expensive, because the telephone connection was used an average of only 2 percent of the time, and unreliable, because if the telephone connection failed communication ceased altogether. In packet switching, data was transmitted not by a dedicated communications line, but by converting it into "packets," rather like telegrams, containing the address of the sender and recipient. A packet-switched network contained many communications lines interconnected by small, message-processing computers—now called routers—that directed the flow of packets in the network.

The pioneering packet-switched network was Arpanet, initially connecting just four "host" computers in 1969, which was funded by the U.S. Department of Defense's Advanced Research Projects Agency. Development of the Arpanet was contracted out to a group of American universities, and this led to a uniquely democratic, occasionally anarchic, culture. By 1971, Arpanet had 23 computers attached to it. Originally, the network had been designed so that users could make use of specialized computers remote from their place of work. However, it turned out that the main use of the network was for electronic mail, something the designers had never envisioned.

In the period 1975–85, other computer networks sprang up around the world, usually based on some form of packet switching. Some of them were commercial networks, while others were private networks owned by governments or MULTINATIONAL CORPORATIONS. The early 1980s also saw the development of on-line computer services such as CompuServe and America Online (AOL) for home computer users. The problem with these networks was that they could not communicate with each other. For example, users could e-mail only people within their own network, and could access only the information located on their particular network. However, in the late 1970s, the Advanced Research Projects Agency—the sponsor of Arpanet—began to addresss this problem, which it called inter-networking, or simply the Internet.

It devised a set of rules—known as a "protocol"—for communication between networks. This was the Transmission Control Protocol/Internet Protocol, or simply TCP/IP, a mysterious acronym familiar to most experienced users of the Internet. Gradually many of the world's non-military networks began to connect with one another. Thus, the Internet is simply a network of computer networks, but it was a miracle of cooperation, each network adding to the telecommunications infrastructure piece-by-piece without payment from any centralized funding authority. By 1988, there were 50,000 host computers attached to the Internet. Three years later there were a million. The early 1990s saw the first commercial Internet Service Providers (ISPs), which gave inexpensive commercial and domestic access to the Internet. The issue of the Internet became highly politicized in the Clinton-Gore election campaign in 1992, in which the candidates expressed the need to provide Internet access to all Americans, just as earlier generations had had access to the postal service and the telephone.

Increasingly, the Internet came to be viewed not as a computing and communications resource but as an information repository, but it was difficult to access this information unless one was a trained information researcher. In 1989, a young, British-born researcher at the CERN nuclear research laboratory in Geneva, Tim Berners-Lee, invented a method of organizing information that he called the World Wide Web (WWW—or simply the Web). To view information on the Web, one would use a "browser" to view an on-line document, using navigation buttons and links to move within the document or to another document. The information itself, however, would be effectively disembodied in cyberspace—existing on computers here, there, and everywhere.

The World Wide Web liberated the Internet. In 1993, the primary users of the Internet had been academics and scientists; five years later, there were 130 million users around the world from all walks of life. The Internet became increasingly commercialized. One of the major commercial successes was the Netscape Corporation, whose Netscape Navigator browser, introduced in December 1994, did much to popularize the Internet. Other corporations such as Yahoo and Lycos were commercial spin-offs of "search engines" originally developed in universities to help locate information on the Web. In 1995, Microsoft introduced its Internet Explorer browser and the Microsoft Network (MSN), seeking to dominate the Internet as it had the personal computer. However, as the content of any one network was dwarfed by the riches of the Internet as a whole, full-service providers such as CompuServe, AOL, and MSN quickly changed their business model to become Internet Service Providers and mere "portals" to the World Wide Web.

By 1996, there were 10 million host computers on the Internet, a number that was doubling every 18 months. By 2000, there were more than 70 million. The Internet enabled a new commercial paradigm, based on the reduction of economic friction by eliminating middlemen and physical inventories. The best-known example was Ama-zon.com, the on-line bookstore established by Jim Bezos, a 30-year-old entrepreneur, in 1995; five years later it had more than 10 million customers. The Internet was a Klondike for so-called dot-com entrepreneurs, with hundreds and eventually thousands of new businesses being formed, such as travel agencies, "e-tailers," stockbrokers, and on-line auctioneers. By 2000, all significant businesses, whether new economy or old economy, found it necessary to have a Web "presence."

See also COMPUTER INDUSTRY; INTERNATIONAL BUSINESS MACHINES.

Further reading

Abbate, Janet. *Inventing the Internet.* Cambridge, Mass.: MIT Press, 1999.

Berners-Lee, Tim. *Weaving the Web: The Original Design and Ultimate Destiny of the World Wide Web by Its Inventor.* San Francisco: Harper, 1999.

Martin Campbell-Kelly

Interstate Branching Act (1994) A banking law passed by Congress, and the first significant change in the structure and geography of banking since the 1920s. Also known as the Riegle-Neal Interstate Banking and Branching Efficiency Act, the law allowed bank holding companies to merge across state lines. They were also allowed to merge their operations into national networks. In some cases, banks had been able to do so previously but were required to open subsidiary operations in another state. The act abolished the need to establish specialized subsidiaries.

Interstate banking had been seriously constricted since Congress passed the MCFADDEN ACT in 1927, prohibiting banks from opening de novo (new) out-of-state branches. The original act was an attempt to prevent bank expansion at the same time that CHAIN STORES were spreading across the country and was widely seen as an attempt to prevent banks from becoming truly national by expanding in the same manner.

In the years between 1927 and 1994, banks were sometimes able to open limited banking operations in other states through subsidiary companies, but the ultimate decision lay with the banking authorities in the state in which the subsidiary was proposed. As a result, interstate banking was effectively prohibited until the McFadden Act was replaced with more liberal banking regulation. The cost of opening and operating subsidiaries in those states that did permit out-of-state banks to operate was also expensive and proved a hindrance to many banks that thought of expanding operations.

After the act was passed, U.S. banking entered a consolidation phase that witnessed the merger of many bank holding companies across state lines. Among the largest was the merger between NationsBank of North Carolina and the BANK OF AMERICA, with headquarters in California. Other regional banking MERGERS also occurred, enabling banks to widen their operations if not to become truly national, spreading into all states. The states also had to change their existing laws concerning out-of-state banking in order to comply with the new law. The law was one in a series of banking deregulation laws passed during the 1990s.

See also FEDERAL RESERVE; FINANCIAL SERVICES MODERNIZATION ACT.

Further reading
McLaughlin, Susan. "The Impact of Interstate Banking and Branching Reform: Evidence from the States." *Current Issues in Economics and Finance* 1, No. 2 (May 1995).

Interstate Commerce Commission (ICC)

A federal agency established by Congress in 1887 to regulate the RAILROADS. The ICC was created by the Interstate Commerce Act. The original emphasis of the commission was to control the railroad practice of granting rebates to the largest customers, thereby eliminating price discrimination. Many of the railroads had granted rebates to their largest customers, and industrialists such as Andrew CARNEGIE and John D. Rockefeller used the rebates to their benefit in accumulating

monopoly power in their own industries. In addition, the law required railroads to publish their rates and entrusted the ICC with enforcing the new regulations.

The ICC's power temporarily was curtailed in 1897 when the Supreme Court denied its power to set maximum railroad rates. Congress responded in 1906 by passing the Hepburn Act, which again gave the agency power over rates and extended its jurisdiction to oil pipelines. After World War I, the agency was given additional power under the Esch-Cummins Transportation Act to consolidate the railroads into 20 operating systems and to regulate minimum rates as well. In 1935, the Motor Carrier Act brought the trucking industry under ICC regulation, and in 1940, the Transportation Act brought water carriers under its jurisdiction as well.

After World War II, the tide began to shift against the ICC as railroads began to lose market share to trucking and other forms of transportation. DEREGULATION in the 1980s made the agency's original powers less important to fair competition and the economy, and calls were heard in the late 1980s for its abolition. After the deregulation of rail rates and practices in the STAGGERS RAIL ACT of 1980, and subsequent motor carrier deregulation, the ICC shrank considerably. When the decision to abolish the ICC finally was made by Congress in 1995, REGULATION of railroads was further reduced, and almost all of the former ICC responsibilities were transferred to the Department of Transportation. The new successor agency, the Surface Transportation Board, began with an almost entirely railroad-oriented set of responsibilities.

The ICC formally was abolished at the end of 1995, and many of its powers were assumed by the Surface Transportation Board (STB). The ICC Termination Act of 1995 established the STB as a three-member independent agency affiliated with the Department of Transportation. Its three members are appointed by the president, serving staggered five-year terms.

The demise of the ICC is one of the few examples of changing trends in transportation and industry having a negative effect on the regulator originally charged with overseeing a particular sector of the economy.

Further reading

Hoogenboom, Ari, and Olive Hoogenboom. *A History of the ICC from Panacea to Palliative.* New York: Norton, 1976.

Kerr, K. Austin. *American Railroad Politics, 1914–1920: Rates, Wages, and Efficiency.* Pittsburgh: University of Pittsburgh Press, 1968.

Interstate Highway Act   Technically, the name of this legislation was the Federal-Aid Highway Act of 1956, one of a series of laws passed over a 50-year period that created the federal highway system. The word "interstate" is used to distinguish it from its predecessors because this act created the interstate highway system currently spanning the United States—a roadway that stretched coast-to-coast rather than simply from city to city as the older model provided.

The first federal highway act was passed in 1916 and designated $50 million to be used to create a system of rural roads to be used for mail delivery. The program originally was known as the Lincoln Highway, and it linked many existing roads rather than building new ones to complement them. In 1923, the program was expanded to include a series of highways designed to link major cities. Federal money was matched by states in order to build the roads. The government allocated about $75 million per year during the 1920s to the program. The program was enhanced when federal highways were extended into urban areas, and secondary roads were added in the 1930s and 1940s. The interstate system was authorized in 1944, but funding and work did not begin seriously until the 1950s.

Interstate highways originally were envisioned as part of the national defense system during the Eisenhower administration. The president remembered the terrible condition of the country's road system at the end of World War I and advocated upgrading highway transportation even more than it had been in the 35 years since that war ended. It was viewed both as an economic- and defense-related issue. The system encompassed 42,500 miles of new highway at a cost of $25 billion, with the federal government assuming 90 percent of the cost. The 1956 act called for uniform design standards. The project became the largest public works project in American history and is responsible for many distinct changes in the nature of American life. It aided the expansion of the economy that began in the 1950s and enabled truck transportation to supplant RAILROADS as the major method of transporting freight, and the automobile as the preferred way of transporting people. When the STAGGERS RAIL ACT was passed in 1980, it was an acknowledgment that truck transport of freight had overtaken the railroads as the major source of long-distance hauling. One result was the eventual demise of the INTERSTATE COMMERCE COMMISSION, the agency originally created to regulate the railroads; it was replaced by the Surface Transportation Board in 1996.

Many unique American developments can also be traced to the increased use of the automobile and truck, including shopping malls, the decline of inner cities, and the general trend toward the suburbs after World War II. The development of the first mass-scale housing development at LEVITTOWN, Long Island, in the 1950s was testimony to the rise of car and truck transportation.

Further reading

Lewis, Tom. *Divided Highways: Building the Interstate Highway, Transforming American Life.* New York: Penguin, 1999.

Rose, Mark. *Interstate: Express Highway Politics, 1939–1989.* Austin: University of Texas Press, 1990.

———. *Interstate: Express Highway Politics, 1941–1956.* Lawrence: University Press of Kansas, 1979.

investment banking   The part of banking that is concerned with securities underwriting and trading as well as other specialized financial services. Most investment banking activities

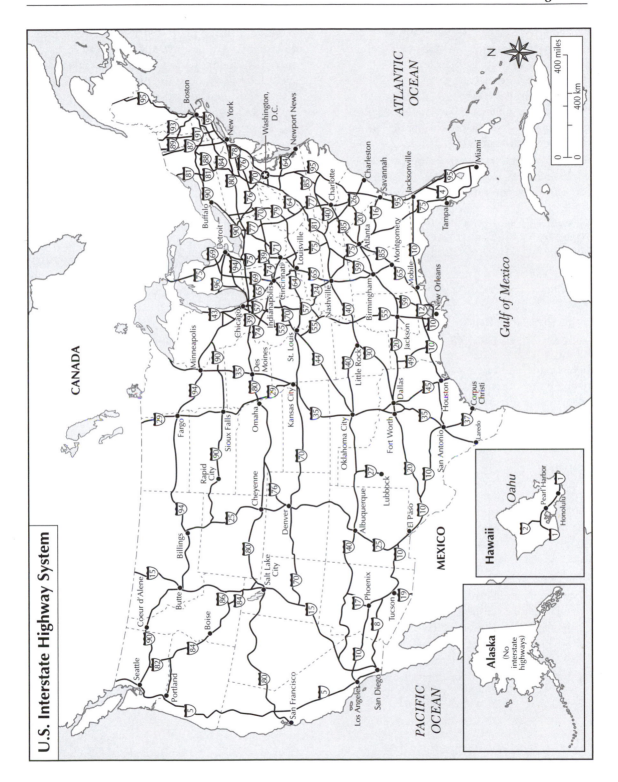

charge a fee for their services, unlike traditional commercial banking, which relies upon the spread, or difference, between interest paid on deposits and the interest earned on loans.

The industry began in the early part of the 19th century when private banks began to help companies sell stock to the public. Investment banking firms that began before the Civil War included Riggs & Co., CLARK DODGE & CO., Alex. Brown & Co., and Vermilye & Co. Prior to the Civil War, investment banks were crucial in selling TREASURY BONDS during wartime. The best-known bank engaging in this specialty was Jay Cooke & Co.

Traditionally, investment banking encompassed the underwriting of new securities and advising companies on MERGERS and acquisitions. After the Civil War, many investment banks underwrote securities for the RAILROADS, enabling them to expand westward to California and link major markets. After the 20th century began, investment banking expanded to include trading in the money market and the sale and trading of securities in the secondary markets such as the NEW YORK STOCK EXCHANGE. After a congressional inquiry in 1912, many banks organized themselves by founding the Investment Bankers Association, the first trade group dedicated to the industry. The group was later renamed the Securities Industry Association. Prior to the 1930s, investment banking was part of the general service of banking for companies, practiced along with COMMERCIAL BANKING or private banking under the same roof. Those operations that were solely for the brokerage or sale of securities were practiced by stockbrokers.

The modern investment banking industry inadvertently was created by the Banking Act (Glass-Steagall Act) of 1933, which forced a separation between commercial and investment banks. Many banks that engaged in investment banking divested their security affiliates in order to comply with the law, and the modern investment banking industry was born. Notable investment banks created at the time included MORGAN STANLEY & CO. and the First Boston Corp. In the 1950s and 1960s, traditional stockbrokers such as Merrill Lynch began to expand into the full array of investment banking services and helped revolutionize the business by making the services available to the small, or retail, investor. Until that time, investment banks never dealt with the public but only with companies. The only exception had been the private banks, which catered to wealthy individuals.

Most investment banks remained partnerships until the 1970s, when they slowly began to sell stock and go public. Increased need for capital and an expanding marketplace made partnerships obsolete; by 1999 no significant private investment banks remained after GOLDMAN SACHS went public that year. When the Financial Modernization Act was passed in 1999, it allowed mergers between commercial bank holding companies and securities firms again for the first time in more than 60 years. The merger of CITIBANK with Travelers Insurance in 1998 was the first of its type in the post-1933 era because Travelers already owned investment banks Smith Barney & Co. and SALOMON BROTHERS, bringing both under the Citigroup banner.

See also DILLON READ & CO.; DREXEL BURNHAM LAMBERT; KIDDER PEABODY & CO.; MORGAN, JOHN PIERPONT; SELIGMAN & CO., J. & W.

Further reading

Carosso, Vincent. *Investment Banking in America: A History.* Cambridge, Mass.: Harvard University Press, 1971.

Geisst, Charles R. *The Last Partnerships: Inside the Great Wall Street Money Dynasties.* New York: McGraw-Hill, 2001.

J

Jobs, Steve (1955–) *computer designer*
Steven Paul Jobs was born in California in 1955 and adopted by a machinist and his accountant wife. While passing through local schools in Mountainview, California, Jobs began displaying an aptitude for electronics and mechanical tinkering. He managed to secure a summer job at the nearby Hewlett-Packard computer firm, where he met and befriended Steve Wozniak, a fellow computer enthusiast. Jobs dropped out of college in 1972 and spent several years studying Eastern philosophy while designing games for the Atari computer firm. After a spiritual foray to India, where he caught dysentery, Jobs came home to California and reunited with Wozniak in 1975. Both young men began experimenting with the concept of a low-cost, high-speed computer for home and personal use and founded the Apple Computer Company in Jobs's garage. A working model, christened Apple I, was designed in 1976 and offered to Hewlett-Packard, which turned it down. However, it sold relatively well on its own, and a legend was born. This was followed by an even more advanced design, Apple II, in 1977, which opened the age of desktop information processing. Sales of this revolution-ary technology proved phenomenal and reached $200 million by 1980. However, as other companies invested in small computers, fierce competition erupted for the growing marketplace. Jobs subsequently stumbled badly in 1980 when his new Apple III computer proved overpriced and prone to technological glitches. A newer design, the Macintosh, was introduced in 1984, but it also sold poorly. By 1985, Apple Computers had lost half its market share to IBM, so Jobs resigned as chairman and voluntarily departed.

Undeterred, Jobs founded a new company, NeXT, in 1985 with $100 million of his personal assets. Thereafter he dedicated himself to designing revolutionary computer hardware for research and educational purposes. Innovative machines emerged from the company, but marketing and sales proved lackluster. Jobs, wishing to diversify, then purchased a small computer animation company named PIXAR from renowned film-maker George Lucas in 1986. He immediately realized the potential for computer-generated film effects and poured $40 million into new technology and programming while entering into a film deal with Walt Disney Productions. In 1996, PIXAR released *Toy Story,* the first completely computer-generated film, to rave reviews, and company stock rebounded accordingly. Within a year, PIXAR's assets were worth more than $1 billion. Jobs also enjoyed a measure of revenge when Apple bought out his NeXT Company and solicited his return as chief executive officer.

In 1997, Jobs again made headlines when Bill GATES of Microsoft Corporation unexpectedly joined forces with his erstwhile rival Apple Computers. Moreover, Jobs invested $150 million into the ailing firm in exchange for a nonvoting minority in the company. The alliance between Gates and Jobs, two legendary giants of the computer world, has rendered them a formidable force in terms of both hardware and software development. But Jobs scored an even greater success with his revitalized PIXAR company. Over the past decade five highly successful PIXAR films have yielded more than $1 billion in profit for both companies, with Disney receiving the lion's share. However, in the spring of 2003, PIXAR made and released the animated film *Finding Nemo* for Disney, which grossed more than $300 million. This made it the most successful animated film in history and induced Jobs to reevaluate his relations with Disney CEO Michael Eisner. He demanded a complete overhaul of their working relationship, reversing the arrangement whereby PIXAR received a pittance. Jobs insisted that PIXAR receive the majority of profit from all future releases, whereas Disney's take would be reduced to 10 percent. Failing that, Jobs was willing to offer PIXAR's services to any one of a number of well-financed Hollywood competitors. Despite his growing relationship with the MOTION PICTURE INDUSTRY, Jobs remains indelibly associated with the rise and triumph of the home computer market. "We started out to get a computer in the hands of everybody," he declared, "and we succeeded beyond our wildest dreams."

See also COMPUTER INDUSTRY.

Further reading

Butcher, Lee. *Accidental Millionaire: The Rise and Fall of Steve Jobs at Apple Computer.* New York: Knightsbridge, 1990.
Deutschman, Alan. *The Second Coming of Steve Jobs.* New York: Broadway Books, 2000.
Malone, Michael S. *Infinite Loop: How the World's Most Insanely Great Computer Company Went Insane.* London: Aurum, 2000.
Stross, Randall E. *Steve Jobs and the NeXT Big Thing.* New York: Athenaeum, 1993.
Wilson, Susan. *Steve Jobs: Wizard of Apple Computer.* Berkeley Heights, N.J.: Enslow, 2001.

John C. Fredriksen

Johnson, Hugh Samuel (1882–1942) *army officer, public official, and author* Born on August 5, 1882, in Fort Scott, Kansas, Hugh S. Johnson was the son of Samuel L. Johnson, an attorney and rancher, and Elizabeth Mead Johnson. Educated in Wichita, Kansas, and Alva, Oklahoma, he graduated in 1903 from the U.S. Military Academy and was commissioned a second lieutenant. He then married Helen Leslie and had one son. In 1915, he received his bachelor's degree from the University of California and in 1916 his J.D.

Johnson's army career was significant by allowing him to meet and work with individuals and agencies that helped his career. Between 1903 and 1919, Johnson served as a quartermaster of refugees in the aftermath of the San Francisco earthquake, superintendent of Yosemite National Park, deputy provost marshal under General Enoch Crowder, with the responsibility of enforcing the Selective Service Act, and assistant director under General George Goethals of the Purchase and Supply Bureau. He also worked under Bernard BARUCH of the War Industries Board during World War I. In 1919, Johnson, a brigadier general, retired from the army. He became vice president and assistant general manager, then general counsel, and, in 1925, chair of the board of directors of the Moline Plow Company.

By 1927, Johnson, having already worked with George Peek on the McNary-Haugen programs for farm relief, was again working with Baruch until in 1933 president-elect Franklin D.

Roosevelt called upon Johnson to help finalize NEW DEAL plans for economic recovery. Johnson's contributions to the National Industrial Recovery Act were so important that Roosevelt appointed him the director of the NRA. It was in this capacity that Johnson implemented his ideas on industrial self-government through the codes of fair competition for nearly 480 different American industries. Unfortunately, despite the hopes and euphoria surrounding the NRA and its Blue Eagle, the program began to fail quickly until, in September 1934, Johnson was forced to resign. He remained within the New Deal as director of the WPA in New York only briefly. In 1935, Johnson left public service and began his "Hugh Johnson Says" column for the Scripps-Howard newspaper chain; he gradually came to oppose FDR's later New Deal programs and openly broke with the president in 1940.

Brusque, vituperative, and alcoholic yet brilliant, Johnson ("Old Iron Pants") died of pneumonia in Washington, D.C., on April 15, 1942.

Further reading

Johnson, Hugh S. *The Blue Eagle from Egg to Earth.* New York: Doubleday, Doran, 1935.

Ohl, John Kennedy. *Hugh S. Johnson and the New Deal.* DeKalb: Northern Illinois University Press, 1985.

Michael V. Namorato

junk bonds   The term given to bonds of less than investment-grade quality. There are two types of these bonds: those that were initially sold when the issuing company was low rated and those that were originally investment-grade bonds but later were downgraded in quality by the rating agencies.

Bonds of the latter type were previously called "fallen angels." Traditionally in the U.S. capital market, only companies with investment-grade credit ratings were able to borrow on the bond market. Companies with less than investment-grade ratings were normally forced to borrow from banks at higher interest rates and for shorter periods of time than they would have preferred, often altering their capital investment plans.

The market for original-issue junk bonds, technically high-yield bonds, was developed in the 1970s by Michael Milken at DREXEL BURNHAM LAMBERT. Many of them were issued as original-issue discount bonds, meaning that their coupons were set artificially low so that their yield to maturity would reflect their risk. When the bonds matured, the borrowing company would have to repay the full face amount—an amount above that which was raised originally. Many companies that were excluded from the corporate bond market made use of the junk market, and by the mid-1980s it had become a major corporate bond market sector in its own right. Junk bonds were also widely used in the corporate takeover and merger trend that developed in the mid-1980s.

Junk bonds became popular after the DEPOSITORY INSTITUTIONS ACT was passed in 1982, allowing thrift institutions to purchase them in limited amounts, reversing a long-standing prohibition against limited-purpose banking institutions buying corporate securities originally found in the BANKING ACT OF 1933. Their relative lack of liquidity in the secondary market became an issue after the savings and loan crisis in 1988, and the RECESSION in 1990–91 caused some junk bonds to default. But the market recovered in the mid-1990s, and junk bonds have become an accepted form of finance for companies that have not gained investment-grade status.

See also INVESTMENT BANKING; TREASURY BONDS.

Further reading

Bruck, Connie. *The Predators' Ball.* New York: Simon & Schuster, 1989.

Yago, Glenn. *Junk Bonds: How High Yield Securities Restructured Corporate America.* New York: Oxford University Press, 1990.

J. Walter Thompson   New York advertising agency opened in 1871 by J. Walter Thompson; it made a fortune in the ADVERTISING INDUSTRY.

The agency transformed magazines into eye-catching issues that were underwritten by advertising and reached millions of homes. It began when Thompson took over the Carlton & Smith agency (founded in 1864). Once there, he focused his attention on soliciting business for general magazines. Thompson, more than any other agent, worked up a vast amount of advertising revenue for an array of magazines, such as *Good Housekeeping* (1885), *Vogue* (1892), and *House Beautiful* (1896). In fact, Thompson bought virtually all the magazine space available to advertisers and controlled nearly all the advertising space in American magazines as late as 1898.

As early as the 1890s, the company established branch offices in Boston, Chicago, and London. The agency also began to create advertisements, develop trademarks, and design packages for its clients.

When J. Walter Thompson hired Stanley Resor and his brother to establish a Cincinnati office, they brought Helen Lansdowne along as the sole copywriter, later moving to the New York office. A group headed by Stanley bought out the retiring Thompson in 1916, and the following year Stanley and Helen married. The husband-and-wife team ran the agency together; he managed client services, and she supervised ad creation. The agency's billings more than tripled, from $10.7 million in 1922 to $37.5 million by the end of the decade, making it the industry leader in total billings, a position it maintained for the next 50 years.

The agency's president, Stanley Resor, the first major advertising executive with a college background, fostered a scientific approach to advertising. J. Walter Thompson's demographic study, combined with the Curtis Publishing Company's findings, provided a factual base on which future marketing researchers would build. In 1912, Stanley Resor commissioned a study entitled "Population and Its Distribution," which listed demographics of the population by category and state. The agency continued to update the research to describe more precisely the con-

sumer population, to track the growth of wholesale and retail stores in large cities, and so on. In 1915, the company established a research department and hired behavioral psychologist Dr. John B. Watson and other experts in the social sciences who would advance marketing research. These professionals applied motivational studies to advertising, initiated the use of scientific and medical findings as a basis for copy, and established the consumer panel, composed of families whose buying habits were surveyed and passed on to clients.

In the early 20th century, J. Walter Thompson handled many products that were purchased by women. Helen Resor's insight added the feminine point of view. Her words and visuals embraced women's hopes, fears, desires, and dreams regardless of what they did for a living. The powerful style worked in promoting Woodbury's Facial Soap ("A skin you love to touch"), Crisco vegetable shortening, Maxwell House and Yuban coffee, Lux soap, and Cutex nail polish.

During the 1920s, J. Walter Thompson led the ad industry in both innovative copy styles and the variety of services offered to clients. The agency pioneered the dramatic shift from selling goods and services to using well-known psychological appeals to reach customers. The agency's advertisement for products such as Fleischmann's yeast, Odorono deodorant, and Lux soap successfully incorporated fear, sex, and emulation appeals. The company's innovative methods included the sophisticated use of testimonial advertising, such as employing royalty and socialites in Pond's advertisements, and the use of photography in advertisements. The agency also provided the best opportunities for women, with its Women's Copy Group handling the majority of the agencies' soap, food, drugs, and toiletries accounts.

Thompson expanded into the new medium of advertising—radio. At this time, single sponsors underwrote most of the popular shows, while their agencies served as the producers. During the 1930s and 1940s, the Radio Department produced some of the most popular shows on the air, including the *Fleischmann Yeast Hour* with crooner Rudy Vallee, the *Chase and Sanborn Hour,* and the *Kraft Music Hall.* Next, Thompson brought its success in radio to the new medium of television, producing the first variety show, *The Hour Glass,* and first dramatic show, *Kraft Television Theater.* When the networks assumed the programming function in the late 1950s, Thompson continued to help develop *Father Knows Best, Naked City, Wagon Train, Ozzie and Harriet, Kraft Music Hall, Bat Masterson,* and *Have Gun Will Travel.*

At the same time, the agency dominated the international field. The company had already established itself abroad as the first American agency with offices in Great Britain in 1899 and on the European continent in the 1920s. GENERAL MOTORS took the agency into Latin America in the following decade. By the end of World War II, the agency was operating 15 foreign offices and quickly added another 14.

In 1969, J. Walter Thompson became a publicly held corporation. In 1980 the firm reorganized to form a new HOLDING COMPANY, JWT Group, Inc., with J. Walter Thompson as the largest subsidiary, along with advertising, public relations, and marketing subsidiaries, which Thompson had acquired during the previous decade. During the 1980s, however, global marketers pushed international advertising expenditures to unprecedented levels. The subsequent mega-merger activity amidst agencies signaled the growing importance of putting worldwide capabilities in place to handle global clients. And in 1989, the London-based WPP group acquired both the J. Walter Thompson Company and the Ogilvy Group.

Today the J. Walter Thompson Company continues to be an industry leader, with more than 8,000 employees in 150 cities and 86 countries. In 2004, the company ranked as the fourth-largest global agency and the largest U.S. agency. The company's roster of multinational clients includes Rolex, Kraft, Kellogg's, Ford, Unilever, Pfizer, Reckitt Benckiser, and Schick.

Further reading

Fox, Stephen. *The Mirror Makers. A History of American Advertising and Its Creators.* New York: Vintage Books, 1983.

Marchand, Roland. *Advertising the American Dream.* Berkeley: University of California Press, 1985.

Juliann Sivulka

K

Kaiser, Henry J. (1882–1967) *businessman and entrepreneur*   Kaiser was born in New York in 1882. After holding a number of menial jobs, he moved to Spokane, Washington. He learned the construction business and began to bid on public works projects, first in Canada and then in the United States. He also participated in building the major Cuban highway in 1927 before returning to the United States.

During the early years of the Depression, he bid for work on the proposed Boulder Dam on the Colorado along with a group of other construction companies. It was the largest building project ever proposed until that time. After successfully completing it, his company worked on other large public works projects, including the Bonneville Dam on the Columbia River. The Grand Coulee Dam followed. He also worked on the Shasta Dam in California, not as a contractor but as a supplier of cement. By the late 1930s, he had developed a reputation as an efficient builder who brought projects in under schedule and at great profit to himself.

World War II saw Kaiser enter the shipbuilding business, doing contract work for both the British and American governments. He began building ships for troop and cargo transport and often completed them in as little as one week, breaking all records in the process and acquiring a reputation as one of the war's best-known entrepreneurs. After the war he continued in the steel business, and Kaiser Steel became one of the country's major manufacturers. He also dabbled in automobile production and developed a car named after him, the Kaiser. One of his major investors was Cyrus EATON, but the cars went out of production after several years due to competition from the Big Three automakers. In the 1950s, he turned his attention to land development and helped develop a sizable portion of Waikiki on Oahu, in Hawaii.

At his death in 1967, he was still chairman of Kaiser Industries, an organization that involved steel, home building, and aluminum. Kaiser's lasting legacy is found in the health care organization that evolved out of his own organization, in which it provided health care to his construction workers. The Kaiser Permanente Medical Care Program became one of the earliest and largest of what later became known as prepaid health maintenance organizations, or HMOs.

See also NEW DEAL.

Henry J. Kaiser (LIBRARY OF CONGRESS)

Further reading

Adams, Stephen B. *Mr. Kaiser Goes to Washington: The Rise of a Government Entrepreneur.* Chapel Hill: University of North Carolina Press, 1997.

Foster, Mark S. *Henry J. Kaiser: Builder in the Modern American West.* Austin: University of Texas Press, 1989.

Kennedy, Joseph Patrick (1888–1969) *financier, U.S. government official, and diplomat*
Kennedy was the progenitor of an American political dynasty. Despite poor marks in economics, after graduating from Harvard College in 1912, Kennedy was drawn to a career in banking, serving as a Massachusetts assistant state bank examiner between 1912 and late 1913. In early 1914, Kennedy played a pivotal role in rescuing the Columbia Trust Company, which his father had helped found, from absorption into a larger concern, and was elected to the bank's presidency at the age of 24. Shortly afterward, he married former Boston mayor John Fitzgerald's eldest daughter, Rose, who would eventually bear him nine children.

With the United States' intervention into the First World War, Kennedy served as assistant general manager of Bethlehem Steel's Fore River Shipyard, south of Boston. Shortly after the armistice Kennedy became office manager of the brokerage of Hayden, Stone and Company, where he developed a particular interest in what were, at the time, new entertainment-related technologies. Unable to interest any buyers in a foundering film production and distribution outfit that he had been commissioned to sell in 1922, Kennedy bought Film Booking Offices of America with a small syndicate of Boston investors in early 1926 and became the company's president.

Between 1926 and 1930, Kennedy spent much of his time in California, overseeing not only his own interests, but also serving as a special business adviser to a number of other studios and production companies. Beginning in December 1927, Kennedy, Radio Corporation of America vice president David SARNOFF, and Keith-Albee-Orpheum vaudeville circuit general manager J. J. Murdock brought about a number of stock transfers that intertwined the holdings and corporate structures of RCA, FBO, and K-A-O. By May 1928, Kennedy, Sarnoff, and Murdock had formed the Radio-Keith-Orpheum Corporation, thereby effectuating the largest merger to date in Hollywood history.

"Untouched," as Kennedy put it, by the Crash of 1929, he divested the bulk of his film holdings and left Hollywood permanently in 1930, returning to the East Coast to resume the stock trading practices for which he was already becoming notorious. He supported Franklin Roosevelt's presidential candidacy in 1932 and assumed the chairmanship of the newly formed Securities and Exchange Commission two years later, despite his reputation on Wall Street. By the time of his resignation in September 1935, the commission's successes in helping to end abusive trading practices and in regulating the formerly autonomous exchanges won Kennedy overwhelming praise both among his administration colleagues and in the political press. He returned to the private sector briefly as a consultant to RCA, William Randolph Hearst, and Paramount Pictures, before assuming his second government posting as chairman of the U.S. Maritime Commission in April 1937.

He resigned his chairmanship after only eight months in order to become the U.S. ambassador to the Court of St. James's. Despite a warm welcome in London, as war approached Kennedy's unwavering advocacy of American neutrality made him unpopular on both sides of the Atlantic and ultimately ended his once cordial relationship with Roosevelt. Returning to the United States in October 1940, Kennedy entered a state of semiretirement. During the war he maintained a number of his earlier business interests, invested extensively in Manhattan real estate, and purchased the Chicago Merchandise Mart. In the late 1940s, he endowed a foundation in memory of his eldest son and began to focus much of his attention on the public careers of his surviving children.

See also NEW DEAL; SECURITIES EXCHANGE ACT OF 1934.

Further reading

Beschloss, Michael R. *Kennedy and Roosevelt: The Uneasy Alliance.* New York: Norton, 1980.

De Bedts, Ralph F. *The New Deal's SEC: The Formative Years.* New York: Columbia University Press, 1964).

Goodwin, Doris Kearns. *The Fitzgeralds and the Kennedys.* New York: Simon & Schuster, 1987.

Amanda Smith

Keynes, John Maynard (1883–1946) *British economist, public servant, and writer*   Son of a Cambridge logician and political economist, John Maynard Keynes was educated at Eton and King's College, Cambridge. In 1906, he sat for the civil service exam and placed second, receiving one of his lowest scores in economics. He took a position in the India Office and spent much of his spare time writing a dissertation on probability, which he submitted for a fellowship at Cambridge. It was subsequently published as *A Treatise on Probability* (1921). He became a permanent fellow of King's College in 1911 and remained active in the life of the college throughout the rest of his life, combining the roles of lecturer in economics, bursar of King's College, and editor of the *Economic Journal.*

During World War I, Keynes served in the British Treasury and after the war took part in the peace negotiations at Versailles. He resigned in protest over the severity of the reparations being demanded, believing they would lead to economic collapse. He developed his objections in *The Economic Consequences of the Peace* (1919), a best-selling polemic that was translated into many languages and gained him worldwide fame.

Keynes's other books included *Indian Currency and Finance* (1913), *A Tract on Monetary Reform* (1923), and *A Treatise on Money* (1931). The *Treatise,* in which Keynes began to develop the theory for which he would become famous, received a harsh review by Friedrich Hayek from the London School of Economics. During the 1930s, economists at the LSE and Cambridge vigorously debated the appropriate remedy for prolonged unemployment. LSE economists thought the problem was that wages needed to adjust to correct problems of the labor market. Keynes and other Cambridge economists believed the problem was a deficiency of aggregate demand. The LSE solution was one of laissez-faire: Tolerate unemployment and allow wages to adjust downward. The Keynesian solution was to boost aggregate demand through deficit financed government spending. In an open letter published in the *New York Times* in 1933, Keynes urged Franklin D. Roosevelt to adopt an expansionary policy for the United States. In *The General Theory of Money, Interest and Prices* (1936),

Keynes attempted to provide theoretical justification for his policy prescription. Keynes's ideas have often been described as a blueprint for the NEW DEAL, but his influence was more indirect. Franklin Roosevelt's advisers were aware of his work, but FDR was reported to have disliked Keynes personally.

Keynes was the chief British representative at Bretton Woods in 1944 where, along with Harry Dexter White, a system of fixed exchange rates was formulated that became known as the BRETTON WOODS SYSTEM; its fixed parities would remain in place until the early 1970s. Throughout his life, Keynes maintained an interest in the arts and the artistic life. Keynes established and largely financed the Cambridge Arts Theater and was a trustee of the National Gallery. After years of suffering with heart disease, Keynes died at his home in Sussex in 1946.

Further reading

Colander, David C., and Harry Landreth. *The Coming of Keynesianism to America: Conversations with the Founders of Keynesian Economics.* Brookfield, Vt.: E. Elgar, 1996.

Moggridge, Donald. *Keynes.* Toronto: University of Toronto Press, 1993.

Skidelsky, Robert. *John Maynard Keynes: Hopes Betrayed, 1883–1920.* London: Macmillan, 1983.

———. *John Maynard Keynes: The Economist as Savior, 1920–1937.* London: Macmillan, 1992.

Fiona Maclachlan

John Maynard Keynes (LIBRARY OF CONGRESS)

Kidder Peabody & Co. A private Boston banking firm founded by Henry Kidder, Francis Peabody, and Oliver Peabody in 1865. Previously, the firm had been known as Thayer & Co., founded by John Eliot Thayer in 1824. The firm became one of the better-known private banks and investment banks in the country by the 1890s, performing traditional banking and securities related services for corporate clients.

Kidder Peabody also became an adviser and major shareholder in the Santa Fe Railroad and by the turn of the 20th century became allied with J. P. Morgan & Co. Originally the firm was the banker to what would become the AMERICAN TELEPHONE AND TELEGRAPH CO. but had to delegate some of the business to Morgan. That alliance led to Kidder being named one of the members of the "money trust" by the Pujo Committee examining American banking in 1912.

The firm's long alliance with Morgan also led to its rescue in 1930 after the firm failed. After being reorganized, it again assumed a premier position among investment banks with a stronger presence on Wall Street. It continued to be an ally of Morgan and extended its activities into MERGERS and acquisitions and trading as well. After the Glass-Steagall Act was passed, the firm remained on the top of Wall Street's leading investment banks and was continually ranked among the top 10 underwriters until the 1960s. It also continued a strong presence in mergers and acquisitions and developed its investment advisory services, which had begun in the 1920s.

When investment banks began to expand in the 1960s, the firm fell behind. In the mid-1970s, it acquired the old firm of CLARK DODGE & CO., mostly for its investment advisory services, and merged them with its own. For the next 20 years, Kidder remained a medium-size firm slightly outside the top rung of Wall Street firms.

A lack of capital caused the firm to be sold to the GENERAL ELECTRIC CO. in 1985, and the conglomerate maintained control until 1995, when Kidder was sold to Paine Webber. A scandal in the Treasury bond department caused large losses for the firm and its parent, and GE finally divested itself of the investment banking firm rather than pour more money into it. Paine Webber eventually closed the firm after repercussions from the scandal continued to plague Kidder, and its name disappeared from Wall Street, 170 years after the firm was originally started in Boston. Along with DREXEL BURNHAM LAMBERT, it was one of the few major Wall Street houses to disappear in the 1990s.

See also INVESTMENT BANKING.

Further reading

Carosso, Vincent. *More Than a Century of Investment Banking: The Kidder Peabody & Co. Story*. New York: McGraw-Hill, 1979.

Geisst, Charles R. *The Last Partnerships: Inside the Great Wall Street Money Dynasties*. New York: McGraw-Hill, 2001.

K-Mart   A department store chain originally founded in 1899 by Sebastien Sperling Kresge (1867–1966), a tinware salesman, as the S. S. Kresge Co. The original stores were known as "five and dime" stores, selling all merchandise for either 5 or 10 cents. Kresge previously was in a partnership with J. G. McCrory, a prominent retailer at the time, but quickly set out to open his own stores. Within a decade, he had 85 stores grossing more than $10 million per year, and he incorporated in 1912. In 1918, the company stock was listed on the NEW YORK STOCK EXCHANGE.

The company remained a "variety" store selling inexpensive items throughout its early history. It opened a chain in Canada in the 1920s and remained successful throughout the pre–World War II years because of its low prices and inexpensive product lines. As a result of his success, Kresge founded the Kresge Foundation in 1924. But by the late 1950s, the store chain was being seriously challenged by other retailers, which were becoming more full-service stores and were moving into the suburbs and into newly constructed shopping malls. In 1962, it introduced a new concept store called K-Mart in Garden City, Michigan. The store was a no-frills discounter of a wide array of clothing and other household items and became extremely successful, leading the company to a record $483 million in sales the first year of operation.

Within four years, more than 160 K-Mart stores were opened in addition to the 753 Kresge stores in operation, and sales topped the $1 billion mark. In 1976 alone, the company opened 271 K-Mart stores, the largest amount of retail space ever opened. By 1977, 95 percent of the company's sales were generated by K-Mart, and the company officially changed its name. The phenomenal expansion hit its peak in 1981, when the company opened its 2,000th store. By the late 1980s, the Kresge stores had been sold, and the company no longer had any links to its former founder or name. The company had become the second leading retailer in the country behind SEARS, ROEBUCK.

In the 1990s, the company began an acquisitions program, adding more retailers to its operations. It acquired the Sports Authority, Builders Square, Borders bookstores, and OfficeMax before subsequently selling them off. But the expansion and loss of market share to the leading retail chain, Wal-Mart, put the company under severe financial pressure, and it filed for Chapter 11 BANKRUPTCY protection in 2002. After reorganizing, it emerged from bankruptcy a year later with new management. In 2004, it was announced that K-Mart would merge with Sears, the largest retail merger in history—creating a rival to number-one retailer Wal-Mart.

See also CHAIN STORES.

Further reading

Hendrickson, Robert. *The Grand Emporiums: The Illustrated History of America's Great Department Stores.* New York: Stein & Day, 1979.

Kresge, Stanley S. *The S. S. Kresge Story.* Racine, Wisc.: Western Publishing, 1979.

Turner, Marcia Layton. *K-Mart's Ten Deadly Sins: How Incompetence Ruined an American Icon.* Hoboken, N.J.: John Wiley & Sons, 2003.

Kuhn Loeb & Co.   Investment banking firm founded by two German immigrants—Abraham Kuhn and Solomon Loeb—in 1867 in New York. The two were merchants from Cincinnati who had already opened a New York City dry goods store before trying their luck at banking. Kuhn returned to Germany, where he offered a job in his bank to Jacob SCHIFF, who arrived in the United States in 1873. From that time, Schiff became the dominant figure at the firm and rivaled only J. P. Morgan as New York's senior banker.

The firm remained small for the first decade after Schiff arrived but found its fortune in restructuring the UNION PACIFIC RAILROAD after Jay GOULD was no longer involved in its operations. Other significant financings included those for the Southern Pacific Railroad, Pennsylvania Railroad, Royal Dutch Petroleum, and Shell Transport & Trading. In most cases, the firm underwrote the companies' bonds and acquired a reputation as a bond financier.

The firm began to expand its number of partners in the late 1890s, adding Paul Warburg and Otto Kahn, among others. Schiff served as an adviser to Theodore Roosevelt and was opposed to the development of the FEDERAL RESERVE when the idea of a new central bank was first discussed in the years before 1910. After World War I began, out, Kuhn Loeb participated in the large war loans of the day for the European allies, although the firm deliberately refused to participate in the largest loan to date, the Anglo-French loan of 1915. Partners of the firm remained sympathetic to the plight of European Jews during the war and were incorrectly labeled pro-German as a result.

Jacob Schiff died in 1920, and Otto Kahn assumed leadership of the firm. The firm's business remained much the same as it had during the days of Schiff: It underwrote mainly bonds and provided financial advice to its corporate clients. MERGERS and acquisitions became one of its specialties and remained as such for decades. It also acquired something of a flamboyant image because of Kahn's affinity for Hollywood and being seen in public, a diametrical shift from the days of Schiff. But the firm could not survive the postwar years without changing. Being a partnership, its capital base remained very small compared to the larger investment banks dominating Wall Street in the 1970s.

Rather than expand or go public, the firm agreed to be bought by LEHMAN BROTHERS in 1977, and its independence came to an end. As a partnership to the end, Kuhn Loeb's reputation was inextricably linked with the personalities of its senior partners, most notably Schiff and Kahn. In the last two decades of its independence, it remained one of the better-known Wall Street merger firms, acting mostly as adviser.

See also INVESTMENT BANKING.

Further reading

Birmingham, Stephen. *"Our Crowd": The Great Jewish Families of New York.* New York: Harper & Row, 1967.

Geisst, Charles R. *The Last Partnerships: Inside the Great Wall Street Money Dynasties.* New York: McGraw-Hill, 2001.

L

laissez-faire A French term meaning "allow to do," it was transformed into an economic theory stating that business should be allowed to operate with as little government interference as possible. In economics, laissez-faire generally has been taken to mean hands off and to be the direct opposite of mercantilism, which suggested strong government interference in the private sector in the 18th and 19th centuries.

Laissez-faire succeeded mercantilism in the 19th century as the economies of the United States and Europe began to industrialize. Its best known exponents were from the British classical school, led by economist Adam Smith, who maintained that humans are most productive when they are motivated by unfettered economic self-interest, free of outside control. Competition flourishes when government influence is minimal, and a full array of goods and services will follow, subject only to the demands of the market.

The doctrine became very popular in the United States, especially during the period of rapid industrialization in the 19th century. Business developed at a much faster pace than government's ability to keep pace with it, and the term became a synonym for a government's generally lax industrial policy. But even during periods when laissez-faire economics appeared to be working, some protectionist government policies still intervened, such as the TARIFFS imposed against imports.

In the late 19th and early 20th centuries, the policies of progressivism began to attack the lenient attitude of government toward business. The administration of William McKinley was the last in which a hands-off policy toward business was evident—until the 1920s when Republicans controlled the White House and Congress. But stronger antitrust policies that began with the administration of Theodore Roosevelt, the founding of the FEDERAL RESERVE, and the regulations passed during the NEW DEAL all signaled a less permissive atmosphere for business than was the case in the 19th century. Similarly, the founding of many government-sponsored enterprises between the 1930s and the 1970s demonstrated that various administrations were not willing to allow certain sectors of the economy such as residential housing, the financing of higher education, and farm financing to be left totally to the private sector.

After the 1930s, the term was used to describe the lack of government interference in the marketplace rather than a specific economic policy. It is still used today to denote a general hands-off attitude of government toward business.

See also ANTITRUST; DEREGULATION.

Further reading

Faulkner, Harold U. *The Decline of Laissez Faire, 1897–1917.* New York: Harper & Row, 1968.
Fried, Barbara H. *The Progressive Assault of Laissez Faire.* Cambridge, Mass.: Harvard University Press, 2001.

Lamont, Thomas W. (1870–1948) *banker* Born in upstate New York, Lamont's father was a Methodist minister. Thomas was sent to private boarding school at Phillips Exeter Academy and graduated from Harvard in 1892. After graduation, he went to New York City and became a newspaperman at the *New York Tribune,* where he rose to become assistant city editor.

Not satisfied with journalism, Lamont invested in a food processing company, but it ran into financial difficulties in 1898. He then reorganized it with his brother-in-law Charles Corliss, and the new firm became known as Lamont, Corliss & Company. As a result of the reorganization, Lamont came to the attention of many New York bankers, one of whom was Henry Davison, who invited him to work for the newly formed Bankers Trust Co. in 1903. In 1909, he moved to a senior post at the First National Bank of New York. After serving as the bank's secretary and treasurer, he was lured away by J. P. Morgan with an offer to become a partner in Morgan's bank in 1911. After becoming Morgan's youngest partner, he remained with the bank for the rest of his career.

After arranging large loans for Britain and France during World War I, Lamont was chosen to represent the U.S. Treasury at the Paris Peace Conference in 1918. He subsequently worked on German war reparations and became a supporter of the League of Nations. In the same year, he also purchased a controlling interest in the *New York Evening Post.* He played a central role in the terms and conditions of the peace negotiations as well as the reparations placed on Germany after the war. He also was sent to Japan as a financial delegate in the 1920s to discuss Japan's role in Manchuria and its role in international financial affairs. The period was notable for financial diplomacy especially, led mainly by J. P. Morgan Jr. and his partners.

Lamont was involved in most of the other major international financial transactions and international diplomatic events of the 1920s, including the Dawes plan, named after Charles DAWES, and the plan to stabilize the French franc. At the time of the stock market crash of 1929, he helped organize a market stabilization plan while at J. P. Morgan & Company, but the plan failed despite the efforts of senior bankers. In 1931, he helped organize the Bank for International Settlements.

Lamont became chairman of J. P. Morgan & Co. after the death of J. P. Morgan Jr. in 1943. The bank went public in 1940, and Lamont became the major shareholder. After 1943, his role in actively managing the bank was limited. During his lifetime, he was a major benefactor to many charities and to Harvard College and Phillips Exeter as well. He is best remembered as a major figure in American banking in the 20th century who provided the Morgan bank with leadership during a time of transition.

See also MORGAN, JOHN PIERPONT; MORGAN, JOHN PIERPONT, JR.

Further reading

Carosso, Vincent. *The Morgans: Private International Bankers, 1854–1913.* Cambridge, Mass.: Harvard University Press, 1987.
Chernow, Ron. *The House of Morgan: An American Banking Dynasty and the Origins of Modern Finance.* New York: Simon & Schuster, 1990.
Lamont, Edward M. *The Ambassador from Wall Street: The Story of Thomas W. Lamont, J. P. Morgan's Chief Executive.* Lanham, Md.: Madison Books, 1994.

Land, Edwin H. (1909–1991) *physicist, inventor, and manufacturer* Born in Bridgeport, Connecticut, Land studied at Harvard, where he became interested in the physics of polarized light. After leaving college without a degree, he developed a polarizing material that was inexpensive and easy to manufacture. From an early age, Land was preoccupied with the idea of polarized light, and he opened a laboratory in his home while still a college student. In 1929, he applied for a patent for a polarizer that resembled a sheet of glass. In 1932, he announced at a Harvard conference that he had developed a complete solution for polarizing light.

Building on this success, he opened the Land-Wheelwright Laboratories in collaboration with George Wheelwright in Boston and began selling his products to the Eastman Kodak Company. In 1937, he and Wheelwright founded the Polaroid Corporation, which began producing polarized products for civilian and military use. When World War II broke out, the company's sales soared as it began selling rifle sights, filters, periscope filters, and goggles to the military. After the war, the company's sales plunged, and Land began seeking new uses for his inventions.

In 1943, he conceived the idea of a camera whose pictures could be developed within 60 seconds. The first Polaroid camera produced sepiatone photographs quickly after being taken. In 1950, black and white pictures were available, and in 1963, the camera was adapted to produce color pictures. As a result, the company became one of the best-known American success stories of the immediate post–World War II period.

The Polaroid camera underwent several generations of development. In the early 1970s, the SX-70 model was able to produce a fully finished, or laminated, photograph within a minute of being taken. Land went on to collect more than 500 patents during his lifetime before retiring from the company in 1980. He was active in the 3-D movie process that was developed to great fanfare in the early 1950s. One of his later ideas, that of instant movies, proved a failure and never

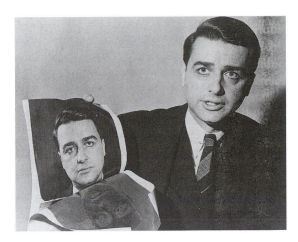

Edwin H. Land (Library of Congress)

saw the light of day. During his retirement, he devoted his time to the Rowland Institute of Science, an organization he founded in 1960.

Although Land never graduated from college, he later became a professor at the Massachusetts Institute of Technology and also lectured at Harvard. He was inducted into the National Inventors Hall of Fame in 1977. The Polaroid Corporation became one of Wall Street's favorite stocks in the 1960s and was one of the 50 most popular among investors because of its cutting edge technology. Despite the introduction of new models, the company began to lose market share and fell out of favor on Wall Street. Developments in digital photography put the company under further pressure, and it filed for Chapter 11 bankruptcy protection in 2001.

See also Eastman, George.

Further reading
McElheny, Victor K. *Insisting on the Impossible: The Life of Edwin Land.* New York: Perseus, 1999.
Olshaker, Mark. *Instant Image: Edwin Land and the Polaroid Experience.* New York: Stein & Day, 1978.

Lazard Freres An investment banking company founded in New Orleans in 1848 by

Alexandre, Lazare, and Simon Lazard, originally as a dry goods store. The three had emigrated from France in that year but a year later were forced to move the business to San Francisco because of a citywide fire in New Orleans. The gold rush had just begun in California, and the business soon began trading gold. Four years later, they opened a branch in Paris, now firmly established in the gold business.

By the end of the Civil War, Lazard was a full-fledged international bank specializing in gold trading. A London branch was also established, and in 1880, a New York office was opened by Alexandre Weill; it became known as Lazard Freres. The New York office was only one of the branches of the bank; it specialized in gold trading and underwriting of some securities issues but remained a small operation until World War II. During the war, Andre Meyer arrived in New York after working in the firm's Paris office. Meyer already had a substantial background in finance, although he was not from an old family, as were the Weills. He took control of the office. After the war Lazard Freres emerged as a specialist in MERGERS and acquisitions as well as maintaining its business in underwriting.

The firm benefited from the postwar merger boom in the United States. Meyer and a younger partner, Felix Rohatyn, aligned themselves with Harold GENEEN at the ITT Corporation, and Lazard became ITT's major merger banker. The firm helped the corporation with many of its major acquisitions as it built itself into a conglomerate and also served other companies. Much of the firm's success in the 1960s and 1970s was built around the relationship with ITT. Meyer died in 1979, and Lazard remained primarily a merger specialist but was also a partnership through the late 1990s, when most other investment banks had gone public.

In the late 1990s, the firm began to suffer a loss of rank and prestige on Wall Street because of its small size and limited capital base. It was reorganized by Bruce Wasserstein, a Wall Street merger specialist who became the senior partner

of the firm in 2001. The firm remained private, being the last of the traditional Wall Street private partnerships choosing not to sell shares to the public. It finally went public in 2005.

Further reading

Geisst, Charles R. *The Last Partnerships: Inside the Great Wall Street Money Dynasties.* New York: McGraw-Hill, 2001.

Reich, Cary. *Financier: The Biography of Andre Meyer.* New York: William Morrow, 1983.

Lee, Ivy L. (1877–1934) *public relations expert* Lee is generally considered the father of modern public and corporate relations. Born in Georgia, Lee attended Emory University and graduated from Princeton in 1898. After doing postgraduate work at Harvard Law School he dropped out when his money ran out. He then became a newspaperman at the *New York Times* and the *New York World,* specializing in business and finance while studying English at Columbia, before opening his own public relations firm.

Along with George Parker, he opened the public relations firm of Parker & Lee in 1904. He then worked on assignment from the Democratic National Committee as a publicist and writer. Lee provided the creative side of the business, while Parker provided the connections and clients. Recognizing a market for corporate public relations in the era of the MUCKRAKERS, Lee began providing the public with the business and industry side of business and social issues as a way of countering the attacks of writers in the press and in books. His method was to provide facts rather than advertising, in the hope that newspaper and journal editors would print both sides of a financial or business story. In 1906, he joined the staff of the Pennsylvania Railroad as a full-time executive in charge of the company's public relations, which were not in the best of shape. He continued to work for the railroad until 1914.

In 1915, Lee began working for John D. Rockefeller Sr. after the "Ludlow Massacre" in

Colorado. The assignment proved successful, and the Rockefellers, like the Pennsylvania Railroad before them, adopted a new, more straightforward public relations policy than in the past. In 1916, Lee opened a new firm. After World War I, his reorganized firm took on many diverse assignments. He worked during the 1920s for greater acceptance of the Soviet Union, believing that a free flow of ideas and greater international understanding of Russia would lead to the demise of communism. He wrote several books on the Soviet Union and on the use of statistics. Throughout this period, he worked for many of the most visible financiers and the largest companies in the country.

During the early 1930s, his firm worked for several Wall Street investment houses that were being investigated at the Pecora hearings in 1933 about the causes of the stock market crash of 1929. A year later, work he had done on an assignment for a German company controlled by the Nazis led to his being investigated by the House Un-American Activities Committee. He died of a brain tumor in 1934 at age 57.

Further reading

Ewen, Stuart. *PR!: A Social History of Spin.* New York: Basic Books, 1996.

Goldman, Eric. *Two Way Street: The Emergence of the Public Relations Counsel.* New York: Bellman Publishing, 1948.

Hiebert, Ray E. *Courtier to the Crowds: The Story of Ivy Lee and the Development of Public Relations.* Ames: Iowa State University Press, 1966.

Lehman Brothers An INVESTMENT BANKING house founded by Henry Lehman in Montgomery, Alabama, in 1845 as a dry goods merchandiser. Lehman was born in Germany in 1821 and immigrated to Alabama, where he established his general merchandise store. Lehman died in 1854, and the store passed to his two brothers. Emanuel Lehman opened an office in New York City in 1858, trading in cotton. Another brother,

Mayer, had close ties with the Confederate government in Richmond, and the company prospered before the Civil War supplying the Confederate Army. They became so prosperous trading commodities that they were able to loan the state of Alabama $100,000 after the war.

In 1868, the New York City office continued to prosper, but the firm remained primarily a commodities trading firm until the 1890s. It was a member of many of the futures exchanges in New York, including the New York Cotton Exchange and Coffee Exchange. It was also a member of the NEW YORK STOCK EXCHANGE, having joined in 1887. The firm began turning its attention toward investment banking when Philip Lehman entered the firm in 1882. Born and educated in New York City, he became a partner five years later.

In the 1890s, Lehman Brothers began establishing banks in New York, the best-known of which was the Trust Company of America, founded in 1899. After the turn of the century, the firm began a rapid entry into the investment banking business. It underwrote stocks of newly emerging companies in growing industries, notably retailing. Before World War I, it joined with GOLDMAN SACHS in underwriting many new issues, the best known of which was for SEARS, ROEBUCK & CO. in 1906.

The first nonfamily member of the firm was not admitted to a partnership until 1924. Most of the partners were members of the Lehman family. The best-known outside of banking circles was Herbert Lehman, who became a partner in 1908 and retired in 1928. Subsequently he was elected governor of New York and a U.S. senator from New York.

In the first quarter of the century, Lehman underwrote new stock issues for companies such as the Underwood Corp., the Studebaker Corp., and the F. W. Woolworth Corp. After the Glass-Steagall Act was passed in 1933, Lehman Brothers became purely an investment banking firm and remained a partnership in the post–World War II years. From 1928, the firm was run by

Robert "Bobbie" Lehman, the son of Philip Lehman, who was responsible for shaping the firm for the remainder of the 20th century.

In the 1970s, Peter G. Peterson became chairman of the firm. He helped reorganize it after several years of poor performance and was succeeded by Lewis Glucksman. In 1977, the firm acquired KUHN LOEB & CO., and in 1984, merger talks were held with Shearson American Express. Lehman Brothers was acquired by Shearson, and the company changed its name to Shearson Lehman American Express, becoming the second-largest securities house on Wall Street. In the mid-1990s, AMERICAN EXPRESS began to restructure itself, and Lehman Brothers was spun off as a public company, assuming its original name. It remains one of Wall Street's best-known and oldest investment banking firms.

Further reading

Auletta, Ken. *Greed and Glory on Wall Street: The Fall of the House of Lehman.* New York: Random House, 1986.

Geisst, Charles R. *The Last Partnerships: Inside the Great Wall Street Money Dynasties.* New York: McGraw-Hill, 2001.

Levittown   A suburban town on Long Island, New York, that was the first purpose-built suburb in the United States. The town was built by Levitt & Sons, a family-run firm founded in 1929 that first conceived the idea in 1947. The firm was headed by William J. Levitt, who got into the real estate and building business when he sold a home for his brother. The success of the small transaction encouraged them, and Levitt & Sons was formed.

The firm first attempted a large-scale housing development in Norfolk, Virginia, in 1945, when it built 1,600 small houses. The marketing for the homes was unsuccessful during the war. The company did not make a profit for its efforts, but it did not abandon the concept. William Levitt realized that the millions of returning servicemen discharged after the war would need housing. Using knowledge acquired from other small developments built during the war, the idea of Levittown was born.

After purchasing a 1,000-acre farm located midway between New York City and the Long Island towns where major defense contractors were located, the company proceeded to build more than 17,000 ranch-style homes on the site. Each unit averaged about 750 square feet and had amenities built in that were not often used in mass housing, such as built-in storage units, appliances, and kitchens located in the front of the house rather than the rear. The homes sold for $7,990 each, considerably less than competitors' homes. But they still made a profit for the company because of the quantity built.

Levittown marketed its homes to whites only and lured city dwellers from Brooklyn and Queens. The community contributed to the urban flight that characterized the 1950s and 1960s and was a major factor in the rapid suburbanization of Long Island. It also indirectly applied pressure on New York banking laws, which until that time prohibited New York City banks from crossing county lines. Many banks lobbied for changes in the laws so that they could follow the exodus.

In 1967, Levitt & Sons was sold for $92 million to conglomerate ITT, which viewed Levitt's communities as a potential customer for many of its diverse products. The suburban concept was imitated many times around the country as builders adopted the marketing concept of building many units at smaller profit margins than on larger houses. For future generations, the name Levittown became a metaphor for the advantages and disadvantages of suburban living in America and was also the model for hundreds of similar projects around the country that capitalized on the post–World War II demand for new housing.

See also CONGLOMERATES.

Aerial view of Levittown, 1954 (LIBRARY OF CONGRESS)

Further reading

Kelly, Barbara M. *Expanding the American Dream: Building and Rebuilding Levittown.* Albany: State University of New York Press, 1993.

Sobel, Robert. *The Great Boom, 1950–2000: How a Generation of Americans Created the World's Most Prosperous Society.* New York: St. Martin's Press, 2001.

Lewis, John L. (1880–1969) *labor leader*
Born in Iowa to Welsh immigrant parents, Lewis became a miner while still in his teens. In his late 20s, he began serving in the UNITED MINE WORK-ERS OF AMERICA (UMWA) and became acting president of the union in 1919. Also, in 1911 he became an organizer for the AMERICAN FEDERA-TION OF LABOR (AFL). He was elected president of the UMWA in 1920, holding the job until he retired in 1960. In his 40 years as head of the union, he often clashed with other unions and embarked on long strikes.

His bitterest clash with other unions occurred when he split with the American Federation of Labor and formed the Committee for Industrial Organization, or CIO, in 1935. Unions that joined Lewis were expelled from the AFL, stirring great animosity within the union movement. His new efforts were successful, however, because by the late 1930s the CIO had more members than the AFL. In 1938, the CIO changed its name to the Congress of Industrial Organizations and began organizing unions in the heavy manufacturing, mass-production industries.

Originally a Republican, Lewis became a supporter of Franklin Roosevelt and endorsed him in 1932 and 1936. Lewis decided to support Wendell Willkie for president in 1940 and threatened to resign from the CIO if the president stood again and won reelection. Lewis then made good on his promise and resigned as president of the CIO after Roosevelt won the election; two years later the UMWA withdrew from the CIO.

During World War II, the public became increasingly disillusioned with the miners because of many strikes called during wartime. Most were successful, however, in winning increased wages. In 1946, immediately after the war, the UMWA again joined the CIO but broke away the following year. Congress responded to the uneasy labor situation by passing the TAFT-HARTLEY ACT in 1947.

A coal strike in 1948 during the Truman administration led to a crisis in industrial relations and finally led to a moderation in Lewis's tactics. Lewis also helped create the UMWA Welfare and Retirement Fund in conjunction with the federal government, and it was signed into law during the Truman administration. The fund provided health care to coal workers. He retired from the union in 1960, administering the fund until his death in 1969.

See also GOMPERS, SAMUEL; MEANY, GEORGE.

Further reading

Alinsky, Saul. *John L. Lewis: An Unauthorized Biography.* New York: G. P. Putnam's Sons, 1949.
Dobofsky, Melvyn, and Warren Van Tine. *John L. Lewis.* Urbana: University of Illinois Press, 1977.
Wechsler, James A. *Labor Baron: A Portrait of John L. Lewis.* New York: William Morrow, 1944.

John L. Lewis (LIBRARY OF CONGRESS)

Livingston, Robert R. (1746–1813) *diplomat* Robert Livingston was born in New York City on November 27, 1746, the scion of an influential colonial family with roots dating to the 17th century. Raised in an aristocratic environment, Livingston was well educated privately and graduated from Kings College (now Columbia University) in 1765. He was admitted to the bar three years later and commenced a lucrative business in concert with his partner, John Jay. At that time, the first rumblings of revolution were manifested against such British policies as the Stamp Act. Livingston urged caution, but once hostilities finally commenced in 1775 he reluctantly endorsed independence as a necessary evil. That year, Livingston attended the Second Continental Congress as a New York delegate, where he was appointed to serve with the committee drafting the Declaration of Independence. Returning to New York, he subsequently took an active role in drafting the New York constitution of 1777 and was rewarded with an appointment as chancellor of the Court of Chancellory. Livingston resumed his seat in Congress two years later, and after independence he functioned as secretary for foreign affairs. In 1788 he attended the constitutional convention in Philadelphia as a delegate, and the following year Livingston administered the oath of office to the new president, George Washington, in the temporary capital of New York City.

Though conservative by nature and nominally a Federalist, Livingston felt increasingly at odds with the faction headed by Alexander HAMILTON and its promotion of the Jay Treaty, which he felt sold out to Great Britain. In concert with Thomas Jefferson's newly emerging Democratic Republican Party, Livingston was strongly disposed to support the French Revolution. This made him a pariah in conservative circles, but in 1801 the new president, Jefferson, appointed him minister to France. It was in this capacity that Livingston made indelible contributions to the United States by successfully negotiating the purchase of the Louisiana Territory from First Consul Napoleon Bonaparte in 1803. This virtually doubled the size of the young republic and, by dint of acquiring New Orleans, facilitated internal trade via the Mississippi River. It proved one of the greatest diplomatic coups in history and a crucial step in the economic viability of the young nation. Livingston remained in Paris two more years before returning home to his estate at Clermont, New York, to engage in scientific farming. He was especially interested in the breeding of Merino sheep and penned several noted tracts on that subject and on agricultural progress in general.

Livingston's reputation as a leading economic figure in American history dates to 1797, when he became actively involved in steam navigation. The nascent technology seemed promising but had proved untenable after many failed experiments at building a viable steamship. It was not until 1802 that he agreed to underwrite noted inventor Robert FULTON in a similar endeavor. Many years of trial and error lapsed before the steamship *Clermont* finally made its historic passage up the Hudson River in 1807. This voyage ushered in the age of steam navigation in America, along with the rise of monopolies to control its employment. Livingston never obtained the national celebrity of Fulton, but his extensive backing proved instrumental to their mutual success. He then used his political leverage to acquire a monopoly for shipping on both the Hudson and Mississippi Rivers. But despite the promise of profit, the limitations of the new steam technology remained legion and failed to produce the windfall anticipated, although the practice of states granting steamship monopolies was vanquished by the U.S. Supreme Court in 1824. By the time Livingston died at his estate at Clermont on February 26, 1813, his varied, far-ranging, and multifaceted career in politics, diplomacy, and science had proved of considerable importance to the young republic. He also provided an undeniable impetus to the commercial applications of steam technology, which successfully matured a few decades after his passing.

Further reading

Brandt, Clare. *An American Aristocracy: The Livingstons.* Garden City, N.Y.: Doubleday, 1986.

Dangerfield, George. *Chancellor Robert R. Livingston of New York, 1746–1813*. New York: Harcourt, Brace, 1960.

Wiles, Richard C., and Andrea K. Zimmermann, eds. *The Livingston Legacy: Three Centuries of American History*. Annandale-on-Hudson, N.Y.: Bard College, 1987.

John C. Fredriksen

Long-Term Capital Management

A giant hedge fund in Greenwich, Connecticut, the near-collapse of which in September 1998 shook Wall Street and drew public attention to the role of hedge funds in the marketplace. The fund was established in 1994 by John W. Meriwether, a bond trader at SALOMON BROTHERS who had hired a team of mathematicians and economists from academia to give his unit an edge in the fierce competition for arbitrage opportunities.

When Meriwether left Salomon Brothers in 1994 after a trader he supervised was caught manipulating bids on TREASURY BONDS, most of his intensely loyal traders followed him to Long-Term Capital. He also recruited, as partners, Robert C. Merton and Myron S. Scholes, who later were awarded the 1997 Nobel Memorial Prize in economic science, and David W. Mullins, a former vice chairman of the Federal Reserve Board. As a group, the fund's partners believed passionately in rational, efficient markets, and their trading strategies reflected those beliefs.

The celebrity-studded fund, whose investors included top banks and institutions from around the world, was enormously successful at first. Trading largely with borrowed money, the fund produced returns, net of its own fees, of 43 percent in 1995 and 41 percent in 1996. But in 1997, as arbitrage opportunities faded and Asian currency devaluations roiled markets, it earned just 17 percent after its own fees. As that year ended, the fund's still-optimistic partners decided to return roughly $2.3 billion to their outside investors, paring the fund's capital to about $4.7 billion, from roughly $7 billion at its peak.

It was an ill-timed decision. The fund's core strategy was to bet that volatile security prices in markets around the world would gradually become more stable. But in 1998 global markets grew ever more treacherous. By August, when Russia defaulted on its debt, risk-averse investors were buying only the most liquid Treasury bonds, driving down the prices of virtually everything else. Meriwether's capital, which totaled $3.7 billion at mid-August, was simply melting away. By mid-September, the fund was on the brink of collapse. Since it owed money to almost every major bank on Wall Street, its dire condition drew the attention of the Federal Reserve Bank, which feared that the fund's failure would trigger a marketwide panic. On September 23, 1998, after long negotiating sessions at the Federal Reserve Bank of New York, a consortium of 14 American and European investment firms agreed to inject $3.6 billion into the fund, in exchange for most of the partners' equity. By that point, every dollar invested in the fund had shrunk to 23 cents, net of fees.

The rescue, which drew widespread public criticism, kept the fund afloat for another year, but its returns were meager. The stock and bond markets became very unsettled during the months following the collapse, and GOLDMAN SACHS, one of the fund's trading partners, had to postpone its initial public offering as a result. By early 2000, the consortium had retrieved its capital, and the fund was essentially liquidated. By then, Meriwether and many of his partners were once again managing other people's money from their offices in Greenwich.

Further reading

Dunbar, Nicholas. *Inventing Money: The Story of Long-Term Capital Management and the Legends Behind It*. New York: John Wiley & Sons, 2000.

Lowenstein, Roger. *When Genius Failed: The Rise and Fall of Long-Term Capital Management*. New York: Random House, 2000.

Diana B. Henriques

Lorillard & Company, P[ierre]. One of the first American tobacco producers, the company was founded by Pierre Lorillard (1742–76). Born in France, Lorillard immigrated to the United States and established an operation for curing tobacco on Chatham Street in New York City in 1760. Tobacco had been an important and sought-after crop since the time of Columbus and attracted many Europeans because of its popularity. Lorillard sold pipe tobacco and snuff from the New York location and soon prospered because Americans were fond of his various tobacco blends, all using Virginia tobacco as their base.

After his untimely death during the Revolutionary War, the business was carried on by his sons Peter and George. They soon began to advertise their product in New York newspapers, featuring an Indian smoking a pipe. The ads became the basis for the cigar store Indian that would later stand outside many tobacconist shops around the country. In 1792, the manufacturing operation was moved from lower Manhattan to the Bronx, and mail-order sales were begun in the early 1830s. Lorillard diversified its tobacco products and included chewing in addition to smoking tobacco. The Beech-Nut brand of chewing tobacco in particular became extremely popular, and its advertising was found on many barns and stores around rural America. The name Lorillard was one of the first to become identified with the powers of marketing.

The Lorillards also employed incentives for consumers to use their products, including mail-in coupons for clothing and household items. They also began producing cigarettes in addition to pipe tobacco. In the early 1900s, the company became part of the "tobacco trust," better known as the AMERICAN TOBACCO CO. headed by James B. DUKE. After the breakup of the company ordered by the Supreme Court in 1911—one of the classic ANTITRUST cases—the company reverted to being an independent as P. Lorillard & Co.

The Lorillard family became well known as socialites and developers of real estate. Pierre Lorillard IV helped develop Newport, Rhode Island, into a resort for the rich and also helped turn his estate outside New York into Tuxedo Park, a sporting and residential club catering to the wealthy.

Further reading

Gruber, Lewis. *Lorillard and Tobacco: The 200th Anniversary of P. Lorillard & Co., 1760–1960*. New York: privately published, 1960.

Heiman, Robert. *Tobacco and Americans*. New York: McGraw-Hill, 1960.

Robert, Joseph. *The Story of Tobacco in America*. New York: Alfred Knopf, 1949.

lotteries Games of chance in which individuals are sold tickets, giving them the opportunity to win a drawing of cash or some other prize. Lotteries originated in Italy in the 16th century and spread to England and other parts of Europe. A lottery affecting America was conducted as early as 1612 in London for the benefit of the Jamestown settlement in Virginia. During the colonial period, lotteries became the first organized method of raising money for such public purposes as the colonial army.

Before the banking system developed on a regional level, lotteries proved to be the only effective way of raising large sums of money for varied causes. They also proved useful when borrowing by institutions was not considered ethical or practical in many parts of the country. As a result, selling lottery tickets to large numbers of people was the predecessor to INVESTMENT BANKING on the East Coast.

The popularity of lotteries quickly spread in the 18th century. They were established to raise money for a host of public and private projects before independence and multiplied after the Constitution was ratified. After independence, colleges such as Harvard, Yale, and Princeton used them to raise funds. Proceeds were also used to build canals, TURNPIKES, and such public works projects as the Washington Monument.

Some of the early lottery agents, such as Simon and Moses Allen of New York State, used the lottery ticket sales business to eventually enter the banking business.

Lotteries proliferated after the Civil War as many southern states sought to raise funds during Reconstruction. The best known was the Louisiana State Lottery, begun in 1868. It soon expanded to selling its tickets nationwide. It also developed a reputation as being somewhat corrupt and drew many attacks from the press and the public. Many other lotteries prospered at the same time, but many eventually were shut down because of public protests about state governments supporting gambling. In 1899, Congress passed a law prohibiting the use of the public mail for distributing lottery tickets, putting an end to Louisiana selling its tickets nationwide. The lottery continued to distribute tickets privately, using courier services, until Congress passed prohibitions against this as well. An appeal was launched, and the case reached the Supreme Court. In 1903, the Court upheld the law in the case *Champion v. Ames*.

In the 1960s and 1970s, lotteries were instituted in New Hampshire, New York, and New Jersey and quickly became popular in many states. Originally used to raise money when capital markets were not developed, lotteries later became an additional source of raising funds for state government projects that did not rely upon public sector borrowing.

Further reading

Chafetz, Henry. *Play the Devil: A History of Gambling in the United States from 1492 to 1950.* New York: Clarkson Potter, 1960.

O'Findlay, John M. *People of Chance: Gambling in American Society from Jamestown to Las Vegas.* New York: Oxford University Press, 1986.

Sullivan, George. *By Chance a Winner: The History of Lotteries.* New York: Dodd, Mead, 1972.

lumber industry   From the time of the first European settlements in the early 1600s, the lumber industry has been vital to the growth of the nation. Lumbering requires three basic components for sustained, long-term success: the availability of woodlands, the development of a market for forest products, and a means by which timber can be efficiently harvested and marketed. Through the 1930s, the history of the American lumber industry was largely one of lumbermen harvesting all the desirable timber in an area and then quickly moving on to the next area—all the while trying to keep costs to a minimum. This usually meant clear-cutting the land, moving lumber to market quickly and cheaply, and then selling or abandoning the land.

The ever-growing demand for more wood pushed lumbermen to continually improve harvesting and delivery methods. The technological improvements in saws and transportation developed to increase the output of the woods, in turn guaranteed a continual search for new timber supplies. Until the late 1800s, the ready availability of more woodland led many to believe the timber supply to be unlimited. But in the 1910s and 1920s, dwindling timber stocks and excessive production caused lumbermen to reassess how they did business, leading in some instances to cooperative efforts between private industry and government. With its tentative embrace of sustained-yield management and regeneration by the 1940s, the lumber industry signaled its willingness to adapt in order to assure future timber supplies.

The Northeast, comprised of New England plus New York, Pennsylvania, New Jersey, Maryland, and Delaware, was the center of America's early lumber industry. Lumbermen had to meet not only domestic demands, but also early industrial needs. Iron furnaces, which required huge quantities of wood charcoal to smelt ore, on average consumed 20,000 acres of forest over about a dozen years. Furnace operators found themselves competing with urban households for fuel wood. Besides wood for home construction, furnishings, and tools, it took between 10 and 20 acres of forest to supply the fuel burned by one home fireplace annually. By the 1780s, competition between iron furnaces and home consumption in urban areas had drawn farmers into the lumber supply trade. Farmers clearing land up to 100 miles away could profitably deliver lumber to urban markets, despite the expense and difficulties of transporting to market.

Regional and overseas trade developed soon after settlement. The first supply of New England white pine, used mostly for masts, reached England in 1634, and trade was well established within 20 years. Blessed with vast stands of highly coveted white pine, and good rivers and ports, Maine became the leading lumber producer in the years following the American Revolution. It sent white pine to Boston and other eastern port cities and competed directly with Canada's New Brunswick in exporting to the British colonies in the Caribbean. The fierce competition led to a brief armed standoff in 1839 between New Brunswick and Maine lumbermen in what became known as the Aroostook War. War was narrowly avoided, but the dispute has colored lumber trade relations with Canada, historically the largest exporter of lumber to the United States, ever since.

By 1820, though Maine outpaced all others in lumber production, its days as leader were already numbered. As settlers moved into western New York and Ohio, they turned to cheaper local supplies instead of importing lumber from back east. New York eclipsed Maine as the leading lumber producer by 1839, and Pennsylvania soon replaced New York as the lumber industry followed settlers westward. The Northeast led the nation in lumber production until 1879, when the lake states region overtook them.

As the lumber industry migrated west from the Northeast toward the Great Lakes in the mid-1800s, lumbermen also harvested timber in the central states along the way. The central states (Illinois, Indiana, Ohio, West Virginia, and Missouri) did not experience the spectacular rise and subsequent decline of production of the Northeast or the lake states because they lacked the large volume of valued softwood timber in those regions. From the mid-1800s until 1916, when the South surpassed it, the central states were the most productive hardwood region in the country (often around 90 percent of the region's production was in hardwoods).

Though the region contributed a small portion to the total lumber production for the nation, the central states have always been important to the transport and distribution of lumber. The upper Mississippi River and the Illinois-Michigan Canal, completed in 1847, provided the "highways" to move the rafts of logs and lumber and transformed the small town of Chicago into a booming trade town. The canal allowed Chicago wholesalers to sell Michigan and Canadian lumber to buyers in the prairie region for 50 percent less than eastern lumber. By 1856, Chicago had replaced Albany, New York, as the nation's leading wholesale lumber market.

As settlers pushed out onto the Great Plains, demand for wood tied the economies of the lake states and prairie regions together. The lake states region, consisting of Michigan, Wisconsin, and Minnesota, also possessed white pine and, like New England, had an extensive waterway network by which to move timber. But the era of large-scale lumbering in the region was relatively brief. As the harvesting of the lake states forests accelerated, production hit its peak years in the 1870s and 1880s. Between 1869 and 1889, lumber production jumped from 3.6 billion board feet (one board foot is equal to one foot square by one inch thick) to nearly 10 billion board feet before starting to decline. It bottomed out in 1932 at 289 million board feet. It has since recovered, and in 2002, the three states produced nearly 1.6 billion board feet, or 3 percent of the national total.

It was in the lake states region that the buying and selling of land became integral to the lumber business. Starting in the 1860s, Frederick WEYERHAEUSER, Orrin H. Ingram, and other lumbermen made their fortunes by buying up forests, cutting the timber, and supplying it to the prairie farmers. Then they would sell the cutover land to newly arriving farmers before having to pay taxes on it. Lumbermen then moved on to the largely untouched forests of the South and the Pacific Northwest. In some cases, an entire company-owned logging camp—buildings and all—would be placed on railroad cars and moved to the next location.

Before large-scale lumbering got underway in the South in the 1870s and 1880s, the southern lumber industry mostly consisted of supplying live oak trees for shipbuilding and the production of naval stores. In fact, from the 1830s until the outbreak of the Civil War, naval stores (masts, turpentine, pitch tar, resin) had become almost as big as the COTTON INDUSTRY. In areas too poor for cotton farming, settlers often worked in the lumber and naval stores industries.

But the depletion of white pine stands in the Northeast and lake states led northern lumbermen

Repair work on an enormous cut-off saw at a lumber mill (FOREST HISTORICAL SOCIETY)

to embrace southern yellow pine. Between 1890 and 1920, lumber production in the South rose from 1.6 billion board feet in 1880 to 15.4 billion board feet in 1920, peaking in 1912. The South was producing 37 percent of all the lumber of the United States during that time, and output continued to rise over the remainder of the century. In 2002, the region produced 21.58 billion board feet, or 46 percent of the nation's total output.

Federal laws such as the Weeks Act (1911) and the Clark-McNary Act (1924), which encouraged fire protection and scientific forest management on state and private lands, helped lay the foundation for the revitalization of the southern lumber industry. The development of a pulp industry based on southern pines during the 1930s provided the monetary incentive for private landowners and the timber industry to undertake forest management. The influx of wood-based industries to the region and the increasing value for pines led many lumbermen to embrace forest renewal and management practices on a widespread basis. Pine plantations for pulp production became big business and brought much-desired industry to the region by 1940. The dominant source of pulpwood since the 1940s, the South increased its share of production to more than three-quarters of the country's pulpwood in 1993. Within 40 years of implementing the Weeks Act, the amount of annual growth in the southern forest outpaced timber removal, though it should be noted that abandoned farmland reverting to forestland contributed to some of this recovery. Southern forests were not only recovering but also providing a model for reforestation efforts around the country.

In the 1880s, the lumber industry turned its attention not only to the South, but also to the Rocky Mountains and the Pacific coast states of Washington, Oregon, and California. Because of the arid land and difficult terrain, the lumber industry largely by-passed the Rocky Mountain states of Idaho, Montana, Wyoming, Utah, Nevada, Colorado, Arizona, and New Mexico as it moved to the more productive forests of the Northwest. Production in the Rockies peaked in 1925, dropped during the Great Depression (as it did nationally), and rose again in the postwar construction boom. The lumber industry remains an important industry in Montana and Idaho, which together produced 6 percent of the nation's lumber in 2002.

When the continental railroads reached the West Coast in 1869, the land rush began on the Pacific coast. With the high cost of shipping timber back east by rail, it was initially more economical to sell the wood to regional markets or ship it overseas to South America and Asia. But once the Great Northern Railroad sharply slashed its freight rates in 1893, it became affordable to ship lumber back east. When production in the lake states region began to decline sharply soon thereafter, shipping lumber over 1,000 miles by rail finally became profitable for northwestern lumbermen. Although timber production rapidly increased, not until 1900 did a western state appear among the top 10 producers. By 1910, Washington and Oregon ranked first and third respectively among all states in production. Since 1940, Oregon, Washington, and California have consistently been among the top three producers. In 2002, they combined to produce 30 percent of all U.S. lumber.

Casting an eye toward the future, even before lumber production had started declining in the lake states, Frederick Weyerhaeuser and other lumbermen began buying forestland in the Pacific Northwest region. At one point his company held 1.9 million acres of land in the Northwest. The creation of federal forest reserves in the 1890s and early 1900s reduced available acreage and drove up prices, eventually leaving timber ownership concentrated in the hands of a few large companies.

With the continuing availability of more land until the 1920s and 1930s, it made little economic sense for lumber companies to hold cutover land and pay taxes on land of no value to them. Instead, companies either sold the land to settlers or let the government take it back instead of paying delinquent taxes. The 1920s, with no new lands to purchase, marked the end of the frontier phase of lumbering. Lumber companies began investigating and even undertaking sustained-yield management (regulating the annual amount of timber cut so it corresponded to the amount grown annually) and selective cutting of timber as a way to regenerate forests by the early 1930s. Even though tax laws made it more costly to replant than to buy mature timberlands, the Weyerhaeuser Timber Company adopted policies of selective cutting and sustained yield and created one of the first industrial tree farms in 1941.

By regenerating the forest, major lumber companies cleared the way for a younger and more vigorous forest with an annual growth rate that would far exceed that of the original forest. In contrast, small local firms and independent lumbermen in the region hastily cut their timber to make a quick profit. The resulting overproduction drove down prices and forced many of these lumber companies out of business by the late 1920s. With most of the easily accessible timber harvested, only large timber companies could afford the machinery to open up and develop the interior regions.

The enormous size of the logs initially presented problems for sawmill operators in the Pacific Northwest. Consequently, many of the innovations in the lumber industry came out of that region. Steam-driven circular saws brought west from the Great Lakes and the South enabled the lumberjacks to cut more timber and at faster speeds, but they could not easily handle the mammoth logs. The introduction in the 1870s of double and even triple saws replaced circular saws, which could not cut more than half their diameter. A decade later the band saw replaced these earlier saws; its one continuous loop of blade could cut through an entire log.

Saw blade technology had to adapt because of technological advances in the woods. A pioneer working by himself and using a single-bitted axe could expect to clear 12 acres a year. Lumberjacks started using the long-handled, double-bitted axe widely after 1878. They combined that with the crosscut saw in the 1880s, dropping by nearly four-fifths the time it took to cut down a tree. The introduction of the gasoline-powered chainsaw in 1947 further sped up the process, and that was supplemented by machines such as fellers and harvesters that can clear several truckloads of timber per day.

To move logs to the mills, lumbermen began replacing oxen with the steam donkey engine in the mid-1880s. The engine used steel cables to drag, or skid, fallen timber and allowed lumbermen to remove larger logs at a faster rate. As technology permitted, ever-larger machines replaced those engines. The massive and complex water flume systems constructed to send lumber down water slides from upper elevations to the mills below were first replaced by RAILROADS and then, after the 1920s, by logging trucks. Truck logging had its greatest impact in Oregon because it opened up areas in the Cascade Mountains that could not economically be tapped by railroad logging. Areas untouched before World War II became accessible and economically feasible after the war because of war-surplus trucks. The use of trucks allowed most sawmills to remain at permanent sites, further lowering costs, and largely helped bring to an end the migratory nature of lumbering.

During the Great Depression, the bottom fell out of the national lumber market. Overproduction drove prices down and touched off a cycle of declining output and prices. William Greeley, David T. Mason, and George S. Long, all of whom had been instrumental in introducing scientific forest management in the Pacific Northwest, pushed for greater cooperation between private industry and the government in an attempt to equalize production and consumption. Concerned about the continual economic problem faced by lumber communities, Mason, a private forester and former U.S. Forest Service employee, argued that private companies should be able to combine public timberlands with adjacent private

holdings to develop better management plans. Doing so would stabilize supply and demand. Mason's new definition of sustained yield became the cornerstone of the Sustained-Yield Forest Management Act (1944) and assisted several lumber towns in the West. The stability this provided made labor union organizing easier during the immediate and prosperous postwar period; later, mechanization and automation of all aspects of the production process, along with industry consolidation, brought worker layoffs and weakened the unions.

Under pressure from lumber companies and politicians not to impede economic prosperity after the war, the U.S. Forest Service continually raised the harvest limit in national forests over the next three decades. In the 1970s, the Forest Service argued that advancements in areas such as logging machinery and regeneration would allow it to intensively manage certain parts of a forest and produce higher amounts of timber through clear-cutting, while leaving other parts of the forest for recreational use. Continued controversy over clear-cutting led the federal government in the late 1980s and early 1990s to remove large areas of federally owned land in the West (the Rocky Mountain and Pacific coast states combined) from harvest. Many western mills dependent on federal timber were forced to reduce production dramatically or to close. The proportion of lumber produced from the West slowly fell to just under half by 1999 as a result of declining levels of timber from public lands and increasing levels of production in the South.

In 1990, the South became the nation's largest lumber producing region, accounting for 36 percent of all softwood lumber and 78 percent of all hardwoods. Of the region's 215 million forest acres, 89 percent is privately owned, which in part gives private industry the ability to increase lumber production. Total lumber production in the North (the northeast, central, and lake states combined) remained fairly steady from 1965 through the early 1990s but more than doubled to 10.2 billion board feet by 1999, nearly all of it in hardwood lumber production. This was largely the result of better forestry practices and more intensive use of remaining timber.

The drop in domestic production did not mean a reduction in consumption. The United States remains not only the largest producer but also the largest consumer of lumber in the world. To meet demand, lumber imports to the United States from all countries totaled 19.9 billion board feet in 1999 (93 percent of it from Canada), an all-time high. New nonresidential construction accounted for about 7 percent of lumber consumption, manufacturing for 12 percent, shipping (pallets, containers, and packing materials) for 10 percent, and 11 percent for all other uses. Overall, about 60 percent of lumber consumed in 1999 was used in housing construction.

The manufacturing of lumber and wood products has fallen from the fourth-ranked overall industry in 1900 in terms of dollar value to a ranking of 13th, within just the manufacturing sector, in 2000. The forest products industry employs approximately 1.7 million people in forest and paper production, or 1.1 percent of the U.S. workforce. Although lumber is no longer the dominant industry it once was, the lumber industry remains one of the nation's most vital and important industries, due in large part to the industry's willingness to adapt to changing economic and environmental conditions.

Further reading

Andrews, Ralph W. *Glory Days of Logging.* Seattle: Superior Publishing Co., 1956.

Cox, Thomas R., et al. *This Well-Wooded Land: Americans and Their Forests from Colonial Times to the Present.* Lincoln: University of Nebraska Press, 1985.

Williams, Michael. *Americans and Their Forests: A Historical Geography.* New York: Cambridge University Press, 1989.

Jamie Lewis

M

Macy, Rowland H. (1822–1877) *business-man and retailer* Born in Nantucket, Massachusetts, to a seafaring family, Macy made several attempts to open a dry goods store but failed on each of them. After failures in Massachusetts, he went to California during the gold rush and opened a successful operation. He eventually returned to Massachusetts with a small nest egg of $3,000, opened another operation in Boston, but again failed to make it successful.

Leaving Massachusetts, he made his way to New York City and opened a dry goods store on Sixth Avenue near 14th Street in 1857. His first-day sales amounted to $12, and his store quickly became a success. Two years later, he spent $2,800 on advertising and generated more than $85,000 in yearly sales in its first full year. He used a simple formula of spending more on advertising than his competitors while also using cash for both buying and selling rather than using credit. Capitalizing on his success, Macy's store became one of the best known in New York City by expanding its offerings from simple dry goods to a full range of consumer products.

After the Civil War, Macy continued to introduce marketing devices designed to attract and keep customers. In 1870, he employed the first in-store Santa Claus, designed to attract families at Christmas. Continued success led to the opening of the flagship store at Herald Square in New York in 1902. By the turn of the century, it was a full-fledged department store. The store expanded beyond dry goods and now carried a wide array of consumer products under one roof.

Macy did not live to witness the success or expansion of his stores. He died in Paris at age 55, and the store was taken over by Charles B. Webster. Webster invited the Strauss retailing family to purchase part of the store 10 years later, and by the 1890s, when Webster sold them his remaining share, they gained control of Macy's.

One of Macy's buyers, William Titon, invented the first tea bag in 1912. By 1924, during the heyday of department and CHAIN STORES, the Herald Square store was the world's largest department store and held its first Thanksgiving Day Parade, a tradition that continues today. But unlike other retailers, Macys did not participate in the expansion boom of the 1920s. The store began to expand to suburban shopping malls only after World War II, when it became a chain.

Rowland H. Macy (Library of Congress)

After a series of acquisitions and management problems, it filed for Chapter 11 bankruptcy protection in 1992. It was acquired by Federated Department Stores after emerging from its reorganization in 1994 and, in the name of greater efficiency, began to shed some stores it had opened or acquired.

Further reading

Harriman, Margaret Case. *And the Price Is Right: The R. H. Macy Story*. Cleveland: World Publishing, 1958.

Hower, Ralph. *History of Macy's of New York, 1858–1919*. Cambridge, Mass.: Harvard University Press, 1943.

Trachtenberg, Jeffrey. *The Rain on Macy's Parade*. New York: Times Books, 1996.

Malcolm Baldrige National Quality Award

Named after former secretary of commerce Malcolm Baldrige, the award is actually four awards given annually to American companies to recognize their achievements. The fields in which the awards are given are manufacturing, service, small business, and education and health care.

The awards were established by Congress in 1987 to recognize American businesses. They were initiated to emphasize quality, which Baldrige felt was essential for American companies if they were to maintain their edge and fight off foreign competition. In the 1970s and 1980s, American companies developed a reputation for poor quality and shoddy products, and the awards were a method of emphasizing quality in a more global business environment.

Each company winning an award must meet specific criteria for excellence, including leadership, customer and market focus, strategic planning, process management, business results, and information and analysis. Companies winning awards since 1987 were Dana Corp., AT&T Consumer Communications Services, Cadillac Motor Division, Xerox Corp., Ames Rubber Corp., IBM, and the Ritz Carlton Hotel Co., among others. The IBM Corporation used the award to challenge itself to turn around the company in the late 1980s, once again becoming known for producing quality products.

Malcolm Baldrige (1922–87) was secretary of commerce under Ronald Reagan from 1981 until his accidental death in 1987. Before entering government service, he was chief executive officer of Scovill, Inc., formerly a brass mill that he transformed into a diversified manufacturer of consumer and industrial goods. The award was named after him posthumously in recognition of his championship of quality in both manufacturing and the service industries.

Further reading

Boyett, Joseph H., Stephen Schwartz, Laurence Osterwise, and Roy Bauer. *The Quality Journey: How Winning the Baldrige Sparked the Remaking of IBM*. New York: Dutton, 1993.

Brown, Mark G. *Baldrige Award Winning Quality: How to Interpret the Baldrige Criteria for Performance*. New York: Quality Resources, 1997.

managerial capitalism
When professional managers run companies; characteristic of the period of American business development when

family members yielded control of their companies to professionals. The term helps distinguish the early period of American business, leading to the Civil War, with the period that followed, when businesses began to be run by professional managers trained in various specialty disciplines.

This period coincides with the widespread emergence of stock companies, when many companies sold stock for the first time in order to expand. In the 1840s and 1850s, manufacturing and RAILROADS (especially railroads) began to grow exponentially, requiring managers with more than one set of skills. After the Civil War, as the railroads continued to expand westward, the need for professional managers became more pronounced as the organizations grew larger and more complex. Quite often, business organizations would still be run by family members, although they were increasingly staffed by professional managers, hired from the outside.

After the turn of the 20th century, as the need for managers became more recognized, many business school programs were instituted to provide graduate, and later undergraduate, training for this new managerial class. The Harvard Graduate School of Business was the first graduate program in the country instituted for this purpose.

In the 20th century, the trend became more clear as fewer and fewer companies remained in family or founders' hands. The rise of the modern CORPORATION after World War I was an excellent example. The size and complexity of DuPont and GENERAL MOTORS, the latter headed by Alfred SLOAN, showed that the 20th-century corporation had become too large to be ruled from the top and now required skilled and trained managers at various stages and levels of organization.

The success of larger business enterprises managed by professionally trained managers became the cornerstone of American business in the 20th century. In many cases, this success can be seen in the MERGERS and acquisitions trend that characterized several decades of the 20th century and the rise of the conglomerate organization in the 1950s and 1960s. In addition, many business disciplines created "managerial" tracks in the post–World War II years, and such disciplines as managerial accounting, finance, economics, and information sciences now exist and are designed to train potential managers in decision making and cooperative planning.

See also DuPont de Nemours & Co., E. I.; Harvard Business School; Taylor, Frederick Winslow.

Further reading

Chandler, Alfred D., Jr. *The Visible Hand: The Managerial Revolution in American Business.* Cambridge, Mass.: Harvard University Press, 1977.

Marris, Robin. *Managerial Capitalism in Retrospective.* New York: St. Martin's Press, 1998.

mass production The process of producing a large amount of manufactured goods by standardizing parts and production techniques. By doing so, the producer is able to lower the cost of production and therefore lower the cost of the product to the consumer.

The method began with the manufacture of muskets for the U.S. Army around 1800. Inventor Eli Whitney had contracted with the government to produce muskets but was unable to meet his production schedule because the parts he used were not standard. He demonstrated to the army that if he were able to employ machine tool techniques, he would be able to produce a standard, efficient musket rather than the handmade variety, which had been the only method used until that time. When he began producing muskets with standard parts, the process was born. Workers were often taught only one part of a system so that they could produce their own specialized part of the process quickly and efficiently.

When standard parts and mass production began to be used widely, the factory system came into general use. Factories had been used previously to produce textiles, and the principles were the same, although the process was more simple and produced only a simple good. Even relatively simply manufactures would become mass produced after the Civil War. Items of clothing, such as shoes, were mass produced in the first two decades after the war ended, leaving hand production to be more of a higher priced specialty art that defined its products as those of artisans rather than factory workers.

I. M. Singer began employing these techniques to produce sewing machines in the 19th century. In 1865, his company produced about 3,000 machines per year, but within 10 years production multiplied to more than 250,000. But mass production is generally considered to have begun with automobile manufacturing in the 20th century. Mass production was successfully employed by Henry FORD in Detroit. Ford employed the assembly, or production, line when producing his Model T automobiles, and the number of cars produced multiplied exponentially between 1915 and 1925. Unlike other assembly lines, Ford's moved, meaning that workers could remain stationary while the cars passed before them for finishing. As the number increased, the price began to decline, producing economies of scale for Ford and other manufacturers. It was the introduction of the assembly line that brought the idea of mass production into the modern industrial age. Ford's methods relied upon simple styling and models, which did not change every year, allowing the process to proceed without interruption. Ford remarked that his customers could have their choice of color as long as they liked black. It was the only color he produced. The Model T was succeeded by the Model A, whose price also fell as a continuing result of mass production.

In 1918, the American National Standards Institute was founded in order to set standards for manufacturing and to study methods of production around the country. Both world wars also helped the process develop further, since standard grades were needed for military armaments. In the post–World War II period, many new products became standardized, and separate industries developed widely accepted methods of producing their goods. More recently, the assem-

bly line has been using robotic machines rather than people in an effort to reduce error in the process and speed production.

See also WHITNEY, ELI.

Further reading
Allen, Frederick Lewis. *The Big Change: America Transforms Itself, 1900–1950*. New York: Harper & Brothers, 1952.

Hounshell, David A. *From the American System to Mass Production, 1800–1932: Development of Manufacturing Technology in the United States*. Baltimore: Johns Hopkins, 1985.

Rosenberg, Nathan. *Technology and American Economic Growth*. New York: Harper & Row, 1972.

Rupert, Mark. *Producing Hegemony: The Politics of Mass Production and American Global Power*. New York: Cambridge University Press, 1995.

McCormick, Cyrus (1809–1884) *inventor and businessman* McCormick produced the first successful mechanical reaper, which revolutionized agriculture in the 19th century. He was born on the family farm in Virginia and tinkered with mechanical reaping devices from an early age, learning from his father, who was an inventor of farm equipment. He produced his first in 1831 and received a patent for it in 1834 after discovering that a similar device had been invented by Obed Hussey. He later purchased an iron works with his father, but they lost substantial amounts of money during the Panic of 1837. The reaper developed slowly as a result.

The mechanical development of the device and its sales were initially slow. McCormick sold only two of his machines in their first year of production (1840) and in 1843 sold 29. But after a trip to the Midwest, McCormick realized that his device was more suited to the wide plains of the breadbasket states than it was to the rougher, hilly terrain of Virginia, even though he had invented a machine that could be used on sloped ground. By 1848, he had relocated his business to Chicago and started producing improved reapers. His factory was one of the first examples of assembly line production, and it came into existence as his patent for the machine was running out. By 1856, the factory produced more than 16,000 reapers and related devices, and his invention was considered the best on the market.

McCormick also employed advertising to sell his product. He purchased a newspaper called the *Farmer's Advance* in which he extolled the virtues of his machine. The paper had a circulation of more than 300,000. His machines sold for $120 each and came with one of the first money-back guarantees. By the time the Civil War ended, his machine was the most popular in the country and had made him a rich man. By 1880, profits exceeded $1.2 million a year. He also tried his hand at politics and ran unsuccessfully for Congress in 1864. But McCormick's invention had a profound effect upon the economy in the post–Civil War period. Before the reaper, farming was much more labor intensive, requiring many more men to harvest wheat and other grains. His invention helped free labor from dull agricultural work at a time when labor itself was in short supply, especially during and after the carnage of the war.

Before the Civil War, McCormick was a strong defender of SLAVERY, although he opposed secession. He used some of his wealth to purchase the *Chicago Tribune* so that he could make his views known, but they proved extremely unpopular in the city. After his death, his company was run by his son, Cyrus H. McCormick Jr. In 1902, the company merged with a major competitor, the Deering Co., to form the INTERNATIONAL HARVESTER COMPANY. The banker to the consolidation was J. P. Morgan & Company. The new company continued to be run by McCormick, who owned almost 50 percent of the stock.

See also DEERE, JOHN.

Further reading

Casson, Herbert. *Cyrus Hall McCormick: His Life and Work.* Chicago: A. C. McClurg, 1909.
Hutchinson, William T. *Cyrus Hall McCormick.* New York: Century, 1930.
McCormick, Cyrus. *The Century of the Reaper.* Boston: Houghton Mifflin, 1931.

McCulloch v. Maryland   A landmark ruling by the Supreme Court of the United States that established lines of demarcation between the power of the states and that of the federal government. The case involved a suit brought against a branch of the BANK OF THE UNITED STATES, located in Baltimore. Two issues were at stake. First was the matter of Congress's ability to incorporate this second national bank, while the other involved the right of a state to tax an instrument of the federal government.

The Second Bank of the United States was chartered in 1816. In 1818, Maryland passed a tax on all banks operating in the state that were not chartered by the state legislature. James McCulloch, its chief cashier, refused to pay the tax, and the case went to the courts, where Maryland won; the bank appealed to the U.S. Supreme Court. Chief Justice John Marshall, delivering the unanimous decision of the Court, overturned the ruling of the lower court and ruled in the bank's favor. The bank was a legitimate instrument of the United States and therefore had a right to exist, despite strong attacks by advocates of states' rights. Following upon the bank's legitimacy, the Court also ruled that Maryland's right to tax was subordinate to the Constitution, which gives the federal government precedence over the laws of states. As a result, the state could not tax an instrument of the United States because it had no authority over it.

One important result of the decision was the notion of tax immunities between the states and the federal government. Following the *McCulloch* decision, interest on municipal bonds would be treated as exempt from federal income taxation, while interest on TREASURY BONDS would be treated as exempt from state income taxation. It should be noted that this did not become a practical issue until the Sixteenth Amendment to the Constitution was passed.

The tax interpretation used today came after a series of other decisions in the 19th and 20th centuries that reiterated the idea that the federal government and the states were generally immune to each other's taxes—based upon *McCulloch*. As interpreted today, it allows municipalities to borrow money and pay interest free of federal tax to investors as long as certain criteria of the U.S. Treasury are met.

See also BIDDLE, NICHOLAS; INCOME TAX.

Further reading
Gunther, Gerald, ed. *John Marshall's Defense of McCulloch v. Maryland.* Palo Alto, Calif.: Stanford University Press, 1969.
Hammond, Bray. *Banks and Politics in America from the Revolution to the Civil War.* Princeton, N.J.: Princeton University Press, 1957.

McFadden Act   Passed by Congress in 1927, the McFadden Act prevented interstate banking by commercial banks for 67 years, until the INTERSTATE BRANCHING ACT was passed in 1994. In the interim, banks tried a variety of strategies to expand into other states but with very limited success.

The act was a response to the desire of many states to keep larger banks out of their local markets. During the 1920s, many small banks failed, especially in agrarian and rural states. An average of two per day were failing when the law was passed. Many state banking authorities feared that the failing banks' markets would be taken over by out-of-state banks and so pressed for protective legislation. Restrictions against operating a bank within a state were always regulated by the host state's banking laws. According to the McFadden Act, banks were prohibited from opening de novo (new) branches across state lines. This would effectively prevent national banks from branching into states that were not their home base of operations.

The McFadden Act was cosponsored by Representative Louis McFadden (1876–1936) of Pennsylvania and Senator George Pepper of Pennsylvania. The original resolution did not contain any specific references to prohibiting bank expansion. Instead, the original intent was to allow nationally chartered banks, registered with the comptroller of the currency, the same sort of privileges within the various states that were usually reserved for state banks only. However, the act became the cornerstone of the fragmented banking system in the United States that lasted for more than 60 years.

The act also authorized the comptroller of the currency to allow commercial banks to begin underwriting equity securities. Although banks began to do so, the provision did not contribute to the Crash of 1929 because the banks did not have enough time to underwrite large numbers of securities before the crash occurred. Once the BANKING ACT OF 1933 was passed, this power was effectively rescinded, and COMMERCIAL BANKING was separated from INVESTMENT BANKING.

The prohibition against branch banking was lifted in 1994, when Congress passed the Interstate Branching Act, allowing bank holding companies to establish themselves in more than one state. Despite the fact that bankers lobbied for years to have the act removed, it proved remarkably resilient and defined COMMERCIAL BANKING for almost seven decades.

Further reading
Geisst, Charles R. *Undue Influence: How the Wall Street Elite Put the Financial System at Risk.* Hoboken, N.J.: John Wiley & Sons, 2004.
Kroos, Herman, ed. *Documentary History of Banking and Currency in the United States.* New York: Chelsea House, 1983.

Meany, George (1894–1980) *labor leader*
Born in New York City, Meany became an apprentice plumber at age 16 before becoming involved in labor unions. He first was active in the United Association of Plumbers and Steam Fitters and became a business agent for his union local in 1922. He was elected vice president of the New York State Federation of Labor in 1932 and then its president from 1934 to 1939.

Meany also served as secretary-treasurer of the AMERICAN FEDERATION OF LABOR (AFL) from 1940 to 1952. In 1952, he became president upon the death of William Green. In 1955, he became president of the AFL when it merged with the Congress of Industrial Organizations (CIO). He served as president of the combined organization until he retired in 1979.

A dispute with another labor leader, Walter REUTHER, led to the United Auto Workers leaving the union in 1967. Meany was a key figure in expelling the Teamsters Union, led by Jimmy Hoffa, from the AFL-CIO in 1957. He was also strongly opposed to communist influences in American labor and supported American military involvement in Vietnam. He took strong political stances, some of which helped affect the outcome of elections.

Meany led the traditionally Democratic union to a neutral political position after 1972, refusing to support either of the major candidates for president in that year. As a result, Richard Nixon won the election, although Meany later accused him of being sympathetic to big business at the expense of labor. When Nixon's political troubles began with Watergate, Meany openly called for his resignation, reversing some earlier support. He also had a falling out with Jimmy Carter, who he originally supported, refusing to support Carter's economic policies. Strongly dogmatic and individualistic, Meany is considered one of the major figures in labor union history.

See also GOMPERS, SAMUEL; LEWIS, JOHN L.

Further reading

Buhle, Paul. *Taking Care of Business: Samuel Gompers, George Meany, Lane Kirkland, and the Tragedy of American Labor.* New York: Monthly Review Press, 1999.

Goulden, Joseph C. *Meany.* New York: Atheneum, 1972.

Robinson, Archie. *George Meany and His Times: A Biography.* New York: Simon & Schuster, 1981.

meat packing industry Prior to 1830, the meat trade was a highly decentralized business, drawing together individual farmers who produced the livestock, drovers who transported the animals to population centers, and butcher-merchants who processed the meat and made it available to consumers. In rural areas (where most Americans lived), meat was locally produced outside of market relationships, as farmers harvested their livestock for home use and sold selected cured products to local stores.

Beginning in the 1820s, entrepreneurs discovered that, whenever possible, it was cheaper to move the slaughterhouses and meat processing facilities to the animals than to ship live animals to major population centers. So long as the meat could be kept from spoiling and transported economically, large-scale production facilities near livestock sources permitted economies of scale in meat production. Growth of internal transportation, principally roads, canals, and steamboat shipping on inland and coastal waterways, allowed nodal points to emerge for packing cured meat, preeminently pork.

Its advantageous geographic location helped Cincinnati become America's leading antebellum pork processing center. Perched on the banks of the Ohio River in rich farming country, Cincinnati was a favorite destination for farmers eager to take advantage of its superior outlets to southern and eastern markets. Annual production levels exceeded 100,000 hogs in the 1830s and reached 400,000 on the eve of the Civil War. Production was seasonal, with operations commencing once the weather became cold enough to chill the slaughtered meat, and ending in the spring once the rivers became sufficiently clear of ice to ship out the finished product.

Cincinnati's pork packers were businessmen who rarely soiled their hands by actually cutting meat. Rather than functioning in a daily market gauging sales through personal interactions with customers, Cincinnati's meat men gambled on long-term demand for pork products in distant ports and cities, anticipating that pigs purchased in November would be sold as bacon, ham, and lard six months later. They were more merchant than industrialist, better attuned to the vagaries of credit and demand for commodities than the mechanics of turning live animals into meat.

By the late 1850s, Chicago was challenging Cincinnati as the nation's leading pork packing center. The expansion of the nation's rail network explains much of this change, along with the continued westward movement of agriculture. As railroad track mileage grew to 9,000 in 1850 and 31,000 by 1860, canals and rivers became less desirable means for transporting meat. RAILROADS had two principal virtues in comparison to water transport: Trunk routes could convey food to eastern markets on a year-round basis, and feeder lines could enter the countryside and bring livestock from landlocked farms directly to central markets. Located astride this rail network, Chicago took full advantage of its transportation advantage and passed Cincinnati as the nation's leading meatpacking center during the Civil War. By 1870, Chicago produced $19 million of cured pork products, twice as much as Cincinnati.

Cincinnati and Chicago, along with other smaller meatpacking centers, depended on pork for their major product prior to 1880. American consumers preferred their pork cured and their beef fresh; in an era before reliable refrigeration, only cured products could be processed and then distributed from centralized packing facilities. Beef production remained a local business well into the 1880s, as the only way to provide fresh supplies was for cattle to be slaughtered near to where it was consumed.

The emerging large meat packing firms, especially those led by Gustavus Swift and Philip Armour, rose to dominance by exploiting new technology in the beef trade. Expansion of the rail network opened the Great Plains to the commercial livestock business by connecting eastern urban areas with midwestern packing centers. Refrigeration, both of the packinghouses and railroad cars, allowed firms to operate year-round and sell to customers far removed from where the animals were slaughtered. Swift was

the first meat packing firm to use refrigerated railroad cars to convey meat processed in midwestern plants to eastern population centers. Armour and other companies quickly followed Swift's lead. Backward integration, in the form of ownership of central stockyards, assured the large midwestern plants of a reliable supply of livestock, while forward integration, with the creation of wholesale meat outlets (known as "branch houses"), gave them entry into thousands of American communities.

The large meat packing companies were true national concerns with thousands of employees by the early 20th century. Trained livestock buyers scouted for quality livestock in the central stockyards of cities such as Chicago, Kansas City, Omaha, and Sioux City, aided by company-employed "cowboys" who directed the cows, pigs, and sheep through the sprawling stockyards. Thousands of packinghouse employees turned the animals into meat, watched closely by platoons of supervisory employees. In the branch houses spread all over the nation, skilled butchers processed the carcass beef and pork into cuts suitable for butcher shops and restaurants. Hundreds of clerical employees tracked perturbations in livestock prices, took orders, monitored production, and tried to be the eyes and ears of the plant superintendents and company executives who managed their far-flung enterprise.

The meatpacking oligopoly was firmly established by World War I. In 1916, Armour, Cudahy, Morris, Swift, and Wilson killed 94.4 percent of the cattle processed in the 12 cities that produced 81 percent of the nation's beef. These five firms also controlled 81 percent of the hog slaughter in those centers. The structure of meatpacking changed little between World War I and the NEW DEAL; the Big Four firms (Armour acquired Morris in 1923) accounted for 78 percent of the total value of meat products sold in 1937.

The seeming stranglehold of the Big Four lasted for a half century. By the 1960s, however, their era was over; in 1962 the old-line firms con-

Hog slaughtering and pork packing in Cincinnati, Ohio, 1873 (LIBRARY OF CONGRESS)

trolled only 38.1 percent of the meat products sold in America. Hundreds of new firms sprang up in the 1950s and 1960s and took advantage of new and more efficient methods of production and distribution to take chunks of the market away from the old dominant companies.

The collapse of the Big Four's branch house system facilitated the entry of new firms. Two interrelated developments rendered the branch houses obsolete. First, large supermarket chains proliferated after World War II. These national food retail companies bought meat in large amounts from packing firms, processed it at central warehouses, and then distributed it to local stores. As the importance of independent local retailers waned, the branch houses lost their central role in most urban centers. Second, the enormous expansion of the highway network after 1945 eliminated the locational advantage of the plants built in the rail hubs, and allowed newer, rural facilities away from rail lines to ship their meat to supermarket warehouses for lower distribution costs. Federal grading of meat helped these independent packers to compete on an equal footing with the old companies in their sales to supermarket CHAIN STORES.

Concomitant with the decline of the branch houses was an enormous increase in meat jobbers, known as "breakers" and "boners." Used primarily by the new independent beef packers, these jobbers took beef quarters from slaughterhouses and further processed the meat in preparation for resale to retail outlets. As their names imply, these wholesalers "broke" the meat down from quarters into basic subprimal cuts such as ribs, loins, and rounds, "boned" them, and then shipped to supermarket distribution centers. Retailers used the wholesalers because they provided more flexibility in the choice of cuts offered to the consumer; independent packers used wholesalers because these new companies needed to do no more than simply kill and minimally process their product, reducing initial capital investment and labor costs.

Declining concentration was a transitional phase before a new oligopoly took control of the meatpacking industry. Astute packers such as Iowa Beef Processors (IBP) founder Currier Holman and Missouri Beef Packers president Gene Frye saw an opportunity to dominate the beef trade by attaching "boning and breaking" operations to their slaughterhouses that would assume the tasks of beef wholesalers. This innovation quickly became known as boxed beef because of the containers in which the meat was shipped.

Boxed beef reduced costs in two ways. Meatpacking companies saved money because they no longer paid to ship unusable bones and meat scraps. Savings in transportation expenses allowed them to undercut prices of firms that shipped beef in carcass form and to increase their margin on each pound of beef. Retailers saved money because boxed beef eliminated the skilled and high-paid butchers who had fabricated the carcasses.

With this cost advantage, boxed beef became the new method for controlling the distribution of beef, much as the branch houses had served the Big Four at the turn of the century. In less than two decades boxed beef grew from a supplementary source of supply to the preeminent method of marketing beef. Sales of boxed beef more than tripled between 1971 and 1979 to 4.8 million pounds, and accounted for one-half of all federal beef slaughter at the end of the decade. Boxed beef constituted only 20 percent of the retail market in 1972; by 1989 boxed beef's national market share exceeded 80 percent. A survey of leading supermarkets revealed that beef shipped in the form of cattle quarters—the old method of transporting beef—accounted for only 4 percent of their receipts in 1986.

Boxed beef was a particularly important source of dominance for a few large firms that mastered this technique of production and distribution. The smaller independent concerns of the 1950s and 1960s rapidly lost ground to the new industry giants in the 1970s as boxed beef flooded the market. The leading four firms accounted for 60 percent of boxed beef sales in 1979 and 82 percent in 1987. IBP alone produced 40 percent of the nation's boxed beef in the late 1970s. Forward integration into boxed beef emulated the techniques of the old Big Four at the turn of the century; and it was equally effective as a method of dominating the industry, albeit under altered circumstances.

Dominance in beef allowed the large companies to assert control over hog slaughter in the 1980s. Pork is sold in processed form far more than beef, and consumer preference for "brand" products protected Oscar Mayer, Hormel, and other pork processors from new competition. Nonetheless, aggressive entry into pork slaughtering by the large packers prompted the older pork-based firms to concentrate on the processing of meat and to abandon their killing operations. By 1990, the pork industry had bifurcated into slaughtering and processing sectors, each dominated by a handful of firms, albeit different ones.

By 1990, a new dominant set of firms had emerged. The new "Big Three" of IBP, Excell (a subsidiary of Cargill), and ConAgra were almost as powerful as Armour, Cudahy, Swift, and Wilson in their heyday. By 1989 the Big Three slaughtered almost 70 percent of the nation's steers and heifers and 35 percent of its hogs. These impressive figures understate their power over the distribution of meat in the United States. In 1990, these three companies produced more than 75 percent of the nation's boxed beef, the form in which most supermarkets receive meat.

The contrast between meatpacking in 1955 and 1990 is striking. In the old stockyard districts of Chicago, Kansas City, and Sioux City, several plants slaughtering a variety of livestock each employed several thousand workers and were located in close proximity to each other. By the 1990s, most meat production was from dispersed plants specializing in either beef, pork, or lamb, usually employing less than 1,000 workers, and widely scattered through the midwestern countryside. Yet much seemed familiar. A small group of firms controlled the industry, drawing on animal supplies from the hinterlands to supply a nation of city dwellers. And technology remained the key to moving large amounts of supplies from farm to refrigerator for the hungry American public.

Further reading

Broadway, Michael, and Donald Stull. *Slaughterhouse Blues: The Meat and Poultry Industry in North America.* New York: Wadsworth Publishing, 2003.

Halpern, Rick. *Down on the Killing Floor: Black and White Workers in Chicago's Packinghouses, 1904–54.* Urbana: University of Illinois Press, 1999.

Horowitz, Roger. *"Negro and White, Unite and Fight!" A Social History of Industrial Unionism in Meatpacking, 1930–1990.* Urbana: University of Illinois Press, 1998.

Walsh, Margaret. *The Rise of the Midwestern Meat Packing Industry.* Lexington: University Press of Kentucky, 1982.

Yeager, Mary. *Competition and Regulation: The Development of Oligopoly in the Meat Industry.* Greenwich, Conn.: JAI Press, 1981.

Roger Horowitz

mergers The process of combining companies by friendly or hostile means. The term refers to both a discrete activity at many Wall Street investment banks specializing in advising on such deals, as well as the generic types of mergers that can result. The process is tied closely to antitrust and antimonopoly activities as well.

Since the Civil War, there have been several acknowledged merger periods—the 1890s and 1900s, the 1920s, the 1950s and 1960s, and the mid-1980s to the 2000s. In all cases, small companies were purchased by larger ones and consolidated into their operations. In the latest period, small companies have bid on larger ones as well. The consolidation trend has often led to close scrutiny by antitrust regulators when violations of the SHERMAN ACT or the CLAYTON ACT were alleged. Each period has had its own distinct characteristics setting it apart from the others.

The period of the 1890s and the 1900s was the period of trust formation, whereby large companies, assembled as trusts, purchased the stock of other similar companies, forming enormous agricultural and industrial organizations. It began in the aftermath of a Supreme Court ruling, *United States v. E.C. Knight Co.* in 1895, favorable to trust formation and ended with decisions ordering the breakup of both the Standard Oil Co. and the AMERICAN TOBACCO CO. in 1911. The second period, in the 1920s, began with the Harding administration and ended with the stock market crash in 1929. It was characterized by consolidation in the UTILITIES industry, retailing, and CHAIN STORES, among others. The third period, in the 1950s and 1960s, witnessed the growth of the CONGLOMERATES. These forms of industrial organization became known as the third type of merger, along with horizontal and vertical mergers. Horizontal mergers occur between two companies in the same sort of business, while vertical mergers occur between companies in the same supply chain. In the 1980s and 1990s, the merger trend was very broad, especially in the wake of DEREGULATION of many industries previously separated, including utilities, banks and financial service institutions, airlines, retailers, and producers of capital equipment and machinery.

In the late 1960s, outside the bounds of the four broad periods, the hostile takeover bid was first employed. This occurs when a company makes an unwanted bid for another, setting off a chain of events that may lead to bids and counter-bids from others also interested in the target company. With the advent of the hostile takeover, bids have also become larger over the years and have become tied to new issues in the stock and bond market since financing for such large transactions can become very complicated. Because of this new twist, Congress passed the Williams Act in 1968, requiring potential buyers to register with the SEC once they had accumulated 5 percent or more of a company's stock. Also appearing in the wake of the hostile takeover bid were defense measures employed by companies designed to fend off unwanted suitors, including poison pill defenses and other measures colloquially known as shark repellents.

Greenmail also appeared during the 1980s. Often, a potential bidder would acquire a block of a company's stock with the apparent intent of taking control, but with the actual aim of being

bought out at a higher price by the company's directors. When the company complied, the process became known as greenmail.

Another popular technique used in mergers and acquisitions is the leveraged buyout—a technique developed in the 1970s and designed to buy the existing stock of a company and make it a private company. Leveraged buyouts, or LBOs, became popular during the merger trend that began in the 1980s. By borrowing large sums of money, potential buyers could bid for the existing stock of a company. Often, the borrowing was a combination of bank loans and JUNK BONDS. Usually, the plan was to restructure the company and sell off some of its nonessential assets in order to repay the debt. The result would be a more efficient, productive company.

The best-known LBO of the 1980s was the buyout of RJR/Nabisco by Kohlberg, Kravis, Roberts, a specialized buyout firm that was one of the first to employ the concept successfully. Borrowing almost $23 billion through a variety of sources, the small boutique firm bought the company and took it private, making it both the largest merger and largest buyout to date. Another type of leveraged buyout is referred to as the management buyout, a deal in which the management of a company decides to buy its outstanding stock, converting it to a private company. The buyout may be done to fend off a hostile bidder or to raise a company's stock price if management believes that its policies can better be executed without shareholders. The funds used to purchase the stock are usually borrowed from the junk bond market or banks and then repaid after the company is restructured. Because of the borrowing factor, this type of buyout differs from a leveraged buyout only by the fact that the buyers are insiders of the company rather than someone from the outside.

See also INVESTMENT BANKING.

Further reading
Baker, George P., and George D. Smith. *The New Financial Capitalists*. New York: Cambridge University Press, 1998.

Geisst, Charles R. *Deals of the Century: Wall Street, Mergers, and the Making of Modern America.* New York: John Wiley & Sons, 2003.

Henriques, Diana. *The White Sharks of Wall Street.* New York: Scribner's, 2000.

Smith, Roy C. *The Money Wars: The Rise and Fall of the Great Buyout Boom of the 1980s.* New York: Dutton, 1990.

Wasserstein, Bruce. *Big Deal.* New York: Time Warner, 1998.

Merrill, Charles (1885–1956) *stock broker and businessman* Merrill was founder and chief executive officer of Merrill Lynch & Co., the first of the financial retailers that came to dominate Wall Street in the latter part of the 20th century. His firm started as a retail-oriented brokerage and rose to become the largest securities house in the country.

Merrill was born in Florida in 1885. After studying briefly at Amherst and the University of Michigan, he went to New York to find employment on Wall Street at the small firm of George H. Burr & Co. He opened Charles H. Merrill & Co. in 1914, specializing in underwriting stocks of small companies and selling to retail clients. His major competition at the time came from such firms as E. F. Hutton. He also hired a friend, Edmond Lynch, who became a partner shortly thereafter. Their original business catered to small investors and was concentrated mainly on stock brokerage, but they did engage in small underwritings, many for emerging retailers such as Kresge.

In the 1920s, the two also became involved with the silent movie industry, becoming owners of the Pathé Frères Cinema. They later sold their interest to Joseph P. KENNEDY and Cecil B. DeMille; it was eventually transformed into RKO Pictures. By the late 1920s, Merrill was losing interest in the securities business; immediately after the Crash of 1929, he effectively withdrew from the industry, transferring his operations to E. A. Pierce & Co. For the remainder of the

1930s, he busied himself with his private holdings, one of which was a controlling interest in Safeway Stores.

Merrill returned to the firm he founded when Pierce ran into financial difficulties. In 1940, the old firm was resurrected with the Pierce and Merrill names and returned to Wall Street. A year later, the firm merged with Fenner & Beane to become Merrill Lynch Pierce Fenner & Beane. In the early 1950s, Beane was dropped and Smith was added to the corporate name becoming Merrill Lynch, Pierce, Fenner, and Smith. Charles Merrill died in 1956, just before his firm expanded to become a major Wall Street investment bank.

By the late 1960s, Merrill Lynch vied with older, more established Wall Street firms for the leadership in underwriting and sales. The firm went public in 1971 and then became listed on the NEW YORK STOCK EXCHANGE, the first exchange member to be listed on the exchange itself. By the 1990s, the firm had become the largest securities dealer in the country in terms of capital and underwriting activities in addition to its traditional stock brokering activities. By the late 1990s, it also led Wall Street in many other specialized financial services such as MERGERS and swap finance.

See also INVESTMENT BANKING.

Further reading

Geisst, Charles R. *The Last Partnerships: Inside the Great Wall Street Money Dynasties.* New York: McGraw-Hill, 2001.

Perkins, Edwin J. *Wall Street to Main Street: Charles Merrill and the Rise of Middle Class Investors.* New York: Cambridge University Press, 1999.

Meyer, Eugene (1875–1959) *financier and newspaperman* Born in Los Angeles, Meyer interrupted his studies at the University of California in order to follow his family to the East Coast after his father became a partner at LAZARD FRERES in New York. After graduating from Yale, his father offered him $600 to stop smoking, which he accepted. He invested the money, accumulated around $50,000, and purchased a seat on the NEW YORK STOCK EXCHANGE, beginning his career on Wall Street.

Meyer became an aggressive investor during the Panic of 1901 and accumulated many stocks at very cheap prices. When World War I began, his net worth was estimated at $50 to $60 million. He was a major investor in the Allied Chemical Corp. and the automobile industries. In 1918, Woodrow Wilson appointed him director of the War Finance Corp., where he gained invaluable experience in farm financing, among other specialties. Calvin Coolidge made use of that experience by appointing him to the Federal Farm Loan Board, and in 1930 Herbert Hoover named him to the Federal Reserve Board. His nomination was vigorously opposed by Representative Louis T. McFadden of Pennsylvania, author of the MCFADDEN ACT, but he was confirmed nevertheless.

Ideological differences with Franklin Roosevelt's administration forced him to retire from public service. In 1933, he purchased the *Washington Post* with the intent of turning it into a major national newspaper. After a shaky start, the newspaper succeeded and became nationally recognized. He also purchased the *Washington Times Herald* and a radio station.

Meyer returned to public life in 1946, when Harry Truman appointed him the first president of the World Bank (International Bank for Reconstruction and Development), which had just been created at Bretton Woods, New Hampshire, along with the International Monetary Fund. After helping organize the institution, he resigned and became chairman of the Washington Post company. He died in Florida in 1959. A daughter, Katherine Meyer Graham, eventually succeeded him at the newspaper.

See also FEDERAL RESERVE; NEWSPAPER INDUSTRY.

Further reading

Graham, Katherine. *Personal History*. New York: Knopf, 1997.
Pusey, Merlo J. *Eugene Meyer*. New York: Knopf, 1974.

military-industrial complex   The term given to the close alliance between the military and defense contractors during the 1950s and 1960s under which preferential contracts were given by the military through the Defense Department for weapons, ordnance, and aircraft. The term was first used by President Eisenhower upon leaving office in 1961, when he described the tight relationship that had developed between the two sectors. "We must guard against the acquisition of unwarranted influence, whether sought or unsought, by the military-industrial complex," he stated in his farewell speech from office.

The origins of the military-industrial complex can be traced to World War II, when the general mobilization brought many companies into direct contact with the government. Many began producing tanks and other armaments for the government on a large scale. During the 1950s and 1960s, the Department of Defense continued the tradition in peacetime when it awarded many military contracts to aerospace and industrial companies to produce all sorts of military weaponry, aircraft, and vehicles. In the United States, the government does not produce its own ordnance and weapons as do some other countries, so the reliance on private contractors was necessary.

As a result of the tensions created by the cold war and the influence of the military, many CONGLOMERATES won valuable defense-related contracts that contributed to the rising prices of their stocks in the 1960s. Although they were highly diversified companies, many conglomerates relied heavily upon defense contracts, awarded to their manufacturing and aerospace divisions, to produce a substantial portion of their revenues. Often, they hired senior military officials away from the armed services to serve as consultants and executives, giving rise to the close relationship between the sectors and prompting further criticism by those opposed to such close collaboration between the military and private industry.

The term has fallen out of favor in recent years, although it is still used to describe the relations of armaments producers and of administrations that spend a large amount of the federal budget on defense.

Further reading
Hooks, Gregory. *Forging the Military-Industrial Complex: World War II's Battle of the Potomac.* Urbana: University of Illinois Press, 1991.
Proxmire, William. *Report from the Wasteland: America's Military-Industrial Complex.* New York: Praeger, 1970.

mining industry   Although basic geology dictated that the mining industry would not play a leading role in the early economic and political life of the United States, many early colonists came to the eastern shores of North America with hopes of finding vast gold and silver mines like those exploited by the Spanish in South and Central America. Leaders of the London-based Virginia Company directed that a crew of 20 men with six pickaxes begin searching for minerals within a week of their arrival in Virginia in 1607. Yet the colonists soon discovered that the mountains of gold and silver they had expected to find were not readily evident anywhere along the banks of the Chesapeake. Captain John Smith wrote of his disappointment that the mineral wealth of the immediate region looked rather unpromising, though he remained optimistic that further exploration would likely reveal "mines very rich of diverse natures."

John Smith was eventually proven correct. The North American continent did hold many rich mines, not only of gold and silver, but also of copper, lead, iron, and other metals. Unfortunately for Smith and the colonists, the fabulous gold and silver mines were thousands of miles from Virginia in what would eventually become the American West. Although disappointed by the absence of precious metals, early American colonists did find and exploit less valuable minerals, quickly developing small and widely scattered deposits of bog iron ore to make nails and basic tools. But mining bog iron was no path to

easy riches. The American colonies would undoubtedly have developed in a strikingly different manner if geology had layered with gold the rivers of Virginia instead of California. As it was, the absence of precious mineral deposits in eastern North America ensured that neither the colonies nor the subsequent early American republic were much concerned with the mining industry. As late as the 1780s an aging Benjamin Franklin could accurately proclaim, "Gold and silver are not the produce of North America, which has no mines."

By the time of the Revolutionary War, the small American mining industry primarily exploited modest eastern deposits of copper, tin, and iron. Typically owned and operated by individuals or small partnerships, these early mining enterprises paid a royalty, or percentage of their production, to the government, a system that was a hold-over from colonial days. Shortly after the American Revolution, the Continental Congress voted to increase the royalty from a fifth to a third in hopes of speeding the repayment of a large war debt. However, the policy was not reenacted after the dissolution of the Continental Congress, in part because during the next few decades there was little reason to think much income would be gained from the meager eastern mineral deposits.

The course of the American mining industry began to change after the 1803 Louisiana Purchase, when the U.S government became the new owner of lead and zinc mines in the upper Mississippi Valley. These mines had already proved fairly valuable to the French and Spanish, and in the light of growing tensions with Great Britain, which would later lead to war, President Jefferson was eager to secure a steady supply of lead for bullets. To that end, Jefferson successfully pushed Congress to adopt the Lead Leasing Act of 1807, establishing a system whereby the government leased the mines to private operators in exchange for a percentage of the lead. Although the leasing system was plagued by corruption and inefficiency, it did succeed in encouraging a significant early mining rush into the upper Mississippi Valley, where miners could develop the surface veins of lead with relatively little capital and simple technology. By mid-century lead mining in the area had become a significant part of the regional and national economy, yet the industry remained largely decentralized and technologically primitive—particularly in comparison to many European mining operations of the time.

An exception to this primitive early state of the American mining industry occurred in the development of eastern coal mining during the 19th century. The American coal industry's exploitation of the huge coalfields of Pennsylvania, West Virginia, and other states grew steadily during the first half of the 19th century in concert with the demands of early industrialization. Well before the Civil War, coal mining operations in towns such as St. Clair, Pennsylvania, had developed into large operations using sophisticated technologies, similar in size and scope to European mines. Mining machinery inventors abounded in the Pennsylvania coalfields, busily making improvements in pumping machinery, rock drills, ventilation, and a host of other areas where deep coal mining raised obstacles. Yet few of these mechanically minded miners and businessmen had any formal technical education. Rather, much like the civil engineers trained on great public works projects such as the ERIE CANAL, early coal mining engineers and managers learned their trade on the job through informal apprenticeships with practicing engineers.

While the coal mining industry flourished, hard rock mining remained underdeveloped during much of the first half of the 19th century. Yet, as further acquisition of western lands created a nation stretching from "sea to shining sea," the conditions were ripe for a major reorientation of the American mining industry. If geology had been stingy in providing precious mineral deposits to the eastern half of the nation, the opposite proved true in the West. The ink had scarcely dried on the 1848 agreement making Spanish California part of the United States when a millwright discovered placer gold deposits near Sacramento, California. By summer, some 5,000 miners were working in the gulches and streams of the western Sierra Nevada; by year's end they had washed out nearly $10 million worth of gold from the gravel stream beds—and the California gold rush had only just begun.

Most of the so-called 49ers who arrived in the next few years mined alluvial gold fields located on federal land, pursuing gold that had, over many centuries, been slowly eroded from rocky deposits in the mountains and been carried by water downstream to settle out in river beds and flood plains. The miners had no clear legal right to take gold from federal lands, yet neither did the law explicitly prohibit it. The government simply had no formal policy for selling, leasing, or even monitoring public mineral lands. For the first two years of the gold rush the new territory was administered by the U.S. Army, which essentially allowed the miners free run of the federal lands—in part because the mining was a boon to the development of western trade. By 1849, the busy mines in California had already produced almost 2 million ounces of pure gold worth somewhere in the area of $40 million—a stunning amount of wealth in an era when the entire federal budget for the same year was slightly more than $45 million.

For a brief time, the California gold fields offered a genuine, if exceedingly slim, chance for any American to strike it rich, if only they could find the cash to somehow get to the West Coast and purchase a few basic tools and supplies. To an even greater extent than with the earlier lead mining rush on the upper Mississippi, the California gold deposits could be mined with simple tools and little capital, and the federal government's inertia in developing a coherent policy for managing the gold fields meant that miners could essentially take whatever they found for free. Still, the vast majority of the early 49ers found little or no gold, while those who arrived in subsequent years discovered that most of the best claims had been taken. Further, as the richest and most easily mined deposits gave out, mines run by individuals increasingly gave way to mining companies with the capital needed to pursue large-scale operations. By consolidating many claims into one operation, these companies could use water cannons and giant dredges to profitably break up large placer deposits and remove the gold. While highly profitable, such techniques created wide-scale environmental damage and angered downstream farmers whose fertile lands were flooded with silt from the mines. Hard-fought court battles eventually led to severe restrictions on hydraulic mining in California, constituting some of the earliest significant environmental REGULATION of the American mining industry.

As downstream placer deposits gave out, prospectors moved up the rivers and into the Sierra Nevada and beyond in search of the "mother lode," the ultimate source of the gold encased deep within the Rocky Mountains to the east. By the 1860s, intrepid prospectors had found hundreds of new deposits, two of which were large enough to ignite their own mining rushes: the Colorado gold fields and the famous Comstock Lode silver mines in Nevada. As had been the case with the early placer mines, a lone miner or modestly financed partnership could profitably develop some of the richest and most easily accessible hard-rock mines. But as miners followed the veins of gold or silver deeper down into the earth, the costs rose exponentially. To profitably develop the gigantic silver deposit at the Comstock Lode, for example, required a complex system of mine timbering, massive hoisting machinery, and expensive concentrating and smelting operations. As a result, ownership and management were once again increasingly consolidated into the hands of a small number of large mining companies, many now capitalized by a growing group of mining financiers based in Boston, Philadelphia, and San Francisco.

In 1866, some 17 years after the California gold rush began, Congress finally began to create a coherent federal mining policy. By this point the mining industries in California, Colorado, and Nevada had become powerful big businesses, and mine operators and promoters with tremendous fortunes effectively used their economic clout to influence legislators. The result was the 1866 lode-mining law, which essentially legalized the previous informal policy of free access, no royalty payments, and cheap out-right sale of public mineral lands. Several years later, Congress combined the 1866 law with several others to form the famous—and still operational—1872 Mining Law, which preserved the earlier laws' basic principles while also increasing the size of claims to facilitate large-scale mining. Under the "free and open" access principle, any citizen was guaranteed the right to begin mining on federal land without needing to notify the government. Miners who wished to buy their claim had to file with the government, but submitting a so-called patent claim was not in any sense a request for permission to mine. Permission had already been granted. As a result, the government essentially abandoned its power to manage and control public mineral lands, retaining for the U.S. Department of the Interior, the administrator of the mineral lands, the power to grant title to the land when a miner (or more likely, a mining company) proved he had done $500 of work, filed the proper papers, and paid the small patenting fee.

Thanks in part to the extraordinary giveaway of public mineral wealth legalized by the 1872 law, the development of western hard rock mining grew at an astonishing rate. Although some opportunities continued to exist for small independent miners, increasingly the mining industry was dominated by technologically sophisticated and highly capitalized lode mining companies that were eager to move beyond the rapid boom and bust pattern of early mining rushes and develop long-term profits. An emphasis on efficiency, planning, and prudent management began to replace the previous "get rich quick" spirit of mining. In 1879, Congress recognized the growing economic importance of this evolving mining industry and its technical needs by creating the U.S. Geological Survey, which began to provide the geological maps and expertise critical to large-scale mining. During the same period, the mining industry increasingly depended on the services of formally educated mining engineers, many being graduates of the leading European schools of mining. Yet as the American demand for mining engineers outstripped supply, the industry and the profession worked to improve domestic educational opportunities. Already prominent institutions such as Columbia University and MIT began offering degrees in mining engineering, and a number of state and privately funded colleges such as the Colorado School of Mines sprang up soon after. Schools such as Columbia and MIT also took the lead in providing their students with considerable training in business management and economics, a recognition that many engineers often ended up in managerial positions with the large mining companies. By the early 20th century, the quality of mining engineering education in the United States equaled or surpassed that of the Europeans, laying the foundation for the industry's subsequent technological progress.

As a result of these developments, the American mining industry underwent dramatic changes in the late 19th and early 20th centuries. For much of the half century following the 1849 California gold rush, the industry had grown by fits and starts. Cycles of boom and bust dominated as mining companies discovered fabulously rich deposits of gold and silver and developed the famous mining districts of the West, many of which became equally famous ghost towns not long afterward. The Comstock Lode, Cripple Creek, Leadville, Virginia City, Bannack, and a host of other names chart the erratic rise and fall of western hard-rock metal mining. Old-fashioned gold rushes continued to occur—most notably the Klondike rush of the late 19th century—but gradually the dominance of silver and gold began to yield to industrial metals such as copper, zinc, and lead. In 1849, the first year of

the California gold rush, the United States produced 1,935 ounces of gold and only about 800 tons of copper. However, 40 years later American gold production had declined to 1,589 ounces, while copper production had shot up to almost 130,000 tons. Large, well-capitalized corporations dedicated to developing industrial ores (often mixed with small amounts of gold and silver that helped fatten profit margins) began to dominate. Americans valued silver and gold for bullion and for use in jewelry, tableware, and other luxury items. But the copper, lead, and zinc from western mines (as well as the important iron and coal output from other regions) were the raw stuff of American industrialization, the material basis of the emerging modern society of electric power networks, RAILROADS, and steam engines.

The rapid growth of the mining industry and its signal importance to the developing industrial and consumer economy of the early 20th century led Congress to create an agency dedicated to mineral extraction, the U.S. Bureau of Mines. Established in 1910, the Bureau of Mines (BOM) was initially designed only to increase the safety and efficiency of the coal industry. Yet the agenda of the BOM soon expanded. As western hard-rock miners of copper, zinc, and other critical industrial metals began to face difficult new challenges from low-grade ores and ever-deeper and larger mines, the BOM increasingly came to their aid, offering expert advice and creating technological advances through research and development. The agency set up regional research stations in California, Utah, Arizona, and Montana, where the BOM staff worked in concert with major mining companies to solve technical problems. The BOM also collected and disseminated detailed economic statistics on the mining industry in hopes of improving long-term planning and management. Technically and economically, the BOM played a critical role in aiding the development of the large-scale modern mining operations of the 20th century.

This development of modern large-scale mines—a "mass extraction" equivalent to the better known MASS PRODUCTION—was first and most fully realized by the copper mining companies of the American West. Early in the 20th century the engineers and managers of the Utah Copper Company began development of what would later become the massive Bingham open-pit mine near Salt Lake City, Utah. Faced with a rising demand for copper for national electrification, paired with the approaching exhaustion of the richer high-grade copper mines in Michigan and Montana, Utah Copper created a new "factory system" for mining that combined steam shovels, railroads, and a massive concentration of machinery into a seamless technological system so efficient that it could profitably mine ore that had previously been dismissed as worthless. The Bingham mine was also unique in that it required financiers to provide an unheard-of amount of capital years before significant amounts of profitable ore would be mined. Fortunately for Utah Copper and its investors, the Bingham mine quickly became one of the most successful copper mines in the world, providing large amounts of inexpensive copper just as the American demand began to soar.

While certain precedents can be found with the open-pit operations of the Minnesota Iron Range or the deep-level mines of the Idaho Silver

Men and machinery in a mine (LIBRARY OF CONGRESS)

Valley, in its massive capitalization, stunning efficiency, and technological sophistication, the Bingham open-pit copper mine was arguably the first truly modern mining operation of the 20th century. The mining industry quickly adopted these basic principles for use in many other types of mining. By mid-century, the hard-rock mining companies used large-scale open-pit operations wherever geological conditions allowed, and by 1963, some 90 percent of all the metal produced in the United States (including the precious metals) originated in open pits. Further, where conditions necessitated deep underground mining, mining engineers developed block-caving technology that allowed efficiencies of scale and speed approaching those afforded by surface operations. These highly capitalized large-scale mines were critical to meeting the huge increases in metal consumption during World War II, as well as providing the material basis for the postwar explosion in American consumption of such metal-intensive products as automobiles, refrigerators, and new homes. Simply stated, the mining industry's open-pit operations made possible the much-vaunted "American Way of Life" of the postwar years.

The ability of mass extraction mining to profitably mine extraordinarily low-grade ores has allowed the mining industry to extend the life of many hard-rock operations for decades beyond earlier forecasts. Operations continued into the 21st century, for example, at the Bingham pit mine, where the ore now contains only .5 of 1 percent copper. However, beginning in the 1970s many mining companies shut down or scaled back operations at western hard-rock mines in Montana, Idaho, and Arizona, leaving state governments with daunting challenges as they struggled to recover from the sudden loss of thousands of jobs and millions in tax payments. In part, this decline simply reflected the exhaustion of profitably exploitable reserves—improvements in efficiency could not extend the lives of declining mines forever. Equally important, however, was the increasing internationalization of

American mining companies, which found that their overseas mines could be developed more profitably—in part because foreign environmental standards were often lower than those in the United States. Indeed, in the decades before the passage of federal clean air and water laws in the 1960s and 1970s, the American mining industry had created vast environmental problems. Some of the most efficient and productive hard-rock mining districts of the West, such as those at Butte, Montana, and the Silver Valley of Idaho, were designated for federally funded clean-up under the Superfund program.

In a final irony, nearly a century after the American mining industry shifted its emphasis from precious minerals to copper and other industrial metals, gold mining has once again become a mainstay of western mining. During a period of high gold prices during 1980s and 1990s, American and international mining companies rushed to develop open-pit, cyanide heap-leaching gold mines all around the western United States. Even the richest of these deposits average only about .20 ounces of gold per ton of rock, or slightly more than one six-millionth of 1 percent. In the average open-pit gold mine the operator thus mines almost three tons of ore to produce enough gold to make one small wedding band—and the remainder of the ore is transformed into huge volumes of hazardous waste.

Thus, in the first decade of the 21st century, one of the most daunting problems facing the American—and now international—mining industry is an environmental one. For almost a century, steady improvements in the efficiency and size of American mining operations provided the raw material for industrialization and the modern consumer society. Now the global appetite for many of the same minerals threatens to dwarf even the enormous American consumption. A key question facing the 21st-century mining industry will be whether it can create a more environmentally sustainable system for supplying the raw materials of industrial civilization.

Further reading

Paul, Rodman W. *Mining Frontiers of the Far West.* New York: Holt, Rinehart & Winston 1963.

Peterson, Richard H. *The Bonanza Kings: The Social Origins and Business Behavior of Western Mining Entrepreneurs, 1870–1900.* Lincoln: University of Nebraska Press, 1971.

Rickard, T. A. *A History of American Mining.* New York: McGraw-Hill, 1932.

Smith, Duane A. *Mining America: The Industry and the Environment, 1800–1980.* Lawrence: University Press of Kansas, 1987.

Young, Otis E. *Western Mining: An Informal Account of Precious-Metals Prospecting, Lode Mining, and Milling on the American Frontier From Spanish Times to 1893.* Norman: University of Oklahoma Press, 1970.

Timothy J. LeCain

Morgan, John Pierpont (1837–1913) *banker*
The most powerful banker of his generation and the second head of the banking house that became known as J. P. Morgan & Co. Pierpont, as he was known, was born in 1837, the son of Junius Spencer Morgan. He spent a year studying at the University of Göttingen before entering the banking business in the United States.

Morgan started in 1857 with the firm of Duncan, Sherman in New York, beginning a career that would eventually bring different firms together as the House of Morgan. He also became a partner in Drexel & Co., a well-established Philadelphia banking firm headed by Anthony DREXEL, and the new Drexel Morgan & Co. became the American agent for J. S. Morgan & Co. of London, his father's firm. Morgan inherited his father's banking business upon Junius Spencer's death in 1890 and expanded it into the most powerful issuer of new securities on Wall Street.

Pierpont was accused during the Civil War of profiteering at the expense of the Union when he bought a consignment of rifles and resold them to the army at a much higher price. After that incident, he was much more controlled in his dealings and became more conservative in his business practices, following the example of his father. He became a notable banker in his own right, participating in many financings for RAILROADS and industrial companies in the 1870s and 1880s. In 1871, after his father arranged a merger with Drexel & Co. of Philadelphia, an established investment bank, the combined firm represented Junius Morgan's interests in the United States as well as doing a substantial business of its own underwriting new securities of many railroads and U.S. Treasury issues as well.

Morgan's interest in railroads led many in Congress to believe that he was devising a plan to consolidate many railroads under one roof in 1887. Although the plan failed because many of the other railroad executives, including Jay GOULD, could not agree on a unified plan, Congress nevertheless passed the Interstate Commerce Act, the first legislation attempting to control the railroads while also establishing the INTERSTATE COMMERCE COMMISSION, the first U.S. governmental agency devoted to REGULATION of an industry.

By 1890, the Morgan banking interests were the most powerful in the country and also among the most respected in Great Britain. Junius Morgan died in 1890 while vacationing in Italy. A reorganization of the partnership followed, and J. P. Morgan & Co. emerged in 1894 as the most powerful member of the firm. Pierpont was contemplating retirement when a financial crisis erupted in the United States that persuaded him to remain active in the bank.

The financial crisis on Wall Street in 1893–94 was precipitated by a steady loss of the U.S. Treasury's gold reserves. Morgan and other bankers, including August Belmont, assembled in Washington and advised the government on how to restore the supply and end the crisis. The operation proved successful, although the bankers were criticized for adding to their own fees while the government was helpless to intervene. But Morgan had attained fame for saving the country, and his reputation grew considerably.

In 1901, he further enhanced his reputation by buying Carnegie Steel from Andrew CARNEGIE for almost $500 million, making the transaction the largest in history. The United States Steel Corporation was born as a result. Other Morgan-orchestrated deals during that general period included the formation of GENERAL ELECTRIC from Thomas Edison's previous small company, and AMERICAN TELEPHONE & TELEGRAPH. Morgan also created the INTERNATIONAL HARVESTER COMPANY by merging the McCormick reaper company with several others. All of these consolidations were established companies purchased by Morgan and consolidated into even larger companies during the period of intense merger and acquisition activity that occurred before the First World War.

John Pierpont Morgan (LIBRARY OF CONGRESS)

During the Panic of 1907, Morgan again came to the aid of the New York banks, the stock exchange, and the nation itself by helping to provide funds to stabilize the markets, ensuring that the panic would end quickly. He also used the occasion to strengthen U.S. STEEL by buying ore fields from John D. Rockefeller in order to provide the company with the commodities necessary to operate cheaply. Despite the assistance provided, Morgan and his banking allies came under close scrutiny during the congressional hearings in 1912 known as the Pujo Committee hearings.

J. P. Morgan & Company had become the acknowledged leader of the "money trust," a group of New York banks accused by Progressives of controlling the nation's credit and access to the securities markets. He and others were called to testify about the activities of the putative money trust. It was the first time that anyone from a banking family had appeared publicly before a congressional hearing, and Morgan defended his banking empire by admitting to none of the accusations or even acknowledging some of the criticisms of banking practices in general.

Also at issue at the time was Morgan's interest in insurance companies. Morgan and his various partners sat on the boards of many banks and trust companies and in the 1900s began showing an interest in life insurance, mainly because of the large amount of captive funds held by the life insurers. The bank bought an interest in Equitable Life, a company with large reserves that had been the target of a New York investigation several years before, examined by the Armstrong Committee.

The Pujo hearings ended inconclusively, and Morgan traveled to Europe for a vacation shortly afterward. He died several months later, in 1913, just as the new FEDERAL RESERVE came into existence. He was succeeded at the bank by his son, John Pierpont Morgan Jr., better known as Jack. In addition to his banking and industrial interests, Morgan was also known for his extensive art collection, reputed to be the best in the country and most of which he housed at his New York City mansion.

See also BELMONT, AUGUST; MORGAN, JOHN PIERPONT, JR.; MORGAN, JUNIUS SPENCER.

Further reading
Carosso, Vincent. *The Morgans: Private International Bankers, 1854–1913.* Cambridge, Mass.: Harvard University Press, 1987.
Chernow, Ron. *The House of Morgan: An American Banking Dynasty and the Rise of Modern Finance.* New York: Simon & Schuster, 1990.
Strouse, Jean. *Morgan: American Financier.* New York: Random House, 1999.

Morgan, John Pierpont, Jr. (1867–1943)

banker   The son of John Pierpont Morgan, he was born in Irvington, New York, and attended St. Paul's School before attending Harvard. "Jack," as he was known, graduated from Harvard in 1889. After an apprenticeship period at the family bank, he was sent to J. S. Morgan & Company in London in 1893 to learn banking before returning to the United States in 1901. He assumed a partnership at J. P. Morgan & Company in New York and then took the reins of power at the family bank after his father's death in 1913. Under his guidance, J. P. Morgan & Co. continued to assert its preeminence as Wall Street's best-known private bank.

The bank maintained its influence in industry and on Wall Street. During World War I, J. P. Morgan & Co. became the major financier to the Allies, the main procurement agent for Great Britain and France, and helped arrange large war loans for the Allies in 1915. As the country's best-known banker, Jack Morgan was also the target of extremists. He survived an assassination attempt at his home in 1915. Between 1917 and 1926, the bank arranged almost $12 billion in international bonds for the major European governments and Canada. He and several partners also served on an international committee that sought to reorganize German war reparations in 1922, a year before the Dawes Plan.

In 1920, one of Pierpont Morgan's most famous companies, the U.S. STEEL CORP., was found not to be a monopoly operating against the public interest. It had been sued almost a decade before for being a monopoly, but the Supreme Court found in its favor. During the 1920s, J. P. Morgan & Co. organized several large holding companies that consolidated different UTILITIES. Jack Morgan was the main witness in the Senate hearings originally called in 1932–33 to investigate the causes of the stock market crash and its consequences. When the BANKING ACT OF 1933 was passed, Morgan and his partners opted to remain a commercial bank and divested themselves of their securities operations. MORGAN STANLEY & CO. was formed by former partners of the bank and continued to act as an investment banker to the many Morgan-formed companies and for the bank's other established clients. At the same time, relations with Drexel & Co., established in 1871, were effectively severed, and the banks went their separate ways.

Another part of the Morgan empire was dismembered in 1935, when Congress passed the PUBLIC UTILITY HOLDING COMPANY ACT, limiting the expansion of utility holding companies and putting them under the supervision of the Securities and Exchange Commission. J. P. Morgan & Co. had been instrumental in forming the United Corporation, a giant utility HOLDING COMPANY with electric power production capacity in many states. As a result of the legislation, investment bankers were effectively precluded from the management of the holding companies.

Morgan and his partners again found themselves the subjects of a Senate inquiry in 1936, when they were called before the Nye Committee investigating bankers' behavior during World War I. Since the activities being investigated were more than 20 years old, the committee could not establish a link between bankers and war profiteering, and the hearings ended without much fanfare. J. P. Morgan & Co. finally went public in 1940, ending the bank's history as a partnership. Jack Morgan died in 1943, ending family control of the bank.

See also INVESTMENT BANKING; MORGAN, JOHN PIERPONT.

Further reading
Chernow, Ron. *The House of Morgan: An American Banking Dynasty and the Rise of Modern Finance.* New York: Simon & Schuster, 1990.

Hoyt, Edwin Palmer. *The House of Morgan.* New York: Dodd Mead, 1966.

Morgan, Junius Spencer (1813–1890) *banker*
Morgan was the founder of the banking firm that came to be known as the House of Morgan. He was the father of John Pierpont Morgan and the grandfather of John Pierpont Morgan Jr., better known as Jack. He was born in Massachusetts in 1813, the son of Joseph Morgan, a successful businessman and one of the founders of the Aetna Insurance Company. He was apprenticed to a Boston businessman when he was 16, and his father bought him a partnership in a New York private bank that became known as Morgan Ketcham & Co.

Morgan did not remain in banking but moved to Hartford, where he began a successful career in the dry goods business with Howe, Mather & Co. He remained in Connecticut for 15 years, until a trip to London brought him into contact with George Peabody, an expatriate American banker who was looking for an appropriate partner with whom to share the responsibilities of his banking business. Peabody had no heirs to whom he could entrust his firm and needed to find someone who could succeed him.

Morgan accepted a partnership offer in the London banking house of George Peabody in 1854, which retained its name until Peabody retired in 1859. The name of the firm then was changed to J. S. Morgan & Co., and the business remained in London. Despite its American origins, the firm was one of London's better known merchant banking houses and participated in several rescue operations organized by the Bank of England to bail out other London bankers, including the London office of Brown Brothers. In 1857, it was the recipient of bailout funds provided by the Bank of England and Brown Brothers as a result of the Panic of 1857 in the United States.

Junius's son, John Pierpont Morgan, entered the banking business in 1857 with the firm of Duncan, Sherman in New York, beginning a career that would eventually bring the different firms together as the House of Morgan. At the suggestion of Junius, he became a partner with Anthony DREXEL in the Philadlephia banking house of Drexel & Co., which then changed its name to Drexel Morgan & Co. The firm became one of the best known on Wall Street and served both domestic and international interests as an agent of the London bank.

When Junius Morgan died in 1890, the bank passed to John Pierpont Morgan. The name was changed to J. P. Morgan & Co. Of the three Morgans in the banking family, Junius was the most conservative and set the tone for the policies his bank would pursue for three generations, until it went public in 1940.

See also BROWN BROTHERS HARRIMAN; MORGAN, JOHN PIERPONT; MORGAN, JOHN PIERPONT, JR.

Further reading
Carosso, Vincent. *The Morgans: Private International Bankers, 1854–1913.* Cambridge, Mass.: Harvard University Press, 1987.

Chernow, Ron. *The House of Morgan: An American Banking Dynasty and the Origins of Modern Finance.* New York: Simon & Schuster, 1990.

Strouse, Jean. *Morgan: American Financier.* New York: Random House, 1999.

Morgan Stanley & Co.   An investment bank created in 1934 by J. P. Morgan & Co. after the Glass-Steagall Act (BANKING ACT OF 1933) was passed. Underwriting of securities was spun off to the newly created partnership headed by Henry S. Morgan, a son of J. P. Morgan Jr., and Harold Stanley, both partners of J. P. Morgan & Co. Morgan's former investment banking clients passed to the new partnership, since the 1933 legislation forbade commercial banks from underwriting corporate securities and J. P. Morgan & Co. had decided to be solely a commercial bank after the law was passed.

Morgan Stanley became the premier investment bank on Wall Street in the 1930s and maintained its position into the latter part of the 20th century. In the late 1940s, the Justice Department filed suit against Morgan and 16 other investment banks in *United States v. Henry S. Morgan et al.*, charging the investment banks with violations of the antitrust laws. The case was dismissed in the early 1950s, when the presiding judge ruled that the government's case had not been proven.

Over the years, Morgan Stanley was the primary investment banker to many large U.S. corporations, including AT&T, GENERAL MOTORS, and IBM. In the 1960s, its power was challenged by other Wall Street securities dealers such as GOLDMAN SACHS and SALOMON BROTHERS because the firm remained a traditional underwriter and was slow or neglectful in adapting to newer trends in the investment banking business, such as sales and trading of securities. Despite the omission, the firm always maintained a presence in the top 10 rankings of underwriting and mergers and acquisition advisers. It began to develop as a full-service investment bank in the 1970s, when it finally added institutional securities sales to its services, followed by investment management and brokerage.

In 1997, the firm merged with Dean Witter & Co. to form Morgan Stanley Dean Witter, although the name reverted to Morgan Stanley in 2001. Through the merger it became more of a full-service financial firm after the expansion during the bull market of the 1990s, while earlier it had been content to be a deal maker primarily in securities underwriting and mergers and acquisitions. After the merger, it added a large retail sales distribution network by acquiring all the Dean Witter branches and brokers.

In 2003, it was one of 10 Wall Street firms involved in a large settlement with federal and state regulators over investment banking practices during the 1990s bull market. It paid a multimillion-dollar fine without admitting guilt.

See also AMERICAN TELEPHONE & TELEGRAPH CO.; INTERNATIONAL BUSINESS MACHINES.

Further reading
Chernow, Ron. *The House of Morgan: An American Banking Dynasty and the Origins of Modern Finance.* New York: Simon & Schuster, 1990.

Geisst, Charles R. *The Last Partnerships: Inside the Great Wall Street Money Dynasties.* New York: McGraw-Hill, 2001.

Morris, Robert (1734–1806) *businessman and financier* Born in Liverpool, England, Morris came to the American colonies while still an infant, and his family settled in Oxford, Maryland, on Chesapeake Bay. He later moved to Philadelphia and, after attending school for only a short time, joined a firm of shipping merchants. In 1754, he was made a partner of the firm at age 20. He was responsible for exporting American commodities and importing British manufactured goods. Becoming very successful, he became one of Philadelphia's best-known businessmen.

In 1765, he joined a committee to resist the Stamp Act. At the beginning of the Revolutionary War, he was elected to the Continental Congress and served on a secret committee charged with finding ways to raise money to fight the war. Between 1775 and 1777, Morris's firm made more than $800,000 in profit by supplying the army with goods needed to fight the war. He came under considerable criticism for his efforts.

Representing Pennsylvania, Morris was one of the signers of the Declaration of Independence after initially opposing it. During the Revolution, he served as superintendent of finance. After the Continental currency collapsed in 1780, Morris's leadership in finance became crucial to the success of the colonies. Since the Continental Congress did not possess the ability to tax, Morris needed to devise a system of raising money under extremely limited circumstances. He developed a system called "specifics," whereby states that could not afford to contribute money to the war effort could otherwise contribute food, cloth, or any other sort of commodity that could be used by the Continental army. Following upon that success, he began to float public loans and raised $63 million to support the army. Still short of funds, he then turned to borrowing from foreign countries and again was successful, borrowing $7.8 million from France, Holland, and Spain.

After assuming the superintendent of finance job, Morris urged that a bank be established to handle government finances. In 1782, the Bank of North America was established with capital of $10 million. The capital came mostly from private hands, although the government did subscribe to $200,000. The government became its first borrower.

Morris was also a land speculator and used the North American Land Company as a vehicle for buying and selling millions of acres of land, mainly in New York State. He became overextended and lost most of his holdings, landing in debtor's prison between 1798 and 1801. He was released when a federal bankruptcy law was passed. He died five years later, bankrupt and supported by his wife at the time of his death.

Morris is also remembered as being a prolific correspondent. Hundreds of letters that he wrote to many contemporaries in the preindependence era and during the Revolutionary War form a valuable picture of the period.

See also DUER, WILLIAM; HAMILTON, ALEXANDER.

Further reading

Grayson, Theodore J. *Leaders and Periods of American Finance.* New York: John Wiley & Sons, 1932.

Oberholtzer, Ellis P. *Robert Morris, Patriot and Financier.* New York: Macmillan, 1903.

Wagner, Frederick. *Robert Morris: Audacious Patriot.* New York: Dodd, Mead, 1976.

Morse, Samuel F. B. (1791–1872) *inventor and artist*   Born in Charlestown, Massachusetts, Morse graduated from Yale in 1810 and went to London to study art a year later. He returned to the United States in 1815, hoping to pursue a career as an artist specializing in historical painting. In order to earn a living, he turned to portraiture and became quite successful, painting portraits of President James Monroe and Eli Whitney, among others.

In 1826, Morse and others founded the National Academy of Design, and he became its first president. He later was appointed professor of art at the University of the City of New York (today New York University). He also became involved with a native political movement opposing immigration, Roman Catholicism, and the abolitionist movement. But his earlier studies at Yale would lead to his greatest success as an inventor rather than an artist.

Morse had studied the new phenomenon of electricity while in college and in the late 1820s again began studying the medium, this time exploring the possibility of transmitting data through electricity. He began experimenting with the TELEGRAPH in 1836 with a university colleague, Leonard Gale. They improved upon a design by another academic, Joseph Henry of Princeton University, and introduced the electromagnetic telegraph in 1837. He obtained a patent for the invention in 1840 and two years later received a congressional grant to build a line between Washington and Baltimore. In 1844, he demonstrated the device successfully by tapping out the message "What hath God wrought" over the wire.

After a series of legal suits over the origin of the system, Morse finally enjoyed success, and the telegraph became the standard electrical communications device. It became the first international means for the electrical transmission of messages and information when Cyrus FIELD finally succeeded in laying a transatlantic cable between North America and Britain in 1858.

Morse also developed the Morse Code, the standard system of dots and dashes used to send messages over the telegraph. The device and the code revolutionized communications prior to the invention of the telephone by Alexander Graham BELL and helped modernize the stock exchanges, enabling them to become more national in their coverage and price reporting than had been the case to date. Although Morse is remembered chiefly for his inventions, he also ranks as a substantial American artist of his period.

Further reading

Coe, Lewis. *The Telegraph: A History of Morse's Invention and Its Predecessors in the United States.* New York: McFarland & Company, 2003.

Kloss, William. *Samuel F. B. Morse.* New York: Harry N. Abrams, 1988.

Prime, Samuel I. *The Life of Samuel F. B. Morse, Inventor of the Electro-Magnetic Recording Telegraph.* 1875. Reprint, New York: Arno Press, 1974.

Staiti, Paul. *Samuel F. B. Morse.* New York: Cambridge University Press, 1989.

motion picture industry   The motion picture industry is the crown jewel of the multibillion-dollar entertainment business. Although its annual box-office take of approximately $13 billion is easily surpassed by the revenues of the U.S. TELEVISION INDUSTRY, the film business is perhaps more important both for its cultural impact and for its position as a springboard for other products. For example, the Sunday evening news regularly reports the weekend box-office totals of new film releases. The annual Oscar ceremony is a global media event second only to the Super Bowl in sports. A film's box-office take is still the most reliable indicator of its value in the home video and broadcast markets. And each year, films serve as the pegs on which to hang thousands of toys, T-shirts, posters, paperbacks, comic books, soundtrack albums, and video games. In most instances, this tie-in merchandise would have little or no value to consumers without the release of a film to support it.

Early film technology had its roots in existing apparatuses used in scientific investigation and in forms of visual amusement. Most historians point to the serial photography experiments of Eadweard Muybridge and Etienne-Jules Marey as important precursors to the first motion picture cameras and projectors. Moreover, while the invention of movies was spurred by the ongoing development of technology for still photography, many other forms of visual entertainment, such as zoetropes, magic lanterns, stereopticons, phan-

tasmagoria shows, and illustrated lectures, had a lasting and dynamic influence on the shape taken by the early film business.

Working in the Edison laboratory, W. K. L. Dickson became the foremost American inventor of early film technology. Although prototypes of the basic equipment were developed throughout the early 1890s, the commercial film industry proper might be said to have begun with the first public demonstration of Thomas EDISON's kinetoscope in 1893 and the Holland Brothers' opening of the first kinetoscope parlor about a year later. Motion picture projectors were developed in France, England, Germany, and the United States starting in 1895, the same year that the Lumiere brothers' cinématographe—the first commercially successful projector—debuted at the Grand Café in Paris. Edison's company entered the field of film projection in 1896 with the Vitascope, a machine that simply refined aspects of Thomas Armat and Francis Jenkins's phantoscope, which had been publicly demonstrated a few months earlier.

Many of the first film programs were seen in vaudeville houses. Early exhibitors often organized several short films into a larger grouping that was varied in terms of genre and subject. Traveling showmen, such as Lyman Howe, also played an important role in bringing film to the public by operating as part of carnivals, circuses, scientific expositions, and the illustrated lecture circuit. Nickelodeons—storefront theaters specializing in motion pictures—became the dominant sites for film exhibition by 1905. The typical nickelodeon seated between 100 and 200 people and offered anywhere from 10 to 60 shows each day. With an admission price of 5 to 10 cents, the average nickelodeon earned several hundred dollars per day in box-office receipts.

Early film production was highly entrepreneurial, with equipment manufacturers and traveling showmen serving as the most important producers. Not surprisingly, Edison's company led the field, followed by Vitagraph, Selig, and Lubin. By 1903, Edison's chief rival was Biograph,

Thomas Edison (right) and George Eastman with motion picture camera, ca. 1925 (LIBRARY OF CONGRESS)

a company founded by his former employee W. K. L. Dickson. The two companies engaged in a series of copyright and patent disputes throughout the 1900s that eventually ended with the formation of the Motion Picture Patents Company in 1908. The MPPC was established as a patent pool, but the effects of its formation were more far reaching as it established royalty rates, licensing arrangements, and guidelines for distribution and exhibition. In principle, the MPPC tried to limit the production and distribution of motion pictures to Edison, Biograph, and eight other licensees collectively known as "the Trust."

Although initially successful, the MPPC foundered due its failure to invest in film exhibition and its resistance to the feature films being produced or imported by independent companies. Already on the decline, the coup de grace for the MPPC came in 1915 with the resolution of a government antitrust suit against the company. While its existence was brief, the MPPC established the contours of the industry's oligopoly structure and stabilized the business through the use of copyrighted technology as a major barrier to entry.

During the 1910s, the film industry shifted its main production base from New York to Hollywood, then a relatively small town made up of retired midwesterners. Hollywood offered a warm climate year round and a varied topography that was especially suited to the production of westerns, the preeminent genre of the period. With the ascendance of the studio system in the next decade, Hollywood became virtually synonymous with a particular style and mode of production in American filmmaking.

The rise of the studio system was aided by the emergence of two parallel trends: the development of the continuity script and the movie star. Often credited to director Thomas Ince, the continuity script functioned as a written template for motion picture production that enabled directors and producers to efficiently plan a film's budget and manage its shooting schedule. Similarly, the movie star's emergence as a cultural phenomenon in the mid-1910s proved to be a major economic boon to the industry, although film companies had been advertising particular performers as early as 1909. As something that drew audiences to particular films, stars helped to stabilize demand for motion pictures and served as a form of product differentiation that afforded certain companies an edge over their competitors.

In 1919, Paramount embarked on an aggressive program of theater acquisition, becoming the industry's first vertically integrated company and encouraging several others to follow suit. The studios' ownership of theaters proved to be a key to their domination of the industry from 1920 to 1950. While the studios owned less than 20 percent of the total number of theaters in the United States, they owned the vast majority of first-run theaters and consequently received more than 70 percent of all film rentals. These studio-owned theaters were protected by a complicated run-zone-clearance system that categorized theaters for all cities and towns in the United States. After a film had completed its first run, a clearance period of one to four weeks would pass before it entered a second-run house located within the same geographic zone. After the second run, a comparable clearance would

ensue before the third run, and so on. This system maximized profits for the studios by encouraging consumers to pay top dollar to see the films in their first-run houses rather than wait for subsequent runs in nonaffiliated theaters. It also created a barrier to entry for independent producers, who were limited to showing their films in nonaffiliated theaters.

In addition to their investments in exhibition, the major studios also benefited from their highly rationalized system of production. With a well-established corporate hierarchy organized around the specialization and division of labor, the studios were structured around individual production units that were serviced by specific departments devoted to make-up, costume, set design, music, sound, editing, film processing, and even food preparation. Because of this complex division of labor, the studios were often described as "dream factories," and their productions compared to that of the assembly line.

During the 1920s, both the Warner Bros. and RKO used their investment in sound technologies to become major players in the industry's oligopoly structure. Following an aggressive program of expansion, Warners' innovation in sound was virtually assured success both because of the initial popularity of *The Jazz Singer* (1927) and because of Warners' licensing agreements with other studios. RKO, on the other hand, was founded in 1928 as a result of RCA's failed attempt to make its Photophone sound equipment the industry standard. Having lost out to Warner Bros., RCA pursued the European market and created its own vertically integrated corporation as a way of amortizing the costs of Photophone's research and development. With its ties to RCA, RKO was part of America's largest entertainment empire, with links to radio, music publishing, and recorded music enterprises.

By 1930, the eight majors consisted of the Big Five—Paramount, Fox, MGM, Warner Bros., and RKO—and the Little Three—Universal, Columbia, and United Artists. The former were all vertically integrated companies, while the latter functioned just as producers and distributors. The onset of the Great Depression threatened the industry's fortunes as many studios went into receivership. The industry rapidly recovered, however, partly due to the favorable treatment it received from the NATIONAL RECOVERY ADMINIS-TRATION. The ironically titled "Code of Fair Competition for the Motion Picture Industry" was enacted in November of 1933. Through it, the industry received government sanction for several collusive trade practices, including admission price discrimination; the use of runs, zones, and clearances; and block booking, a practice that tied the sale of a particularly attractive upcoming release to one or more other titles much less in demand.

While the Depression posed one set of problems, a more serious threat to the industry emerged in the proliferation of state and local censorship boards as well as pressure groups concerned about the regulation of film content. Fearing government intervention, the industry adopted the Motion Picture Production Code, a set of policies that established guidelines and prohibited certain types of objectionable representations. Initially established in 1930, the Production Code Administration was strengthened and reorganized in 1934. Although many filmmakers found ways of getting around its proscriptions, the Code banned profanity as well as explicit representations of sex and violence.

During World War II, Hollywood actively participated in the war effort through its work with the Office of War Information. Many filmmakers made documentaries and propaganda shorts about the war, while others produced combat and "homefront" features that celebrated the values and fighting spirit of America and its Allies. After the war, however, Hollywood became an important target of government investigation and regulation. The House Un-American Activities Committee (HUAC) conducted hearings on communist influence in the motion picture business during the late 1940s and early 1950s. The hearings resulted in the blacklisting of more than 200 people due to past political affiliations. A government ANTITRUST suit posed more serious legal problems. The suit began in 1938 but was not decided until December of 1946. The resulting decree radically altered the industry by prohibiting several collusive trade practices, such as block booking, the fixing of admission prices, and the maintenance of clearance periods between a film's various runs. More importantly, after an appeal by the eight majors, the Supreme Court also ordered the divorce of the studios' theater circuits.

Facing serious changes in industry structure, declining box-office revenues, suburbanization, and competition from television, the studios retrenched in the 1950s by shrinking their production schedules and selling off their backlots. By restricting their supply, the studios hoped to increase consumer demand. The 1950s were also a

Poster for The Jazz Singer (LIBRARY OF CONGRESS)

period of enormous technological ferment as the industry tried to draw people back to theaters with films that, in Cole Porter's words, featured "Technicolor, CinemaScope, and Stereophonic Sound." Even 3-D and Smell-O-Vision enjoyed brief moments in the sun as novelties, although they had little lasting impact on the business as a whole.

Over time, the industry developed several strategies intended to spread its financial risks. For one thing, studios increasingly focused on distribution, ceding much of the actual labor of production to independent companies. In a typical deal, the majors offered financing and distribution to independent producers in exchange for a distribution fee and approval over the film's budget, script, director, and cast. For their part, independent producers were given more freedom and the opportunity for profit participation, but only after all of the negative production costs had been recouped. Besides the shift toward deals with independent producers, the studios also attempted to spread their risk through strategies of horizontal integration. Throughout the 1950s, the majors sought to diversify their holdings by acquiring or starting up record subsidiaries, music publishing houses, radio stations, and television production companies. For film companies, such diversification spread the risk by using other divisions' revenues to offset periods of weak performance at the box office.

During the 1960s and 1970s, many of the majors were swallowed up by larger CONGLOMERATES. Transamerica's ownership of United Artists, Gulf & Western's control over Paramount, and Coca-Cola's later proprietorship of Columbia Pictures were symptomatic of this shift toward conglomerate structures. The 1960s also saw the dissolution of the Production Code Administration. In 1968, only two years after it was revised, the Production Code was replaced by a rating system, which introduced the now familiar designations of "G," "PG," "R," "X," and later "PG-13" and "NC-17."

Since the 1970s, the production and marketing of blockbusters has become a focal point for the industry. Following in the footsteps of such films as *Jaws* (1975), *Star Wars* (1977), and *Batman* (1989), these blockbusters tend to be expensive, special effects–laden spectacles that strive for almost immediate payoffs at the box office. With extremely wide release patterns, these films are typically released during peak seasons (summer and Christmas) and depend heavily on huge opening weekends and foreign grosses for their success. Nowadays, it is not uncommon to see an "event film" playing on at least three or four different screens at the local multiplex.

The era of the elephantine conglomerate is also over, with most film distributors operating as part of smaller but still diversified media corporations. When compared with the first emergence of the studio system in the 1920s, many of the players are the same (Fox, Paramount, Warner Bros., Columbia, Universal), but they now function as parts of a larger media oligopoly comprised of companies such as News Corporation, Viacom, Sony, Vivendi, AOL/Time Warner, and Disney/ABC. During the 1980s and 1990s, film companies sought to benefit from their place within media conglomerates by exploiting "synergies" in the cross-marketing of products across a number of different divisions. With strong ties between film producers and distributors, television networks, cable channels, Internet providers, book publishers, video distributors, and music companies, a single successful project could, in theory, drive activities in several different divisions of the corporation.

Still, while the oligopoly structure of the industry remains intact, it has bifurcated into two interrelated tiers of companies. While the majors constitute one tier, the other is made up of boutique distributors, such as Miramax, Fox Searchlight, and Sony Pictures Classics, that have parent corporations among the majors but operate with independent management and marketing teams. Specializing in smaller, more "cutting edge" fare, these companies serve an important niche market, and the films they distribute serve both as a training ground for new talent and as a site of artistic innovation. Much of the industry's prestige is bound up with these "indie" films since they sometimes garner great word of mouth, rave reviews, and many year-end critics' awards.

With their glamor and global reach, movies are America's most important cultural export. Yet many film critics and scholars are wary of the ramifications associated with a more globalized media culture. With its almost total domination of film markets around the world, the economic power of Hollywood is a chief cause of concern. It is ironic that an industry so invested in dramatizing the tales of underdogs plays Goliath to hundreds of Davids around the globe, small industries making a handful of films each year and struggling to show them within their own markets. In this situation, the losers surely are global media consumers, who must seek out other outlets for their indigenous cultures' cinematic heritage and traditions.

Further reading

Allen, Robert C., and Douglas Gomery. *Film History: Theory and Practice*. New York: Knopf, 1985.

Balio, Tino. *The American Film Industry*. Rev. ed. Madison: University of Wisconsin Press, 1985.

———. *Hollywood in the Age of Television*. Boston: Unwin Hyman, 1990.

Fell, John L. *Film Before Griffith*. Berkeley: University of California Press, 1983.

Gomery, Douglas. *The Hollywood Studio System*. New York: St. Martin's Press, 1986.

Kindem, Gorham A., ed. *The American Movie Industry: The Business of Motion Pictures*. Carbondale: Southern Illinois University Press, 1982.

Litman, Barry R. *The Motion Picture Mega-Industry*. Boston: Allyn & Bacon, 1998.

Musser, Charles. *The Emergence of Cinema: The American Screen to 1907*. Berkeley: University of California Press, 1990.

Schatz, Thomas. *The Genius of the System: Hollywood Filmmaking in the Studio Era*. New York: Pantheon, 1988.

Jeff Smith

muckrakers   The term given to journalists and writers of the 19th and early 20th centuries who attempted to expose the shortcomings and foibles of big business. The term was originally used by Theodore Roosevelt, who borrowed it from English poet John Bunyan.

The muckraking tradition is as old as American politics but grew significantly after the Civil War. It is usually understood as a response to the rapid expansion of the railways and of industrialization that transformed the United States into an industrial society. Later, it became identified with the Progressives, who advocated better working conditions, corporate accountability, and political activism. The muckrakers generally came from the ranks of liberal journalists and essayists, many of whom established significant reputations on the basis of their exposes.

The first significant piece of muckraking was published in 1871, when Charles Francis Adams and Henry Adams published *The History of Erie and Other Essays,* outlining the foibles of Jay GOULD and Jim FISK at the ERIE RAILROAD and Gould's attempted gold corner in 1869. The book came at a time when railroad regulation had become a popular public issue and helped contribute to Gould's notorious reputation.

Muckrakers generally were considered hostile to big business, but their tone and purposes varied. The essays and books that followed the development of such industries as John D. Rockefeller's Standard Oil Co., described in painstaking detail by Ida Tarbell in *History of the Standard Oil Company* (1904), tended to be straightforward corporate histories that showed the techniques and methods employed by industrialists in building their empires. Others were more general, such as William Demarest Lloyd's *Wealth and Commonwealth,* a combination of a discourse on society's ills and a general diatribe against the evils of big business. Still others, such as Gustavus Myers's *A History of the Great American Fortunes,* showed in great detail how the great industrialists accumulated their fortunes while flaunting public convention. One of the last of this genre, Matthew Josephson's *The Robber Barons,* was published in 1934. Other notable writers included Lincoln Steffens and Edwin Markham.

Not all muckraking literature was nonfiction. Upton Sinclair's *The Jungle* exposed poor sanitary and working conditions, while Frank Norris's *The Octopus* described the inadequacies of large industrial companies. Sinclair Lewis's *Babbitt* painted an avaricious picture of businessmen in general, while Norris's *The Pit* depicted commodity traders in Chicago in a less-than-sympathetic light. However, when taken as a whole, muckraking literature was a powerful force that captured the public imagination for almost 70 years before evolving into a more formally investigative journalism.

See also ROBBER BARONS.

Further reading

Filler, Louis. *The Muckrakers.* State College: Pennsylvania State University Press, 1976.

Weinberg, Arthur, and Lila Weinberg. *The Muckrakers* New York: Simon & Schuster, 1961.

multinational corporation A business enterprise having substantial operations in several countries. Rather than simply sell its goods or services from home, acting purely as an exporter, multinationals set up manufacturing and distribution facilities in other countries in order to have greater access to the foreign market. Multinationals accomplish this by making a direct investment in other countries, representing an outflow of capital from their home country into long-term investments abroad.

Traditionally, companies have sought foreign facilities in order to seek new overseas markets, find commodities unavailable at home, find less expensive labor, or seek foreign expertise unavailable in their domestic market. By seeking to invest directly in a foreign country or countries, companies choosing this route often find themselves exposed to a host of challenges and problems not found at home, including a wide

range of political, socioeconomic, and trade problems.

Companies became multinational slowly, beginning in the 19th century when some developed a technological superiority for their products and discovered a substantial foreign demand for them. One of the first American companies to develop overseas operations was the SINGER SEWING CO., which established manufacturing facilities in Scotland in the 19th century. Most of the current American multinationals date from the late 1940s, after World War II, when companies moved their operations abroad. Since then, many of the Fortune 500 companies have become multinational in one form or other, with the largest manufacturers such as GENERAL MOTORS and Ford leading the way. Later they were joined by service-oriented companies such as Citigroup and the BANK OF AMERICA. Many CONGLOMERATES have also become multinational by purchasing overseas subsidiaries or making substantial direct FOREIGN INVESTMENTS.

In the 21st century, the term *multinational enterprise* has become more widely used. The term implies a broad range of activities and also includes multinationals that may not necessarily be corporate, such as international government agencies. The term *enterprise* also suggests that the relationships between the parent companies and their overseas operations may be changing as well, with joint ventures, shared facilities, and minority investment becoming more and more popular as foreign direct investment becomes broader and more capital intensive.

Multinationals, and especially those from the United States, have been subject to widespread criticism as being meddlers in other countries' monetary and foreign policies and having an undue political influence in many developing countries. Labor unions have contended that moving operations offshore increases unemployment at home, a criticism that particularly was heard when the NAFTA was passed. Other complaints about the activities of multinationals have included their ability to avoid INCOME TAX through such techniques as transfer pricing and their ability to exploit cheap labor or resources and then divest in the host country quickly afterward.

Despite the criticisms, multinationals have led the way toward more uniformity in the world economy and led the march toward globalization while bearing the brunt of criticism from those opposed to the trend.

See also CORPORATIONS; FOREIGN INVESTMENT.

Further reading
Madden, Carl H., ed. *The Case for the Multinational Corporation.* New York: Praeger, 1977.
Vernon, Raymond. *Sovereignty at Bay: The Multinational Spread of U.S. Enterprises.* New York: Basic Books, 1971.
Wilkins, Mira. *The Emergence of Multinational Enterprise: American Business Abroad from the Colonial Era to 1914.* Cambridge, Mass.: Harvard University Press, 1970.

mutual funds An investment vehicle developed in the United States beginning in the 1920s. The idea was borrowed from the London financial market, where unit trusts had been packaged and sold for a number of years. In a traditional mutual fund, investors buy shares in an investment company, which invests in a wide array of stocks or other financial instruments.

The packager of the mutual fund diversifies the holdings of the company, and the individual's investment is thus diversified in the same manner. For the share price of the fund, the small investor is able to mitigate risk for a relatively small investment—something impossible to do otherwise. When mutual funds were first packaged and sold in the 1920s, originally as unit trusts, many were not fully diversified but invested in other mutual funds or companies in which the manager had a special interest. When the 1929 crash occurred, many became almost worthless after originally commanding a high share price. As a result, they became the subject of a congressional investigation in 1933 looking into the causes of the crash and the behavior of brokers and investment bankers.

As a result of the investigation, Congress passed the Investment Advisors Act in 1940, requiring investment companies selling funds to the public to follow the guidelines for public offerings outlined in the SECURITIES ACT OF 1933. The funds' rate of growth remained relatively slow until the 1950s, when they began to pick up during the bull market of the 1950s and 1960s. Their next and greatest period of growth occurred in the 1980s and 1990s, after Congress passed legislation creating self-directed retirement plans and allowing greater portability among the plans.

By the end of the 1990s, there were more mutual funds in existence (approximately 8,000) than there were common stocks listed on the stock exchanges. As a result, the funds' behavior in the stock market had a great effect upon individual stock prices and the market indexes as well. After the bear market of 2001, a major scandal erupted in the industry when it was discovered that many mutual funds were allowing other institutional investors to use their facilities for trading after the markets were officially closed, in clear violation of rules established for their own behavior.

A more recent phenomenon has been the growth of a related fund, the hedge fund. Reserved for wealthy and institutional investors, hedge funds are not yet required to be registered with the SEC. As a result, many of their activities and portfolio compositions are not made public. Many of the hedge funds use the facilities of mutual fund companies to trade their own portfolios. Although their investment strategies can be markedly different from those of a traditional mutual fund, the two are related conceptually and have similar appeals although to different investors.

See also STOCK MARKETS.

Further reading
Geisst, Charles R. *Wall Street: A History.* New York: Oxford University Press, 1997.
Henriques, Diana B. *Fidelity's World: The Secret Life and Public Power of the Mutual Fund Giant.* New York: Scribner, 1995